How to Make Movies

HOW TO MAKE MOVIES

Low-Budget / No-Budget Indie Experts Tell All

KEVIN J. LINDENMUTH

Foreword by Eric Red

McFarland & Company, Inc., Publishers

Jefferson, North Carolina, and London

ISBN 978-0-7864-7106-5
softcover : acid free paper ∞

LIBRARY OF CONGRESS CATALOGUING DATA ARE AVAILABLE

BRITISH LIBRARY CATALOGUING DATA ARE AVAILABLE

On the cover: (inset) Tiffany Shepis in the 2012 film
Wrath of the Crows (Photograph courtesy of Marija Obradovic);
video camera © 2013 Studio Smart

Manufactured in the United States of America

*McFarland & Company, Inc., Publishers
Box 611, Jefferson, North Carolina 28640
www.mcfarlandpub.com*

Special Thanks to

Kate Lindenmuth
Tim Ritter
Dave Hayes
Barry Waddell & Seasons of the Wolf
John & Nancy Lindenmuth
and all the filmmakers involved with this book.

Table of Contents

Preface

It's been nearly a decade and a half since I first started penning my very first book, *Making Movies on Your Own* (1998). Although the '90s were not as lucrative as the '80s, during which time home video machines came into play, it was entirely possible to make a modest living as an "independent filmmaker." The big video store chains were amenable to taking on micro-budget sci-fi and horror, so instead of selling a handful at conventions you'd be selling thousands of copies in one fell swoop. Alas, many of those retail video chains have folded up in place of direct-by-mail rentals or video downloads, which take far fewer titles and pay a small percentage of what they used to. Yes, every so often there's a movie shot for next to nothing by an independent producer/director, like *Blair Witch Project* or *Paranormal Activity*, that ends up making millions for a studio, but only a comparable pittance for the original filmmaker.

This huge decrease in revenue from the genre films was one of the reasons I had switched gears about a decade ago and began producing/directing independent documentaries that were broadcast nationally on PBS. Rather than recouping and making money by selling DVDs this was done by getting it accepted by PBS, then finding underwriters/sponsors for the broadcasts. Generally, this made up for the year of time spent creating the program. And probably far more people have seen my documentaries than have my horror films. I still have a love for independent features and have penned a few scripts the past few years and worked, in varying capacities, on other people's productions to satisfy that "itch." And, in fact, I plan on returning to the horror genre by shooting a particularly disturbing film soon, simply for the satisfaction of creating something creepy and unique.

While a lot has changed since the '90s in the technology and distribution, a lot has also stayed the same, primarily the persistence and dedication of independent filmmakers, whether they are making shorts, features or documentaries. The individuals in this book aren't doing it for riches — they are doing this because they are the foremost independent filmmakers in the truest sense of the word.

Why make a movie? Because you want to.

By reading how these filmmakers go about the process of making a film, you'll be able to take away useful information on how to go about making your own film and hopefully avoid the avoidable pitfalls.

Kevin J. Lindenmuth

Foreword by Eric Red

A warning: This book is not for the faint of heart.

Making a low budget film will kill you.

But seriously.

Everyone knows you don't need millions of dollars to make a good picture, particularly in the horror genre where many of the best examples are — and always have been — lower-budget efforts. Anyone working on a very tight budget wanting to make a feature film will find lots of tips on how to prepare and mount the production and what to expect along the way from the topics comprehensively covered in this volume. Kevin Lindenmuth assembles a diverse group of low-budget horror filmmakers used to working and delivering under extreme limitations and picks their brains on all the major stages of the filmmaking process. Covering everything from financing and production to distribution, the result is loads of common-sense, practical advice from the trenches. From technical decisions to handling actors and crew to production situations, these war stories from the micro-budget front lines cannot help but be useful to any filmmaker trying to "get it in the can." While many of the indie directors interviewed in this book obviously have different approaches to the various aspects of the process, often they are in agreement about the best solutions and share similar experiences. Benefiting from proven tactics of filmmakers who learned by doing is especially worthwhile for readers making their own film where it's their time and money on the line. Because while the book deals with making horror films, it's really about the hands-on work of making movies.

People ask me all the time what makes a film director.

A film director is somebody who gets their film made.

Period.

Eric Red is a Los Angeles–based motion picture screenwriter and director whose films include The Hitcher, Near Dark, Body Parts, Bad Moon *and* 100 Feet. *Recent published short stories have been in* Weird Tales Magazine, Shroud Magazine *and* Dark Delicacies III: Haunted, *an anthology. His first novel* Don't Stand So Close *was published in July 2012.*

Making Movies

The very first films I ever made were Super 8mm shorts when I was ten years old. This continued through my teenage years, and one of my creations even made the cover of *Cinemagic* magazine, which was a boost for my beginning filmmaking career. While I also wrote short stories at the time, making a movie was so much more immediate — you could watch the tale you were trying to convey. And I think that's the main reason for the interest: to make something that people could watch. Yes, Saturday Morning Creature Features like Detroit's own *Sir Graves Ghastly* definitely left a mark, as had all the drive-in fare like *The Corpse Grinders*, *Dr. Phibes* and the *Planet of the Apes* movies. That's why the majority of my features were of the horror and sci-fi genre. The first was *Vampires & Other Stereotypes* (shot in 1990) and the last was a short for a ill-fated anthology called *Goregoyles* (2002).

Yet, with such low budgets, there was always minimal crew and everything was largely controllable, so I knew the productions would get done. I was doing the majority of the work and I always finished something I started. I was always making the movies I wanted to make.

In the late '90s I gradually switched gears and began producing/directing non-fiction feature documentaries, many of which were broadcast on PBS. Rather than creating something that was based on a screenplay, I was creating something that was basically based on people and experts answering questions, whether it be on food allergies (*"I'm Not Nuts": Living with Food Allergies*, 2009) or perceptions and opinions about death (*The Life of Death*, 2011).

But as with the features, this was something I could pretty much do on my own. In fact, I would produce, shoot and edit the entire productions. And ironically, far more people would watch these documentaries than ever viewed the genre movies, as they were broadcast nationally. One documentary was even broadcast worldwide (*Solanus Casey*) by EWTN (Eternal World Television Network). I don't think those people ever realized I was best known for vampire films.

So it is indeed possible to branch out as an independent filmmaker. If you want to make science fiction films, you can. If you want to create comedies, go ahead. If you desire to make people aware about a real-world problem, shoot a documentary. The possibilities are endless. The only thing it hinges on is you.

The Filmmakers were asked:
What are your influences and aspirations and what inspired you to make movies? What drives you to make films?

Glenn Andreiev: I always had a passion for creating and telling stories and marvel at the ingredients that go into making a great movie. For example, I just saw *The H-Man*

3

again, a 1950s science-fiction movie with a blob-like creature. In one scene the "blob" slithers around a room. I read that this "creeping blob" effect was achieved using a room set built inside a large wooden cube with bolted down furniture and a bolted-down camera. This cube-set was rotated on a large tumbler and the blob substance rolled around the moving set. The resulting effect shows a steady, normal-looking room, with this blob skittering about. I love creature-feature-engineering stuff like that!

John Borowski: Growing up I was enthralled by the films of Alfred Hitchcock. Not only did he know how to create the perfect atmosphere for a thriller film, Hitchcock planned every shot in the minutest detail to create the ultimate psychological affect on the audience viewing the film. Like all great art, film really works when it creates an emotional response from the audience. Atmospheric horror films inspired me to create docudramas on serial killers where I can explore the horrific aspects of the killer's crimes and also focus on the historical aspects of the time period in which the killer lived. I believe that film is almost like magic where the reality on-screen is actually an illusion. When every aspect of a film comes together properly through acting, cinematography, music, lighting, et cetera, then a film is truly something to admire.

Keith Crocker: My influences are very simple; I came from a large family of six children. Television was a big thing in those days, a great way to entertain a large family for cheap. Watching *Chiller Theater* with the whole family gathered around the TV was a life-altering experience for me. First off, the movies horrified me and literally gave me nightmares. I distinctly remember seeing *The*

Natasha Warasch goes over the screenplay with director Keith Crocker during the interrogation sequence of *Blitzkrieg: Escape from Stalag 69.*

Beast with Five Fingers, the Peter Lorre classic that also featured Robert Alda. When I went to bed that evening, I had a horror in that I swore I was going to see that dismembered crawling hand creeping up the wall by my bed. Talk about trauma! My mom was oblivious, I don't think she had any clue how much these films were messing with my brain. Over the years, a strange transformation began to happen — I began to love horror films. I guess what they were doing was kind of an interactive therapy that was working out a lot of my internal fears. I developed a love affair with genre cinema, in particular horror films. My interest grew in such a manner that I started collecting books on the subject. One of the first film books I bought was *Heroes of the Horrors* (1975), written by *Castle of Frankenstein* zine editor Thomas Calvin Beck. It was there and then that making the art of movies into my art took hold. First, I started by drawing the photos from certain films that were featured in the books I collected. Then I started to paint those same type of pictures. I'd literally stretch canvas, draw the scene right from the photo and paint it. The filmmaking aspect came in during the summer of 1978. A friend of my brother, who knew of my interest in movies, brought over a Super 8mm camera and asked me if I ever considered shooting a movie. Well, I pulled together my brothers friends and my first film was a 15-minute epic called *Dracula Is Alive and Well and Living in Hewlett* (Hewlett, New York, is the town I was brought up in).

Richard Cunningham: I have quite a lot of influences. Early on, Rod Serling and *The Twilight Zone* fascinated me. I would watch marathons of the show on TV. I was captivated by the cleverness and social commentary underlying the concepts and the stark imagery in which they were set. I even painted the opening narration on the walls of my childhood bedroom. Similar science fiction by authors like Ray Bradbury and H.G. Wells also drew me into more visually imaginative storytelling. Films such as *Braveheart*, and a bud-

Writer/director Richard Cunningham

ding interest in classical studies, laid the groundwork for my attraction to the period genre.

I've long admired filmmaker Wes Anderson's trademark dialogue. Along those same lines, a 1957 movie called *The Sweet Smell of Success*, made a deep impression on me with its biting metaphors and rhythmic language. I think also there are certain movies from the '80s that sparked the imagination of kids growing up during that time, and of course continue to have an impact — *Star Wars* or *E.T.*, *Indiana Jones*.

When I started developing the techniques of my animation, I was watching a lot of cartoons and anime at the time, a lot films by Hayao Miyazaki, episodes of *King of the Hill*, *Frisky Dingo*, *Archer*, and various comic book animations. They had their obvious differences. So in watching the various forms of animation, I was aiming to pick up on the subtleties that ultimately make any animation more convincing.

I think what drives me to make films, first and foremost, is my genuine passion for storytelling, for creating some form of escape for people (myself included), and the sense of accomplishment that comes out of it. Storytelling is a craft fundamental to many of the best artists, and to all of civilization, really. Our history and culture are handed down by it. Our religions are based on it. Our economy is supported by its production and consumption. It can broaden and sway minds, or awaken deep emotions in us, or simply serve as a much-needed distraction from reality. I think that as this craft has evolved alongside society, we have come to identify ourselves by pieces of history and characters of fiction alike.

Films also appeal to me simply because they bring together so many different disciplines of both art and craft, all of which must congeal ultimately into the story's final form.

Maurice Devereaux: Growing up an only child surrounded by comic books and toys (G.I. Joe, Big Jim, Mego Super heroes, Johnny West, et cetera) I would invent my own stories. It was always a need, either it was born out of the fact that I had no one to play with, or it was there all along. I need to tell stories. At first I wanted to be a comic book artist, but after seeing *Superman, Star Wars,*

Close Encounters of the Third Kind, Raiders of the Lost Ark, et cetera, I wanted to be a film director like Spielberg. As I teenager I read *Fangoria, Starlog, Cinefantastique, Made Movies,* et cetera, and just watched a ton of films. I grew to admire Kubrick, Romero, Carpenter, Cronenberg, DePalma, Polanski, Argento, Hitchcock, Coppola, the Coens, Lynch and so many more. Sam Raimi was also a huge influence on me jumping into making my first feature at 17, after reading about how he made *The Evil Dead.*

Donald Farmer: There was always a movie camera around the house when I was growing up. My parents documented every vacation, birthday party and holiday with our Standard 8mm film movie camera. The results were projected on our roll-out home movie screen mixed with Castle Films one-reelers like *Dracula, Woody Woodpecker* and *Howdy Doody.*

So after a few years of this, I thought, "Here's the camera ... there's some extra film laying around. Why don't I shoot something

Writer/director Maurice Devereaux on the set of *Lady of the Lake*.

Maurice Devereaux directing his first film, *Blood Symbol*.

myself?" Only I didn't want to shoot vacations and birthday parties. I wanted to film my friends pretending to murder each other.

I was 12 years old when I made my first little 8mm epic. I edited in camera as I shot, and the 50-foot reel gave me a running time just a little short of four minutes.

I was kind of aware of a crime movie playing back then (late '60s) called *In Cold Blood*, so I named my little masterpiece *In Hot Blood*.

My inspiration was *Mad Magazine* and those movie parodies they ran in every issue like *Rosemary's Boo Boo* and *Balmy & Clod*. They always used the original film's title for some groan-inducing pun. And I thought, "What's good enough for *Mad Magazine*..."

Keep in mind I knew absolutely nothing about the particulars of *In Cold Blood*— not that it was based on a true murder case, not that it involved an entire family being slaughtered in their farmhouse, nothing about the writer Truman Capote and his borderline disturbing obsession with the killers. All my 12-year-old mind digested was that *In Cold Blood* had something vaguely to do with murder, plus it was the perfect title for me to have a little fun with. So I set to making *In Hot Blood* with three of my friends and a bottle of ketchup.

Even at that age I knew I needed a celebrity in my cast to give my debut film that extra zing. Years later I would get in the habit of hiring relatives of ex-wives of celebrities, like when I got Charlie Sheen's uncle for *Demolition Highway*, David Bowie's ex-wife for *Demented*, or Stallone's ex for *Compelling Evidence*. But at the age of 12 and living in Manchester, Tennessee, the closest thing to a celebrity in those days was a little girl named Sally — hands down the most drop-dead gorgeous 12-year-old girl walking the halls of Westwood Junior High. Like most of my male friends, I was in absolute awe of Sally but knew she would never agree to participate in something as dubious as my shady movie project. So I went after the next best thing ... one of her relatives!

I didn't want Sally's big brother ... he was three grades older than me and went to the local senior high. Plus he kind of scared me. But Sally's cousin Ronald was in my same grade and seemed up for the suggestion. And I thought, "Maybe if Sally sees her cousin doing my movie, she'll think it's not so bad and agree to star in my NEXT one." That never happened, but I could dream.

So we filmed *In Hot Blood* in about two days flat, sent the film off to the local drug store to be developed, and my first movie was a wrap. I showed it to the actors and that was about it. The thought of doing a follow-up film didn't occur to me until six years later when I'd moved up to Super 8mm film and had learned a little about editing. No more editing in the camera ... this time I'd shoot my idea of "coverage," plus mix in clips from one of my Castle home movies. Namely in one scene where the female lead is watching television, I edited in clips from the Castle edition of *This Island Earth* to represent the TV show she was watching. I thought I needed a really original death scene this time, so I filmed the lead actress being strangled to death with a stretched-out condom ... a scene that did NOT amuse my father. Finally, I knew this movie should be way longer than *In Hot Blood*, so I ended up with about 30 minutes of edited footage including titles.

Over the next three years I would grind out five more of these little Super 8mm movies. The first two were melodramatic soap operas with a few murders tossed in, but the fourth was my 40-minute horror epic *The Summoned* ... the first time I had anything approaching special effects make-up. Very low-end effects, mind you. For a scene where a zombie is shot in the chest, I taped a firecracker to a piece of cardboard, taped a balloon full of movie blood on top of that, then taped board, firecracker, and balloon underneath my actor's shirt. Oh yeah ... and we put some cotton in his ears, too. I'm pleased to report he survived.

Several years later, the two stars of *The Summoned* showed up in some of my better-known movies. Robert Tidwell played the video store clerk in *Demon Queen* and Larry Herren played a supporting role in *Scream Dream*. Larry was actually another in my long line of "relatives of the stars." His cousin, Roger Herren, had played the boyfriend of Farrah Fawcett in her 1970 movie *Myra Breckinridge* and was even man-handled by Raquel Welch in one scene. I was endlessly fascinated to know that one of the stars of a Raquel

Welch movie actually hailed from my little town ... and that "I" was friends with his cousin. To say that Larry was less impressed with his cousin's achievement would be a serious understatement.

I did the last of my six Super 8mm movies in 1976, then decided I should stop fooling around with home movies and get a real job. So I used my college journalism major to get on with Nashville's daily paper, the *Tennessean*, and branched out to covering film production for *Fangoria* and a couple of other magazines ... plus launched my own horror fanzine *The Splatter Times*. But being on so many movie sets as a reporter eventually got me interested in filmmaking again and I started making plans for my first feature-length movie, the project that would eventually become *Demon Queen*.

Jeff Forsyth: I would have to say my major influence as a filmmaker has always been Steven Spielberg. As the years go by I am still trying to quantify what that exact quality that Steven has that is so unique. There is a certain magic to one of his films, regardless of content. His films possess a level of quality in every aspect of the craft, from the cinematography to the acting. It's an X factor he has that I continue to try and understand.

I think I have always wanted to make movies. As a child my favorite TV shows would get canceled. That happened with *Star Trek*, and I always wanted to make more [episodes]. I would force my brother to help me act out episodes or new adventures for the characters. As I look back on it, much of our imaginative play was "cinematic" — we would make up characters that were adventurers or space explorers. I kept talking about making a movie — a *Trek* movie at the time. When I turned about nine or ten years old, my mother bought me a Super 8mm film camera. That was it for me. I loved it. Strangely enough, I fought the exact kind of barriers then as I do now: time and money. I made a few little bits with the Super 8. I animated my *Star Wars* action figures after viewing a very inspirational

behind-the-scenes documentary of *The Empire Strikes Back*. I made a few-minute film of my brother playing Spiderman in *Spiderman vs. The Ninja*. They were fun little things. But ultimately I was discouraged by the format. My camera had no sound, and a ten year old doesn't have the funds or the knowledge to edit and shoot enough [footage] to make a feature.

It's a bit of an insane compulsion really. I am in love with absolutely every aspect of the process and I'm unable to "shut it off." I think about it all day and night. "This would look great," or I think of a line that should be in a script. I feel a need to be creative, but in the end I just think the whole process is just fun and I can't think of anything as a hobby or an occupation I would enjoy more.

Richard W. Haines: I became interested in filmmaking at a very early age. I was "glued to the tube" as a child, watching old feature films around the clock on WOR's *Million Dollar Movie* and on the *Late, Late Show*. My parents were movie buffs, so we went to the Hollowbrook Drive-in during the summer to see double bills, and indoor cinemas the rest of the year. The Westchester theaters were owned by Ron Lesser. Lesser's Beach Cinema 1 was set up for 70mm, which was the only house in the area that used the large format.

In 1971, my folks bought me a Sears Super 8mm camera and I started making amateur films. It had a frame-by-frame option, so I created stop-motion animation as well as live-action. I used stop-motion to make my G.I. Joe action figures appear as if they were fighting. I recall staying up late at night editing them, which made me exhausted the next day in school. When they were finished I recorded some music on an audio cassette machine and projected them for friends.

I purchased the Kodak Ektasound 140 camera in 1973 and started making sound shorts. I rounded up high school friends and made a Spaghetti Western spoof and other novelty films. I enjoyed making my amateur movies. I wanted to make professional feature films as a career. I still have most of my Super 8 shorts and, since they were shot on Kodachrome, they didn't fade. I transferred them to DVD and store the originals in my archive.

William Hopkins: I can't remember any time in my life when I didn't want to be involved in filmmaking. I was one of those "monster kids" who grew up watching the Universal horror classics on TV and spending my allowance on Aurora model kits and magazines like *Famous Monsters* and *Castle of Frankenstein*. Back then, before home video, you had to choose between what was playing at the local theater and what was playing on TV, and since it seemed most of the movies my local theater booked were a little too mature in subject matter for a kid, I ended up spending a good part of my childhood with

my head glued to the TV set. I studied *TV Guide* magazine each week as soon as it arrived, circling all the movies I wanted to see and pretty much scheduling all my free time around what was showing on *Creature Features, Chiller Theater, The 4:30 Movie* and *The Late Show*. My diet consisted mostly of horror, sci-fi and fantasy films, including Universal's classics, films from Ray Harryhausen, Hammer and Amicus and, of course, the Japanese giant monster movies. Even stuff that was relatively new at the time, like *Night of the Living Dead* and *Rosemary's Baby*, I first saw when they ran on TV. Those movies, along with shows like *The Outer Limits, Star Trek, Dark Shadows* and *The Twilight Zone*, all made a great impression on me as a kid and, by the

time I was in junior high, I had pretty much made up my mind what I wanted to do with my life. My father, who first introduced me to films by plunking me down in front of the set at four or five years old to watch *King Kong, Dracula* and *Frankenstein*, ended up regretting it later when I announced my career plans. He didn't think it was a practical way to make a living, and he was right. But I wouldn't discover that until many years later.

As a kid, even though I was familiar with names like James Whale and Tod Browning from reading *Famous Monsters Magazine*, I tended to think of the contribution of writers and directors as being secondary to the work of the special-effects and make-up artists. I hadn't developed my critical faculties enough to be able to judge the quality of

Writer/Director Bill Hopkins

things like writing, cinematography, editing or overall storytelling ability, but I was able to tell which monsters looked cool and which effects worked, so guys like Ray Harryhausen, Willis O'Brien, Jack Pierce, Dick Smith and Rick Baker were the ones I paid attention to. To me, as a child, the jobs that seemed most important were the special-effects and make-up artists. So that's what I wanted to be.

I did a lot of experimenting with animation, using clay models and a Super 8 camera, and taught myself the process of making rubber masks from reading the few books that were available then on the subject. Anyone who knew me in those days probably remembers me as the strange kid with the Super 8 camera in one hand and rubber monster mask in the other. But it didn't take me too long to realize I didn't have the patience or dedication that animators and make-up artists need to have. I also came to understand that the effects and make-up guys were almost always in the position of realizing concepts that others had come up with, and I really wanted to be the one coming up with the ideas — the story, the characters and so forth. So I began to develop a greater appreciation for the work of the director and the screenwriter and started paying more attention to people like Hitchcock and Kubrick and the other greats of filmmaking.

Then, in the mid '70s, *Jaws* and *Star Wars* were released, and they made a big impression on me. While both films were thematically very much like what I had been watching for years, the quality of the direction and writing took them to a new level. They weren't just great monster or sci-fi movies, they were great movies. And my parents and the other adults around me expressed enthusiasm for them, too, which was almost never the case with the other horror/sci-fi films I obsessed about. The sophistication of the filmmaking and the storytelling in those films was a huge leap beyond most of what had come before in that genre. So I was inspired to focus on developing my skills as a screenwriter and pursuing that as a career.

I can remember the day when I made that decision to commit to screenwriting. I was still in my teens, still living at home with my folks, and my room was littered with all the modeling clay, paint and rubber masks from years of experimentation. I cleared it all out, packed it up and moved it to the attic and installed a big electric typewriter in my room. I'm sure my parents were happy to have all that mess cleared up, but the typewriter made so much noise — it sounded like a machine gun when you typed on it — they probably lost a lot of sleep on those nights when I was up late working on my first screenplays. But, as it turned out, their suffering was not completely in vain. The first script I wrote in my last year of high school was optioned but never produced, but the second script I wrote, *Children of the Night*, was actually produced. It received fairly wide distribution on home video through Columbia Tristar and on cable TV. That I was able to make a sale on my second screenplay was certainly encouraging to me. I still remember showing my father the check I received from the sale. He stood in the middle of the living room holding the check out at arm's length and squinting at it in disbelief. It was a relatively small amount for a script sale but a huge amount to him, probably a third of his yearly salary at the time. He said, "They paid you that much for one of your scripts?" He couldn't believe it. He got out his glasses right away and sat down in the kitchen to read the script, which is something he hadn't done with anything I had written up to that point. But he wanted to see what I could possibly have written that anyone would be willing to pay that much real money for.

Both of my parents passed away not too long after that and didn't get a chance to see the film that was made from my screenplay, which is probably just as well. I don't think they would have thought much of it. But at least they lived long enough to see me make that first sale.

In the years after that, I continued to write scripts and shop them around. A few were optioned. I was commissioned to write scripts for a couple of projects, but nothing ended up being produced, so it was a frustrating period. I did make some important contacts, though — people I'm still in touch with and still doing business with.

By the end of the '90s, as new technology became available (like digital camcorders and nonlinear editing software), I decided to try raising money to shoot my own films so I'd have more control over the productions and get more of whatever profits there were. From that decision came *Sleepless Nights*, which I did with Howard Nash and Frank Cilla as the producers, and more recently, *Demon Resurrection*, which I did with Frank Cilla and Edward Wheeler.

Steve Hudgins: I've always been a writer and storyteller since as far back as I can remember. Making movies is just another way of telling a story. I specialize in horror/thrillers. More often than not, I'm very disappointed by most of the movies being produced within that genre. I really want to bring originality back to those types of movies.

Rolfe Kanefsky: I fell in love with movies when I was around four years old. My father introduced me to the films of Abbott and Costello. I remember catching the very end of *Abbott & Costello Meet Dr. Jeckyll and Mr. Hyde* and I was hooked. Growing up in New York, they would run their films every Sunday morning at 11:30. I watched them religiously, from age 4 to 14. Of course, I watched things beside Abbott and Costello. I became a fan of Alfred Hitchcock movies, Blake Edwards, Steven Spielberg, John Landis, The Marx Brothers, Neil Simon, and John Carpenter. I've always said my three favorite films of the 1980s are *E.T.*, *The Blues Brothers* and *Psycho II*, with *After Hours*, *Fright Night* and *The Stepfather* running a close second.

I received my first video camera when I was 13 and started making my own short films inspired by my favorite comedies. I began writing before I could actually write. I would tell my stories to babysitters and have them

translate them to paper. I eventually learned to write and at age 15 took a screenwriting course at HB Studios in New York. I learned the proper screenplay format by this course and by reading other screenplays.

Around the age of 14, I knew I wanted to be a director, and started seriously trying to figure out how to break into the business. I realized that most first-time directors started with horror films, so I decided to rent every horror film on video to study the genre. Sam Raimi's *The Evil Dead* became a big influence, and I loved John Landis's *An American Werewolf in London* and Tom Holland's *Fright Night*.

At 15, I made a 52-minute flick called *Undead* which was a *Sleuth*-influenced horror flick. At 16, I spent two years working on my first independent feature called *Strength in Numbers*, an action-comedy thriller in *The Goonies* tradition. I also started working as a P.A. [production assistant] during the summers and did a stint at Troma on *Troma's War*. My senior project in high school was *Murder in Winter*, a comical Agatha Christie murder mystery done on stage and filmed.

Around this time, I was becoming restless and wondered how long it would take to write a low-budget teen horror film. I wrote the first draft of *There's Nothing Out There* in five days. I did it as an exercise but couldn't get myself to do just a straight teens-killed-by-alien story. I had seen so many horror films by this point that I was wondering why nobody in a horror movie has ever seen a horror movie. So, I thought it would be fun to have a character who is a horror fan and comments on all the stupid things that people do in horror films. He would be like the audience and I could poke fun of all the overused conventions of horror films, like the cat scare and people standing in front of an open window, going out alone, dropping the knife, et cetera. That's how my first real film was born. Wrote it in 1987 and filmed it in 1989.

Basically, I got into film because I enjoy telling stories and entertaining people. For a time, I wanted to be an actor, but in high school I was stuck in a lot of bad plays and I realized that it takes so much work but if the end result is weak, what's the point? So, I took control and started directing films myself, moving behind the scenes to tell my stories for the sheer joy of entertaining people. Later in life, taking jobs for money came into play, but I've always tried to make even the worst projects something special and a little different.

Brett Kelly: My main influence was my dad. When I was a kid I used to fight going to bed, kicking and screaming. My father would often let me come back downstairs once my sister fell asleep and we would watch the late

Top: Writer/director Steve Hudgins. *Bottom:* Writer/director Rolfe Kanefsky on the set of *Nightmare Man.*

movie on CBC, often they were monster films, MGM musicals or films noirs. I loved them. What drives me to make films is an obsession with telling stories. I always used to play make-believe as a kid. My friends and I would pretend we were *Star Wars* characters or *Teen Titans* or something like that. I used to wish I could afford a Fisher Price video camera that existed at the time that recorded video onto audio tape somehow. I have just always needed to tell stories.

Chris LaMartina: One of my earliest memories is demanding my aunt sit down at the typewriter while I dictated scary stories to her. None of them made much sense, but the sessions instilled a sense of showmanship in me that has yet to cease. During my early years, I became enthralled with Hammer horror flicks, Universal Studios, '80s slasher movies, and Troma (seeing *Toxic Avenger* because I thought it would be like the cartoon, *Toxic Crusaders*, basically ruined my life). Around age 11, I discovered the family camcorder and

I began to emulate the films I loved. Every day after school I produced short films. I have VHS tapes of hundreds of little projects — comedies, horror movies, stop-motion animations, even a western or two.

There was something so exciting about creating and telling stories. It's a passion that still persists in my life because I enjoy the process of relating experiences to other people. Someone once told me, "The only reason anyone does anything is for a good story" ... and while I don't know if this is completely true, I come back to it a lot.

Jim Mickle: When I was 13 years old I saw *Army of Darkness* and discovered *The Evil Dead* trilogy. I always enjoyed watching movies, but that was the first moment where it all clicked and I realized there were all of these decisions being made behind the camera to create the personality of those films. From there I spent my teens soaking up genre films that had real craft behind them. I fell in love with the works of David Lynch, John Carpen-

Writer/director Chris LaMartina (*President's Day, Witch's Brew*). Photograph by Josh Sisk.

Writer/director Jim Mickle (Mulberry Street, Stake Land)

ter, Dario Argento, Peter Jackson, Sam Raimi, and Robert Rodriguez. At first I made little backyard movies on a VHS-C camcorder with my neighbors and tried out a lot of the tricks from the movies I loved. Over time you start to find your own personality by telling stories that excite you or have some personal connection. That's what still keeps me in love with making movies.

Damon Packard: My influences came out of growing up in the '70s and early '80s. At that time there was a lot of idealistic enthusiasm and a burning need to explore the realm. I still have the drive to make films, but it's different. Since that initial desire and drive never actually materialized a form of graduated success in the field, the kind of limited potential you're repeatedly dealing with on a no-budget scale becomes less and less vital and purposeful as the years pass.

Brad Paulson: When I was a little kid I was at a friend's house and *Superman II* came on. The other kids went out to play. It was like

I was Gollum (in *Lord of the Rings*) and the Ring was calling to me. I stayed in to watch the movie. I've always been like that. It's purely instinctual for me. Every year when the family gathers around to watch football for the holidays, I'm watching movies. It feels like it was something I was born with. I've always loved movies and that is what has driven me the most to make my own. Since I was a little kid, the first section I've always opened in the paper was the entertainment section. Then, maybe the comics. I've always been at least as much a fan of watching movies as I have been of making movies. And I'm glad to say I still have that enthusiasm. I just wish I had the money to go along with it so I can do it full-time.

As far as influences, I've loved comic books since before it was "in" to do so. I believe they've always been a highly underrated and amazing art form. Comic books, to me, serve as templates for movies. Remember when *Sin City* came out and everyone thought that movie was so innovative? It was just doing a faithful adaptation of the material. The same thing with the movie *300*. Those movies are now widely ripped off and people think they're brilliant. It's the original source that was brilliant. The good filmmakers are just honoring it by not making it unrecognizable. Whenever Hollywood strays too far from the source material, that's when things go wrong. This is why I've always been a fan of Kevin Smith. He interjected his love of comic books into movies early in his career and that established an instant connection with me as a fan. When a movie connects with you in a way, that's helps to fuel your passion for making movies. It's such an amazing forum for mass communication. As far as other influences, I'm a big fan of the unusual. Case in point, if there's a dwarf in a movie I'm instantly down to see it. Other oddities seem to compel me as well. I definitely grow tired of the same thing over and over again. I'm certainly not a snob of watching what is familiar, but I also like a heavy dose of variety. Directors that have embraced a different type of style interest me as

Brad Paulson directs a college short film.

well. Guys like Dario Argento, Peter Jackson, Sam Raimi, John Waters, The Coen Brothers, et cetera. I love writers like David Mamet. Who doesn't love *Glengarry Glen Ross*? Some of my other favorite authors include Joe Lansdale, Jack Ketchum, Edward Lee, Edgar Allan Poe, Jack London, Roald Dahl, Charles Bukowski and Steven King. If you're strapped for movie ideas, all you need to do is read. It activates your imagination unlike anything else. I'm also into metal, doo wop, drunken outlaw country music, cheesy '80s action movies, '80s comedies like *Back to the Future* and the John Hughes flicks. I think *The Breakfast Club* was a fantastic template for a micro-cinema movie. Very few characters, primarily one location. It could have easily been boring and one to hit the fast-forward button to, but with its fantastic script and energy it became an instant classic. It proved heart transcends budget any day of the week. The same applies with French New Wave cinema. Mostly one take, very lim-

ited locations, mostly dialogue. This is great stuff to watch for making your own inexpensive movie. I'm also a fan of hard-to-find cult movies, puppets and pop culture. Basically I'm kind of a weirdo, but it's only an outside projection of what I find amusing and entertaining. At my core, I'm surprisingly normal and adjusted. I believe art has provided me a great outlet and balance.

Jose Prendes: I was influenced early on, like most people, by the magic of movies. I remember watching one of the early *Superman* films and wanting desperately to do "that." What "that" was became clearer as I got older. I grew up watching the films of Frank Capra and Steven Spielberg and learning how things work and don't work cinematically when it comes to movies. I discovered Kurosawa films and the rest of the fantastic films in the *Criterion Collection*, and I just absorbed it all like a sponge, taking what I wanted and growing my knowledge base.

I knew from a very early age that movies were for me, regardless of the struggle and hardships. I hated everything else except movies, so it was kind of a no-brainer.

Paul Scrabo: My "real" job is as a crew person for network television, so I'm involved in projects that are highly commercial in nature and insist on your dedication and skill, but you may not have any emotional interest or passion with the subject. So my own projects are not necessarily commercial or trendy. I already make a living in that world. Making movies on your own is tough enough, so it might as well involve an idea you're interested in pursuing.

The movie theater experience itself may be my biggest influence, at least how it was in my youth. They were sacred places. Your normal life was put on hold when you entered. It's a bit different today, with actual commercials playing on a the screen when you walk in. There is no transition.

Indie producers live in an incredible time today with so many venues — the internet, streaming, DVD, Blu-ray, iPod, and now web movies can be displayed on your television. They're not locked into the computer screen anymore. But it's wonderful when low-budget films get the chance to play at film festivals. Despite all these new outlets, I think the one place every filmmaker wants his film shown is a real theater, with a real audience. That's when your film becomes a movie.

Eric Shapiro: When I was around 12 years old, in 1990, my dad bought a camcorder, I think for a family vacation to Florida. I started using it to make ridiculous movies with my friends; we were always ripping off the *Airplane!* and *Naked Gun* films. The more I used the camera, the more I started getting a feel for the medium, and wondering what it would take to make my stuff look as good as the stuff I saw on TV or at the movie theater. There's something dynamic about the medium — the way it combines drama, literature, music, photography, and so much else.

Writer/director Eric Shapiro

Anthony Straeger: The first thing that influenced me into making anything was that I was working for the BBC on a children's series called *For Amusement Only*, a "seven strand" piece, and my strand was called *Judge Jugular*. After shooting three episodes it was obvious to the director that there wasn't that much to this strand and it was bubbling along fine, whereas another strand featuring lots of kids was way behind its schedule. As the director/series producer at the time, Peter Leslie, had limited resources in terms of second-unit directors, he allowed — get this — the temporary secretary/assistant to take over the directing of it. Obviously, she had no idea [of what to do], but I had a good cameraman and a good sound guy, so every time she tried to be a director and got it wrong, I took over directing

Sarah Paul and Anthony Straeger block a scene for an independently made film.

myself. At the end of the 13th episode, the crew came up to me and shook my hand saying, "You were great and you should give directing a go!" I thought f * * k it ... why not! I then wrote, produced and directed my first short, *The One We Came in For.*

The other great influence for me in terms of my approach has been Peter Jackson. His first movie, *Bad Taste*, is the proof that filmmaking at grass roots is about initiative. He worked out all of his stunts, special effects and even built his own jib. It took him four years to produce using friends and family and became a fabulous cult movie. He is the only person that could have taken on something like *Lord of the Rings* and come in on budget.

The influence for me loving horror movies comes from my mother, who, when I was but a young boy, would let me stay up on a Friday night to watch the *Midnight Movie*, which tended to be one of the Hammer House of Horror films. I loved the stylization and, even at that age, the sexiness.

The thing that got me into wanting to make a movie was simply that I had made several shorts, some good, some bad, some just down

right ugly... But I had been learning. And all the while I had been writing feature-length scripts and failing to sell them. It reached a point in 2008 that I thought I have to either ... make a movie or simply give it up. Now that I have made a movie, what drives me to continue is that I want to make a better one, I want a larger budget, more time. And what I aspire to is making something I really feel makes me bristle with pride so that I can say, not to friends or peers, but myself ... I did that... Well done, my son!

Marc Trottier: I've always enjoyed horror movies, even as a child, such as *Friday the 13th*, *A Nightmare on Elm Street* and *Evil Dead*. I would've loved to make movies growing up, but I only got into acting and had access to a camera when I was 22 years old ... so I had a late start. After I discovered acting, I began wanting to make films that I could act in. I'm not sure if I'd want to make/direct a movie that I couldn't be a part of as an actor as well. Since I started acting and making films, my big influences, as far as directors, were M. Night Shyamalan (earlier works), Steven Spielberg, and more recently J.J. Abrams. They just

Writer/director/actor Marc Trottier

make the kind of stuff that I'd like to make and act in. I make films because I'm an artist, and it gives me a creative outlet ... and because films are fun!

Mike Watt: I've been a film-lover since a ridiculously young age. My parents are both film buffs and most of my earliest memories are of sitting between my parents in various darkened theaters and drive-ins. The first movie I remember seeing was George Pal's *Doc Savage*. It was the one luxury our poor family would make sure we could afford and we went on a near-weekly basis from the time my sister and I were toddlers. At home things weren't much different. Before cable and VCRs, we'd sit down as a family to watch movies on TV in the evenings, what I consider to be the staples of my childhood: *The Magnificent Seven, The Wizard of Oz* and *Bringing Up Baby*.

Through my father, I was educated in movie language without being aware of it, particularly with regards to westerns and *film noir*, a term he hated, incidentally. He called these exercises in shadow, light and morality "hard-boiled movies."

Also fortunately, he was and is a bibliophile, and the house was filled to overflowing with books of all topics. Anything I wanted to read, I just had to find. These are the foundations of my love of storytelling. A book I carried with me a lot as a kid was a paperback entitled

Movie Magic, which gave the history of special effects from the Lumiere Brothers up to, I believe, *Jaws* or *Star Wars* (two more fundamental movies of my make-up). I distinctly remember watching an episode of *Mork & Mindy*, where Robin Williams played both Mork and himself in one scene, and being thrilled because the book told me how the effect was achieved in all its *Patty Duke Show* ingenuity. Then I tried to explain the process to other kids in the first grade. Needless to say, the words "traveling matte" didn't keep me from being beaten up a lot.

In all honesty, all I've ever wanted to do in my life is tell stories, regardless of the medium. I've been lucky enough (or dumb enough) to have had the chance to do just that as a published author, journalist and, on a more limited scale, filmmaking.

Throughout my formative years, I spent time doing what most budding filmmakers did, shooting little Super-8 movies with school equipment (which I was unable to borrow; I didn't get my first VHS camcorder until my senior year of high school), moving toys and bits of clay around in attempt to bring them to life two frames at a time. What I lacked in any kind of technical talent I made up for with strong storytelling and structure. By the time my junior year rolled around, I'd already been professionally published in very, very small scholastic journals, but these minor achievements had weight.

Once I got to film school, the post–Vietnam War–era equipment (Frezzolinis, CPs, Arri-S's) proved time and again that I was hopeless as a cameraman, a director of photography or a sound engineer. And these failures taught me to align myself with those who were talented in those areas. My strengths — writing and editing — grew stronger with the love I had for those two arenas. To me, that's where the movie comes together, the blueprint and then the crafting. Not surprisingly, given my antisocial nature at heart, these two things are done best alone. Production, on the other hand, alternately bores me and stresses me out to no end.

Writer/director Mike Watt shooting a scene from *The Resurrection Game*.

But once the piece is created, once it's up on a screen for the world to see, that's what keeps me going. Regardless of audience response, any movie I've had a hand in exists because of work I put into it, by myself or with my filmmaking family. This *movie* did not exist before us.

Chalk it up to fatalism or fear of mortality, but I make movies in order to leave some of myself behind when I'm gone.

Ritch Yarber: I have been a film fan my whole life. I grew up watching every genre of movie, including horror, westerns, gangster films, musicals. As a kid, my friends and I were steady customers every Saturday at the old matinees where you got two movies for one price. Our summers were spent at the drive-in with my best friend's older brother chauffeuring us around in one of his beat-up junkers. Every new horror movie or exploitation film on the circuit was eagerly absorbed by our hungry eyes. The noon movie on television introduced me to the likes of Cagney, Bogart, Grant and all the rest. I especially loved films that drew me into a story that I really did not want to end and that would leave you thinking and wondering, "What else happened?" after the movie was over. Some of the movies that I often reflect back on for inspiration are *The Graduate, Night of the Living Dead, That Man from Rio, Raiders of the Lost Ark, It's a Mad Mad Mad Mad World.* I am driven to make films that entertain foremost, and that tell an interesting story with unique characters that you either love or hate, but that, hopefully, you will remember and comment on long after you have viewed it. I try to deliver more in my films than may be initially expected from the audience so that the viewer will know that, as a filmmaker, I appreciate and respect the time that they have chosen to devote to watching my product and that, despite the budget, I have attempted to earn the opportunity to entertain them. Of course, my production company is a little different. I prefer to call it a "film group" since the goal is to create opportunity in our productions for people to showcase their talents in an actual movie product or "feature-length résumé," as I have termed it. I make films because my personal goal is to one day be paid to create scripts or direct films. I feel that the best way to get noticed is to establish a history of successes. So, as I perform my duties as writer and director, other talented people contribute their best work to the production, and, hopefully, the end result will be that actual paid opportunities will come about based on the successes of these films, for one or more of us. We have had a few success stories. Some of our actors have since appeared opposite Will Ferrell, John C. Reilly and Michael Madsen in productions on television and on the big screen. My work and success on my microbudget productions has created opportunities to write for other filmmakers, for radio advertisements and for local cable television.

Ivan Zuccon: I remember, as a kid, watching Sergio Leone's movies, I wanted to try my hand at cinema and I even started writing a script for a sci-fi western movie, something combining my two all-time favorite films, *The Good, The Bad, and the Ugly* by Leone, and *Escape from New York* by John Carpenter. Perhaps I already knew that I would end up behind the camera, even though I went through many phases and many other passions, like music or drawings and comics. My influences are mainly literary. My imagination has been struck by writers such as William Burroughs and J.G. Ballard. They've opened my mind, and made me seen things that I could not even imagine. Then came the movies. Bergman and Buñuel's cinema have marked me deeply. When you watch their films it's like jumping into a boat and taking a very personal journey into the worlds created by them. Two of their movies that changed my life are Bergman's *The Silence* and Buñuel's *The Discreet Charm of the Bourgeoisie.*

Writer/director Ivan Zuccon

Film School

In my professional film/video work no one has cared if I went to film school or not. In fact, they are usually surprised (which I don't know is a good thing or a bad thing) when I tell them I have a B.A. from the University of Michigan. Everything I learned, I learned practically, hands-on, on-the-job, from audio to lighting to shooting to editing. While in school I worked as staff at a local community-access television station and made my own movies, independent of classes. Would I have made my short films if I wasn't attending film/studies classes? Yes. However, seeing films in film school that I'd never normally see — from *The Umbrellas of Cherbourg* to *Barry Lyndon* to *Out of the Past*, gave me an aesthetic sense. Learning why and when to use certain angles, framing and lighting was also useful in conveying feeling and situation. Basically, film school teaches you the art of making a movie.

The one advantage of going to school is that you'll meet other people interested in the same thing — and you'll be able to get like-minded people to work on your projects. And, who knows, you may make some connections that will help your future films. However, if you have the intention of becoming a Hollywood director once you graduate, you'll probably be disappointed. Most likely, you will be going for the same "production assistant" job as someone who has never set foot in a film seminar. Making and directing a movie that gets distributed and "out there" to an audience makes you a director.

I've met hundreds of independent filmmakers and half of them have gone to school, while the other half learned it on their own. Is there a difference in the quality of their films? No — there's an equal amount of good and bad movies. Will going to film school or not going to film school determine if you make a movie? It depends. Ultimately, going to school is a personal decision of the individual filmmaker.

The Filmmakers were asked:
Do you recommend going to film school or learning in the field? What do you think are the advantages/disadvantages of each?

Glenn Andreiev: If possible, do both. First, you'll meet fellow film students who will become future collaborators. If the film instructor is good, you'll learn a lot of great stuff that will prep you for the real world. Unfortunately, I had some film teachers that focused on their own unrealistic, filmmaking agendas.

Working on a film set is also a great learning experience. While I attended the School of Visual Arts, I worked on the cult movie *Street Trash*, as the transportation captain, and I learned so much about keeping a low-budget shoot afloat, on schedule, and on budget. I was lucky to work on *Street Trash*, which was made by ingenious professionals. I could have wound up working on a film made by people who have no concept of making a film.

John Borowski: Even though I graduated from film school, I don't think it is necessary to go to film school. The tools to make films are affordable and so much can be learned online and by watching the "making of" extra features on DVDs. I would recommend buying a camera and editing software and learning on your own. Watch great films and analyze how they are made. Much can be learned at film school if you are taught by experts in their field because they have real-world experience, which is invaluable. In college, I created my own curriculum based on my desire to be a well-rounded producer/director. I took lighting, screenwriting, sound, editing, camera, and even acting classes. Learning how to wrap audio cables is essential!

Keith Crocker: I'm a film school graduate, but, personally, I'd have rather received my education in the field, or at least continue to self educate. I don't resent my college education — I honestly think that everyone needs some sort of structuring once they leave high school; college or the military is most certainly the way to go, as you get life experience out of both. However, filmmaking is a field that offers no promises. In most cases you have to go out and make it work for yourself. I honestly believe I could have done this without college. On the other hand, tuition at the time was far cheaper than renting film equipment from a rental house (we are talking the mid–1980s). We were shooting on film then, so the instruction was important if you didn't want to keep screwing up your product. Plus, all the equipment and crew people were there for the asking. I left college with a decent 16mm film résumé, but in the real world that meant shit. Furthermore, by the time I got out of college technology was changing, most folks shot video (which I deplored), analog video editing was all the rage, all the stuff I learned about 16mm was starting to go the way of the dinosaur. And although I knew film was expen-

sive, when it came time to start shooting my first feature, *The Bloody Ape*, I had to shoot it on film, even if it was Super 8mm. I just couldn't stand the look of video-shot product. In terms of what is the best way for someone to proceed into filmmaking, either college or field work, I say that's determined by the person's comfort level. If you try to get ground-level film work, and of course you won't be in the union, you had better believe you'll be working for free, whether it's big or low budget, and you had better believe that will continue for a while until you land your first paying gig. And more than likely you'll be getting people coffee, not setting up shots. College, on the other hand, is not the real world, so yes, you can pass directly to a director's position in college, but once you get out of college, unless you're doing your own films, you are not going to be handed a director's chair.

Richard Cunningham: I'm inclined to think film school is something that's for some people and not for others. I suspect it's great for getting a formal and well-rounded education on the process of filmmaking, and for developing networking skills, and finding production groups to form.

But I never went to college for film. I did go for writing, and the competition was so incredible that I was quickly, however halfheartedly, becoming a classical studies major. So I left and started production of my first major self-produced film.

Aside from meeting a talented group of friends and writers with whom to collaborate, the college experience didn't work for me. And now, seeing the debt some of my colleagues face from their earned degrees and the obstacles they continue to face securing work in their respective fields, I can't say I regret going my own route. I feel like degrees have lost considerable value in the workforce, while the costs of higher education continue to climb. The recent Occupy Wall Street movement in the news, with people getting hosed and teargassed in protest, attests to the hopelessness a lot of educated young people are experiencing in the face of unemployment. They feel like they bought into a system that didn't pay them back, and I think that was my impression of it as well.

Learning in the professional field is the best way to go about it; if you're fortunate enough to live by the industry and/or a location that attracts film/TV productions. If you can work on a professional movie or television set, you will observe how a production operates, and that certainly gives you a good idea of how a movie is properly broken down and streamlined. You might also see how the big movies are at the mercy of some of the same forces as the micro-budget productions. Learning in the field, like starting out as a production assistant, you instill yourself into a system, where in order to advance your position you have to put in a lot of hours. This not only quickly familiarizes you with the filmmaking machine, it introduces you to the grueling hours put into lighting and camera setups, rehearsals, and the dozens of other elements at work during a day's shoot. An average shift on a professional set is 12 hours; and for a PA, it's a lot of running around for people, with little recognition for your efforts. It definitely seems like a make-it-or-break-it kind of job, but if you can become part of the crew, you will be making connections that will secure you work on further productions, and you are creating an incredible educational and networking opportunity for yourself.

Beyond that, I recommend immediately immersing yourself in the craft of filmmaking: buy some good books on it, watch YouTube tutorials, get yourself an HD camera with an external-mix jack, start filming your family and friends and pets in order to practice framing and lighting shots, or for editing and soundtrack material; or try shooting no-budget trailers or shorts to develop and understand the craft more intimately.

Whatever approach you take, it all comes down to practice. Naturally, the more hours you put into fine-tuning your skills as a filmmaker, the more precise you become in telling the story to the audience; but also, the better your workflow runs, and, ultimately, the more confident you become in taking on new challenges offered in film.

Maurice Devereaux: I went to film school in a college in Montreal, but it wasn't a very advanced course and I was quickly bored and then decided not to go to university, and just pursue making films on my own. But I still met so many friends in film school who were important to my career, that, looking back, I do believe it was well worth it to go to school to "meet" fellow cinema nuts. Also one of my cinema professors, Pierre Pageau, was very nice to me — he helped me out for years after I was no longer a student, giving me access to equipment, et cetera. The drawback to going to film school, I guess, would be the cost (especially to a high-end school in the U.S.) as you could make a feature for the cost of tuition. So it's pretty much 50/50. So if you're already surrounded by filmmakers, actors etc, then school might not be necessary. If you're alone with your passion, in the middle of butt-fuck nowhere town, definitely go to film school.

Donald Farmer: I suppose I went to my own version of film school. All those movie sets I visited on assignment for *Fangoria, Fantastic Films* and other magazines gave me a chance to watch George Romero, John Carpenter, Sam Raimi and other favorite directors up close. Plus I was doing interviews with lower-budget filmmakers, like Herschell Gordon Lewis, Joel Reed and Fred Olen Ray for my *Splatter Times* fanzine, so before long I was itching to try features on my own.

Actually, the first film set I ever visited was a country-music movie called *W.W. and the Dixie Dance Kings*, directed by John Avildsen. He'd just done *Joe* with Peter Boyle and *Save the Tiger* with Jack Lemmon — two films I was a huge fan of. I found out where he'd be filming in downtown Nashville and showed up to see what making a major motion picture looks like. Burt Reynolds was the star, so lots of teenage girls were clustered around his trailer — screaming every time he poked his head out.

This was during the height of his '70s popularity—he'd just made *Deliverance* and was churning out two or three movies a year. I saw very little actually being filmed during my visit but spent the day hanging out with the movie's very affable stunt coordinator ... a guy named Hal. Only a few years later when *Smokey and the Bandit* came out did I make the connection that the director of that film, Hal Needham, was the same Hal who'd been telling me stories all day about working with John Wayne, Jack Nicholson and Raquel Welch.

By the time I got the gig to cover the making of *Day of the Dead*, I was ready to see what I could learn from watching George Romero at work firsthand. Unfortunately, the only thing I saw Romero direct were some zombie crowd shots where he just said things like "growl" and "move your arms!" I was one of those zombies ... the producer had enlisted all visiting reporters to play bit parts in the movie. But with multiple cameras shooting endless coverage, I could pick up very little about Romero's approach to filmmaking. He had a huge crew and it looked like everything was being delegated. All the assistants had assistants ... the production seemed to have limitless resources. Not exactly the situation I'd find myself in with *Demon Queen* two years later, with a measly five-man crew. At least I had the good fortune to nab one of Tom Savini's make-up crew for my debut feature—an insanely talented guy named Rick Gonzales. Anything worthwhile about *Demon Queen* is because of him!

That same year I was on location with John Carpenter's *Starman* for another magazine report. I was still buzzing from seeing Carpenter's *The Thing* and figured the man could do no wrong. When it came time to start filming, Carpenter at least looked through the camera viewfinder a little more than Romero. Still, he had the maddening habit of whispering directions to his stars (Jeff Bridges and Karen Allen). He'd pull them over in a corner before each scene so no one else could hear a thing. Then when he went for a shot, his as-sistant director yelled "Action," and "Cut." I didn't hear Carpenter's voice the entire time I was there!!

I'd just wrapped *Demon Queen* when I had the change to cover the filming of Sam Raimi's *Evil Dead 2* in North Carolina. And—finally—here was a director that I could really learn from. Raimi had just as big a crew as Carpenter and Romero, but this was a guy who believed in the micro-management approach to filmmaking. There was absolutely no job or no crewmember too minor for Raimi's full attention I watched him take time out for mundane chores like interviewing a potential assistant gaffer, overseeing the day-to-day progress of his production, and make-up staffs (inspecting every last prosthetic appliance and animation model) and spending hours on even the filming of background plates—a chore most major studio movies would delegate to a second-unit crew.

Raimi clearly had the entire movie in his head, right down to every edit and zoom-lens shot. When he described a scene to me he would be shooting later that week, I realized, "Here's a guy who knows his movie COLD ... before he shoots it." Raimi would probably agree with a line I read once from Brian De Palma. The director of *Carrie* and *Scarface* said flatly, "I think coverage is a dirty word."

Hanging out with Raimi, all the flaws of *Demon Queen* seems so magnified now I could barely stand to watch it. Sure he had a little more money than me ... about ten million versus my three grand. But there were lessons to be learned here, and I now I was determined to make my next movie something I could be just a little bit more proud of.

Jeff Forsyth: There are both tremendous advantages and disadvantages to attending and not attending film school. I was not able to attend film school, although I would have liked to. The chief advantage that I see in attending would be being surrounded with like-minded individuals. People that actually understand you and what drives you can be a great advantage as a support system. Not only

Jeff Forsyth films actors Lexie Davies and Frank Tropepi in a scene for *C.A.I.N.* The motorcycle is on a rented trailer, and the camera is in the back of a pickup truck, allowing for a stable shot.

as technical and artistic help, but as emotional support as well. The obvious disadvantage is the cost. A filmmaker could make several low-budget films for what it costs for tuition. You'll gain far more "hands on" experience just diving in and creating. Film school can't teach you to be an artist. Either you are you aren't.

Richard W. Haines: In my case, attending NYU's film school was helpful. I learned how to work in 16mm film, which included editing, negative matching and sound mixing. Since my first feature was shot in that format, then blown up to 35mm, I was able to save on costs. Of course, today the emphasis is on digital movie-making in colleges, so that aspect would not be applicable. I also studied with historians William K. Everson and Leonard Maltin, which inspired me to get into that field as a supplement to my directing career.

However, if a person was interested in the technical areas of the industry I don't think film school would be necessary. Their best bet would be to get a job as a production assistant on an independent production, then work their way up to some area they wanted to focus on, like cinematography, sound design or editing.

William Hopkins: I'm probably not the best person to ask, because I'm pretty much self-taught. Whether it was screenwriting or special effects or photography or editing, I pretty much figured it out myself without formal training. I saw a lot of films and read a lot about the ones I liked, but I certainly never learned anything about filmmaking from sitting in a classroom. The end results may not always be the best, but, for better or worse, it's all my work, all done in my style and using the techniques I developed through trial and error. I did go to film school back in the early '80s but I didn't have a very good experience, and I didn't graduate. Maybe others would've gotten more out of it. Maybe film schools have gotten better since my day. I hope so. But, for me, it seemed a waste of time and money. On the very first day we heard things from our instructors like, "None of you are going to have careers in the film industry because there just isn't enough work," and "You'll only get out of this school what you put into it." I couldn't disagree with either statement, but it was a little discouraging to hear these things from the people we were paying to train us in the business — and to hear such honesty only after making our first tuition payments. But film schools are businesses. There are plenty of rich folks who are willing to indulge their children by paying for them to be trained in things they have very little chance of ever making a career of. And there are plenty of schools that are only too happy to take the money.

Many of the instructors at the place I went seemed to be rather unhappy people who hadn't had much luck in the film business themselves, and so they ended up teaching. There were exceptions, though. I took a class in film history given by William K. Everson and that was certainly worthwhile. Being introduced, by someone as knowledgeable as Everson, to great films I probably wouldn't have known about otherwise was practically worth the cost of the tuition in itself. So the classes in film history and theory were worthwhile, but the rest seemed a waste. It's possible, too, that I was just not in the right place, mentally and emotionally, to be able to really benefit from my time there. I wasn't mature enough to be able to see the value in the experience. In the years since, the school I attended turned out a few successful filmmakers, so maybe there was something going on there I just didn't appreciate. Or maybe they've gotten better since I left.

But I don't think anyone should feel they have to go to film school to be a filmmaker. If you don't have the money to be able to go that route, put what little money you have into getting a camera and an editing system and get started making your own films. The most valuable education you can get comes from just making movies.

Steve Hudgins: Learning in any aspect is a positive. But there is absolutely nothing that can replace actual hands-on experience. I re-

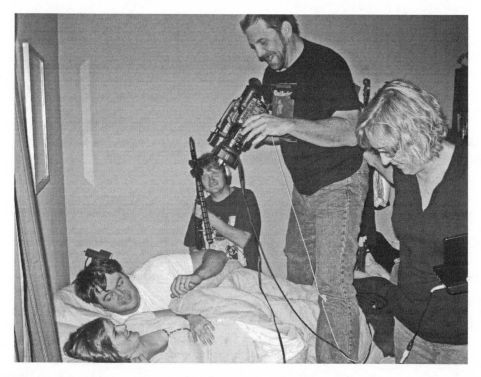

Preparing to shoot a scene for of *The Creepy Doll.* Pictured (left to right) are Kristine Renee Farley; Justin Veazey; Mark Cotton (boom operator); Steve Hudgins (cameraman); and PJ Woodside (holding monitor).

cently saw a Q & A with William Friedkin, who directed *The Exorcist, The French Connection* and a ton of other movies, and his advice to film students was to drop out and start making movies. He said anything you need to learn about film making you can learn by watching Alfred Hitchcock movies.

Rolfe Kanefsky: You can't beat learning in the field. Film school is good for learning the basics and possibly very good for meeting people, networking, and making connections that can be very important career-wise. I was totally obsessed with making movies by the time I was ready for college. I had already made two feature-length films. My parents wanted me to go to a good college that had a film department. I wanted to go to a film department that had a college. We settled on Hampshire College. They had a film program that wasn't very good, but everyone loved the idea of making movies so they had a lottery to determine who would get into the class. I lost twice and then finally just forced my way in, supplying my own Super 8 camera (that's what was being used back then). I did all the assignments and made some fun shorts. One short, *Just Listen*, plays in the beginning of *There's Nothing Out There*, and I put the whole 12-minute film on the new release of *There's Nothing Out There* that Troma put out in 2011.

Anyway, I remember showing these "horror" shorts in class and getting bad responses from the teachers. They hated anything Hollywood, and especially horror. However, that summer I worked on a slasher film, *Posed for Murder*, as a production assistant and made friends with the director and producers. I showed them my short and they were very important. The director even, some say, ripped off a shot I did for his movie. So, I quickly learned there is a big difference between the academic world and real world of the film business. When I took a semester off to make *There's Nothing Out There*, my college advisor read my script and said that I wasn't going to learn anything from making this horror movie. I still find that comment to be incred-

ible. Writing and directing a $150,000 dollar movie in 1989 at the age of 20 and I wasn't going to learn anything?!! Well, after shooting, I did go back for one more semester and told him that I think I learned some stuff. He told me to write down what I learned and maybe I could get some credit for the film. I wrote a 144-page book called *Making Nothing at the Age of 20*. The book is online at www.theres nothingoutthere.com and is written for other aspiring filmmakers, relating my experiences. After that, I left college to pursue my career full-time.

So, like I said, it's good to learn the equipment and meet other like-minded filmmakers but take everything you learn in school with a grain of salt. Being on a real movie set, you'll learn a lot more about how the business really works, for better and worse.

Brett Kelly: I think the main advantage of film school is the networking opportunities that it provides. Making movies is a collaborative art, and that's a great place to meet people to collaborate with. I personally didn't go to film school, but I did take television broadcasting at college for a short time, until my student loan ran dry. It taught me a lot in the short time I was there. I think it's important for aspiring filmmakers to know the "language" of film and to learn the techniques that a film school will (I assume) teach you. Whether or not you can do that from school, from being an intern on a film set or what have you, it's important to learn the rules before you can properly call yourself a filmmaker. In my opinion anyway.

Chris LaMartina: Prior to my undergraduate film school experience, I attended a magnet high school with video production courses. Both high school video class and film school were invaluable experiences to my development as a storyteller.

They allowed me to explore my craft, discuss tactics through student critique, and provided crucial networking opportunities that I still rely on to this day.

Could I have learned visual storytelling

outside of school? Absolutely, but film school is what you make it. I learned both inside and outside of the classroom, never letting the education process evaporate at edge of campus.

I will say this, however: if you're serious about filmmaking a career, consider minoring, or perhaps even majoring, in business. Too many filmmakers forget that this is show *business*. We all want to be artists, but paying your rent is good, too. A business degree allows for a nice counterbalance to your strong aesthetic voice.

Jim Mickle: There's no right way to get into the film business. I went to NYU undergrad for film production and I enjoyed the hell out of it, but I also spent a lot of time working on films as a grip, a storyboard artist, and an editor. Ultimately I think I absorbed a lot from both, and I can attribute a good amount of success to both, but I think it's totally up to the individual. Film school was great for meeting like-minded people and learning theory, but mostly for having a structured environment for creating short films with limitations, and growing from that. But now, with the costs of film schools rising, and the availability of impressive cameras and technology exploding, I think the most important thing to do is go out and create as much as you can and learn from mistakes and find out what you're good at and what you enjoy the most about the process. Start interning and production assisting on films as soon as possible because that's where the most hands-on experience comes from. At first you probably won't get paid, but if you have a good attitude and show an eagerness to learn, good jobs and opportunities will come. I was always amazed that most directors on movie sets are the least-experienced people on the sets. Having real experience in pre-production, production, and post makes it a lot smoother when you're shooting and working with crews. Editing is the single best place to learn about storytelling because you're forced to create a narrative out of whatever material has been delivered. I've learned a lot about coverage through years of editing as a day job.

Damon Packard: Well, I went to film school briefly in 1988, mainly to borrow equipment and meet people, but I'd already been making films for six or seven years. I think the best way is just to start doing it on your own. But, of course, these days, with easy-to-use extremely hi-quality (and cheap) camera and editing equipment available at everyone's fingertips, film school is just a self-contained social environment for a collective group of kids to make and exhibit their films. In the filmmaking age things were a bit different as you had to learn how to use Super 8mm, 16mm and 35mm film cameras, flatbed editors, full-coat dubbing, syncing dailies, et cetera. It was infinitely more complex and prohibitively expensive.

Brad Paulson: Education is a wonderful thing, and I would never discourage anyone against it. You can never do yourself wrong by getting out there and learning more. My parents are educators and they've done a lot of good for this world. I have a lot of respect for all they've accomplished and the wonderful influence they've had. However, there are different ways to learn. Basically, for me, it's a money-and-time thing. If you've only got six months to live and making a movie is the last thing on your bucket list before you die, I wouldn't waste it going to film school. I'd skip right to making the movie. If money isn't an issue, I'd recommend it. If it is, you're better off using that money to make a movie. There are a few other factors that come into play as well. It all depends on what school you're going to. If you're going to a small school in the boondocks, where you're not going to get any guest speakers, then I'd definitely save your money. If you're going to some place like UCLA where they have tons of great guest speakers who are actually making a living making movies and it's in a place where film is all around you and you have the money, I'd say go. Don't put yourself in debt to do it. But if you have the money, go. You don't want to spend the rest of your life paying off loans in something that you have a minuscule chance of making a living at. I know that sounds brutal to say, but it's the truth. There are millions of people who move to L.A. to be either a writer, director or actor. Unfortunately, it's an industry that keeps it's guardians very close to the door. If I had to do it over again, I wouldn't go to film school. I'd go to school for something I knew I'd be able to make money in. Then, I'd make movies on the side. The longer you're in L.A., the more you'll see that what most people are making their money on out here is screen-writing seminars and "how to" film classes. This is primarily for two reasons — number one, because there's a sucker born every minute, and number two, because these people aren't making enough doing what their classes are charging you hundreds to thousands of dollars to learn how to do. Having said that, I still go to some of these classes, provided they're cheap enough. You can always learn something from a seminar. You just have to be cautious about which ones you pick and how much money you spend. There are a lot of predators out there and your money is what they're hunting. Be careful who you give it to. Teaching you how to make movies is guaranteed money for them. The only guarantee with making movies on your own is that it will be a high-risk venture.

The best thing about film school, to me, was not the school part. Many of the friends I met there I'm still close to, to this day: the fellow weird kids that taught an even weirder kid all about cult movies. I had never heard of Dario Argento before I went to film school. I had never heard of Lucio Fulci. A fellow film nerd showed me *The Beyond* and would describe the movies in his collection as art that changed his life forever. The fellow film nerds I quickly befriended had an infectious enthusiasm that I quickly absorbed and, in turn, they absorbed the movies I was passionate about. We made a great team and had a blast working on each other's projects as we avoided our responsibilities in the real world while we were in the bubble that is college.

The school part involved mostly teachers reading from books and telling everyone their projects sucked. And then they showed us their movies, which proved why they weren't making them professionally. Not to say they were all bad, by any means. There were some passionate, non-biased teachers there who I respected and had a great time in their classes and learned from. I wish we had more like them. Unfortunately, several were not very nice to us. Film professors, to me, are like cops. There are good cops are there are bad cops. There are cops who truly care about helping people and doing the right thing. Then, there are the corrupt sons of bitches and the bullies: people who are jaded about life and are on a constant power trip. Some of my professors fell into that category. There was a lot of bitterness going around that school. I don't believe there's any excuse for this. I've had plenty of things not go my way and I don't take it out on other people. They were supposed to be there to inspire us but spent most of their time telling us we were going to fail. I think they saw us as competition in a strange kind of way.

My main beef about film school was that there was a lack of nurturing on the teacher's part for the students' individual visions. The department seemed to have an agenda about the type of films they wanted to see representing the school, and if you didn't make those kind of movies the teachers would be the opposite of supportive. There were clearly a lot of politics involved. To me, this didn't make sense because it wasn't high school. Everyone was paying to be there, and that was paying the teachers' salaries. They should have been happy to help the students make the kind of movies they wanted to make. Unfortunately, it wasn't that way at all. Also, there was no effort to teach us anything about the business side of things, even making budgets. When we graduated they provided zero help in finding us jobs. I'm still struggling to make even the simplest ends meet.

I remember I went back to visit one teacher

I interned for who was a complete ass when I walked into his office. I told him I was making movies and all he did was tell me how the students who graduate never give enough money to the alumni department. I tell you this right now. If I ever do have any money, he's the last guy I'll give it to. The least you can do in this life is not be an asshole 24 hours out of the day. If you can't follow that simple rule, you don't deserve any money. Film school can be a great place, but, not unlike the government, there are too many politics at play. There needs to be some changes made to put the students first and make it worth the money to attend.

Jose Prendes: Film school is not necessary. You will learn so much more doing it on your own. I learned a hell of a lot more working on my first feature, *The Monster Man*, than I did in the previous two years of film school. There are some things that film school cannot teach. However, I think some people do well in a school environment. Others, like me, hate school. I found my film school lacking, so I learned what I wanted to learn and moved on.

One of the biggest advantages of film school is that they teach you the lingo. This is important if you want to work on professional sets, because you get to learn what a C-47 is, or how a call sheet works, or what exactly an Abby Singer shot is. However, if you pick up a book or work on a few sets as a PA, you will learn the exact same thing!

If you have the money and your parents want you to go to college (which was my situation) then do film school, but you DO NOT NEED A MASTER'S DEGREE! I got an associates degree just to get my folks off my back, because I wanted to jump into movie making. I was hungry and I felt school was holding me back. You only need a master's degree if you want to teach, and if that is the case, then go for it. If not, stay away from film school, save your money and make your first movie! You will be so happy you did.

Paul Scrabo: I'm from a generation where the idea of a "film school" was amazing. My God, if you have the money for film school, go. You can go to college ... and master in film? I can't take it serious. It may be an amazing racket, and I'm all for it. It is certainly legitimate for networking and being with like-minded folks. I would certainly recommend any courses that would improve one's writing ability. That's valid. It's a shame the school game is life-backwards — when you are older, that's when you appreciate the importance of education. Imagine spending a few years where all that's expected of you is to learn? Sounds like a fine deal to me.

Eric Shapiro: Learning in the field is probably better. I started off at Emerson College as a film major, but hated it and switched to writing, literature, and publishing. The technology made me crazy; I realized I was far more interested in the script and performances (which is still true), and had no patience to learn about loading film into a camera. So, for me, there was a disconnect at school between what they were teaching and what excited me about the medium. The advantage of the field is that you get the business side drilled into you and you learn from doing. School really doesn't have an advantage over the field; there's no substitute for experience. Certainly not theory!

Anthony Straeger: Okay, lets start with the advantages and disadvantages before I make a recommendation: What are the advantages of going to a film school? Simply, you are in a like-minded environment, you have the facilities at your disposal, from cameras to lights to sound. You have instant crew. You have a great opportunity to experiment and discover yourself within the safety of the school. In short, you have everything that you could need to hand with the bonus of mentors and people that have sound technical knowledge of filmmaking.

The disadvantages of going to film school, first and foremost, is cost. It's an expensive business. I know that the main two in London, the London International Film School runs a two-year, all-around course, and the

National Film School runs a three-year specific course. Both run at several thousands of pounds per year. Which is okay if you:

1. Can get a grant
2. Get sponsored
3. Come from wealthy parents

I was trying and succeeded in getting into London International Film School, but couldn't raise the finances or get enough support to make it viable. If you can go, then select a good school that is well recommended. You need to learn the basics of everything — sound, lights, camera and then management.

The advantages of not going to film school... Well, they say that sometimes it's better to learn on your feet and in the midst of the action. And this can be very true — especially these days when so many people are making shorts and movies. It's relatively easy getting involved in any number of productions where you can learn at first-hand other people's mistakes and skills. If you have the right attitude, this can be a less expensive route, though with low/no budget productions you won't get paid in cash, only experience. The disadvantages are almost part of its advantages. You can get to work with some real idiots and end up wasting a great deal of time, but that's the way it is.

There are many great books out there on lighting, camerawork, producing and directing an independent movie. With the right kind of research and with the good sense to start small, you can grow as a producer/director/writer and learn from your own mistakes. As to whether I recommend that you should go to film school, the answer is — YES — If you can, you should.

Marc Trottier: I've never been to film school (as I've mentioned, I started late), but I'm sure I would've loved it. I also think that learning in the field is invaluable, regardless of what you've learned in school. You need to make mistakes and try new things to find out what you like and what works for you (and hopefully you'll get to do that in school). You

can only learn so much from reading a book, no matter who wrote it. Get out there and play and have fun ... and in the process, you'll gain experience and confidence in what you enjoy doing.

Mike Watt: I'm a big supporter of film school for the fundamentals, particularly if you get to work with "archaic" equipment. At Pittsburgh Filmmakers, so much of our equipment had been bought from or donated by television studios and pro- and semi-pro photographers. Much of it was in rough shape. But it was pointed out to me by my longtime friend and filmmaker, Justin Wingenfeld (*Skin Crawl*), that filmmakers taught us how to "make movies under the worst possible conditions." Nothing ever worked the way it was supposed to, so we learned early on how to improvise, MacGyuer a camera so that it worked for at least one shot, wrap a microphone cable to override the neighbor's television signal, et cetera. I think this end of film school is priceless.

The mechanics of filmmaking, when it comes to the physical equipment or the visual language of filmmaking over the last century, is essential knowledge. You simply cannot move ahead as an artist without some knowledge of what came before you. Maybe you can instinctually know that something is wrong if you broke the 180-degree rule. But if you know what the rule is in the first place, it goes a long way towards avoiding rookie mistakes so you can concentrate on glorious new fuck-ups, which sometimes yield great rewards as well as heartbreak.

But none of the mechanics or history will help you as an artist if you don't *love* the medium. That's obviously something that can't be taught. So many filmmakers I know make movies because they "like to," and refuse to watch anything that was made before the year they were born. No black and white movies, nothing foreign — hell, nothing that isn't *horror*, in many instances. And that's why we're continually plagued with "masked killer slashing up pot-smoking asshole kids" movies, *sans* anything of depth. "You've never seen kills like these," one kid told me. Then looked blankly at me when I asked, again, "What is it *about*? What makes this movie special? Why is this story one you *have* to tell?"

If all you want to do is entertain yourself and your friends, then there's nothing wrong with "liking" movies or "liking to make" movies. But history is so much richer than just what you think your preferences are. One argument I get into a lot involves the Italian "spaghetti westerns." I have a real tough time when someone insists that Sergio Leone made the best westerns in history, offhandedly dismissing all of Leone's influences — John Ford, Howard Hawks, Anthony Mann — the guys who *understood* what westerns were and what they meant to our culture, particularly as Americans. It's the difference between experience and vocabulary. You simply cannot discard what came before you because you won't know how to build upon history of which you're ignorant. How would one grow as an artist and a filmmaker without knowing about the past? It's like trying to kill a fly with a shotgun. In the dark. You can imitate, you can morph elements into something of your own, but without that history, that's all you have: imitation.

That being said, personal education grows exponentially with experience. Until you're on a set of any size, all the theory and mechanics in the world won't help you *create* a movie. True creativity comes, in my opinion, not from wealth and controlled environments, but from limitations and ridiculously unforeseen obstacles. After the writing is done, everything else involved in making a movie is physical and so much of that physicality is working *around* whatever problem has been coughed up by the universe. How do you keep that old camera working until the end of the day? What are you going to do for lights if there's no electricity? Why didn't the location scout mention that the set was infested with roaches? This effect didn't work, what do we do?

Working independently forces you — to borrow the cliché — to wear many hats and sometimes all of them. This is where you evolve as an artist: learning what you are *not* good at. Something came up and your DP didn't show up? You'll have to light yourself, and if you don't like the results, even if you understand all the concepts, your choices are to live with it or reshoot. On the other hand, it turns out you have a talent for capturing really good sound. This period of self-discovery doesn't end if you continue to work independently, and that's a good thing. Even when you're working with a tight crew whose habits you know as well as your own, it's still good to know if you've evolved into a *better* DP or what have you. At least you understand what you're doing, even if you're not the best at doing it.

Ritch Yarber: The chance to attend film school is a phenomenal opportunity to learn, understand and use the tools that are part of the craft of filmmaking. It is certainly an advantage to anyone that wants to pursue this art in a serious manner. However, I do not feel that film school in itself will make you become a better filmmaker. It will just make you better informed. The passion to tell stories and affect audiences lies in the soul and mind of the artist. It will certainly be a harder road to travel, but the committed filmmaker will ultimately seek, find and execute the ways and means to deliver their vision with or without the benefit of attending film school. Either way, their works will grow from raw, rough early projects and slowly blossom into more polished and defined productions. I feel that film school is designed to produce filmmakers that may have all of the technical tools to succeed. But that does not guarantee that a person will be a good filmmaker. Those without the advantage of this knowledge are forced to think out of the box and are bringing new and innovative changes to the art everyday. The future of filmmaking is getting exciting again as these new ways are slowly being embraced and welcomed. With this being said, I still wish that I had gone to film school when I had the chance. I tell kids today to "live their passion!" Better to try and fail than attempt to climb back into the game after life has taken you on its path. Follow your heart, as the mind can be easily influenced.

Ivan Zuccon: Schools are important, and it's important to learn in the field. The first thing, though, is not essential, while the second one is. You cannot learn to make movies without having experience on set. Making movies is something you learn, first of all, by watching others do it.

The Script

If someone asked me what I thought I was best at, in terms of filmmaking, I would say it was writing the scripts. I spent far more time writing the screenplays than I spent on shooting the actual productions. And, because of the limited budget, I knew what was possible to do and what wasn't. I kept in mind locations I had access to, special effects I knew I could pull off (for the most part), and used actors that fit the characters. The majority of the script was the idea and the dialogue. It didn't matter if I had to change a location, such as an apartment — and oftentimes, I didn't even see the on-location apartment until I showed up for the shoot. That didn't matter nearly so much as what the characters said and did. The story was all important.

I've come across a great many of wannabe scriptwriters who are obsessed with script writing software, and it was always my impression that they thought the computer program was going to write the screenplay for them. Well, you don't need a program. Just learn the correct format to use. Look up examples of Hollywood scripts on the internet — there are scores of them freely available to download. If you're writing the script with the intention of trying to get an agent for it, it should be as professional as possible and adhere to all the rules. However, if it's just for your eyes only — and for your actors — you need not be so concerned about this.

I have written scripts for other filmmakers, based out their outlines or ideas. However, there were always strange requests with these. One of them was an erotic vampire movie and the director was specific that there needed to be a sex scene every ten minutes. Basically, I came up with the situation and dialogue and then, when the sex scene happened, I simply wrote "They have sex," as I had no idea what he was going to have them do. It didn't affect the story or the dialogue. On another vampire movie, the outline was very much like *Twilight*, so I took that and made it into a spoof, mirroring some scenes and being very sarcastic. I even went further and added an entirely new aspect to it, to separate it from those movies — and other vampires — but the filmmaker didn't quite have the budget to pull it off — so over 20 pages, and the best parts of the script, were excised. With another horror script, about a Golem-like monster, the producer was hung up on certain things, such as having the main female character dressed as a slutty school girl in one scene (for no reason other than to make him happy, since that obviously turned him on). Then, on another script, which had a lackluster idea of someone being possessed by a ghost, I greatly improved the original idea, giving motives and reasons for all the characters' actions. I ended up loving this story, even though the core idea was lame. Yet, when I showed this to the "producer," he wanted me to undo it all and keep to their original outline, which read "He's a ghost. Ghosts can possess people if they want." I received payment for the script, but it was one of the most unsatisfying writing jobs of my life.

I have also co-written numerous unproduced screenplays with other independent filmmakers, and those were written for much larger budgets, intended for production companies that would potentially buy them. I think these are perhaps my favorite scripts. The collaboration worked so well that, reading them now, I cannot remember who wrote what or came up with certain ideas or twists and turns to the story. They are that consistent in style. I think that type of co-writing is a rarity.

With my documentaries there's no script whatsoever to follow. But I do have a list of questions that I want answered — and the purpose of the documentary is to creatively put these "answers/responses" together. For me, it was the polar opposite way of working on a narrative scripted feature. The majority of the creativeness comes in the editing, of how it's all put together. I've heard of filmmakers who have only used a story outline and let their actors improvise all the dialogue. Sometimes that can work and it gives a specific feel to the movie.

On a few occasions I have also directed scripts written by other people. This was a segment of a werewolf anthology, written by an enthusiastic novice (at the time) and a feature drama, *Walking Between the Raindrops: Revisited*. In the case of the drama, it was actually a remake of a film that was shot/produced by the writer a few years before. He trusted me enough to make his script into a new movie. The script was unchanged from the first version. It could not be improved — it was that perfect.

The most important thing, once you are happy with your shooting script, is to make sure you stick with it during the production. For example, with my very first movie, *Vampires & Other Stereotypes*, the finished product represents only about 60 percent of how I wanted it to turn out. This stemmed primarily from being my very first feature, having far too many actors and crew (30 people working at the same time!) to coordinate, and an Italian DP who never read the script and had his own ideas about the movie. On my next feature, *Addicted to Murder*, I made sure to shoot it as well, and that turned out 95 percent of how I envisioned, primarily because I had control over everything. My only crew was a sound man and he never needlessly questioned the nonlinear story.

The one thing to which a low- or no-budget production will always lend itself is the uniqueness of the script, especially if this is something that you're going to do yourself. After all, this isn't filmmaking by group decision, and you're not trying to be politically correct and appeal to the widest possible audience. This is the reason why the majority of my features were based on my own scripts — there was no creative interference.

The Filmmakers were Asked:
How important is your script? Does your budget determine your ideas or vice-versa?

Glenn Andreiev: The script is the blueprint. Many writers use the "no blueprint–no building/no script–no movie" analogy, but I'll use it again. What I do is that I write not worrying about the budget. On your first draft you should focus on the story, the pacing, the characters, not "oh, what will this cost?" On the second draft I figure what would be costly to shoot, and start making changes.

John Borowski: Use the script as a guideline. Don't get caught up in constant revisions and reformatting. It is most important to shoot footage. So many filmmakers get stuck in the writing stage. To me, storyboards are as equally important as the script. They help me visualize the film shots and how they will be edited together. When writing, you must be realistic about what type of budget you have

John Borowski (left) reviews a script for *H.H. Holmes,* as an actor looks on.

and what is possible to film on that budget. Costs add up quickly when filming. Make sure you do not film night scenes as lighting can be very expensive. Other items that can raise your budget include: guns, make-up, and elaborate stunts/special effects.

When writing the script, it helps to have locations, actors, and, props that you know you can acquire. This way you are building the script around aspects that you know you have access to rather than trying to find them later. Moving into the production phase, the worst thing would be to discover that you cannot gain access to a location or that you cannot afford to have a gun expert on the set.

Keith Crocker: The screenplay is vital; it's your roadmap for the making of your film. However, being flexible, and having the ability to improvise, especially on the set of a "no" or "low" budget film is vital. It's very important to be able to keep shooting and not get hung up about exactly reproducing the shooting script. I'm all for getting a film done as opposed to getting a film done perfectly, as that

is a very high expectation to meet on the lower end of filmmaking. As far as writing for a budget is concerned, you do your imagination extreme damage by limiting it. You are better off letting your imagination soar and simply scale down the method of creating your vision. You have to be inventive as a filmmaker, and as original as possible. Following someone else's roadmap will only keep you suppressed. You're best off letting your freak flag fly high and figuring out how much of it you can create once you get to the actual shooting.

Richard Cunningham: To some extent, I think you can relate the process of making a film to that of chiseling a stone sculpture. You start out, a smith of sorts, playing with a general shape, then you work away at that block with your bag of tools, probably hitting little surprises as you progress, that make slight alterations here and there to your original vision — ultimately contributing individual character to the end product. The script, I think, works well as the sculptor's stone. If you're working off a poor quality chunk of rock, one crack can make a statue's arm fall off.

I think it's much easier to produce a quality movie — no matter what the budget — if it's backed up by a good story and genuine-sounding dialogue. Having said that, since I've directed, I've realized that a script also needs some malleability throughout production as well. Unforeseen obstacles or changes are bound to come up that demand script changes for the benefit of the finished piece.

However, I usually don't let budget stop me too much when I'm developing a story. In high school, I wrote a script for a medieval period film, *Lycian*, which I was determined to develop; and ultimately I left college to begin making it. My production team had an extremely limited budget, especially considering the scope of the movie, and it sometimes made rewrites and workarounds necessary. For instance, I remember during a climactic public execution scene, there was supposed by a large audience present, but we only had about 20 extras that day, so I was forced to rewrite the dialogue to suggest that a crowd had not shown up in protest of the execution itself.

But by and large, we stuck to the script, and the ambition that rested within it, we matched by pushing our skills further than we first thought possible. Similarly, my animated short film, *Year Zero*, is an action/drama about a survivor stuck in his New York City apartment during a zombie apocalypse in 2012; it was also my directorial debut.

Essentially, I think it's best to write whatever kind of story piques your interest. It's a big commitment to even write a script, or rather, to finish writing a script. It will likely feel like a lofty, arduous task at times, so passion certainly helps to keep you going after that third rewrite. But if you take that liberty in your writing, also realize that, when production begins, you may need to consolidate scenes or even characters, change scripted locations, and all those other compromises a director makes once the cameras start rolling and the story evolves into a collaborative effort.

Maurice Devereaux: Of course everyone always says that the script is the most important part of the movie, but most indie and studio films neglect this aspect. Most big-budget films throw in lots of money to get good actors, great sets, costumes and effects, but most of the time their biggest flaw is the script. It is the hardest part to get right for many reasons. Sometimes there are too many cooks who throw their ingredients into the pot (various studio heads, producers, et cetera) with suggestions that are not always related to the "quality" of the story ("we need to sell toys, put something we can make a toy out of" or "this actress is hot, change that role of the scientist guy, make him a hot woman scientist and make the role bigger," etc...). And many "artsy" films are often more concerned with aesthetics then telling a compelling story. So problems with the script are usually my number-one beef with most movies I watch.

Of the four films I directed, only the last two had a complete script before the shoot began. The first two were continuously rewritten, and are terrible. Both started out as shorts that became features over the span of many years. Big mistake. The last two, *Slashers* and *End of the Line*, for all the rocks one can throw at them for their weaknesses (acting, sets, effects, overall production value), I do feel the scripts are very solid.

I've also written six other screenplays that are now gathering dust in my closet or hard drive. These unrealized projects make me sad, as unlike a film or book, all the hard work we put into writing a screenplay is unrewarded if the film is never made. A script is not a "finished" medium that can be shared with the world to be loved or hated. I've been toying with the idea of turning two of my screenplays into graphic novels, but even if it would be less expensive than making a movie, it would still cost a lot to get a professional quality artist, colorist, letterer and a print run. The comic book world has also been hit by illegal download (comics and graphics novels are scanned and put online minutes after their release dates), so it would probably be hard to make my money back in this medium as well.

Unfortunately for me, I was never able to tailor my imagination to better suit my budget. All my films have suffered from being too ambitious for my low budgets. Instead of doing a *Blair Witch Project* (three actors in the forest), I did *Lady of the Lake*, an underwater witch in medieval times, with tons of costumed extras, or *Slashers*, a film taking place in Japan, with tons of Japanese extras. Terrible ideas for low-budgets films.

Donald Farmer: The budget is always in the back of my mind when I write a script. I can't put in things like an earthquake swallowing Los Angeles or an army of hundred-foot zombies. On my budgets, that "ain't happening." And I prefer short "concept titles" that basically tell you what the movie is about, versus "generic titles." Usually, the titles I come up with myself—*Demon Queen, Cannibal Hookers, Vampire Cop, Dorm of the Dead*—are almost always "concept" titles that tell you exactly what to expect. But sometimes a producer will insist I use their title, such as the case with *Deadly Run, Blood and Honor, The Strike*, or *Deadly Memories*. These tend to be the more generic titles that don't tell you quite as much.

So I usually start with a title, then do a treatment before I start a script. I can't really get into a script until I have one character I want to identify with — the character whose point of view is most important to me. I haven't done that with all my scripts, but I usually try. Once I have this particular character in mind, whether it's Caroline in *Red Lips* or the sorority pledges in *Cannibal Hookers*, I want these characters to have basic goals or agendas, then use that as a foundation for the rest of the script. All the troubles in *Cannibal Hookers* happened because these two social-climbing girls were so desperate to join an elite sorority. Twenty-five years later, that's pretty much the starting point of David Fincher's *The Social Network*. Everything in the movie

happens because Mark Zuckerberg wanted to get into an elite fraternity.

Jeff Forsyth: The script is crucial to the success of any project. Without it and its frame work the project cannot hold together. At best the final result will be uneven. At worst it will be an unwatchable disaster of a movie.

For me, the budget and ideas go both ways. I certainly have not been successful enough yet to just make anything I want to and "budget be damned." I also have had several meetings where the topic was, "We need to make something we can afford." So I have ideas that follow both of these streams. One interesting thing that happens to me, at times, is that "budget-friendly" ideas I have seem to expand and develop into more expensive ideas. And ideas that were more extravagant have, at times, been downsized to fit restricted budgets. That was the case with *Children of the Sky*. It was conceived as a drama with minimal effects and it grew into a special-effects science-fiction thriller.

Richard W. Haines: Since I make genre films with unique lighting designs and compositions, I storyboard every shot in the script and use that as my blueprint. When I write my screenplays I first find out what locations are available in advance of principal photography. For example, in my last feature, *What Really Frightens You*, I wanted the climax to take place at a Gothic castle. I made sure I could find one first before writing that sequence. I ended up using Wing's Castle in New York. If I couldn't secure a castle I would have rewritten the ending for a different location.

William Hopkins: There are many different factors that will affect an audiences' reaction to your film. The music, the cinematography, the editing, the effects work, the costuming, the format you're shooting in, et cetera. All are important, of course. But the most important things — the crucial things, really — are the cast and the script. We can all think of films with huge budgets, great effects, and wonderful scores that still left us cold because we didn't like the people we saw on the screen and we didn't care about the story being told. So, the first step is to get a good script. And that's something that should take a while. Something thrown together in a week or even a month is probably not going to be good enough. You have to be prepared to go draft after draft, getting feedback and making changes until you get it right, even if it takes six months or a year or longer.

When I first started writing scripts, I did what I imagine most beginners do. I wrote stuff that would've required studio backing and big budgets to produce. The first script I completed, if it were produced today, would probably need a $50–100 million dollar budget to do properly. Naturally, the script was never produced. So, yes, as an indie filmmaker, I think you have to take budget into consideration when writing your screenplays. If you're just writing scripts as an exercise, or if you plan to shop them around to the studios, then I guess you can be a little more ambitious with the scope and scale of the thing. But if you want to shoot the scripts you're writing, then you need to keep the budget in mind. What I do before starting work on a script is to make a list of all the resources I'll have at my disposal in shooting the actual film. What locations do I have access to? What equipment will I be able to use? What size cast and crew can I afford? And anything written with the budget in mind is almost always going to be better because you're forced to refine your work, fine tune it so it'll work even without a big budget.

Steve Hudgins: There is nothing more important than the script. If you don't have a script, you don't have a movie. I don't care how good of a filmmaker you are, I don't care what kind of equipment you have, I don't care what kind of a budget you have, I don't care how good your actors are — if the script is not good the movie will not be good, period. Sure, you can make it look pretty. You can get great shots. You can light it perfectly. But guess what? People don't go to the movies to watch two hours of pretty photography. They go to the movies to be told a story. Have you ever seen a big-budget movie with big-name actors and a big-name director and a big-name producer, but the movie absolutely sucked? Of course you have. We all have. Nothing can save a bad script. The script is everything!

As far as budget determining your ideas, if you are writing a script to make yourself, write within your means. For example, don't write in scene that involves a bus crash, when you know you don't have a bus that you can crash.

Rolfe Kanefsky: The script is king. It's been said, "You can make a bad movie from a good script but you cannot make a good movie from a bad script." It all starts with the script. It is the story you want to tell. If you don't have a good story then what's the point in telling it? I've written a lot of scripts. Many I've directed and some I've sold that other people have directed. I've written scripts on spec just to write. I've been hired to write scripts based on other people's ideas. I've rewritten other scripts or "ghost written" some to help unfinished movies that ran into trouble along the way.

Budget determines a lot when it comes to writing if you are doing it as an assignment. When I'm just writing something that I hope to sell as a spec script to the studios, then budget doesn't matter. In fact, the bigger it is, the better. You want to impress people and not be limited. That's the job for the production team. If I'm hired to write a script based on someone's idea, then I always ask what budget are you trying to do this for so I don't give them something that can't be made. When I'm writing a script that I plan to make myself, I am usually well aware of the limitations and try to write something cool that can be made for modest means. The budgets of my films have ranged from $50 thousand–$1 million, and I've done enough films that I know what I can or cannot accomplish with the budget at hand. Sometimes having limited resources forces one to be more creative, which is a good thing. When you can just throw endless amounts of money at something it doesn't always solve the problem. With horror films, I still believe that what you don't see is a lot scarier than what you do. CGI does not enhance the horror! If anything, it takes you out of the story and reminds the audience they're watching a movie. I used to say that you can make a very good movie for $3–5 million. Now, with digital, you can do it even cheaper but you have to be creative. And you have to care about the characters. If you're not involved in the people and the story, it doesn't matter how slick your movie is.

That said, all scripts are different. If you want to write *Transformers* you're going to need some money. Don't try to write a $200 million movie and then make it for $100 thousand. But at the same time, don't limit yourself, especially in your first draft. There will be rewrites. I usually go for ambitious stuff and then tone it done or figure out how to pull it off inexpensively.

I wrote a script called "The Hazing" that had a lot of effects in it. I knew that I wanted to do most of the effects practically (on set), and knew how to do it. But some people read the script and thought we'd need $5 million for effects alone. I explained that we didn't, but that stopped the script from being made for years. Finally, a producer came in and financed the movie, but during the tech read [where all the main crew members sit around and go over the script and what every department will have to do], the producer panicked. At the end of the meeting, he took me aside and said, "You know, Rolfe, we can't make this movie. I mean, you're never going to pull off your vision with this limited budget." Now, we had a budget of $750,000 for this one and some really good people working on it. I wasn't worried. I've done a lot more for a lot less. So I asked, "Well, are you going to pull the plug a week before we start filming?" He said, "No, but don't expect to get what you want to get." I said, "Well, let's give it a shot," and overall I was very happy with the final result of the film. It was pretty close to my vision. I never changed anything in the script. I just figured out how to shoot things the "right" way.

My advice: Don't start filming your movie until you are 100 percent happy with your script! It's your blueprint. Everything always goes back to the script. When things get crazy on set — and they will — the script is your lifesaver.

Brett Kelly: The script is all important. I usually write, or have someone write for me, within my budgetary restraints. If a company hires me to make a film for them, I get a dollar figure first, then create a script that can be done for that amount of money. I always tell people, if you can't afford an airplane hangar, don't set your film there.

Chris LaMartina: The screenplay is everything. It's the blueprint for production, post-production, and the distribution of the final product. It took me a long time before I realized just how important the script is to every step of the filmmaking process.

First, if you can't tell your story in a single sentence, your distributor is going to have a tricky time selling the film to an audience. Think I'm joking? We learned a lot between *Book of Lore* (our second flick and an intricate mystery-thriller) and *President's Day* (our fourth film, a horror comedy). This is the first step in making the film and it is also the first step in selling the film. The log line for *Book of Lore* was long-winded and barely touched the surface of the story. *President's Day* was to the point: a high school student council election turns deadly when a maniac dressed as Abe Lincoln starts murdering candidates. With the log line of *President's Day*, our audience knew exactly what they were getting, both story-wise and tonally. It was an obvious tongue-in-cheek '80s throwback flick, right down to the title.

By the time Jimmy and I pitched feature number five, *Witch's Brew,* we could tell our basic plot in two words: cursed beer. I say this with a bit of sarcasm, but there is a lot of underlying truth there. The screenplay dictates where you can go, both as a director and as a business person. Don't forget that. They are interconnected as much as the brooding artist in all of us wishes to forget.

Considering production costs is also essential to the screenwriting process. If the script requires multiple locations/actors/effects, you'll need to pony up more cash to make it happen. If it's written with budget in mind, you might find that working with limited resources fuel creative innovation. Plenty of times we've got a jolt of imagination from dwindling bank accounts. This is not always the case, but money is the bane of every micro-budget production. Use limited resources to your advantage.

Jim Mickle: The script is hugely important. I've had the great fortune of working with my lead actor, Nick Damici, on screenplays. He does the hard part of writing every day and pounding out draft after draft, then I sort of edit his work and do clean-up as it gets closer to shooting. The hardest part is getting that first draft out and finished, then the rewriting is like sculpting a big block of clay and giving it shape and dimension. Both *Mulberry Street* and *Stake Land* started as very different first drafts, and evolved over the course of many months into their final forms.

By the time we get to shooting, we know every in and out of each scene and we've explored so many different options that it makes it very easy to improvise or change things up if better ideas come along. So, it's a very necessary blueprint. But I've been lucky to work with very smart collaborative people to help continue shaping things all the way up to the final sound mix.

Most bad indie movies I see were obviously made with bad scripts, making it very hard to give notes or feedback on rough cuts when so much of what doesn't work originated on the page. Spend time getting it right before you start shooting. In both cases we had to do reality passes on the scripts to get them to fit into the kind of budget we were expecting. We knew we'd never get millions to do either film so we set out to write things around locations and resources we knew we could pull off.

Damon Packard: Script is important, but your execution and vision is what mostly counts. And, yes, unfortunately budget DOES determine your ideas. You are always limited to what you can do on limited budgets. Little or no money usually produces the same kind of results you get in the world of micro-budget filmmaking, regardless of how imaginative you are. It DOES require somewhat large amounts of money to realize potential, but not the kind of ridiculous over-bloated budgets Hollywood deals with, that are very difficult to raise and allow you to maintain any creative freedom.

Brad Paulson: I believe the script is the most important part of the movie. A shitty movie can be made from a great script, but it's far more difficult to make a great movie from a shitty script. The script element is something I really don't understand about the Hollywood system. If you go to seminars where agents are guest speaking, they always talk about how your script must be rock solid before anyone sees it. Then the script must be rewritten until it's perfect in the agent's eyes. And, of course, give them hundreds to thousands of dollars and they'll make sure that happens. Or so they say. But how many movies do you see at the theatre with a perfect script? Nearly none. Sometimes, they don't even write the scripts until they start the movie. Look at the *Transformers* trilogy. They have 300 million dollars for the movie and don't give a shit about the script. Don't you think if you're going to invest that much money, you'd want to make the script that much better? Those movies are only good as eye candy, but after 20 minutes, you get bored because there's nothing else to them. And I'm not a pretentious ass like many of the people I went to film school with. I enjoy watching movies strictly for entertainment, but if there's nothing to the movie besides spectacle it quickly becomes not worth your time. Meanwhile, there are amazing scripts out there that will be sitting on the shelf forever. Clearly, a perfect script is not Hollywood's number-one priority.

The budget, unfortunately, does determine

my ideas because if there's something too visually ambitious it's going to be a pain in the ass to try and pull off. Besides, the older I get the less I want to deal with bullshit. In other words, if I'm not making any money off the movie, I can at least make the process enjoyable. I found when we first started making movies we planned for dozens of different locations. Then, we found out that was a real pain in the ass and kept scaling it back. Now, I write for what I like to call two person/one room movies, which are basically as limited in budget, locations, actors and effects as possible. Things will most likely stay this way until I actually get the budget to make things a little more larger scale. However, two person/one room movies doesn't mean a movie has to be less quality. There are some wonderful plays which are basically two person/one room movies. And then there are some plays which you feel like you're being tortured every second you're sitting in the theatre. But it's worse because you feel like you can't escape. The point is, it's up to you. Budget is not the

be-all and end-all. You can write a great script with limited actors, locations and eye candy. It's more challenging but if you have talent you can pull it off and prove you don't need a rich uncle or a studio to make a good — if not better — movie than the big boys.

One last bit on this topic: as a homework assignment, the next time you go to one of those paid-for seminars and someone claims they can give you a well-polished script, ask them what the writers of the last *Transformers* movie got paid and what draft of the script they were on before they started shooting. I guarantee you'll render them speechless, at in the very least, stump them for a bit.

Jose Prendes: I started writing scripts when I was in high school. I taught myself from the hundreds of screenwriting books I read. You can write so much easier than you can direct, because writing is free. So, yes, the script is very important to me. I love writing. But when it comes to budget, that script isn't written in stone.

Budget determines everything in your

Jose Prendes looks through the day's script notes and camera reports.

movie, even for the big-league guys. Maybe you write an awesome helicopter crash, but you can't afford it, so now it is an off-screen car crash. One of the most important weapons in your filmmaking arsenal as a writer/director is being able to write within a budget.

For example, on *The Monster Man*, I wanted to make a massive, blockbuster-style end-of-the-world film. Then I realized all I had at my disposal was a DV camera and a very limited budget, so I wrote with that in mind. The finished script was 45 pages and was originally a tense, serious action picture. You've probably never seen this film, but I will tell you that it turned out to be a comedy. On day two I realized my budget and look would not lend itself to a serious rumination on the end of the world, so I turned it into a slapstick spoof on end-of-the-world movies, and, for my money, it worked better that way. A lot of critics didn't get that I did a lot of "shoddy" things on purpose, because I was mocking shot-on-video movies, but that's neither here nor there.

Consequently, on *Corpses Are Forever*, I had written an ultimate zombie bloodbath with guts and limbs flying everywhere, but even with the move to 35mm film and a larger budget, time and the limited resources, we were forced me to cut out the entire zombie battle and end with a cliffhanger. One which I had hoped to finish in the unfilmed sequel "The Corpse Who Loved Me," but money, fans, or interest failed to materialize.

Ultimately, the script is your bible. Get that to where you want it. I wish I had spent more time on the *Corpses* script, and that is one thing I will always regret. So take your time. Write the movie YOU want to see, but write the movie YOU can afford ... or at least max your cards out on.

Paul Scrabo: The script is the most important thing and, surprisingly, not the most expensive. *Dr. Horror* was designed almost like a film festival, several mini-movies throughout, and I wanted to try to give a DVD buyer his moneys worth — not a 70-minute feature but a "big" no-budget film. There is even a built-in "intermission" so one can come back to the movie later. So, the script was over 120 pages. But I would not recommend that. Would you rather have 120 pages or 90 pages of headaches dealing with producing your film?

I didn't have money to throw at problems so I was forced to use common sense. I had one location — a house. So no one bothered us. I turned the camera around and that was another location as far as I was concerned. There was also a backyard and a lake.

One of our mini-movies featured actor Trent Haaga turning into a werewolf. Now we were lucky to have Mike Thomas, not only as a cast member but also our make-up artist, so he took on the task of Trent's transformation sequences. But the sets for the story included a movie theatre, a photo studio, an apartment, and we had to shoot all of this in one day.

Well, that was a bit unrealistic, so we filmed it as if his life was like a play, onstage. We bought some black fabric and used it as a backdrop. A mirror was the apartment, two seats and a flickering light were the movie theatre.

Eric Shapiro: The script is at the top of my values hierarchy. Actors are a close second. If those two elements are powerful, it matters a lot less where you put the camera. To date, my budget (or lack thereof) has driven my ideas, many of which involve scenarios that take place in one location and/or on a single day.

Anthony Straeger: As far as I am concerned (and I'm pretty sure this will apply to most producers and directors), the script is most important. A house needs a firm building platform or foundations to put walls and windows on and in. A film works exactly the same way. A good script helps create a better film because the director has something to work with and so does the cast. A bad script puts you on the back foot from 'Day One.'

At the beginning (I would assume as with *Call of the Hunter*), the initial meeting takes place between the writer, the director and the executive producer — the man that is putting

Paul Scrabo confers with Nathan Sears and Debbie Rochon on the set of *Dr. Horror's Erotic House of Idiots*.

in the money. At this point is when you are looking at the budget in relationship to the script. This is the moment when you know whether you have enough to realize the ideas contained in the script fully or whether you will have to make some serious compromises.

There is a world of difference between doing a drama, horror or action movie, so all the ideas you have may have to be tailored to exactly how much you can achieve for the money you have. Unlimited funds equals unlimited ideas, limited funds means a more creative approach in achieving a desired effect.

It doesn't matter what the price tag is on the film, each level has its problems — it's just that more money makes it easier to complete. When you are looking to raise private cash and are working with a bare-bones budget, it gets a little harder. So I worked on how much I could realistically do within the movie (*Call*

of the Hunter) and then went out with my cap in hand begging to friends, Romans and countrymen. The initial budget to make it was £25,000. I stayed well within this and attempted to keep the dynamics of SCRIPT verses BUDGET to a perspective that would mean getting the best out of the script we had and the most out of the limited resources I had to work with.

Marc Trottier: I think having a good script is hugely important. Some people pay close attention to scripts and storyboards and what not, and other people maybe go with the flow a little more and let things happen naturally. Regardless, I think the "idea" is the most important thing before even beginning to film. In my opinion, if you're going to film something very short, just for fun and for the sake of practicing, then it's not as crucial. But the longer it will take to film (and the longer it will take in post-production) the more effort should be put into the script, and planning ahead of time in pre-production.

I think the script/budget relationship can go either way. Sometimes you know how much money you have to work with and your ideas revolve around what you can afford to do. Other times you might have an idea that will dictate how much money you'll need to beg and steal to get your project finished. (Note: don't steal money to make your movie!)

Mike Watt: The script is the beginning and end of your project. It's your blueprint for the story and the characters. If it's terrible from the start, you can have all the money in the world and it won't improve the movie (see the *Transformers* movies for the most recent examples). It's at this beginning stage that a lot of pride will have to be swallowed if you want to make a good movie. There is a doctrine that may be one of the most important rules you can ever learn: "knowing how to type doesn't make you a writer," just as everyone with a camera is not a filmmaker or anyone with fingers is a guitarist. Even on the lowest budget where you *have* to wear all the hats, you cannot expect that you'll be awesome at everything. And the script is where it all begins. You can learn how to format a script on your own or use a "schmancy program" like Final Draft, but that doesn't mean you can tell a story. "I just want to entertain people" is not an excuse, nor is watching something bad, and saying "I could do better than that." Most people can't.

I'll say that again because it ties with "no one person can do everything well": *most human beings cannot write.* This was true before the digital revolution, before even the era of moving type. Telling a story that is worth telling and hearing is difficult. I'm not talking about plot. The "plot" is just what you hang the rest of the story on. Anyone can write a plot: A leads to B leads to C; beginning, middle, end. "A killer going around killing people" is not a story. Who are his victims? Why do they have the killer's attention? Is it necessary

to know anything about the killer? Are the victims people you want to see die, or, more importantly, people you want to see live? For that matter, are they people at all, or just juicy gore effects waiting to happen? Humans are drawn to stories, to listen to them and to tell them. Too often in development, however, scripts sound like they were written by children just learning to tell a story. "So then the guy goes up the stairs. And then he opens the door. And then he looks around. And then the bad guy, and then and then." Obviously (hopefully obviously) that's not a story.

The best actors in the world can't do anything with, "Fuck, man, I just wanna get fucked up and fuck. Fuck, yeah!" That's not dialogue. And if that's character development, you haven't created a person; you've created a noise box. *But that's how people talk!* No they don't. And if they do, you really need to go listen to some other people for awhile.

Besides the bad mechanics, the clichés and the profanity-laced dialogue being a large round of *nothing,* let me put it this way: it's been done before. We've all seen terrible movies exactly like that, both independent and professional, that are empty shells of "things happening" to "some kids." So if there are a thousand awful movies that already exist, why would you want to make one more?

If your goal is to become a *filmmaker,* whatever that word means to you, you have to understand story, character and structure. And if you don't, you have to find someone who does. If this particular story means so much to you, get it down on paper and then give it to a real writer. If you're among the small percentage of people in this world who can tell a compelling story, all power to you! But know your limitations. Because there's enough crap in the world already. Make something worth watching.

As far as script begetting budget or vice versa, we've done it both ways. Our first movie, *The Resurrection Game,* called for ten different locations, a cast of at least a hundred, dozens of gore gags, stunts, gunplay, choreographed fights, retro-futuristic props and a friggin' sword fight. Not knowing for ourselves how stupid this would all be to pull together, we moved forward anyway, and thus learned the "MacGyver School of Filmmaking" for ourselves. This school teaches you to be flexible and resourceful. It also teaches you that if you edit anything fast enough, you can hide almost all of the seams of an illusion.

The multiple locations we managed to boil down to about seven. Both the hero's and heroine's homes took place in our own house, in the same rooms, dressed completely differently. The cast of hundreds got whittled down to 30 or so, with many actors doubling ("Shemping" as Sam Raimi would say) and tripling as zombies. For the rest, we begged, bartered and borrowed to bring it all together. The final sequence was meant to take place at a medical amphitheater at one of the local colleges until we learned how impossible that would be, as none of us were college students. So the scenes were rewritten to take place in run-down attic and cellar space we could redress.

We've tried over the years to follow the (early) Robert Rodriguez tenet of writing the script around what you have or can get — *Severe Injuries, Splatter Movie, A Feast of Flesh* and *Demon Divas* were all written around locations we knew we could utilize, but *Razor Days* included an abandoned mine (originally), a diner, a martial arts dojo, and extensive make-up work. So we needed a lot of pre-production time for that one. It's really best to think about what you have first, but sometimes the needs of the story take precedence. With that in mind, I still try to avoid movie ideas involving car crashes, animal stampedes, orgies, the ocean, et cetera.

Ritch Yarber: The script is the most important part of any production. It should be developed fully to take the viewer on a well-planned journey that will leave them satisfied and reflective as they leave the screening. The

Director Ritch Yarber and DP Brian Foster on the set of *Murder Machine!*

script is the cornerstone of the filmmaking effort. It has to be solid and consistent. The filmmaker and the viewer will be unfulfilled if the film is based on a loose, undedicated idea. The holes will show themselves, the patches will be evident and the opportunity to bond with the audience will be lost. The filmmaker will find himself frustrated as the pieces struggle to combine into the desired story. If the story is solid on paper, the vision is easier to achieve on film.

I don't consider budget all that much when trying to come up with script ideas. The important thing is finding a subject or story that will engage the viewer with a solid beginning, middle and end. Once these things have been determined, the budgetary restraints come into play to see how the needed plot points can be intelligently and realistically portrayed. There are always problems on a small budget, but, interestingly, there always seems to be acceptable answers to these problems that an audience will accept "in the spirit" of the production. Audiences are smart. They know if they are watching a high-dollar Hollywood production or a micro-budget independent film, and their level of acceptability is relative to this. If you respect your audience enough to strive at all times to the highest standards of realism possible on your specific budget, they are generally willing to overlook small lapses as long as the attempt to deliver what was promised on the cover of the box is there. Overly grandiose ideas would certainly be foolish to entertain on a micro-budget; however, with a little imagination, these ideas may be able to be morphed down into a solid and attainable product. This was the case with my film *Murder Machine*. The original idea was that of a mysterious killer that used assorted James Bond-type gadgets as his implements of torture and murder. This quickly proved impossible to portray realistically on our $5,000 budget. The idea was "morphed" into the finished version that features a drifter that is adept in the pure art of killing with the goal of becoming the real-life embodiment of a fictional killer, the same as in the original version, just tweaked to fit our budget.

Ivan Zuccon: There was a time when, even with a just a shred of an idea, I used to pick up the camera and start making movies. Now it's not like this. This change is a sure sign of maturity, and now I find myself having many scripts ready. I write and rewrite the scripts until they totally satisfy me, so that the processing of writing takes more time. The lapse between shooting different movies gets longer. However, I am convinced that behind every good movie is a good script. What you do in movies is tell a story, and stories must be good. If they aren't, it's hard to get to the heart of the audience. I seldom write scripts all by myself. I work with good scriptwriters, even if it's based on my own idea, except in cases of adaptation from a novel or a story of classic writers such as H.P. Lovecraft. I usually write quite extensive lines of dialogue, then give my material to the scriptwriter, who makes a first draft. After this step, I personally start working on the second draft, then the third and so on. My latest movie, *Wrath of the Crows*, had ten drafts. Certainly the budget affects your choices and modifies your ideas. If you have a low budget it's a tough to adjust your ideas (or the scriptwriter's ones) to lack of money. But, as they say, every cloud has a silver lining. Working on a low budget pushes your creativity to the highest levels, forcing you to seek effective and cheap solutions. It teaches you how to get the maximum effect and the best performances with little money. There is nothing more valuable than this and it will come in handy when you'll have more money to manage.

Glenn Andreiev: On your own script, if you invent stuff while shooting, you don't have to clear it with yourself. I can't imagine having that on-the-set freedom with another person's script. Would we have to contact the screenwriter while shooting and ask, "We want to eliminate that monologue and replace it with a fight." I imagine there would have to be serious contractual, complicated, costly agreements with the writer(s).

John Borowski: The ideal situation for a filmmaker/director would be to have a screenwriter to write the script. The director must work closely with the writer to convey the themes and feeling he would like portrayed in the film. Once the script is written, the writer and director work together to revise the script to tailor to the director's vision. Hitchcock worked this way. I believe a film changes through each phase of production, morphing into the final creation. Having a vision is important, but understand that after the film is on paper, it will change with bringing on actors, being on set, and when being editing and scored. It should be a constantly evolving art form until it is complete.

Keith Crocker: The obvious benefit of being the writer of your own film is that your vision doesn't conflict with what the writer had in mind because you are the writer. When you shoot someone else's script, and if the writer is on board for the shoot, you risk running into conflict with the writer over the way a certain scene is portrayed. These types of arguments not only hold up shoots but they can lead to a film being postponed indefinitely. Not a good thing to happen at all. However, most writers are best off with someone else interpreting their work on a visual format, so some of the worst writing can still be salvaged and made into a beautiful film by some direc-

tor with a good eye. This, of course, can also occur vice versa, with a good script turned into a shit film. It happens. Only once in my life did I try shooting someone else's screenplay, and the minute I tried to turn the dialogue into something I felt sounded less staged, the guy had a fit. He wanted the dialogue followed to the letter. Hence, I prefer to write my own material.

Richard Cunningham: It's a mixed bag of good and bad, for sure. I've only worked off my own scripts in the past, or on productions where I was a part of story development. But I can offer a little insight on the pros and cons of filming a production with your own script.

The script is yours; you have a clear understanding of where your movie is coming from and what it wants to say; you probably have a close connection to the story and the characters, probably have angles and locations in your head, already; and the casting process could either be inspirational or utterly hopeless, but you definitely know who you're looking for.

The flip side is that all that personal investment can make the writer more resistant to change in a medium that is constantly changing because of anything from a random spark of creativity on set, or unexpected rain ruining a day scheduled for exteriors. I think if you're writing a script to a movie that you're going to produce as well, you just have to be willing to let go of the sanctity a writer can sometimes bestow on a finished work (unless that's just me). There's that fine line of saying, "Screw you, everyone, I have a vision," but still managing to listen when a critic is giving you good advice.

Maurice Devereaux: I've never worked from someone else's script, but I'm guessing that the big difference is that when you write, you have an overall vision of the film. You know the story and the characters by heart. You can answer any question or you should be able to. Because if you can't answer a question, it usually means there are "holes" in your script. Like if an actor asks, "What was my character doing while something important is happening with other characters?" and you can't answer him, because you didn't think things through, it might be a problem. If you've done your homework on a script, you usually know a lot more than what ends up in the final script,. You know about the back stories of each character, what they do when they are not in a scene, et cetera. It might seem superfluous, but it isn't. It means you care and tried to create a "world" with real people in them and the film is capturing moments. You, as the creator, know what is behind those moments and can answer any question about it.

So if you're working from somebody else's script, you might find yourself puzzled by something and would have to ask the writer why some character does something. If the original writer is unavailable, or dead, you might THINK you understand everything in the story. Yet, it will be your interpretation of the original writer's intentions, and it may be completely wrong... When you write it yourself, you should be "God." For better or worse, you should know the why's and what's of everything in the script.

Donald Farmer: The only movie I've directed where I had zero input in the script was the comedy *Bollywood and Vine*, which I co-directed with Edward Jordan. He sent me a package of about five incredibly well-written scripts, so I picked that one to do with him. It ended up winning awards at a couple of film festivals. Two other movies I did — *The Strike* and *Deadly Memories* — had scripts which I completely rewrote.

For the my two-part Civil War film, *Blood and Honor* and *Battle for Glory*, I was given a 300-page book written by the first-time producer (an Atlanta dentist with some celebrity clients), with instructions to turn it into a

script. The book ended with a huge flood washing all these Southern plantations away, so that was the first thing I ditched. I decided anything resembling a credible flood was a little beyond our budget. I came up with a more affordable ending, where the book's villain, a scheming Cajun maid, commits suicide by throwing herself off a waterfall.

The producer also envisioned the movie being a two-part television mini-series, so I wrote a script long enough for a four-hour running time. Even after cutting several scenes my first edit came in at three hours. It was eventually chopped into two separate movies with some overlapping scenes in each. This called for some new narration to be written to help bridge the plot lines of the two movies, so I was basically adding to the script even through post-production. An outside writer, especially one with some industry credits, might not have stood for so much after-the-fact script tampering. So there's advantages to a director also being the primary writer.

Lucky for me, this producer let me play hard and fast with his novel; even inventing whole new characters when I felt the need. His only mandate was the final film should be equivalent to a PG rating, so that killed my plan of making a full-out Southern sleaze epic like *Mandingo*. Our celebrity, Miles O'Keeffe, actually wanted to film a love scene with his leading lady, but the producer had a quick answer for that. "My wife says no love scenes," he barked. Apparently this guy's wife had the last word on everything!

Jeff Forsyth: Up until recently I have only worked on my own scripts. I just recently started developing a short a friend wrote and I'm enjoying the experience. Writing is kind of like torture for me. I never know if it's any good or not. When I read a script that someone else has written, I know.

Richard W. Haines: There's the cost factor. If you write your own script you don't have to pay a screenwriter or license story rights. Since I create my screenplays in the manner I describe, there would be no point in hiring someone to find locations while writing the script. I also incorporate my own background into the stories, which includes my phobias and other personal information that an outsider would not be familiar with. I have hired writers to fine-tune my scripts on some movies. They added character nuance and dialogue without altering my structure or narrative. However, I prefer to own all aspects of my films, which includes screenplay rights. That gives me the option of making a sequel or licensing remakes in the future.

William Hopkins: I've never worked from anyone else's script and I don't expect to in future projects. If you're going to be working on a project for years, you really have to be comfortable with it and feel strongly about it. For me, that means writing my own stuff.

Steve Hudgins: Obviously, when you're working with your own script, you're going to have more freedom. When you're working with someone else's script, it all depends on the agreement that was made. Regardless, all agreements have potential sticking points when it comes to changing or tweaking the script. Before day one of shooting this should be worked out loud and clear so there is no possibility of misunderstanding.

Rolfe Kanefsky: It's very important to know your script inside and out before you start production. Being the writer of the script makes this job easier since it all came out of your own head. When I write a script, I visualize the entire thing so I already have the whole movie shot in my head. Getting that same vision in the camera is always a challenge but I know what I'm going for, and sometimes succeed. Working from someone else's script, you have to figure out how to make it your own. So far, I have written everything I have directed. Even if it started somewhere else, I've rewritten it to a certain extent so it becomes a part of me. The only disadvantage I can think of is if you are so close to the material, you may be a little tunnel-vision and not see other opportunities. But that's why you hire actors,

great crew members, and good editors. I always have a very good game plan but try to keep an open mind for other ideas that can come from anywhere. I believe the script is very important, but it is a blueprint. I like and encourage actors to add their own personalities to the roles, and if a cameraman or crew member has a good idea for a shot or an angle that is better than what I first thought of, I'm all for it. If there's time, I'm open to trying it a different way. Unfortunately, on the schedules and budgets that I usually work with, I rarely have a lot of time. But if an actor wants another take, nine out of ten times, I will let him/her have it. On tight schedules, scripts always have to be simplified. If last-minute changes take place, you need to know how that will affect all the other events/characters in the story. If a script is tight, one little change can have a domino effect and mess up a lot of things. So know your screenplay whether you wrote it or not.

Brett Kelly: What's nice about working from your own script is that you can use shorthand. If you know you are going to be the one directing it, you don't have to hold your own hand, the way a screenwriter might do for you if they felt they had to describe every little thing. I prefer using outside writers, but I always provide a detailed, scene-by-scene treatment of the movie I want to make. Writers always throw you bits that you never would have thought of, and that's pretty cool. I like to think that providing the detailed treatment is a way to make their jobs easier. I'm not sure if they would agree with me, but it's my way of getting the movie script I want.

Chris LaMartina: I write with a partner: my best friend/producer, Jimmy George. We've never worked from another person's script because bringing our stories to life has been the most exciting part of the filmmaking process for us. In addition to satisfying your own creative goals, producing from your own screenplay allows you to write for your available resources and if you're handling post-production: your edit.

Another strong attribute of producing from your own work is the ability to change the script on-set without stepping on someone's toes. We've all heard the tales of lowly writers scorned by self-important film producers (hell, Jimmy and I have had our optioned stories butchered a few times) ... so it's nice to be in charge of your own destiny.

The disadvantages come in the form of self-critique. Artists cannot live in a vacuum. We *always* get script coverage on screenplays before we agree to produce the film. Coverage is where another screenwriter (often times, a more successful or "established" screenwriter) gives you positive/negative feedback. There are plenty of affordable websites that provide this service. A quick Google search will surely pull some up.

If you're not willing to hear some harsh words about your art, you better re-think your filmmaking aspirations. I can guarantee that the script doctors and their coverage will be nicer than the comments you'll see on your film's Netflix page or Amazon product listing. So fix those problems while you can. If it's wobbly on the page, it will be most likely be just as painful on screen.

Jim Mickle: I've always worked in a collaboration with Nick, so it's tough to know what the differences are. In that case it's great to tag team an idea and keep some objectivity, because it can get very claustrophobic very quickly if you're going at it alone. I love being able to bounce around ideas together and discuss why certain things work or how they can be tweaked. It really helps to understand what shapes a story and makes us both more disciplined as storytellers.

Damon Packard: Well, I guess that depends on how much creative control you have over your own or someone else's vision. I personally have never worked with someone else's script so it's hard for me to comment.

Brad Paulson: The benefits of working from your own script is that you know all the answers. You know all the characters and the motivations, the tone, everything. You have

full coherence of everything that's happened in the script. That is, unless you were completely wasted when you wrote it and can't recall the process. Or if you're one of those assholes who plagiarized something and are attempting to pass it off as your own.

I don't know why more people don't direct their own scripts or why Hollywood doesn't encourage it more often. I guess it's because a lot of writers are great at being introverted and not that good with people. It's a shame because they'd have the answers to everything on set because it's all related to script. But the disadvantage of directing from your own script is that you are the only one to blame if things go wrong. You're more attached to it. You're right there and invested all the way. It's far more disappointing when it doesn't go as you planned and you're not quite getting the vision you wanted across on screen. Basically, you've just got to detach yourselves from feelings of disappointment when you make movies because they're going to happen and they're going to happen in spades. The trick is to make it so the same ones don't keep happening over and over and that you keep improving.

Jose Prendes: I'm a writer, that's what I've done the most in my professional career, so I only work with my own scripts. On the off chance that I am working on something with a friend, then I always have to have a hand in the material.

If you aren't a writer, then you WILL NEED someone else's material. There is nothing wrong with this, so don't feel bad that you're not a writer/director like Kevin Smith or Quentin Tarantino.

I like to work with my own script because I know it intimately and I can answer every question ... or almost every question. I sometimes don't even need to look at the script to know what happens next or who says what in the scene because I lived it through the writing and re-writing. One disadvantage is that any negative notes really knock you for a loop. Maybe I'm just sensitive, but working with my script I feel like I'm a daddy and when someone says my baby has a stupid third act I get mad. I haven't lost any friends yet, but it could happen. Working with someone else's material allows you to be ruthless and tear and shred through it, which could be fun.

Paul Scrabo: Quite often, another writer's thoughts and ideas are more apparent than your own! I enjoy it. You're compelled to really work and think clearer.

The script for the third story in our anthology was not yet completed when principal photography began, but there was no rush. All we knew was that Brinke Stevens, a legend in Indie Horror, would be approached to star in that section of the film. It made perfect sense and would round out our cast of fan favorites. And I was stuck on the approach of that third story; I only knew it had to be the best one of the bunch. That's when we finally called Brinke — not to act, but to co-write *The Perfect Woman*.

Eric Shapiro: If you write your own, you have control, but if you work from someone else's, as I did on *Rule of Three* (written by Rhoda Jordan), you have the privilege of admiring the work as an outsider. That's a great thing; you can watch takes in the monitor and get wrapped up in the language and nuances in a way that you might not be able to if they came from your own mind.

Anthony Straeger: The advantage of working with a script I have written is that I have evolved the story. As such, it means I have a definite idea of the vision of the piece from its look to who will be in it. The process of writing may start out with a vague idea or a vague story line, but as you get through draft after draft you start to build a shot-by-shot picture in your head of what you would like to see.

So, when it comes to the production, there is a fully formed baby waiting to be born. Having given birth to this script I feel that I know how it feels, how it breathes. Even if you can't raise the budget to do exactly what you want, you know where you can make squeezes in order to tailor the cloth. You have everything in one guy's head and so there is a single-mindedness driving the script.

The disadvantages of this are simply that you can become "totally tunnel visioned" about it. You think you have written one of the gospels and that only you can be right about everything. It takes courage in this to be able to say to the DP and to your actors, "What do you see, how do you feel, what doesn't work for you?"

The advantage of working with somebody else's script is that you, quite simply, bring a new set of eyes to the project. You can make suggestions and push boundaries that the writer may not have been able to see. It becomes a team process that can help propel the script towards a better look and understanding of itself.

The disadvantages can come in the form of disagreement when a writer is unwilling to budge on something that he sees as integral and important, where you as the director may see it as over explaining or disposable in order to push the movie along.

In reality it doesn't matter. There are no advantages or disadvantages in the low budget/independent movie area, because if you, as the director, have written a good script or have been given a good script, it's happy days. There is only one thing that counts — a good script. A bad script, whether it's yours or someone else's, is simply a bad script. As a beginning filmmaker you need to absorb as much creative energy from as many sources as you can — THAT will help you be a better script writer and a better filmmaker.

Marc Trottier: I think a benefit to working from someone else's script is that you'll probably be less attached to it, and more willing to change things if they need to be changed. A potential disadvantage of working from someone else's script could be that if they're involved with the project, you might not see eye to eye on certain things, which would take more energy to deal with than if the ideas had been all your own.

In my opinion, one of the benefits of working from your own script is that nobody knows the script better than you. Also, you have a better chance of having your ideas translate from paper to film as accurately as possible with the least amount of changes (unless you choose to make changes). I can't see a disadvantage to working from your own script, except that it was one more job that you had to do by writing it in the first place!

Mike Watt: I've never directed anyone else's work. The only times I've ever worked from someone else's script has been as an actor and that's rarely — very rarely — ended well because of my ego. The same thing usually happens when I do screenwriting-for-hire.

Ritch Yarber: The benefits of working from your own script are that you are fully aware of the vision from start to finish and have already carefully planned into your script how to accomplish it. To work from someone else's script, you have to carefully examine every facet of what is written to have a sure understanding of what is intended and then determine what needs to be included or excluded to get to that point. Plot points that are under-developed must be reinforced or reinvented. It is also most important that the director fully understands what the writer expects him to accomplish and "if" it can be accomplished within the means of the script in its present form.

Ivan Zuccon: It makes no difference to me, provided that the scriptwriter understands that the movie belongs to the director. If the scriptwriters were the authors of the movie, then directors would just have to shoot the pages of the script, but this is not how it works. Between the script and the finished film there's a basic step called "staging," and this is the director's work and what the audience finally sees on screen.

Equipment and Production

While the need for creativity and persistence will never change in creating an independent film, production equipment will continually transform. When I shot my very first feature over 20 years ago, I did this with hundred-thousand-dollar broadcast cameras and recorded on Betacam SP tapes, which was the industry standard at the time. I ended up with a Betacam SP tape master, from which VHS copies would be made. When high-quality digital cameras came out, I utilized these, as the five-thousand-dollar cameras looked as good, if not better, than the previous, bulkier versions. Editing, which had to be done in order and by changing physical tapes in the editing suite, gave way to digitizing those tapes into a computer and being able to edit them nonlinearly. Although I had more choices when editing, the advancements in technology didn't make things easier. You had to learn how to use the new equipment, get through the learning curve of understanding a new computer software program — and the actual time it took to put your picture together increased because you had new things

you had to do, like capturing all your footage and outputting it to DVD. With my PBS-aired documentaries, I had to supply them with a Betacam SP copy, which they uplinked to their satellite feed. Most recently, everything has turned to HD — High Definition, and it's now expected that your finished product be in that format and available as a digital file for distribution.

As an independent filmmaker you'll use whatever equipment and technology is available and affordable to you. If you think you need the most up-to-date camera, like a RED, in order to do your production — and it's stopping you from making that movie — then look into using an older camera if you're that determined to make that film. Or you can purchase the most recent, recommended model and expect it to be replaced in a few years. Will you get your money's worth out of it? Don't get hung up on equipment. It's not about technology — it's what you do with what you have. You still have to know how to frame a shot, light an actor, record good audio and put the entire thing together after it's all completed.

The Filmmakers were asked:
What equipment/format do you use and why? How has this differed from when you made your first movie to your most recent film?

Glenn Andreiev: Well, my very, very first film was shot in 1972 with my dad's Regular 8mm Keystone, a hand-wound camera from World War II. My first feature film, *Vampire's*

Embrace, was shot in 1988 with a 16mm Éclair. Of course, video has yet to have the visual richness of 16mm, but it was a bit complicated shooting with film. (For example, I learned the hard way that 16mm camera parts expand in very hot weather, causing light leaks.) Now I use an HDV Sony FX7, and like all video cameras, you see on the spot what you are getting, and the image quality is gorgeous. What's great is that your camera equipment can fit in a backpack — great when traveling and shooting.

John Borowski: I studied filmmaking shooting on 8mm and 16mm FILM, not video. I see this as a bonus since almost everyone is learning and shooting on HD now as opposed to film. There is a difference when you can hold the frames of the film and physically see each individual frame. The editing process when editing on film is very different. Editing on film is where I developed a sense of pacing. The first video camera I owned was the Sony VX1000. I filmed the entire *HH Holmes* film on that camera and loved it. I have been shooting video ever since and really appreciate shooting and then watching the rushes immediately and being able to edit so quickly. I filmed my third film, *Carl Panzram*, in the HD format and the process is basically the same.

Keith Crocker: *Blitzkrieg* was shot on mini-digital videotape. I shot with the Panasonic DVX 100A camera, which I bought at a reduced rate because they were on to 100B by the time I got my camera. My decision to shoot on digital video was brought about simply by my desire to keep costs down, I'm a film purest (to a degree). *Bloody Ape* was sound Super 8mm film, the compilation *Cinefear Sampler* was short works all shot on 16mm. In fact, I began *Blitzkrieg* believing I was going to shoot it 16mm, silent, reversal film stock, and dub in the dialogue when it was transferred to a digital media. However, I started to appreciate my own dialogue about three-quarters into the shooting script, and I really wanted it recorded live. Prior to starting shooting, I did an acting gig on a friend's short film, and they were shooting with the Panasonic DVX 100A. I was quite taken with the image, plus the fact that you could hook up a monitor

and watch what was being shot as it happened. I realized that, with digital video, if you lit it like you'd light film, you were able to create a digital grain. While it's nothing like natural film grain, to the untrained eye you might just be able to pass this format off as film. That is why I made the leap from film to video — the camera finally caught up with my expectations. I don't feel the same way about HD (High Definition). My thought on that is that the image is way too clean and you really can't attempt any film-type look to it. It's way too slick, and film is a mirror of human error. I'm more comfortable with an imperfect image as opposed to a perfect image. I'm real old school. It takes a long time for technology, and I to keep up hand in hand, I admit this freely. I still have a 16mm Canon newsreel-style camera that operates off a large cylinder battery, as well as two sound Super 8mm cameras. I have even have projectors to go with them, the whole nine yards, I still shoot test footage on 16mm or Super 8mm, whatever film I have on the table. Budget-wise, digital video has saved my life, though. *Blitzkrieg* was way too large in scope, and I could not have shot it on film and finished it. Digital video was very liberating.

Richard Cunningham: With *ShE* and *Arcadium* I was working with a team that used prosumer-quality equipment, but I wasn't very technically savvy at the time, not enough to list what they had.

Films since, I've used anything that will work. For my last two movies I used a Canon HV20, a consumer camcorder that shoots in HD. I most recently purchased a Canon Eos Rebel T2i, a popular and affordable SLR digital camera. I've stuck with Canon, because the color is superior, in my opinion.

With my most recent film, *Year Zero*, easily half of the movie's production took place in a ten-year-old Dell Dimension 8200 series desktop that froze up routinely on me. At first I was drawing digitally with a mouse. Then I began using a Wacom pen and tablet for illustrations, and working in effects programs like Photo Impact 6 (old-school) and Adobe Photoshop. Later on, I used a Mac Mini and Adobe After Effects for animating; and for editing, I worked in Final Cut Pro. With all the VO recordings and music I worked off a program called Acid Music, by Sonic Foundry. The microphone for both voice-overs and music is a mid-grade studio condenser model.

On my very first film, *Gemini*, we were shooting on VHS camcorders, editing in between two of them. Superimposing titles was a big thing back then. I think, though, that was when I realized anyone could make a movie, even if you're just a 16-year-old kid living in the sticks, teaching yourself on homemade movies; that it wasn't this mystical process that only took place in Hollywood and New York.

My approach isn't all that different these days, in principle, except now I can certainly play a 30-year-old character more convincingly than I did as a teen.

Maurice Devereaux: My first film, *Blood Symbol*, was shot on Super 8mm and 16mm, *Lady of the Lake* on 16mm, *Slashers* and *End of the Line* on HDCAM. Shooting Super 8 was a nightmare. People today have no idea of the hardships (and costs) it took to make a film on that format. It cost $35 to purchase and develop a two-minute and thirty-second reel of Super 8mm film, and about four times that for 16mm. Then, you had to pay huge amounts to transfer it onto Betacam master tapes and VHS off-line time code burn-in off-line tapes and do color correcting. And since Super 8 reels are so fragile and you couldn't stop and start a transfer to color correct, you had to do it on the fly, so for about 12 weeks I had to edit my 450 reels of Super 8 onto one-hour reels, sorting them by scenes of day, night, and the overall type of color correction that would be needed, so that we would not have to be doing huge color timing shifts for every shot. But manipulating the Super 8 is problematic, as the image is so tiny that a little piece of dirt would be huge in the image. So I then had to manually clean each frame of the film, with medical gloves, and a special cloth and fluid, in a controlled room. This took me about 400 tedious hours. Also, when editing off-line on VHS deck to deck, you had to manually write every "in and out" of the time codes that were burned-in to the image, to be able to re-edit the film later in the more expensive Betacam online suite. *Blood Symbol* had 1,290 cuts. It took me about 700 hours to carefully write them down, because any mistake would be costly later with the online edit. So it was a nightmare. I also did this on *Lady of the Lake*. Digital editing is fantastic, a lifesaver. People who edit digitally today have no idea how easy they have it.

I love the look of 35mm but there is no logical reason to shoot on film today, with all the top-end digital cameras available. Oh, how I wish I had digital cameras and computer editing when I was a teenager. I would've made ten features before I was 22. The first nine would have been bad, but number ten would have been pretty good, and all the experience it took me 25 years to accumulate I would have achieved in only four.

Donald Farmer: I've shot in about all the major formats. A few of my projects have been 35mm—*No Justice, Demented* and *Deadly Run. The Strike* was half 35mm and half 16mm. Several others were 100 percent 16mm, like *Vampire Cop, Compelling Evidence, Vicious Kiss, Demolition Highway, Blood and Honor, Battle For Glory* and *Deadly Memories.*

My first four movies—*Demon Queen, Cannibal Hookers, Scream Dream* and *Savage Vengeance*—were all shot on three-quarter-inch videotape. Time has shown this isn't a format that ages particularly well. It picks up lots of drop-outs and even loses some serious picture resolution. I've seen lots of half-inch videotapes that age better than most three-quarter masters. To be completely honest, I think some of my '70s Super 8mm movies look better now than anything I shot on three-quarter video.

After that, I switched to Betacam SP as my non-film format of choice. I used it a couple

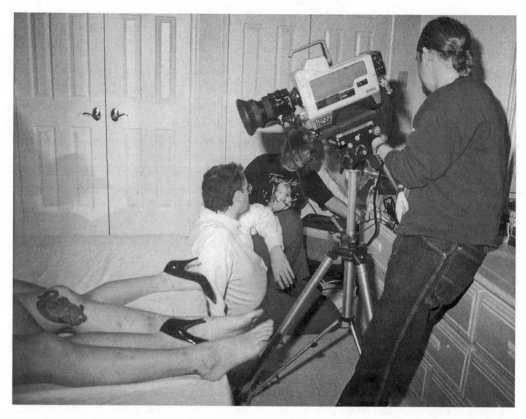

Donald Farmer and crew prepare to shoot a lesbian love scene for *Red Lips*.

of times for *Red Lips: Bloodlust* and *Space Kid*. Now I'm shooting in various High Def formats, as on *Chainsaw Cheerleaders* and my new movie *Shark Exorcist*.

Jeff Forsyth: I've recently stepped into the HDV arena but have not had a chance to shoot anything with it. I'm loving the quality, especially for low-cost micro-budget features. When I started out the only thing available to me was SVHS that I used for videotaping special events. Young filmmakers coming up now have NO idea how great they have it. The equipment available today for the independent filmmaker still amazes me. For a fraction of the cost of even ten years ago a filmmaker can achieve professional quality. The advent of low-cost digital HD, desktop editing and cheap disk space has really been a benefit. When I made my first movie, desktop editing was just coming into the scene. Most of us low-end filmmakers were still shooting in

Super VHS and Hi-8, with the end product being on VHS. I'm mortified when I look at my movie. Not at the feature itself but at the technical shortcomings compared to what I could do now for the same cost.

Richard W. Haines: Since I'm a "filmmaker," I shoot my movies on 35mm film stock. I studied the art of cinematography and I'm able to simulate the look of various genres, including Technicolor movies, film noir thrillers and 3-D pictures. I like the nuance of grain in film stock, which is what generates a dimensional appearance. Not graininess, but how light is reflected on the emulsion from foreground to background. "Painting with light" as Freddie (*Lawrence of Arabia*) Young used to describe it.

I have nothing against digital as a release format. I scanned in the 35mm camera negative of my last movie, reversed the image to a positive, which generated razor-sharp imagery have a "hard copy" of your imagery on plastic. There's no reliable way of preserving a digital image other than out-putting it to a 35mm negative, which is very expensive. It's cheaper to shoot in 35mm to begin with. In addition, digital technology is like a moving target, and no format lasts for long. First, they used 2K resolution, but that was rendered obsolete with the introduction of 4K. Warner is transferring some of its negatives to 8K now. I wouldn't want my master element in a system that will eventually become obsolete, whereas 35mm film stock has been around for over a hundred years. If you have a 35mm negative it can be transferred successfully to any new digital media developed in the future, so I'll stick with 35mm until it's eliminated, at which point I'll stop making movies.

Obviously, the quality of 35mm negatives is superior to a 16mm blowup. In hindsight, I wish I had the money to shoot *Splatter University* in 35mm — but at least I retained the "hard copy" of my images on 16mm stock.

I've used a number of different 35mm cameras over the years. I primarily shoot with an Arri, although we used an old Mitchell for some of the special effects work in *Space Avenger* in 1987 because it had rock-steady registration for superimpositions. Since 1995 I've only hired cinematographers that own their own 35mm equipment, which saves on rentals and guarantees it will be in good running order. *Splatter University* was shot in 16mm, as I mentioned, and we used several cameras, although I don't recall which models 30 years later.

One of the biggest changes has been the switch from analog sound recording to digital. We used to shoot with a Nagra, which used one-quarter-inch analog audio tape. Now we use a digital audio recorder, which is in sync with the 35mm camera, that generates much better sound and doesn't have the problem of tape hiss or other signal to noise-ratio issues when copying it.

William Hopkins: Both of my films were produced before High Definition video be-

Donald Farmer offers direction to actress J.J. North during the shoot for *Vicious Kiss*.

that replicated the grain structure of the emulsion. I'm opposed to shooting a movie on digital since you lose so much of the visual artistry contained on film.

I'm also an archivist and one of the few "indie" filmmakers that is concerned with preserving my negatives. The advantage is you

Director William Hopkins behind the camera on the set of *Demon Resurrection*.

came practical for indie filmmakers so both were shot in Standard Definition digital video. I used the Sony VX1000 for *Sleepless Nights* and the Canon XL1S for *Demon Resurrection*. The Sony was a terrific camera for its day and I never had a moment's trouble with it. But it had a fixed lens that wasn't of the highest quality, so the resulting picture was really too soft for professional filmmaking.

The Canon camera gave us a lot of trouble during the shoot, eating tapes and malfunctioning in various ways almost from the first day. But the image quality was very high, very vivid and sharp, especially when the camera was fitted with a better lens. When we were shooting *Demon Resurrection*, we ran a Firewire cable to a Mac laptop and captured the video directly to a hard drive using the Hack TV app, a process that worked pretty well and helped us to get around the Canon's tape-eating problem.

Steve Hudgins: We use the best equipment that we can afford and/or borrow. A lot of it comes down to personal preference. Our equipment is much better quality than what

we used on our first movie, but my advice is to use what you can. Don't let what kind of equipment you use, or don't use, hold you back from filmmaking.

Rolfe Kanefsky: Well, when I first started making professional films, the year was 1989. I had been doing video productions and some Super 8 shorts, so I was delighted to be shooting my first real feature on Super 16, which looked great when blown up to 35mm. This is what we did with *There's Nothing Out There*; it had a small theatrical release in New York and California. We made five answer prints and showed them at midnight screenings and film festivals as well as the one week long run at the 8th Street Playhouse in New York City. After *Nothing*, I was able to shoot my next project, *My Family Treasure*, on 35mm. From 1996 to 2003, all of my movies were either 16mm, Super 16, or 35mm. I love film and was very happy to move from video to film. And then the business changed. It became digital. I was hesitant to shoot on digital because the look wasn't great and it took just as long to light properly for video if you wanted it to look as good as film. But as the technology improved, the savings from shooting on digital rather than film were impossible to overlook. I also shoot a lot of footage. It's much, much cheaper to do this on video rather than film. In the film days, we would circle takes to determine what would be printed, because printing the film cost money. On video/digital that is no longer an issue. In 2003, I made *Jacqueline Hyde* for a budget of about $75,000. Film was not really an option, so I shot my first film on digital, using the Sony 900. It was a very good camera and I was quite pleased with the look. In fact, we ended up selling the film and having it released on DVD through Warner Bros. Home Video. That proved to me that the days of film were over. If the first video production I did could be released by Warners, I knew this was the new way, despite my love for film.

I have since used all different types of digital cameras. *Nightmare Man* was shot on the Panasonic Vericam and opened in 350 theaters nationwide as part of the *Horrorfest: 8 Films to Die For* festival in 2007. We had to blow it up to 35mm for the release, but it proved that it could be done. My recent film, *1 in the Gun*, was shot on the Panasonic 3000 and looks amazing.

The important thing about shooting digital is that you need really good lenses and know how to light [a scene] properly. Film is more forgiving, so you really need a cameraman who knows what he's doing. The problem with digital is that the cameras are so cheap that anyone thinks they know how to make a movie. Not everyone does. In the days of film, the cost was so expensive that it stopped a lot of people from making movies. Now, everyone is making them for next to nothing. This is a good and bad thing because many filmmakers aren't learning the basic rules of how to make a movie. They just rush into a production, shoot it quickly, slap on some slick box art, and try to get it released. Sometimes they succeed and sometimes they fail.

I don't have a problem with new people making movies — but learn your craft. I made dozens and dozens of shorts and two feature-length videos while just learning to make movies. I'm proud of them but I would never try to release them, except possibly as a special feature on a DVD or Blu-ray. Take your time and make your film the best it can be before shopping it around. The people who are in this business just to make a quick buck and don't really care about the art or quality of their "film" is what upsets me.

Brett Kelly: Nowadays I shoot on HD cameras, sometimes DSLRs. When I first started I shot on SVHS and Hi-8 video cameras. The quality these days is definitely better, but in a way I prefer having tape rather than SD cards. I prefer knowing that a permanent record exists, rather than cards that get erased constantly. It makes me a nervous wreck knowing that a whole days work can get wiped out in an instant. The DSLRs are cool and handy, but at the moment, sound needs to be recorded separately and synced up in post. That's a pain, but the trade-off is the low cost of the equipment, and that makes it worthwhile.

Chris LaMartina: I shot my first feature on a consumer Sony camcorder with in-camera audio and Home Depot worklights. It was absolute trash, but you have walk before you run, right? That film was produced as a learning experiment, to see if I could finish a feature (an anthology, really), and to see if it could get distributed (it did).

With each subsequent film, we got better gear. We shot *Book of Lore* on a Canon XL2, a 24p 3CCD camera with swappable lenses. At the time, we thought it was unbelievable. Now, it looks like a dinosaur, and this is a motif that repeats itself over and over again in the ever-changing technology climate we live in.

By the time we got to *President's Day*, technology was moving so fast that I'd gotten sick of buying a new camera every two years. Instead of buying new gear, we hired a DP/gaffer team that provided their own: a Panasonic HVX with a 35mm lens adaptor setup.

The adaptor looked pretty great. We could use fixed lens and do wild rack focus maneuvers that we'd never done before. However, it required a lot of light. We'd lose about two-and-a-half f-stops with the use of the adaptor. For a simple bedroom scene, we'd be blasting the location with Kino lights. Lighting ate up a lot of production time.

By the time we shot *Witch's Brew*, DSLR cameras shooting HD video become the "it" format. We shot with two Canon 7Ds. Light loss was minimal (except when using an especially long telephoto lens or freakish wide lens). In general, these cameras provided great picture quality for very minimal cost, but just like every format, it had its disadvantages. On hot days, the 7Ds would overheat. A lot. They never blew up, but we didn't take many chances. We'd power them down as often as we could. The DSLRs also had no sync-sound option (recently, I've heard of a "hack" that can work around this issue). We recorded sound to an H4N zoom recorder and it had to be synced-up in post. I used a program called Plural Eyes for this. It uses the wav form of the 7D's camera audio to match up with the wav form of the H4N's.

Another downside to consider with DSLRs is your editing platform. The 7D saved files as H.264s. At the time, Final Cut Pro (my preferred edit suite), couldn't edit H.264's natively and, therefore, I had to convert them to Apple ProRes HQ files. This and the syncing of audio took up quite a bit of post-production time. I spent about two months encoding and syncing the footage. It looked great in the end, but it was very labor-intensive for us.

Jim Mickle: My first feature, *Mulberry Street*, was shot in 2005 on a Panasonic DVX100, which was a 24p Mini-DV camera that I absolutely loved. I edited in Final Cut Pro and we wound up blowing it up to HD and the distributors made a 35mm print for release. On *Stake Land* we shot in 2009 using two RED-One cameras, and I edited in Final Cut Pro and did all the F/X and compositing in Adobe After Effects, working with 4K RAW files. My senior thesis film, *The Underdogs*, was shot in 2001 on 35mm and I edited on an Avid.

I was always a film snob and never thought I could accept digital for feature filmmaking. And while it will never be 100 percent as good as film, I've learned to love digital as a way to do things efficiently and create a workflow where I can do most things by myself. Once it's shot I can import immediately and start editing full-resolution footage in my bedroom that day. Certain cameras also have their own aesthetic, so while the Panasonic DVX100 can't compete with 35mm in clarity, it has its own look and flavor that can be fun to play with. Same for the RED. I've seen it look terrible and I've seen it look great. I've been lucky to work with a great DP, Ryan Samul, who really knows how to exploit all formats.

The technology now is so good, there's no reason not to be making things that can compete with Hollywood.

Damon Packard: At this stage in technology in the micro-budget world I've been using the Canon DSLRs and Panasonic Prosumer cameras. The Red Epic currently seems to be the favored tool in professional circles. The tools are always improving, but nothing will ever replace the photochemical look of film.

Brad Paulson: I use the Panasonic DVX 100a because that's all I have the money for. I can't even remember what the camera was we made our first movie on. I started using shitty handhold camcorders to make my own movies in high school. This was, of course, before the prosumer stuff was around. Never in my wildest dreams at that time would I have thought there would be an affordable camera out there in a few years that would give me a "film look." At that time, I was already seeing Hollywood Video get infested with micro-cinema, so I thought it may be possible for me in the future. When we made *The Van* we didn't even own a camera. So, we went to Fry's [grocery store] in Burbank to look at options. The clerk told us people would buy the cameras to shoot porns and turn them back in three weeks later and get their money back. I looked at my co-directors and said, "Looks like we have three weeks to shoot this sucker." On *The Bloodstained Bride* we started using the Panasonic DVX100a and that's the same camera I've used ever since. Fortunately, I can upgrade if I need to because the prosumer equipment is so much less expensive than it used to be. On the *Bride* our camera was worth 5K. Now it's only worth 1k or less. It still suits my purposes and has been a great little camera. I plan switching formats in the near future, but it has been very good to me over the years.

Jose Prendes: Equipment changes all the time, depending on timeframe and budget, so this is kind of an odd question to answer. My first film, *The Monster Man*, was shot on a dv cam, while *Corpses Are Forever* was shot on 35mm film. It all depends on budget and the tech available at the time.

Paul Scrabo: The past ten years have given us more formats, more codecs, more cameras, more flavors than we can master. I would recommend that if your film contains actors and your goal is to sell to a distributor for cable or home video, you simply rent the best camera you can. You're not saving money by going with a consumer format. The costs of the actors, the script, the lights, the costumes and the permits are the same anyway.

And the sound quality is more important than the picture quality. Clean up the soundtrack and re-record the dialogue, if necessary. A viewer will keep watching your film despite some poor video if he likes the story and can hear the dialogue. But if he can't make out what anyone is saying, forget it.

But if your goal isn't a narrative film with actors, then grab the camera you have and see what you come up with. Have fun with images and editing. Mix and match shooting formats. Go retro. Put those tiny Kodak, Flip and Sony HD cams in places where larger and more professional gear can't go.

Eric Shapiro: I'm not picky as long as it's High Definition. *Rule of Three* was shot in Standard Definition in 2007, and that's haunted us for years. Going around to festivals, it looked different on every screen; sometimes really washed-out and grainy,

Jose Prendes working with a 16mm camera in a film school short.

sometimes sterling and glossy. And when Netflix licensed it for streaming, it got flagged by our distributor's quality-control department for all the grain. So the editor, Randy Stoudt, had to put a soft blur on it and adjust the image. HD is far more stable and can withstand far more transfers and platforms.

Anthony Straeger: I have a number of cameras — all sub £5000 ($7500) cameras, ranging from tape based to solid state SD card based. I made *Call of the Hunter* on a JVC GY-HD200—1280 × 720 at 24fps. This camera is a Mini-DV HDV camera and has the great advantage of having a really good lens on the front of it. Additionally, I had a wide-angle zoom to give me the full range of options. I had no problems with the quality not being full HD (High Definition), i.e., 1920 × 1080.

I very much like the JVCs as they have made their .mov file system very Final Cut Pro friendly — so having the solid-state model has reduced the editing time. I don't really think that one should be too hung up on the camera; there are so many very good, small and low-cost cameras out there that it really is a fantastic playground for filmmakers. There are some amazing developments in low cost cameras at the time of writing, there was a new airing from Canon the *Canon C300* at sub 20k looks like a remarkable camera.

I have some of my own personal sound equipment — I have a Beyer Dynamic MCE 86N(C)S shotgun microphone, which I love because it has a nice mellow tone to it. For voice-over work I have a Blue Yeti USB microphone and, for the money, it was a great buy. Once again I don't have top-end equipment, but the equipment I have does a really good job.

In addition to that, I have amassed quite a lot of lighting running at 2 × 2000-watt Blonde Lamps, 4 × 1000-watt Redhead lamps and a set of four variable Dedos. Add to that a few 200-watt regular house bulbs and I can light anything. These days, when cameras are so sensitive, you don't need the really big 10 and 5k lights under most circumstances.

So, my equipments covers all the main departments, meaning I can actually make anything to a very decent quality. It's good to work out what you have to spend and do lots and lots of research on cameras, microphones etc before you buy. I don't think about things like, "I can't shoot because I haven't got a good enough camera." I shoot because I have bought one and, in most cases, it will do just fine.

Stepping up to say, the RED Camera from my JVC would have inflated the budget and the shooting time for *Call of the Hunter*. So the whole thing becomes relative — Many films are now being shot on the Canon D5 and D7 because they are high quality and easy to use. But once you move to prime lenses then you move the time line along. It gets back to balancing the books — Time versus Equipment versus Budget. Three balls that take a lot of juggling.

I can tell you one thing — after *Call of the Hunter* I will not do anything as insane as trying to shoot in 12 days. Currently Quid In Shrapnel Productions is in negotiations to produce a zombie movie entitled *Blue, Green, Yellow, Dead!* And we are looking at a schedule of 28 days, and 42 if it goes to 3-D. We intend to shoot something like the Red or Scarlet, but that will all depend on the final budget negotiated. Back to juggling and that is all you can do.

Overall, you have to do a serious weighing-up job. The length of the script and the action involved affects the length of shooting time and, therefore, the budget. The camera will affect how you shoot and with what lenses you can shoot with and, as such, affect the shooting time and the budget.

Marc Trottier: Equipment and technology have changed so much in recent years that I re-edited *Darkness Waits* to try and make the quality acceptable with the standards of today (by "today," I mean "2008" which is when I finished it). I was a victim of what I call "Lucas Syndrome" ... which is basically re-doing things to try and keep up with the current standards (like how *Star Wars* was released 37 times ... with a 3-D version scheduled for release over the next few years). I re-edited it a few times and added new footage over a period of seven years!

Since I haven't been active lately (as far as writing/directing) and I worked so long at restoring footage from *Darkness Waits* (which was shot on Mini DV) that I still haven't personally made anything in HD yet — although that would be my obvious choice because the quality is amazing and you have so much more control over the footage. I know, I know ... welcome to the 21st century, Marc!

As far as editing goes, I edited the first part of *Darkness Waits* (originally two short films which were eventually put together to create a feature) on a VCR. Actually, that's how I began editing stuff. The finished product would be a VHS tape, which just seems so ancient nowadays! I currently use Adobe CS5 (5.5) for all my projects. With the Creative Suite, I use Premiere Pro for editing ... After Effects for visual effects, animated titles and color correction ... Photoshop to fix individual frames or create the cover art for the DVD/Blu-ray case, disc and menus ... Audition for special sound effects and adjustments that I can't do in Premiere ... and Encore for DVD/Blu-ray authoring with animated menus and music.

Mike Watt: We started with 16mm film and slowly moved our way through the various incarnations of digital video, finally landing in the HD world. While many of our colleagues are film purists (Amy included), I never preferred it. Everything about working on film is another step. Load it in the dark. Shoot it. Process it. Reshoot because something went wrong. Get a work print. Edit. Conform the negative. Transfer the sound from one format to another. Apologies to all film purists (Art Ettinger at *Ultra Violent Magazine* in particular) but digital is really the way to go.

Demon Divas and the Lanes of Damnation was our first HD movie, with the equipment provided by our crew, DiggerFilm (Steve Villeneuve, Hugo Bissonet and Simon Geraghty).

Shooting *Demon Divas*: Hugo Bissonett (left), and Mike Watt.

In order to edit, I had to upgrade our computer system, editing software and eventually obtain our own HD camera for inserts and reshoots. It was a large expense up front instead of an ongoing expense of the film and processing. Working from P2 cards instead of tape is also a long-term cost saver. And, of course, it's all instant. A couple of menu items in and you can see exactly what you shot, making the "reshoot or print" decision an instant one. Of course, HD comes with its own share of nerve-wracking elements (card interruption, bad reader, corrupt hard drives), but it's nice to focus on filming rather than electrochemistry.

The differences between the production on *The Resurrection Game* and *Razor Days* are night and day. Part of that came from having the budget to keep everyone around for ten straight days, as opposed to one or two weekends per month for two years. More came from that instant gratification of digital.

Shooting fast and tight is always a priority for us, but with film we always heard the dollar signs ticking away as the film exposed. On *Razor Days*, a much more character-driven script, HD gave us the luxury of improvisation. One day in particular during the shoot, we had an elaborate, four-page dialogue scene between the three stars, Amy, Debbie Rochon and Bette Cassett, which also included a choreographed fight scene. Just as we were ready to shoot, the sky opened up and vomited rain in sheets. The actors voted to keep going, but the elements made the scene increasingly difficult to stick to choreography and the blocked moves. So I told them to just go for it. Whatever felt natural, don't worry about the lines, hit the emotional beats. We wound up with three very different takes of the scene, the actors utilizing the full half-acre of muddy space while I, Director of Photography Bart Mastronardi and the rest of the tarp-carrying crew just tried to keep up. There was one section of dialogue in particular that led in different directions each time and it allowed us to focus on each of the three, capturing very special moments that are, miraculously, fitting together beautifully, if a bit subjectively. Were we shooting film with the same budget, those magical moments would have been lost.

This day changed the dynamic of the rest of the shoot. I'd encouraged improvisation during small scenes, but thanks to the digital format, we could just keep going long after the scene was done. We'd get a master, close ups, and then everyone would just let loose, evolving their characters with both new dialogue and prolonged silences. Sure, if I'd had Robert Altman's average budget, we could have done that with film, too. Without the cash, it's the format that allowed us all to find our footing from one scene to the next.

And, of course, with digital nonlinear editing, the post-process comes with its own adventures, too, which is going to result in a movie with a unique look and style from anything else we've ever done.

Ritch Yarber: We shoot on the Canon XL in digital format. Although I am a fan of the Canon XL, the main reason we use it is that Brian Foster, our director of photography, already owned this equipment and the attachments. I added a second Canon XL to our arsenal to complement what he already had. We use Mini-DV because it is economically the most viable format for our budget at this time. Our editing program is Adobe Premiere and Final Cut Pro.

Our first movies were shot with consumer grade Hi-8 cameras and some lights that Brian borrowed from the cable television productions that he worked on. We now use the Canon XLs, small lighting packages, monitors, professional microphones and whatever else we can borrow, beg or steal ... just kidding. We have even dabbled with direct video feeds into on-set computers. Our latest film, *Murder Machine!*, features CGI effects that greatly propelled us as we sought to fully realize our vision of the ultimate killer. We hope to continue this escalating trend with our next feature that will incorporate CGI effects to add an animated character to interact with our live cast, something that we have no clue about but that we have already started to make happen. We know it is a common thing to many filmmakers these days but we hope to present it in an original manner within our usual micro-budget. Another new and growing experience for us and for the talented artists that will contribute to this work and, hopefully, gain future opportunities by making it happen.

Ivan Zuccon: I don't believe the technical means is that fundamental. I shoot my movies in HD quality with very good cameras, like Sony CineAlta, even though I'd love to have enough money to shoot a movie in 35mm.

Compared to my early days, the main difference is that I now shoot in High Definition. But does it really matter if a movie is digital rather than in film format? I don't think so. If the story is good, if characters are believable, if the acting is solid, if photography is well defined, and if the editing is good, then it makes little difference what kind of support every frame has been impressed on. Does it matter if a painting is on canvas or cardboard? Does it matter if a portrait is painted with crayon or oil? I don't think so. It's the subject that matters, it's the stroke, the hand of the painter, the meaning the author wants to transmit through his creation.

Camera setup with the crew of *Wrath of the Crows* (2012). Photograph courtesy Marija Obradovic.

Budget and Funding

The majority of my films, including the documentaries, have been self-funded. I think a large part of this was due to impatience. I wanted to get right to it, not spending months or even years trying to get money from other people. Yes, I had tried that many times through the years while working on my own projects, and it never amounted to anything other than frustration. In trying to get money from investors the one obstacle I kept on coming across, over and over again, is that these potential "producers" wanted a guarantee that they'd make their money back within a certain time period and they wanted this in writing. Some even stipulated that they wanted me to pay them back everything even if the movie made no profit. While I always had the intention of finishing a movie and selling it, I wasn't psychic. So I refused to do any of these deals because I couldn't promise something out of thin air. It was more trouble than it was worth and I didn't want the producers as a perpetual black cloud over my head.

So I did as much of the work as I could myself, borrowed equipment when I didn't have it, and recruited volunteers for crew and actors. I was always up-front about the low-budget aspect of production and always made sure to have food on-set and on location. A well-fed cast and crew is a happy cast and crew. Once a movie was done and I had income from it, I invested that money into the next production and then into the next. To further get more "bang for the buck" I collaborated with other filmmakers by making anthology-type features. They'd produce and fund their own segments and would get a percentage of the profits. This worked out for everyone and we'd only have to spend a fraction of what we would on an individual feature. This worked well for a decade, when it was viable to produce some sort of income from independent filmmaking.

The only time I ever lost money on a film was on the drama *Walking Between the Raindrops*, primarily because I shot that in California and, after the digital movie was completed, had it blown up to a 16mm print for film festivals. This cost about five times more than the actual budget of the movie. However, that particular film remains one of my favorites.

With the documentaries I made my money by getting sponsors/underwriters for the PBS television broadcasts. However, I had to finish the program first — and get it accepted for broadcast — before I could blindly approach these different companies for cash. It always took about a year to shoot and edit a production, as I was doing the majority of the work. Yes, there was always a chance it wouldn't get accepted and I would not make any money at all, but it was a risk I took. It's always a leap of faith believing in the project and that you'll be able to make money on it. Just don't go broke doing it.

The Filmmakers were asked:
How do you handle your budget and funding?
What costs money and what doesn't?

Glenn Andreiev: You want to pay your lead cast members and crew people something. They all have bills to pay and the "we'll all share in the profits" thrill dies awfully fast during production. Also, you want to pay yourself. When shooting, you want to concentrate only on your film, not, "Is the landlord coming around today?" Today, with the indie film market being so weak, you want to target local businesses for funding, saying that their business in your film can be great local publicity, and think of ways of effectively getting local (not national) publicity for them, meaning the seafood restaurant in Jacksonville, Florida, probably isn't concerned about the publicity they'll get in Michigan.

If you're shooting with video on location, always play it very low, with minimal equipment and crew, letting businesses know you'll be in and out of their place quickly. You'll get so many services, locations, even food for free if you prove you're not going to be a big pain in their necks.

John Borowski: There are three major phases of independent film production: funding, production, and distribution. Each of these phases is a mountain to climb. Sometimes I feel I would rather climb Mount Everest as that is how difficult making indie movies can be. Since my films are documentaries, I can make them over a period of years. With a narrative feature film, the entire production budget must be ready when filming commences. Being a 100 percent independent filmmaker, I self-fund my films. I budget my films based on the last film I produced and try to achieve more with a smaller budget each time. Many filmmakers want huge budgets but I want mine as small as possible so there can be some type of a return on investment. The less money spent, the less that has to be made back. If you have investors they must be paid back so you can prove to them that you can make a return on their investment. The costliest budget items for documentaries with reenactments are sets, props, make-up, and costumes. I would recommend to budget at least one-third of your budget for post-production sound (sound effects editing and mixing) and music. When making *H.H. Holmes*, the addition of Hollywood voice-over talent Tony Jay and the excellent post sound work and music really brought the film to a higher level.

Keith Crocker: I simply start out shooting with the notion that I'm going to save every dollar I can. I'll pay for only what needs to be paid for and nothing else. I don't spend money on permits; I steal locations. I pay only for nude scenes from actors and actresses, because nudity is a tall order for actors; it can cause uneasiness and discomfort, and you may lose the performer if you don't give an incentive. I always supply food, drinks and comfort for a cast and crew; you'll lose them if you don't take care of them. I'll pay for supplies needed in regards to make-up and costuming, so the make-up artist does not get stuck with any bills. But most folks know nothing about what they can and can't get for free. They very often spend themselves into a hole and their films cease in production because they run out of money. No need for that to happen if you're careful, smart and very up front about your needs. Most folks want to see a film succeed, and love to help out, provided it's not a miserable trip.

Richard Cunningham: I try to keep budget down to a bare minimum because the funding for my films comes from my own wallet and whichever small team I'm involved with. Day jobs can only afford an amateur filmmaker so much, and debt in general scares the hell out of me, so I try to improvise and use makeshift equipment where I can.

For example, on my last film, I cleared the floor space in my apartment, converting it into a photography studio in which I shot a majority of the hundreds of images seen in the film's compositions. For lighting, I bought a few china balls, a halogen lamp set from Walmart, and I employed translucent shower curtains to soften them, poster board for bounces. I used a piece of sheer Styrofoam sheeting which I illuminated from behind, creating a blank backdrop and clear edges on the objects for when I needed to cut out the image in the illustrating process later. I even used an old crutch to produce some of the characters' more extreme action postures. It obviously makes you look a little less big-time to the other people involved in the project, but using a little ingenuity to fashion your own equipment can save you thousands of dollars in production costs.

Then there are some expenses you can't avoid, like the camera. Still, you can purchase a solid prosumer HD camcorder now for a few thousand dollars; or, if your budget demands it, you can start out even cheaper than that. Sound is also one of the most powerful and immediate attributes that will quickly differentiate a good film from one poorly made, so it's important to invest in a quality microphone. If your film requires a lot of static shots or slow pans, it's also a smart move to invest in a sturdy tripod that offers some real fluidity to the camera's movements.

You can often get friends to help out during a shoot for crew; even actors are often willing to jump on-board for no salary, but in that situation it's wise to plan out a concentrated filming schedule and stick to it — especially if you are paying people little to nothing — because with such favors often conflicts are bound to emerge in schedules the longer that your production goes on.

Maurice Devereaux: To finance my first film, *Blood Symbol*, I sold off my huge comic-book collection that I had collected for years, and worked in odd jobs. I had tried to find outside funding from either government agencies here in Canada (Telefilm and Sodec) but was always refused, as they do not like horror/fantasy films, and the tax-shelter years of *Prom Night*, *Terror Train*, *Shivers*, *Rabid*, *My Bloody Valentine*, et cetera, were over. David Cronenberg would not have had his career if it wasn't for the tax-shelter deals of the time, as his early films were loathed by critics and the government. But unfortunately for me I missed those golden years. Cronenberg, after being a success internationally, has since been accepted by the government-funding agencies, but he's an exception. If anyone else would submit scripts like *Shivers*, *Rabid*, *Scanners*, *Videodrome* or *The Brood* they would get rejected. I ran out of money many times during the six years it took to finish *Blood Symbol*. Eventually I found a producer who convinced a post-production house to pay for all the post and become co-producers, and that's how the movie was finally completed.

For my following projects I tried contacting a few private companies, to no avail, but it's normal as it is very hard for even established directors to get projects off the ground. For *Lady of the Lake*, I took my savings ($15,000) and took out a loan ($10,000) and shot half the film in 1993, edited what I had (50 minutes) and did a trailer. Then I tried for five years to find investors, partners, and money to finish the film. Many promising leads turned out to be wastes of time and it was very frustrating.

In 1998, my friend Martin Gauthier (who ended up composing the score) had inherited some money from his dad, and loaned me the money to finally finish the film.

But I don't recommend taking money from family or friends, as it puts a strain on relationships. Because, unfortunately, it wasn't 100 percent clear between me and Martin that the money he put in was an investment or a loan. This was a big mistake, since we were friends, naïve and clearly not "businessmen." We didn't do things officially with contracts that made everything crystal clear. I thought the money he was putting in was an investment and that whatever money the film made back he would get first and then we would split the rest. He though it was an investment/loan and that I would eventually pay him back, when I could (no time line, a "gentlemen's agreement"). Oh, boy, if I had known, I would never have taken on his generous $100,000 loan, as even the small $10K loan I had taken before took me years to pay off. And a 100K loan would have terrified me. On the upside, we finished the film, Martin was happy with it and started a career as a film composer. On the downside, the film made almost no money back (only about $20,000). Even if Martin never pressured me, it still was an albatross on my shoulder and I felt morally obliged to pay him back. I ended up finally paying him back the $80K about nine years later. Luckily, we're still friends.

For *End of the Line* I took all my savings from my contract work (I edit movie trailers, TV and radio commercials) and partnered with special make-up F/X artist Adrien Morot. He would do all the F/X in exchange for 30 percent of the film's sales. The film cost me around $400,000, but sales for the film were only $185,000 (minus 30 percent for Adrien's share), so I ended up losing lots of money.

So what have we learned is that financing films out of your own pocket is the absolutely worst way to make movies. DO NOT DO THIS! Not only do you lose lots of money, but worse, you don't make any useful contacts for your next film, as no one in "industry" knows you. Once Adrien Morot was doing the special F/X for a horror film shot in my hometown of Montreal, he was talking with the film's producer, who was candidly sharing his feelings about the many problems they were having on the film and how it sucked (terrible script, lousy first-time director who knew nothing about horror films, etc) and Adrien mentioned to him, "You have a horror film expert (*note: His words not mine) in your

own backyard, Maurice Devereaux—why didn't you hire him?" The producer answered, "Who?" He had never heard of me, and the first-time director (who had only done a short film), who was making this four-million-dollar feature, knew someone related to the production and got hired. Contacts ... those are the real gold. Ninety percent of jobs come through them. And, unfortunately, it has never been my strong suit on the filmmaking side.

Well, unless you enjoy working with amateurs, EVERYTHING costs money. Good actors, professional crew, food, gas, locations, insurance, equipment. Until you have made a film, you really have no clue how so many things add up. Even if today some things are way cheaper (camera, editing), there are still so many elements that remain that you need to pay for. Many indie filmmakers think once the film is "in the can," they're done. But for certain sales (TV) you need extra E&O insurance, and you need to make international sound mixes of your film (without the dialogue) to sell to foreign markets. Films are money pits, no matter how professional you are. There is always something you forgot and need to pay for.

Donald Farmer: For my first few movies I funded them partly through co-productions with video production companies. They provided the things that represented major costs on a low-budget film: camera gear, lighting, crew, and editing facilities. If I could get these items for no up-front cost through partnerships with various production businesses, I then would cover the remaining costs myself ... things like actors salaries, make-up staff and supplies, meals, motels, craft services. That's how I worked on my first movie, *Demon Queen*. I found a Nashville video-production company a friend referred to me. The owner and his wife were my "crew." He brought all the camera and lighting gear down to Miami from Tennessee and we filmed for three consecutive days. Then, to give us more running time, I wrote a couple of second-unit scenes set in a video stores that my cameraman shot when he was back in Nashville. That's where I brought in my friend Bob Tidwell from *The Summoned* to play the video store owner.

After wrapping *Cannibal Hookers* in Los Angeles, I moved back to Tennessee and immediately was hired to be production manager and co-casting director on *No Justice*, a 35mm feature with a $350,000 budget and a six-week shooting schedule. This was funded by a local car dealer who would ultimately spend a half million on this and our follow-up movie *Demented*. So here I was finally working with a real budget, even though I wasn't directing and was involved more in organizational aspects of the shoot. Even the director wasn't really directing, since our producer insisted on giving himself sole directing credit. But in reality, the picture was about 80 percent directed by Fred Dresh, whose credits included crew work on the John Saxon film *Cannibal Apocalypse*.

I ended up getting a nice acting scene in *No Justice* opposite Cameron Mitchell, whose phone number I'd saved after interviewing him for my *Splatter Times* fanzine. I'd already lent Mitchell's number out when Fred Olen Ray was casting *The Tomb* and needed another name. Now I had suddenly had the resources to hire Mitchell myself after the producer's negotiations with Charles Napier went south. I had enough in my casting budget for a second, smaller name, so I brought in Camille Keaton, who I'd gotten to know when I lived in Los Angeles. We also had Bob Orwig, who'd just appeared with Charlie Sheen in *Platoon*, but he happily worked for a fraction of what Mitchell and Keaton were paid.

Having such a solid budget on *No Justice* meant we had money for hiring a mostly L.A. crew. We flew everyone to Tennessee and housed them at the local Scottish Inn for six weeks, springing for lavish catering (with a choice of multiple salads and desserts), renting Panavision 35mm camera gear and a full grip truck, paying for multiple locations through our three-county shooting area, and finally, actually editing the movie "on film" to create two actual 35mm prints we would show at local theaters and drive-ins. This would be the last time I'd see such lavish spending on a movie I worked on. Even five years later, when I did four back-to-back movies with a combined budget of 1.2 million, things were considerably more frugal, as it should be.

No Justice could easier have been done for about half its $350,000 budget. The waste I witnessed was a real education in things I wanted to avoid when I started raising backing for my own movies. Why fly a crew in from California when you can hire them locally? Why have a 30-person crew when half that number will do fine? Why cut on film when your primary market is video and television? Why blow cash on fancy catering and wrap beer? If the crew wants beer at the end of the day, they've been paid. Let them buy it themselves!

But there is one useful trick I learned on *No Justice* for stretching a budget. Our producer had the bright idea of approaching companies for product placement spots. Not for cash, but for an agreement to provide camera time for the products in various scenes in exchange for a few cases of said product for free. We did that with Pepsi and Budweiser on *No Justice*. But a few years later, on *Deadly Run* and *Vicious Kiss*, we used product-placement to get free rental cars, RVs for the stars, and lots of lots of free bottled water for the thirsty cast and crew. For any indie directors wanting to score some free drinks or snacks for their crew through product placement, I always recommend the path of least resistance ... namely, go after the smallest brands in each category. If you need free bottled water, don't approach Evian or Aquafina ... go after the obscure regional brands that probably can't afford lots of advertising. Same with snacks ... let them know that your movie will be sort of a permanent commercial for their product that people will still be watching years from now. Even offer to put the company's website and phone number in your end credits roll, if you think that will help. Any movie, no matter how small, is going to HAVE to buy drinks and snacks for the actors and crew ... right? Why not get that stuff for free and have some extra money for your budget?

When I used to shoot on film, the cost of film stock, processing, and sound syncing were hard costs that could never be deferred. But now that everything's gone digital, all those costs have evaporated and low-budget filmmaking is more accessible than ever. Now maybe the biggest hard cost is hiring an effects house to do your CGI.

Jeff Forsyth: All my pictures, so far, have been self-financed. That has extended the production time on a few projects by months. With such an uncertain market I had not previously felt it was the right time for investors. I have one more micro-budget film in me, I think, and then I am going to seek investors.

Richard W. Haines: I use independent investors putting up small amounts of money which limits their risk. I also roll over profits from one film to the next to make sure I retain 51 percent of the equity for creative control.

The way I budget my pictures is I don't take any up-front fees since I own the finished product. That saves on producing, directing, writing and editing costs. I pay the crew what I can afford but give them a check on a daily basis. I know that on some low-budget shoots the producers run out of money and are unable to pay their employees. I discovered it helps their performance if you pay them on a per diem basis.

William Hopkins: Everything costs money, it seems. Everybody has their hand out for money and every aspect of your production will come with a price tag on it. We all hear these stories about films that were made for a few thousand dollars or a few hundred. At least one filmmaker recently claimed his total budget was 50 British pounds. How true those stories are and how much is hype and publicity is hard to say. I suppose if the film is shot on a deferred-payment basis, you can say it cost nothing to make, but that's a little misleading. That's like saying you have no living expenses

Box art for William Hopkins' *Sleepless Nights*

because you put everything on credit cards. Eventually the bill comes due. I would guess the producers of these supposed no-budget films tell the IRS a different story when tax time comes around, especially if the films have had any success in the marketplace.

If you're approaching your production in a professional way, you can expect that every aspect of it will cost something. The equipment you buy or rent, cast and crew's salaries, transportation, food and lodging, costumes, supplies for special effects and make-up, fees paid to secure the locations, insurance for the shoot, expendables like gaffer's tape, batteries, light bulbs, foam core. Obviously, you want to keep the costs down as much as possible, but everything costs something. Very few films that actually cost nothing to make have any real commercial value in a world where just about everybody has access to high-quality cameras and editing software. If a film like *The Blair Witch Project*, which is about as small and simple a production as you can imagine, still cost somewhere between 30 and 60 thousand to make, according to the reports I read, then it's hard to imagine anything with any commercial value being done for much less than that.

For both of my films, the funding came from private investors brought to the productions by our producers. Nowadays we also have indiegogo.com and kickstarter.com to consider. Whether or not those sites will really be useful to indie filmmakers in raising funds for their productions remains to be seen, but I'll certainly be giving them a try.

Steve Hudgins: We are low-budget specialists and handle our own entire budget. To me, the biggest expense is equipment. Depending on who you know, you can often borrow some equipment, but the basic equipment for making a movie like camera, sound equipment, lighting equipment, editing software and a computer powerful enough to deal with it all is where a lot of the money goes.

Rolfe Kanefsky: Ah, the eternal struggle — raising money to make your film. It's not easy. It's never easy. I have written a lot of scripts. I have budgets for many of them. I have multiple budgets for many of them. Different levels the films can be made depending on the money at hand. There are the budgets with name actors and the budgets with non–SAG actors. Basically, most movies can be made for a variety of budgets. When push comes to shove, things can be simplified, favors asked, and films get produced despite the lack of funds.

I know some filmmakers who will not make their movie unless they have enough money to do so. I also know a lot of filmmakers who have been waiting years and years to make those movies and end up making nothing. I've always felt that the more you do, the better you get and every experience teaches you something. It's been frustrating because if

Rolfe Kanefsky and producer Alain Siritzky on the set of *Rod Steele 0014 in Today Is Yesterday Tomorrow*, a James Bond parody and sequel to *You Only Live Until You Die*.

there really is very little money, your film will not have the slick Hollywood look. It might be a good film but it doesn't look like a 20 million dollar film because it ISN'T! But when the choice is to make nothing versus a low-budget independent, I usually choose making the movie.

So, what costs money? Well, everything costs money. That's not to say that you can't get favors. Most do. If you shoot in your own house or a friend is nice enough to lend you their house, then you save money on your location. You can steal shots versus getting permits. You can feed a cast and crew pizza and fast food versus hiring a caterer. You can buy a camera with a 30-day warranty and return it after your shoot. There are many, many ways to beg, borrow and steal to make your movie. With the exception of stealing locations, I have never done those other things. I believe in paying people, even if it's very little. You want to show people you respect their services. All actors get paid. All crew members get paid unless they're an intern in training. But if you can't pay, then you must feed them well. A good meal goes a long way. You also have to pay for film/tapes and you need to light your scenes properly. Unless you know someone who owns their own camera and lighting package, you must pay for this.

Renting equipment on the weekends saves money. You get extras days and, if you return it by Monday morning, you save a lot. I know people who have shot entire films on weekends, renting the equipment every Friday and returning it on Monday. Again, I have not done this but most of my films have been six-day weeks to get the most out of the equipment.

I have usually worked with non-union crews, which saves money when you go over 12 hours, and that often happens. Same goes for actors but even some SAG actors, if they're on your side, might not blow the whistle if they shoot an extra hour or two.

Making a movie, any movie, takes a lot of hours, dedication, hard work, and self-sacri-fice. Find a team who shares your dedication. Treat them well, compliment their hard work, give them real meal breaks and you will save a lot in the long run. It's much better working with a happy crew than a pissed-off, exhausted crew that wants to kill you or the producer for putting them through this. Be cheap but don't be too cheap and, if you're smart, you'll put the money where it belongs ... on the screen!

That's why I started producing myself. I was sick and tired of watching money being thrown away and time wasted on the stupidest things. A long time ago, I worked as a P.A. on a movie called *Jack's Friends*. It was a first-time director and we were shooting in the Hamptons at night in the winter. It was freezing. So, we're shooting this scene where a naked girl is laying in the road to stop a car so she and her boyfriend can carjack the driver. Anyway, we're shooting the scene and it gets to the part where the girl runs to get her clothes and can't find her shoe. Well, the director suddenly wasn't sure if he should shoot a close-up of the shoe that she can't find. He stopped and discussed this for almost 40 minutes with the producers while the actors and crew sat around, freezing, waiting for them to make up their minds. I couldn't believe it! I was screaming inside my head, "Shoot the shoe! Just shoot it so you have it. Then you can decide in post while editing if you want to use the shot or not!!" It would have taken two minutes to shoot the close-up but they wasted almost an hour on set talking about it. Talk about throwing away a lot of money and time. These discussions should have happened in pre-production.

That's why you should always have a good pre-production schedule. Prep is the cheapest period of time during any movie. But what happens quite often is people get some money, rush through prep, run into problems during production and then try to fix it in post. It's always a mistake and always ends up costing you a hell of a lot more money. If you plan it correctly in the first place, it will be better in the long run and save you a bundle.

Brett Kelly: I'm sure a lot of filmmakers

will tell you the advantages of free talent, and that's definitely true. Many actors and composers will work for free at the beginnings of their careers and I've certainly utilized a lot of their services. At this point, I like to pay folks whenever the budget allows, but if you don't have the cash there are people who will work for free in exchange for clips for their reels or to build their résumés. I think the bulk of my budgets tend to go towards feeding cast and crew on set and during post-production. One aspect that often gets forgotten is the cost of deliverables to distributors, that's a biggie. Don't blow your money up front, it's the end that costs the most.

Chris LaMartina: *Witch's Brew* was our biggest production to date. We raised $13K through a site called Kickstarter, which funds creative projects through donations. We found another $2K through investors and ponied-up $1K ourselves. It was our most expensive film to date, at $16K.

Using a Kickstarter was an interesting, exhausting experience. At the time, the site was relatively new and we were one of the first productions to fund a feature film with it. We promoted the link every day through social-networking sites and begged/pleaded with friends, family, and "fans." Will we ever use it again? Probably not. It's sort of a one-trick situation and the months following our successful fundraising, we saw plenty of projects fail because of "Kickstarter fatigue."

Prior to *Witch's Brew*, everything was self-funded with a handful of small investors. We'd take revenue from local premieres and the small advances we'd get for distribution deals and just roll them over into the next film's budget.

Allocating resources and deciding how you'll budget varies on the project. Without a doubt, the most important money spent is on food. Some might find this shocking, but if you don't feed your cast/crew and you work long hours (which is almost a given in the micro-budget world), you will have a mutiny. The bottom line is that people want to feel ap-preciated, and feeding them is the *least* you can do.

Other important budget decisions are special effects, nudity, and costuming/props. If you're making a low-budget flick, you probably won't have a name actor starring ... so your stars are your effects team and, if you're doing something sleazy ... your nude roles.

I'll politely not disclose what we pay for nude roles (it varies based on the scenes), but it's important to pay those folks ... not only for the sake of respect, but because that is a high-selling point to any distributor.

My first three films had zero nudity, and every distributor we talked to promised us they'd be more intrigued to license with a project featuring more skin. When it came time for *President's Day*, I knew what we had to do. There's gore and sex within the first two minutes. We got triple the distribution offers comparatively and we learned a good lesson: sex sells.

Similarly, your body count and/or monster (whatever that may be: a maniac, vampires, werewolves, garden gnomes, etc.) is crucial to audience excitement and public interest. Micro-budget fans love a good gross-out. Don't let them down. They are the most loyal, devoted fans out there and they're consistently disrespected by cheap effects.

Less important, but not to be forgotten, are costuming/props. If your resources are limited, and you don't have money for wardrobe, you can write your screenplay to be cheap. A story that takes place in one day with minimal characters doesn't require a lot of money for costumes. We have a tendency to make ensemble films that are also prop-heavy. Often times, we make up for this by requesting actors to provided *some* of their own costume and digging through attics, thrift stores, and friends' collections.

Jim Mickle: Our first film started off with $10,000 from a friend who had the balls to invest in a little horror movie. From there it gradually grew to $27,500 to have a cut we could deliver to festivals. We sort of got the money piecemeal, because it was so risky we didn't know if we wanted to blow it all at once if the movie turned out to be a piece of crap. With *Stake Land*, a fantastic filmmaker named Larry Fessenden came along and hooked up the financing through Dark Sky Films as part of a slate with two other films.

In both cases I had amazing producers who could handle the finances and keep it off my mind. I've seen a lot of directors get carried away with the business end of filmmaking, and I think it can almost be a form of procrastination to avoid having to start committing to creative decisions in pre-production. But the sooner you can forget about budgets and let producers do their job, the better. Department heads and producers have done this way more than almost all directors, so the best bet is to trust the people around you and team up with people who understand and enjoy their job. It can be counterproductive to have a director who is overly concerned with the ins and outs of the budget or the financing.

Damon Packard: Everything costs money, any kind of production or endeavor. It doesn't matter if it's a film or not. Talent, equipment, wardrobe, props, locations, scale rates, you name it. How I handle my budget is usually a situation where I shoot what I can when I can, simple as that. In other words, shooting is very rare and sparse. The days are few and far between, mostly filled with general survival issues.

Brad Paulson: Stars cost money. Dwarves cost money. A good dwarf is a major commodity just because they are so hard to find. This is also why they can get away with having the attitude that they so often do. But they're worth it because there are so few around. Good-looking normal-sized actors, on the others hand, are everywhere in this town. So, it's a balancing act. Things which I consider production value on the screen are definitely worth the money. Something unique — something you don't see most people use in their movies. Effects are good to spend money on if you have someone who knows what they're

doing. There's nothing worse than shitty special effects. If that's the case, you're better off doing your own. I hate CGI. I'd much rather spend extra money and take extra time while filming to use practical effects. Use production value. Put the money on the screen. If you can't put the money on the screen, use it on food to feed the actors. It's been said a million times before and it's as true today as it has been in the past: a well-fed crew is a happy crew. On my next movie I plan on cooking all the meals for the crew. I'll save money, and I think a home-cooked meal will help to build camaraderie. Plus, I just plain love cooking. When there's a good sense of camaraderie, making movies can be a blast. When people hate each other on the set, it can be hell. It's also usually a good rule of thumb to save money for screeners, rental for the screening, festivals and general post-production costs. You can spend $100 on the movie but if you want it to get out there and get seen you can easily spend thousands on festival entries. This needs to be planned ahead for.

Jose Prendes: Money is the most important thing when making a movie. It dictates EVERYTHING! You write for your budget and try to stick to it, but you almost always go over. Trying to make a movie is basically trying to manage chaos. Things cost more than you think, or you break something and have to replace it, or equipment rentals add up, or a thousand other things can happen in the course of making your movie. For me, I try to get everything for free if it's coming out of pocket. The one thing I don't skimp on when people are working for free is food. I make sure I feed my cast and crew because good food goes a long way to get everyone on your side and keeping them on the team. Funding is a whole other ball of wax and really isn't something I can answer because most of my movies have been self-funded, except for my next one, which is taking forever to land money, and that is the sad truth about funding in general. I don't know why tons of cheesy movies get funding when good projects languish in what is called "development hell," but it happens. If you want to make something, plan for something you can afford, and then make something cheaper.

Paul Scrabo: *Dr. Horror* was self-funded, so the first item I put in the budget was how much I was going to pay myself for the time that I'm taking off from my regular job — how much I could get by with for those three or four weeks. And multi-tasking is a myth — you can only focus on your production, not your day job as well.

Originally, it was planned to have one of the mini-movies featured in the film presented like an old Universal horror film. Finally, I had to get real. Period costumes, sets and cars? Could we get this ready in time? Could I pay for all this? The budget determined that we would shoot the entire sequence like a situation comedy, and we finished it in one long day. Inspiration or desperation? Take your pick!

Eric Shapiro: My first priority is what most filmmakers often see as the last priority: making sure the cast and crew are compensated. Sometimes you can't always make it, but you should do your best to give the people who work on it *something* for doing so. The difference between a compensated group of people and a group that works for free is massive. The former is far more cooperative and happy, even if they're only getting a token payment.

Anthony Straeger: First, I was very realistic about the amount of money I could make the movie for. So putting together a budget that someone can look at and say, "This is feasible," is very important. As this was a very low-budget film I was able to approach friends and like-minded associates.

As far as working a budget out, there are some great templates that will help — all downloadable on the internet for free. What you need to do is break down the component parts from location/equipment/transport, et cetera. You have to be realistic. Get an estimate on absolutely everything — and, if it's an important hire, get at least three quotes. Make sure that you have insurance if you can because that is one thing that could bite you in the ass!

One of the parts to your question is the Chicken versus the Egg. Do you have a specific budget available to you or are you going to take your script and produce the following?

1. Full synopsis and proposal
2. Script/screenplay
3. Budget Top Sheet
4. Estimated time frame
5. Any marketing material, comparisons and relevant projections start or are you going to take your script, budget it.

This information is crucial if you are pitching for money. There are a number of ways to build up interest in you project, such as Social Media, Crowd-Funding, private and public funding bodies. The bottom line is if you plan a budget you can aim for a specific amount of funding, which will guarantee your schedule and requirements. If you just have 10k, then you simply have to tailor your cloth, which can be quite exciting in itself.

One of the biggest costs in low-budget film is accommodation (if necessary) and food. They say an army marches on its stomach. Well, the same applies to cast and crew. Half the shooting budget for *Call of the Hunter* was spent on food/drink and accommodation. Believe me, as an actor having done low-budget and experiencing a bag of chips after 12 hours, I can tell you that it is the best way to breed discontent.

On the other hand, what doesn't cost money in no/low budget is talent. These days, sadly, more and more actors and crew do work for free. If someone (as I did) says, "I don't have the money to pay you," then you have to make a very definite promise to make it worth their while. So this is a list I think every director and producer of a no/low-pay movie should obey. It's short but it's important:

1. The cast and crew have to be treated with respect and looked after.

2. They should, without asking, be supplied with stills and a copy of the film.

Marc Trottier: I look forward to the day when I can make something with a proper budget, where I can pay the actors and the crew what they deserve, as opposed to asking acting friends to work for free ... and to hold the boom for the shots that they're not in. I also taught myself how to use all the editing software because I didn't have money to pay someone else to do it. That's something else I look forward to — paying other people to do post-production work.

The budget for *Darkness Waits* was supposed to be split between four people, including myself. The other three bailed at the last minute, so I ended up funding it alone. So I can't really speak from experience about budget and funding, because up to now, it's always come out of my pocket. Hopefully after reading this book I'll have some better ideas of how to pay for stuff!

I know that there are grants that you can apply for ... but I've never done that.

If you're lucky enough to find talented people to work for free (or really cheap), then you have to at least supply food and beer (I recommend supplying beer *after* filming is complete, if you want things done properly).

Mike Watt: When we started, money from Amy, my and Bill's full-time jobs went towards film, materials and food. There were times when Bill had to build a new prop from scratch because we couldn't afford a pre-built whatever-it-was. The rest of it was to buy and process the film. But a large portion of our limited budget went towards keeping the cast and crew fed, which meant a lot of home-cooked meals, sandwiches, snacks and soda. Since everyone was working for free, over the span of two years, the food went a long way to keeping people coming back.

Over the following years, food was still the top priority. But in place of film costs came travel expenses. Gradually, we prided ourselves in making sure no one was [paying] out of pocket — at the very least — on one of our pro-

ductions. If you can't afford to feed people and get them to where you need them to be, you should rethink your project. It's the first "professional" step.

Further down the line, we've made contact with enough investors to make sure our principal cast and crew are paid for their time and expenses for the duration of the shoot. Sometimes we adhere to contracts; other times we play fast and loose, but nobody leaves empty-handed if we can help it.

For a Happy Cloud Picture the paid-for elements are food, travel, props/effects, insurance and salaries (however small they may be). We've rarely paid for locations, legal advice, publicity or equipment rental (though the latter has come up, over the years we've scrounged nearly everything we need). The best advice for not paying for something is make lots and lots of very disparate friends.

Ritch Yarber: To date, all of our TwistedSpine.com Films productions have been totally funded from our own shallow pockets. The main reason for this is that we consider ourselves a "film group" and not a business venture. We are trying to showcase what each of us can do if given the opportunity. So far, nobody has come forward to the group and announced that they want to showcase their ability to gain funding to make independent films. That would be great. Till that happens, we feel that we are investing in ourselves by spending our own money to produce valuable entertainment that provides us and others with experience, visibility and a sense of successful accomplishment. We have always made our money back on our films and have consistently reinvested that money into the next project. We are finally at the level where our efforts are starting to get us the notice, accolades and opportunities that we hoped for. TwistedSpine.com Films is about everyday people gaining opportunities to become paid entertainment professionals through their contributions to a successful micro-budget production.

The TwistedSpine.com Films attitude and belief is that high-quality productions can be made on a micro-budget by utilizing a grass-roots campaign to attain equipment, talent and props. Passion does not cost money. Passion has you scour thrift stores and flea markets until you find the best costuming and props that you can afford and that will be acceptable as real to the viewer. Passion has you finding great locations and working out ways to get them into your film. Passion has you working to find the best actors for your project. Passion keeps you from settling for the quick and easy fix to a problem. Passion has you finding affordable ways to keep your cast and crew fed, happy and content that their work is appreciated.

The great thing about how TwistedSpine.com Films makes movies is that everybody works as a team, knowing that the success of one will be the success for all. It's not about making money, it's about making opportunities. That makes for a great creative atmosphere with everybody giving their best to the work.

Ivan Zuccon: Managing the budget is the hardest thing to do. No one can deny that everything's expensive, and that making movies at zero cost is almost impossible. In the field of horror movies what costs more, both in terms of time and money, are the special make-up effects. I sometimes get annoyed when I have to wait for hours before shooting, waiting for make-up artists to finish their job. But nowadays it's hard to think about making horror films without special make up effects, unless you decide to use CGI. Yet, this only postpones the problem, and all the chickens will come home to roost during post-production. I have a dream, which is to shoot a horror movie without even a drop of blood in it, to create a scary and creepy atmosphere through the clever use of camera and photography. Unfortunately, it seems that you can't shoot a movie like this in today's times; the password for distributors is "more": more blood, more violence, more sex, more monsters, and therefore, more special effects. You need at least to partially adapt yourself to the trend if you want to recover the money you invested. In the end, making movies is also about business, not just about art.

Production Crew

When you are working on a feature it's extremely important to work with people you can depend on and who you get along with. Your best bet is to work with either individuals you've worked with before, whether it be in film school or a professional production, or with friends. On my films I tried to use the same crew people since they knew what they were doing. The one thing you really don't want to be doing, particularly on a first feature, is training people on the job. You'll have more than enough to worry about. If you need specific skills, post advertisements for the crew members you are searching for, such as for lighting and audio. You'll have to have interviews to make sure you're all on the same page, and state if there is pay or not and the type of hours they are expected to work. I remember several instances where potential crew thought they'd be working on a half-million-dollar budget when I kept on stressing that it was only a $5,000 production. "Oh, you can get money," they insisted. "I'll give you a discount of my day rate." Well, a real day rate for a camera or audio person can be anywhere from $300–$500 a day, and that was not feasible with the lack of budget. It wasn't possible under the circumstances. It was either make the movie as cheaply as I could or not to make it at all.

I've also found that the smaller the crew, the better. On your first production, get only who is necessary. Do you really need a script supervisor or a continuity person? Probably not. But you definitely need a camera person (who can also light) if you're not shooting yourself—and there needs to be a person responsible for recording good audio. A few production assistants also come in handy, as they'll help with everything that needs to be done. A tight-knit group also makes the production go much quicker.

Your crew also has to understand that if you're the producer and/or director that you're calling the shots. This is not a Hollywood "film by committee." By all means, you should be open to suggestions. Someone may have a better or more efficient way to light a scene or frame a shot — and that can only benefit your production. But it's not conducive for someone to be a "backseat director" in front of your other production people.

If you are working with "volunteer crew" then you'll most likely have to work around people's day-job schedules, and that means shooting on weekends. Most people will not give up their weekends unless they have a great interest in seeing your movie completed. So a little enthusiasm on your part goes a long way. No one will be as excited about your movie as you are. Keep up that momentum.

The Filmmakers were Asked
How do you pick and choose your crew?

Glenn Andreiev: All experienced cinematographers and editors know their stuff. Where you want to focus on is their personality. It's a process of elimination. If I know they are talented but are full of themselves, or simply look down at you, go to the next candidate. Ask yourself, are they going to respect you as a director? Are they okay with working on a low budget? Are they going to offer suggestions that are truly to the benefit of the film and not their ego? I worked on a feature film in Florida that stopped for a good three days into production because the editor was a "know-it-all" and berated the director with endless, needless "tough-love" filmmaking lessons. Other crew and cast members started walking off the film — they saw it was doomed for failure because of this constantly yapping editor.

John Borowski: The internet is a great resource for finding crew. I usually put up ads for the crew that I am seeking and receive many responses. Some want to be paid what they are worth, but, unfortunately, my budgets are so small, or nonexistent, that I cannot pay full rates. I am always truthful and up front when hiring crew and cast and explain to them what I would like to achieve and the amount I have to work with. The film industry is an ego-driven business, so you will come across many people with attitudes. It seems that when making every film there is at least one bad apple. I once worked with a director of photography who I was upfront with and once we started filming he complained to the other cast and crew members on the set calling it "ghetto filmmaking." I made sure to write him a letter, letting him know how unprofessional

Director John Borowski (right) discusses framing a scene with DP Jason Satterfield. Photograph by Matthew Aaron.

he was acting on the set and that I would never work with him again. He asked that his name be removed from the film, so I removed his name. Word-of-mouth and references are very important in this industry, so I recommend to people that they always be courteous and professional, as word gets around quickly as far as who is problematic to work with. You have to work long and stressful hours when making films. Try to be pleasant and have fun while doing it.

Keith Crocker: These days I choose crew more by experience than anything else. Years ago the crew was also made up of actors, technicians, friends, and essentially anyone who wandered onto the set. In other words, everyone doubled up on duties regardless of how good they were when it came to a specific job. If you were

DP Jason Satterfield sets up a shot for director John Borowski, while actor David Weiss (rear) awaits his cue. Photograph by Matthew Aaron.

willing to do anything, you got the chance to do it. When I was shooting on 16mm, I tried to do it all: produce, write, direct, shoot, edit (right down to the A&B roll) and draw up the publicity. This helps to explain the exhaustion I'd suffer from making films. It felt like giving birth, except I'm a male and I have none of those reproductive organs to even know what that feels like. But filmmaking, to me, is very

much a birthing process. Anyhow, *Bloody Ape* was the last film that I made taking on way too many hats. I ran myself into the ground, literally, got physically ill and ended up in the hospital. From that point on I vowed to pull together crews to make my life easier. And I did with *Blitzkrieg* and the two promotional film trailers (*Three Slices of Delirium* and *Rasputin on Campus*). In between, when I finished

Bloody Ape and began *Blitzkrieg*, I met a slew of people who had various degrees of skill, guys like Jim Knusch, who had a background in 35mm and 16mm camera work, and was willing to try his hand at shooting digital video. Because of his film background, he was the only man I'd trust to light and shoot *Blitzkrieg* (I knew he'd light it and set up angles like it was film). The same goes for Dan Lipski, who shot two of my latest promo trailers. He has a good digital background but he has shot film as well. And there's Keith Matturro, who did costumes and production design on *Blitzkrieg*. Keith is a collector of memorabilia, who has a big collection of World War II uniforms, and he understands so much about the war that the bulk of us don't know because we don't invest the time in such things. Without Keith Matturro, *Blitzkrieg* could not have been made. In the past, I'd use people I was comfortable with; folks that I knew wouldn't give me a hard time. Now, I'll use folks who I don't always like personally, but I know are reliable and will come through. Filmmaking is work, and you don't always love those you work with. You cooperate and you learn to work with people. I also use people I can learn from — I like folks who have ideas and want to share them. The best films are the ones that have collaboration. I don't like ego, though. I can't stand when I get a "genius" on the set who thinks they know more than anyone and wastes your time telling you just how great they are. It's usually the less experienced people who do this. You should only get wiser with experience. Growing a large ego will do nothing but get you into trouble.

Richard Cunningham: The first crew I was involved with was a couple of friends from high school. We all had particular interests in filmmaking and kind of naturally assumed our roles in production. The guys with whom I collaborated on *America the Mental* and *Year Zero*, I met after I moved to New York City.

Year Zero's cast and crew celebrate the film's world premier at the 2011 Tribeca Film Festival. Left to right: Americk Lewis, Marie-Pierre Beausejour, Pat Rigby, Tim Brennan, and Richard Cunningham.

Producer Tim Brennan I met working on film/TV sets in New York City and another collaborator, Pat Rigby, is a New York City stand-up comedian, who I met through Tim.

I guess it's obvious to pick creative, versatile people for your production team, but I don't think it can be overstated. If you're working on a union film, then you'll have specific people for specific jobs; but on a micro-budget film, it's usually a few people wearing a lot of different hats to get the film completed. So it helps if everyone on the crew/production team is bringing a few talents to the table. Moreover, it's not easy getting the time commitment from a large group of make-up artists, set designers, gaffers, grips, et cetera for a non-paying job, so the more you can boil down the crew, the fewer people you have to depend on.

Maurice Devereaux: Who's good, who can I afford, who's available... There are union books with lists of people, but usually go through other filmmaker friends and their recommendations. Contacts!!!

Donald Farmer: On a small, ultra–low–budget shoot I usually just need a cameraman and a couple of production assistants who can help wherever they're needed. On a bigger budget, I look for a director of photography first, then see if he has recommendations for camera crew, gaffers, or other crew from people he or she has worked with. Most DPs have a ready list of crew they want to recommend to you, so why not take advantage?

If I'm working with a DP for the first time, I want to see clips of things they've shot before. I tend to have some of specific requests in terms of lighting, so I like a DP who doesn't expect total autonomy in this area. I can tell fairly quickly how much I can delegate to a DP — sometimes they will suggest camera placement but I usually do this myself. I'll make the call if a dolly track or any kind of camera movement is used. My big pet peeve: if I don't request camera movement or a zoom lens shot, don't give it to me. I remember feeling beyond pissed once watching rushes from one of my 16mm movies and seeing their zoom-lens moves that I hadn't asked for.

Donald Farmer (with camera) shoots a scene for his first movie, *Demon Queen*.

Jeff Forsyth: My crews have always been minimal, not because I like it that way but because the crew is usually staffed with friends and family that I train to operate in certain jobs.

Richard W. Haines: I've used the same cinematographers on multiple productions, since they understand my shooting style. I allow them to pick the rest of the crew like AC's, gaffers and grips. I pay them but they are sub-contracted out by the DP so he can find people he's comfortable working with. A film crew must operate as a team, so it's better if they use veterans.

William Hopkins: We didn't really have a very large crew on either film. On *Demon Resurrection*, since I was shooting the film myself as well as directing, it really just came down to four or five additional people, two of whom were our producers, Frank Cilla and Ed Wheeler. Everybody did double and triple duty. Several of our actors also helped out behind the scenes when they weren't needed in front of the cameras. It might've been nice to have a few more people to help out, but on a small production like *Demon*, every additional person would've meant more expense and more trouble, frankly, since every extra person brings their egos and little personality quirks along with them, and the likelihood of conflict rises. I'd really rather work with a smaller group of mature, intelligent people, folks I trust and who I know are really committed to the project. I never really felt we were short-handed on *Demon*, or that we were missing out because we didn't have more experienced people crewing the film. We all worked together and if we encountered any problems we kept at it till the problems were solved. We muddled through and came out with a pretty entertaining film at the end of it. So I suppose when I start readying my next film, I'll be looking to the same people, if they're available, or I'll be taking their recommendations on who to hire.

Steve Hudgins: Usually when we send out a casting call, I attach a crew call along with it to see if anyone is interested in helping out with crew. From there we stick with the hardest-working, most reliable and dependable crew members.

Rolfe Kanefsky: You interview, ask filmmaker friends for referrals, and try to continue working with the people you know are good! Sometimes it's trial and error. When you have very little money, you can't afford the best people for the job. You have to settle for the "hungry" people who need to work, or the excited film students looking to break into the business. You have to learn how to read people and hope your judgment is on target. Every now and then you find a really good, talented crew member and then you hold on to him/her for as long as you can. Basically, everyone has an agenda. You need to find someone who has the same agenda as you and then you can help each other. I like being around the same team. It makes it easier to communicate my vision. I also need my crew to trust me. You have to win over that trust. You need to work as hard as you hope your team members on the set will work. James Cameron is a tough boss, but he works his ass off. You either have to stack up to that kind of leadership or walk away. On my last production, we had very limited means and a very tough schedule. We shot for 54 days, six-day weeks, and almost always filmed at night. That is hard, and many, many of the crew members did not last until the end of the shoot. But we found a few great ones and some that really learned a lot. Back 10, 20, 30 years, Roger Corman was famous for hiring young talented kids, teaching them the ropes with his B-movies and watching them graduate to big studio films. Charlie Band with his Full Moon company also did that to a certain extent. On the East Coast, Lloyd Kaufman and Troma Entertainment was the training grounds. Unfortunately, now, that doesn't really exist. It's all independent films that can't put out that slate of productions to keep people working. So, you have to move around and work on as much stuff as you can. I was lucky to work for or in association with Corman,

Setting up for the "Miss Louise" scene in Steve Hudgins' *Spirit Stalkers*. Left to right: Terry Sidell, James Gibbs, Steve Hudgins.

Band, and Kaufman. It was a great training ground and really taught me a lot about stretching a dollar and making it look like a hundred.

But going back to the question, we find people through ads on craigslist, other websites, and through networking. Being at the right place at the right time makes all the difference. That's why luck plays such a big part in the film business. If you have luck, talent, and drive, you can have a career.

Brett Kelly: I tend to work with the same people a lot, but the way I would meet them is from networking opportunities, such as attending screenings of other filmmakers. I also take recommendations from friends I've already worked with.

Chris LaMartina: We will always pick the best person over other attributes. I've spoken with plenty of top-notch craftspeople who were totally rude, inconsiderate, and smarmy. We don't need the drama, and if you're making a cheap flick, neither do you.

Good people bring a lot to a production: energy, camaraderie, and a shared sense of purpose. Obviously, you can't just hire anyone because there are plenty of great folks that aren't interested in honing film skills, but it's about finding a balance.

Take the film student who wants a foot in the door versus the twenty-year veteran who wants a NY Strip Steak for catering. Most likely, your budget will already dictate this decision, but if not, definitely consider it. The bonus to hiring young talent is a fresh take on old ideas. We've learned a lot from green film kids rather than the weathered grumpy old gaffer. He can teach you a lot, too ... but this is an ever-changing industry and passion ranks supreme in our book.

Jim Mickle: I spent a few years working as a best boy grip on a lot of indie movies, and along the way I met a lot of great people who I went on to work with. I met Ryan Samul through that and he had a great DP reel and we clicked creatively, so he went on to shoot both my films. I worked on *Transamerica*, where I met my girlfriend, Linda Moran, and she's been producing movies for 15 years. She's an amazing producer and an invaluable creative partner and she's introduced me to a lot of talented people. My sister Beth Mickle production designed my student films and now she's gone on to be hugely successful in the film world, designing movies like *Drive* and getting nominated for BAFTAs, so her crew was kind enough to get down and dirty and do *Stake Land*. A lot of people, like composer Jeff Grace and sound designer Graham Reznick, came from Larry Fessenden and Glass Eye Pix's team.

That's another great part of living in New York and working in film. There's a whole culture of like-minded people to surround yourself with, so when the opportunity comes to make a movie, you get to work with all your friends.

Damon Packard: It comes down to pure practicality, whoever is available, willing, and agreeable. The logistics of getting everyone available and together on the same day and hoping nobody drops out at the last minute (which often happens) and nothing else goes wrong is a miracle in itself. And this is partly why so many months/years unnecessarily pass for what *should* amount to a week's worth of work!

Brad Paulson: The crew is usually people we've worked with before that we trust. It all kind of revolves around the film school principles, really. Everyone helps each other out on projects. However, this tends to dry up after a bit. There are only so many things people will work on for free. After that, it's time to move on. This is what we've had to do from time to time. This can be a good thing, though. Sometimes, working with new people can reinvigorate things. Since there's so many

people that have moved here to get involved in movies, someone will always respond to a "Crew Needed" craigslist ad. Filmmaking on an independent level is very old school and homegrown. I love that aspect about it. When you're in the trenches with a good group of people, making movies has such a small-town feel to it. It makes you feel like you're doing something good and are far removed from all the corporate bullshit of studio movies. However, I'm looking at a lot of the people I've known over the years who have moved out to L.A. and just got destroyed by the brutal system that exists in this town. Most people don't now how to live broke. I would have been out of here years ago if I hadn't trained myself to live at my means and nothing else. I've disciplined myself to live dead-ass broke out here since the day I made California my home. I'm like the guy in the post apocalypse who's shacked himself up in the hut learning how to survive off nothing for years, just waiting for the nuclear fallout to clear so I can venture out and make a movie again. I really don't know why I stay. It's certainly not for financial reasons. It must be a combination of the fact that I enjoy being around like-minded people and am a glutton for suffering. To live here there has to be something wrong with you, and to move here to pursue a career in filmmaking you have to be insane.

Jose Prendes: If they are willing to work for free and are hungry for film experience, then they are in my crew. That was the original method. Now that I am dealing with union stuff, my crews are selected very carefully and résumés are weighed. But I like to work by instinct. I like to meet the person, talk to them about their favorite movies, why they want the job, and I can usually read a person correctly. I haven't had any crew problems on my sets. I try to make sure everyone is having a good time.

Paul Scrabo: They are friends who also work in media, and are all too familiar with deadlines and budget restrictions. And they know other professionals as well.

Eric Shapiro: I imagine I get my crew like most others in the indie world: based on availability, how conducive their needs are to what you're offering monetarily, and how easy and civil they seem. There's an intensive talent demand for the DP and editor; for the rest, proficiency and competence are acceptable.

Anthony Straeger: There are two ways to pick your crew:

1. From people you know — some may be in the business; some might just want to get into the business.
2. From websites such as Crew United, Casting Call Pro and Shooting People in the U.K. These places are great resource points and you will find many artists more than willing to contact you to find out more about your project.

Other ways of finding cast and crew are through Networking nights, and these can easily be found on Facebook, Google et al.

I chose my crew from *Call of the Hunter*

through a combination of the above. As my crew was very lean, it comprised as follows:

John Slocombe, our executive producer, who provided over 50 percent of the investment in the project. Helped project manage the movie and found the location.

Dennis Morgan was chosen as director of photography because we had worked on a number of projects in the past, ranging through corporate filmmaking through to short films and TV. He is a solid lighting cameraman who has years of experience and always keeps his cool under pressure.

Chris Reading, our soundman, came from an advert I placed on Shooting People. He was straight from college and was looking to build his CV. He had a great personality and sense of calm that was just what I needed for this project.

Stephen Gawtry, our writer, worked as production manager and continuity — in our situation there was a need for anyone who was involved in one capacity to double and triple

On location in a forest shooting the *Call of the Hunter*: Anthony Straeger (foreground), Dennis Morgan (directly behind), Stephen Gawtry (looking down), and Nick Gregan.

up their jobs — He actually helped by supplying a great brew of tea.

Nick Gregan, a photographer friend, fancied himself as a Steadicam operator and so he came on board as Steadicam/second unit. Other duties included gaffe work on the movie.

Richard Unger was brought in as stills photographer and again came through an advert on Shooting People. But once we had met, it was found he had so much equipment that he became head sparky, gaffe and rigging.

Sally Alcott was also found straight from college and via the advert on Shooting People. She was SFX make-up/hair/costume. Once again she was relatively new to the business, having also only recently finished her degree. She coped really well with a very limited budget of less than $1,000.

Martin Shenton and myself go back many years and he was brought in as fight coordinator and stuntman. He'd worked on Bond movies and is very experienced so was glad that he could afford the time to come and do some sterling work for us.

The most important thing about our production was the time pressure and being stuck in one place 24/7 for 12 days. I selected everyone not solely based on ability but on their personality and nature. It worked out really well, and I will be forever in there debt for the amount of work they had to do and how well they did it.

Marc Trottier: I've never had a proper crew, because, like I've mentioned, I've never had a proper budget to pay for it. But I look forward to the day where I'll have a dedicated sound guy, lighting technician, boom operator and director of photography with the proper equipment to assist me.

I've been lucky enough to always have actors who were kind enough — and multi-talented enough — to help out with all the other stuff. But like the song goes, "That's what friends are for..."

Mike Watt: This process varies from film to film. In the beginning, the majority of my crew were either guys at my film school or people I worked with at the lab, whose films I had seen. The ones we had the best relationships with were the ones we continued to work with. As the years went on, we networked with other filmmakers and talents. Jeff Waltrowski graduated a year or two behind me and made the terrific *Project: Valkyrie* and became my DP on *A Feast of Flesh*. Aaron Bernard, an actor on *A Feast of Flesh*, came on as the second-unit director on *Splatter Movie* and also authored that movie's (and *Demon Divas*) DVDs. DiggerFilm's crew originally approached us to take part in their documentary and their stuff was so impressive that we hired them for *Demon Divas*. For *Razor Days*, my longtime friend Alan Rowe Kelly introduced me to Bart Mastronardi (*Vindication*), whose photography and instincts are among the best I've ever seen, and I realized he was the only one who could shoot this movie.

We tend not to "audition," however, or hire based on reels alone. At any end of the business, it's best to find your principal crew among talented people you have either met or know through someone you trust. You have to move too fast and be too flexible to work with any wild cards. If someone comes recommended to us, we'll meet them first and try to gauge if their personality will mesh with the rest of the HCP family. Very rarely a crew member will end up being not what we'd hoped for — great at one thing but not open to improvisation when problems arise is the biggest occasional hurdle.

The more movies you make, your instinct for talent refines and usually blossoms into future collaborations. Movies are horrifically stressful events, more so, I believe, than moving, public speaking or possibly even the death of a spouse. Frustration and exhaustion is inevitable. It's not a point of pride and it's not fair, but it is a true trade secret: every movie needs a "dog" — that one guy everyone focuses their frustration on to avoid everyone killing each other. Sometimes the dog is a volunteer PA or another type of crew with too little experience, to the point they just get in the way. With low-budget shoots, though, particularly when it comes to people who aren't being paid in any way beyond food, it's difficult to just ask these people not to return. "Dogs" aren't usually malevolent, just inexperienced. If they're causing real problems, by all means dump them. But even if they're utterly useless, unless they're knocking down walls or setting buildings on fire, they still provide the purpose of "ire magnet." It sounds very cruel, but a "dog" can be an essential member of the production. Maybe all they come away with is that we're a bunch of dicks, but they still learned from the process.

But you can't assign the role of "dog" to anyone. They have to earn that title. The first day is a freebie. Subsequent days of screw-ups (laziness is not tolerated, but misfiring synapses on a daily basis can add to the stress and adventure) force you to decide if you have the time to replace the "dog" or just let him be the focus of bitching, which takes a lot of stress away from other interpersonal relationships. If the rest of your folks are professionals, there won't be much yelling at the dog, just gritted teeth and forced politeness. On two of our productions we had a pair of dogs, but in each case they wound up working together on other projects and are still cordial to everyone else they worked with.

Ritch Yarber: Our filmmaking group already has a stable under structure. That is, people that have performed the same duties on many of our projects. We add more crew to this structure by having open calls for people that want to do various tasks on a project for the experience. We review the interested people to determine if they "fit" the standards that we are seeking, i.e., talent, temperament and dependability. Once chosen for the project, we try to allow as much input as possible from that person pertaining to their position and to allow them to make true and valuable contributions to the overall project. As the "president" of the group, I make the final decisions and take the responsibility of getting the production to where it needs to be.

Ivan Zuccon: I trained my crew during the years. At the beginning they were just movie lovers with the will to learn a profession. Now they have become high-level professionals who I could never do without.

Actors

Other than a solid, entertaining script, I think the second most important thing for a low-budget production is the actors to bring that script to life. They can make or break a movie as their performance makes the story line believable. Do not cast non-acting relatives in a part just because it's easy. Spend time on having auditions and finding the best actors available in your area. If you live near a major city, this will be easier.

Be up front if there's pay or not, how much time is expected of them, how long the shoot is, just as you would with your crew members. The majority of the time I was unable to pay actors BUT I did promise them a copy of the finished movie and lots of publicity. This was easier with horror films and actresses, as photos of a vampiress covered in blood always made a few genre magazine covers. Quite a few of these actors I've cast in my horror movies have gone on to much higher profile gigs, appearing on such television shows as *Lost*, *Desperate Housewives*, *Party Down*, *Southland*, *CSI*, *Dexter* and *Mad Men*.

The usual process of finding actors is to post an ad, listing the characters and descriptions. It usually took me a few weeks to go through all the head shots and résumés and then another week or so to set up the auditions. I always ask the actors to do a one-to-two-minute monologue, as this weeds out the real actors from the "wannabes" and immediately shows you if they can act or not. It's a given that actors should be able to memorize lines. After you listen to their monologue you can decide to have them read a page or two of the character in the script.

This saves a lot of time. Also, make sure to videotape the auditions because you'll have to re-watch all of them to make your final casting choices. This is also because of the "photogenic factor." Sad to say but some people do not photograph as well as they appear in real life. But the reverse also holds true.

Before the actual shoot make sure to have a reading of the script with all the actors present. It's at this point you answer any sort of questions they have about the script or the characters they portray. I always told the actors to get together and practice their lines. They usually had a month or two to practice, from the time they were cast to the time I started shooting.

During all of this, make sure to treat your actors well. Don't rant and rave during the shoot, don't take out your aggravation on them. They are there to make your vision come to life.

To get the perspective of a low-budget movie actor, I asked actor David C. Hayes, veteran of dozens of genre films, to give an actor's take on low-budget productions.

Interview with Actor David C. Hayes

What is your background as an actor? What first got you interested in acting?

My background as an actor is pretty ... unique. I started as a grip/gaffer type in Chicago and noticed a bunch of horrible acting in the projects I had been involved in. I mentioned to a sound mixer friend that I could "do that stuff," and he hooked me up with a short film and I landed my first role. Untrained and unapologetic about it, I figured I

Actor David Hayes at the first Annual Flint Horror Convention, in 2011.

should learn something, so I began to give a local theatre company free coffee from the Starbucks I worked at. Sooner than later I had landed a role in their 1998 *Rudolph the Red-Hosed Reindeer* show, a transvestite reindeer musical. I went on to be a part of their musical version of *Carrie* and then began to seek out the cult/horror/bizarre films in town. I'd always been a genre fan and decided to focus on these types of projects.

How do you normally prepare for a role?

It depends on the role. What I like to do is to take a piece of my own personality and put it on steroids. I get a lot of weird/creepy roles, for some reason. When I'm dealing with something like that, let's say Motorman Dan in *Machined* or *Reborn*. That is nothing more than amping up the collector mentality in me already. I love collecting comic books, movies, et cetera. What Dan does, he collects serial-killer memorabilia and eventually creates his own serial killer. All he is doing is searching for the ultimate piece to his collection ... just

like me. Before leaving the West Coast I had finished a role in *A Man Called Nereus*. It is a pretty unique animal, a metaphysical action comedy, where I play Nereus. The role called for an autistic-like savant on one plane and a genius manipulator of physics on another plane. On one side I'm just a big kid. On the other side, I consider myself semi-educated and teach college ... just need those steroids.

What was the best acting experience you've had in a film?

The best experience I've ever had was working on *Bloody Bloody Bible Camp*. We wrapped last year and I've recently seen the final cut and I'm pleased. The film is set in the 1980s and is an homage/spoof of the slasher genre. The slasher genre is where I cut my fanboy teeth. Michael Myers, Jason Voorhees, the rip offs ... all of it influenced me so much. So, when I got the chance to play one of my favorite slasher archetypes, the local that warns the campers about the bloodshed and tries to save the day, I was thrilled. We had a great time on set, shooting near Big Bear, in California. I had some great scenes with other genre vets, like Jeff Dylan Graham, Tim Sullivan, the legendary Reggie Bannister, and I got to perform in my third film with Ron Jeremy (all of them clothed ... at least partially).

What was the worst acting experience you've had in a movie?

Hmmm. Rough one. I am going to have to go with a film we'll call the *Cherry Blast* to keep the guilty from getting any real press. That isn't the name of the film, but it will do. I was cast as a cab driver that takes the main character a few places and provides some below-average horror movie exposition and a funny story. Cool, I can dig that. Unfortunately for me, and everyone else, after three excruciatingly long table reads in a loud Mexican restaurant, I find out the director is a raging alcoholic. Right before we shoot my ONE day, he is arrested. So, that shoot is postponed. I feel bad for the kids here, so when he gets out I agree to do my day. I was coming off of another feature the night before so my turnaround was about four hours, and I'm pretty tired. I get to the location only to find out that the director had been fired from his own film. Apparently, his only job was to procure a taxi for the scene and he got drunk and forgot. So, not wanting to waste any more time, the AD/co-writer/co-producer/actress (one of those) took the reigns and rented a gold Cadillac. Thinking quickly, a Tupperware dish was turned upside down and TAXI was written on it with a Sharpie. This was duct taped to the top of the Caddy and, lo and behold, we're ready to shoot. Got there at six A.M. and the first shot was off by noon. Yeah. Great times were had by all. I went to the screening and, well, yeah. It turned out as well as I thought it would.

What would be your ideal role?

I desperately want to play Divine in her life story. She is such an interesting creature, a phenomena cut down in her prime. I've been a huge John Waters fan for many, many years and would love to explore Divine and show the world just how brave and tough she really was.

As an actor, how do you recommend to directors how to do auditions? Give both "good" and "bad" examples.

Auditions. I've been on both sides of the camera as far as auditions go and I'm always more grateful of the more clinical approach. This may be different from every other actor on the planet (but I'm different from every other actor on the planet). I like to walk into an audition, and I'm not there to make friends. I don't care what the guy before me did and I don't care what the director's résumé is. If I'm in that audition that means I have enough information about the project to make it worth my time. Once you've got me that far, don't feel as if I'm waiting with baited breath on your next direction during my cold read of the first draft. I'm not that invested. I can't be that invested. If I become that invested then the eventual rejection (since this is a business of rejection) would be too great to bear. So, the ideal audition is one that I have the proper information for. I come in, say hello politely, hear what the director/casting director is looking for, and perform. I then say goodbye after leaving my picture and résumé and either the production calls or they do not. A bad audition is to hold me there to read with multiple people or to vary the cold reads by degrees. I understand the concept of finding out whether or not someone can take direction, but after two minutes with an actor and seeing how their look fits the vision, a decision has already been made to either move onto the callback or not. Don't waste all of our time. Thanks, and good night.

How should first-time directors deal with actors? What is the most important thing they should do? Again, give both the "do's" and the "don'ts."

It depends on the actor, but there are some universal truths that first-time directors need to deal with: (1) They are never as prepared as they think they are; (2) The specific language of the screenplay is merely a suggestion (if you're me); and (3) You cannot break the rules of proper filmmaking before you've learned the rules of proper filmmaking. We'll take these in order. Firstly, the first-time director is never, ever prepared for what they encounter on an independent film set. This usually revolves around all of the jobs that an indie director has to do that do not involve directing. When I directed my first, disastrous feature I also cooked lunch, produced the damn thing and ran sound. That sucked. I wasn't prepared. As an actor, I've seen it happen lots of times to first-timers. You have to know how to do everything on that set since; invariably, you will have to do it. Secondly, if you, as a new director, are tied to the language of the script as immutable then you don't understand the collaborative nature of film. I guarantee that, if I just walk on some set, I'm a better writer than whoever just "polished" that script. Most actors who've spent some time in the saddle realize how language works, how powerful it

is and how, and let me be clear here, DIFFERENT CHARACTERS SPEAK DIFFERENTLY. Not in funny accents, mind you, but with completely different vocabularies and intents. Characters speak differently to different characters as well. The serial killer can say the same thing to a cop and to a victim, but they will not be the same verbiage. You have to let your actors go with their instincts — unless you hired your friends. In that case you're screwed. Lastly, if you don't understand how to turn on the camera or light a simple scene properly, what the hell makes you think your artistic vision will even be editable? I mean, come on. Some directors may not know this, but postproduction doesn't fix anything ... it is a Band-Aid on an axe wound. In focus, properly lit (meaning, lit for story and meaning and theme) will help your actors bring your script to life. After you've learned how to speak in a cinematic language, you can then change it up a bit and try your Tarantino-esque opus. Until then, learn the right way first.

The Filmmakers were asked:
How do you get your actors? What is the weirdest story you have about an actor/actress?

Glenn Andreiev: Originally I placed an ad for actors in *Backstage Magazine*, and auditioned about 20 people for each major role, and went from there. Now I feel I have an established stock company of fine actors I used numerous times, such as Frank Franconeri, Shawna Bermender, Ashley Wren Collins and Mike Gadinis, to name a few.

You want a weird story — here's one: An actress with a great face and interesting credits came in to audition. At the audition I asked her about her one credit. As a teenager, she was part of a singing trio that performed for President Reagan at the White House. Very seriously, and with great detail, she explained that Ronald Reagan kidnapped the singing trio

and kept them prisoner in the White House basement for many years. She also insisted that if we hired her there could be no shooting during mid-afternoon hours. Those are the peak hours for the evil energy coming from all the local computers, and that energy severely changes behavior patterns.

John Borowski: For finding cast members, the internet is the ideal location to place an ad. Acting publications and websites are also excellent places to place ads for cast members. Make sure to mention if you are seeking union or non-union actors. Usually, Hollywood talent requires you to make the film as a union film, but there may be a contract where you can negotiate hiring of both union and non-union performers. When making *H.H. Holmes*, I sought an actress for the voice of Carrie Pitezel, whose children were murdered by H.H. Holmes. In the ad, I instructed the women to call my answering machine and cry as Carrie would have cried in court. It was a fun experience to come home and listen to all these different women crying on my answering machine.

Keith Crocker: Again, back in the early days, the cast was usually made up of friends and friends of friends taking on roles and not knowing jack shit about acting. One actor that's stayed with me for years is Paul Richichi, who was in all the silent and sound 16mm work I did in the '80s. I always chose Paul because he was 20 years older than me, he had age on his face, that look of experience. You could pretty much drop him in any role you had that required a person of maturity. Now, is Paul a good actor? The answer is no, he's not, but he plays eccentrics perfectly due to the fact that his acting skills are so flawed. His delivery is insane, he speaks without taking a breath between sentences, and there is no human being that logically speaks that way. Some folks think I ruin films by using him, but it's the exact opposite — people remember him, they remember those scenes. He literally has the power to bring a house down. When we had the theatrical showings of *Blitzkrieg*, people in the theater went ape shit over Paul's delivery in the final scene. They applauded, yelled out loud, they loved him. He really drove the film home. We are using an authentic weirdo to play a weirdo. It works.

Now, in terms of weird stories, actors and actresses tend to be weird people to start with. They spend a lot of time admiring and loving themselves and are the most self-absorbed people you are ever going to meet. During *Blitzkrieg* shoot I was using actresses from various parts of Europe. Now, for the most part, a few of them disliked each other simply because they had similar ac-

cents — they felt strong competition with each other for this reason. One actress, who was Slovenian, disliked another actress because she was from Montenegro, and their accents, while not quite exact, were close enough. The Slovenian girl was also half Austrian, and she was tiny and small framed. But the girl from Montenegro was tall and blonde, which I also think was an issue. Two girls from Romania hated my Russian actress simply because Russia had control of Romania (through Communism) for so many years. But when I queried them about not liking her they simply said, "I don't like her acting!!!" And I'm thinking "Hey, let me worry about her acting — you guys just do your job." I teach an adult education filmmaking course and I always tell the students that they have to be part psychologist when it comes to working with actors and actresses because they carry so much mental baggage and can easily derail a film with their bullshit!

Richard Cunningham: I've posted casting notices for open-call auditions in local newspapers and on craigslist (this was back in the day). When you put yourself out there like that to the masses, you're likely to get one or two odd calls, and we did, but we also managed to discover some talented, committed actors. Though my approach today is quite different.

Once I moved to New York City and started doing background and stand-in work

In *America the Mental,* Pat Rigby plays sociopathic stand-up comedian/drug enforcer Rickjack Smitty.

on productions, it became a very convenient environment in which to cast actors, because I was meeting several of them at any given gig. The cast of my film is usually a mix of aspiring actors, willing to work for little or no money for the experience or to acquire clips for a reel, or just because they like the material; that and willing friends and family members.

But there are also casting websites available online, where you can post notices, some free, some pay-sites, like Actor's Access that offer exposure to a large pool of both union and non-union acting talent.

Maurice Devereaux: For my last two films I hired a casting agent, money well spent. Only once, on *Blood Symbol*, my first film, did a "wannabe" actress try to seduce me into being in the film (she wasn't my type for the film or otherwise, although I never did and never will use my position in that way). On *Lady of the Lake*, the night before starting a three-week shoot, everything had been paid for (film, equipment, locations, etc.), my lead

actor calls me to back out of the project. It took a long conversation to convince him to stay on and not destroy me. Also on *Lady of the Lake* there had been a five-year break during the shoot due to lack of funds (half was shot in 1993, the other half in '98), so when I was gearing up for the second part of the shoot, I had to track down my lead actress, who had moved to the Czech Republic. I had to pay to fly her back, and when she arrived (the day before the shoot) she had omitted to tell me she had cut her long curly hair and we had to, in a panic, find a matching wig for the next day ($450 down the tubes). Also, when preparing the second half of my shoot on *Lady of the Lake*, I contacted Angus Scrimm (the Tall Man in *Phantasm*) to play a small cameo part, he graciously declined, feeling the money I would have to pay for his salary, flight and hotel would be better spent on the film itself. But six months later he saw the finished film at the Fantasia Film Festival and loved it! He was quoted in *Cinefantastique* magazine as say-

On location for *Lady of the Lake*. Left to right: Tennyson Loeh, Erik Rutherford, Denis-Noel Mostert, Francis Tessier, and Maurice Devereaux.

ing he thought the film was superb and that he wished he were in it. A classy gentlemen and a terrific actor.

Donald Farmer: I used to get most of my actors through agencies. I'd make arrangements with each agency to set up auditions in their offices, then have the actors come in on a staggered schedule of maybe one every 15 minutes. And Screen Actors Guild performers have to be hired through their individual agents, with a little bit of negotiating back and forth if they have any name value. If you're a producer/director with little or no track records, even minor names want some assurance they'll be paid. For instance, when I hired Cameron Mitchell for *No Justice*, my deal with him was to pay him in cash as soon as he stepped off the plane. If I showed up empty-handed (which I didn't), Cameron let me know he would get right back on the plane and go home. For hiring Brigitte Nielsen there were even more precautions. I was required to put her full salary in an escrow account to guarantee our production company had funds to pay her. But sometimes you can get an actor with minor name value for no more than you're paying everyone else. Bob Orwig had already co-starred in *Platoon* when we cast him in *No Justice*, but he got no more than the minimum daily rate we paid actors. Ray McKinnon has already co-starred in the Oscar-winning picture *Driving Miss Daisy* when I hired him for *Vampire Cop*. He didn't charge anything extra ... neither did an actress in the same movie who'd just does a bit part in *Terms of Endearment* with Jack Nicholson.

But once you hire an actor, there's no guarantee you can keep them through the whole shoot. As I mentioned earlier, I had to rewrite the ending of *Cannibal Hookers* when we lost a male lead due to a broken leg. I also lost the original female lead of that movie, Hillary Lipton, just three days into production. Hillary was a gorgeous blonde who'd been an extra in *Miami Vice* and in the Kevin Costner/Whitney Houston movie *The Bodyguard*. Hillary cracked me up with her story of how Whitney

marched up to her on the set one day and said, "Girl, you've got an attitude problem!" Anyone who knew Hillary could understand what Whitney was talking about. Anyway, I'd already filmed a couple of days with Hillary for *Cannibal Hookers* when we ran into a roadblock. The "roadblock" was a dead body Hillary discovered in the parking lot of our location!

I'd found Hillary through the same talent agency in Ft. Lauderdale that booked her on *Miami Vice*. Apparently this agency was the show's main supplier of background extras. There was a huge photo of stars Don Johnson and Phillip Michael Thomas in the lobby to remind prospective clients of this fact. I needed an office building to film one day and worked out a deal with the agency's director — we could use the location on a Sunday, a day they're normally closed — as long as only Hillary handled the building keys. That was fine with me, so we all arranged to meet there Sunday morning. Hillary showed up a little early and found a car already parked by the front door with a 20-something girl sitting in the driver's seat. Figuring it was another actress waiting for her to show up with the keys, Hillary went over to say hello. Very quickly, poor Hillary wished she hadn't.

Hillary didn't find one of the other female cast members behind the wheel of that car. What she DID find was a freshly deceased female body covered with multiple stab wounds. Hillary, naturally, freaked — police were called, and shooting was suspended ... indefinitely. It turned out the dead girl had been murdered by her boyfriend several blocks away, then driven to our office building. Her body had been propped up behind the steering wheel and left there for some unlucky person to discover. Police quickly traced the victim's address through the car's plates and found a still-bloody crime scene, with the killer in residence. This genius hadn't even attempted to clean up the evidence. As for Hillary, she was so traumatized by the experience she dropped out of the movie. I couldn't use the incomplete footage I'd already shot of her so *Cannibal Hookers* went on hiatus. Several months later I moved to Los Angeles and restarted it with an all-new cast. But when the movie came out on video in France and Belgium, it was a photo of a topless Hillary that appeared on the box cover.

Hiring Dana Plato for *Compelling Evidence* in '94 was the only time I'd had to check with a probation officer for a star's services. Dana had been a huge sitcom star in the '70s and '80s on TV's *Diff'rent Strokes*, but her star had seriously fallen. Now Dana was probation for the 1991 Las Vegas video store robbery that put her back in headlines all over the world. Our casting director, Gerald Wolff, was also Dana's manager and trying his darndest to resuscitate her career. I wanted to fly Dana to Atlanta for the movie but learned that out-of-state employment needed the consent of her probation officer. So I dashed off a letter that I proposed to give Dana "gainful employment" in the state of Georgia for one week, and he granted approval. Once Dana arrived she was a complete professional, nailing most of her shots in one take. I'd given Dana a fairly dialogue-heavy role and needed her to deliver long spiels in several unbroken shots, but she made it seem effortless. One critic said, "Dana Plato gives a funny and solid performance in *Compelling Evidence*. As a fast-talking tabloid reporter, Plato brings to mind Jennifer Jason Leigh's performance in *The Hudsucker Proxy*." Dana was great to work with, a real sweetheart, and I still miss her.

Jeff Forsyth: For my first project I placed an ad for auditions in a local newspaper and had quite a few responses. Also, I had worked on another filmmakers' projects and met several local actors on those sets. Now I do a lot of scouting through the local theatre groups and met actors from all over the country through Facebook and a few other social-networking sites. At this point I have a huge database of actors and actresses I can call on. It's a great feeling to have the contact info of so many people and to have been exposed by

their work and know what they are capable of before we ever get on set together.

Richard W. Haines: As with the crew I've used the same performers for my leads in several features. I shoot very fast and expect everyone to be prepared for working at that speed. It keeps their energy level up, since filming is very exhausting for everyone involved.

For supporting players and bit parts I place an ad in *Backstage* and hold auditions at a rented rehearsal hall. I have a video camera set up and ask the applicants to prepare a short monologue so I can see what they look and sound like. Then I review the footage and call back those who might fit one of the roles, giving them "sides" [script excerpts] to perform with other players, until I find those who have some chemistry together.

After we're cast I rehearse and block out the entire movie in the rehearsal hall. Whatever choices, character nuance or improvisations the actor wants to try needs to be worked out in pre-production. On set there is no time to do anything other than film their performance. This technique works best for me and keeps costs down. I rarely do more than two takes of any shot. I figure if we need a third take someone isn't prepared and we rehearse the shot a few times before shooting another one.

I have many amusing stories about actors, but here are a couple. During the production of *Space Avenger* I thought it would be quirky to hire a porn star for the scene when the female alien has sex with a human. She gets so hot she literally screws him to death, frying him into a skeleton. We hired X-Rated star Jaimie Gillis for the scene. Gillis was one of the few performers in the adult industry who could act. He was good in the role and amused us with stories about his career between takes. We shot one of his scenes in Peekskill, New York, and the local officials got wind of it and tried to throw us out of town. They thought we were making a porn instead of a sci-fi comedy. The co-producers met with the politicians and convinced them we were a legit film production and they allowed us to finish our shoot there.

While we were filming a rooftop scene in *Space Avenger*, Kirk Fogg kept getting tongue-tied. I asked him what the problem was and he told me that the scene was the one he kept auditioning with and he had done it so many times he had a mental block. I took Kirk to a local bar and bought him a few drinks. That relaxed him and he was able to perform the scene without any problem. I wondered if I should create a new Method acting technique based on this remedy.

William Hopkins: For both of my films we ran ads in the trade papers and rented out studio space in Manhattan to audition the people who responded. We got several hundred headshots each time and we winnowed the piles down to a couple of dozen people we thought would be right for the available parts. Most of the best people we saw were folks who were experienced stage actors but had relatively limited film experience and weren't SAG members. On *Sleepless Nights*, a couple of the actors in our cast were actually in Broadway shows during the time of our shoot, and would come to our set after doing their show for the day. One actor actually went on tour with a show while we were shooting *Sleepless Nights*. We had to shoot around him, using stand-ins for him, while shooting the scenes with the other actors. Then we shot all his close-ups about a year later when he got back from the tour.

Our leading man on *Sleepless Nights* ended up leaving the production about midway through. The shoot had been a troubled one and we were way behind schedule. He got a job on another film and left ours, probably assuming it was wise to move on since our film looked like a lost cause. But we didn't give up. Fortunately we were able to shoot all of his close-ups for the remainder of the film on the last night before he left the production. Then we continued to shoot after he left, using stand-ins. It made the editing of the film

rather challenging but we were able to make it work in the end.

On *Demon Resurrection* we tried to avoid similar problems by casting talented actors we felt would be really committed to the production and would stick with us through the rough spots. We also made sure to have everything planned out so we could get through the script in 21 days. It was a grueling shoot and everybody was worn out by the end of it, but we got it done on time. The cast did a spectacular job. Everyone was terrific and completely professional. We really were very lucky to have been able to put together such a great group of people.

Steve Hudgins: We always do an open casting call for the majority of our roles. We let local theaters and agents know. We also post the casting calls on our website and Facebook pages along with any other regional websites that post casting bulletins.

Rolfe Kanefsky: The level of actors has a lot to do with your budget. I've worked with professional casting directors on the bigger projects. I've done casting myself by putting out notices on lacasting.com and nowcasting.com. I've met actors at parties and have had friends/filmmakers recommend certain performers. When you're going after name actors like Brad Dourif, Jeff Fahey and Steven Bauer, you have to get to their agents/lawyers or a casting director who knows them, unless you happen to be friends with them personally. But if you aren't next-door neighbors with Michael Madsen, then you have to make an offer to his representation. And by offer, I mean money. Many times to get them to agree to your project you have to make a pay-or-play deal, which means you will pay them no matter if you make the movie or not. Then, of course, you have to send them (meaning their agent/manager) the script and hope they (again, agent/manager) reads the script, likes it, and passes it on to their client. If the money isn't good enough, this will probably never happen. It's a tricky business, but names are important and many times you need them to get the money to make your movie. It makes the investor/distributor comfortable.

When dealing with non-names, this process is a lot easier. You just put up a notice and bingo, you'll have thousands of submissions. If the part requires female nudity and doesn't pay well, the submissions go down substantially. But that's another discussion. Anyway, on a typical Rolfe Kanefsky flick, we send out a character breakdown on various websites and get a lot of submissions. I then go through the online head shots, read the résumés, and hold auditions. Auditions can go on for weeks or months depending on the project. I also videotape the audition because it's great to have a reference to go back to and see how your actor photographs. Does the camera love him/her or hate him/her? Then come callbacks and eventually you have your cast. Like crew members, I enjoy working with actors that I get along with. I have used many of the same actors. Right now, Robert Donavan is in the lead. I've directed him in 20 motion pictures! Tiffany Shepis is another favorite. We've worked together seven times now. But you're always looking for new talent as well.

In term of weird actor stories, I've found

Scream Queen Tiffany Shepis on *Wrath of the Crow's* set. Photograph courtesy Marija Obradovic.

that most of the time the cast will work itself out. I've had actors drop out at the last minute and be replaced by other actors who are so good in the role that I can't believe I even considered someone else doing it. Every movie has its share of casting stories.

Here's one: I was casting for *Nightmare Man*. A lot of the actors in this film I had worked with before. I knew Tiffany Shepis from *The Hazing* and kind of wrote the character of Mia with her in mind. I had just worked with Blythe Metz in *Jacqueline Hyde* and knew she'd be perfect for Ellen. James Ferris was also in *Jacqueline Hyde*, and he was a perfect Jack. There were four other important roles in the movie. We need an "Ed," a young guy who was supposed to be Mia's boy-toy boyfriend. We found him on nowcasting.com. Ellen's husband was a different issue. One of the producers of *Nightmare Man* was Brazilian, and, in exchange for the money he invested in the film, he wanted all Brazilian rights to the film, which we gave him. He also wanted a hot Brazilian star to play William, Ellen's husband, and suggested Luciano Szafir, who I was told was the "Brazilian Tom Cruise." I insisted on meeting him. He flew into Los Angeles and, after the meeting, I agreed and he got the role, accent and all. Richard Moll happened to live up at Big Bear, where we were shooting the film. One of the other producers, Esther Goodstein, worked with Richard a long time ago. Fate brought the two together and we offered him the role, a one-night shoot minutes from where he lived. He liked the script, accepted the money offer and did the part. Easy in, easy out, and very helpful for getting us press for the movie. He was our only "name" in the cast.

Now, there was one more role: the part of Trinity, the blonde possible heroine of the piece. She had to be beautiful, but also strong and intelligent. We saw a lot of actresses from LACasting and NowCasting for this role. There was nudity required, which limited us a bit, but we found some good possibilities. Well, as we were casting, an actor/friend of mine, Clu Gulager, was eating at Cantor's, a famous deli in Hollywood. His waitress on evening was a very pretty blonde who also happened to be an actress. He talked to her and told her she should come to this bar on Thursday nights where a lot of his filmmaker friends gather to bitch and moan about their careers. She liked the idea and showed up. Myself and Tiffany Shepis happened to go that night as well. I meet her, liked her look, told her that I was audition for the part of "Trinity" and invited her to read for me two days later. She auditioned and surprised us all by being great! She was the best actress I'd seen. She even agreed to do the nudity. I was about to cast her when she called me. She really didn't feel comfortable with doing a topless scene. She had never done it before and said, "If you can't cast me because of that, I understand." I understood her hesitation and because I was also one of the producers of this film, I decided that her acting ability was more important than her boobs. I changed the scene to let her wear a bra, and cast Hanna Putnam in the role. She quit her waitress job for the time being and starred in her first movie. She then later got cast in *Feast 2 & 3* directed by Clu's Gulager's son, John. So, there's the old "waitress-becoming-an-actress discovery" story for real.

Brett Kelly: I ALWAYS audition folks. The reason for that is simple — if an actor earns the job, they will respect it. If they are just tossed the gig, they won't treat it like something they earned. If they don't respect the job, they will waste your time. I have so many weird actor stories — they are an interesting breed of person. I can't even narrow it down. I teach a workshop on auditioning and can go on for hours with mistakes actors make to screw themselves out of a job.

Chris LaMartina: Don't use your friends! Well, okay ... use a couple friends, if they can really act. Otherwise, hold casting calls. Even on our first production with no frills, we auditioned a ton of actors and it paid off. Each

subsequent project, our successes garner more interests and more potential cast members. We posted ads on sites like craigslist, various film Facebook groups, and other actor websites.

It's important to get a quasi-legitimate location for this meet-up. Don't make strangers show up to your apartment to read lines. You can get a hotel meeting room, a library or even a church hall, for super cheap.

At our casting calls, we like actors to set up slots through email so it runs smoother (we still take walk-ins, however). They are emailed sides ahead of time so they can get comfortable with them.

A receptionist (usually one of our girlfriends or wives) greets the talent and hands them a questionnaire. This paper is super important. We ask a few questions: (1) Will you smoke for a scene? (2) Will you do nudity? (3) Will you do partial nudity? (These questions help siphon out actors for specific roles so there's less drama later into the process). The final page of the questionnaire is a calendar with our potential shooting schedule (usually a window of two months) where we request every actor to plug in when they are available and what dates they are unavailable. This is fantastic because it shows who's really too busy to do an indie film. We've loved certain actors who just couldn't do our schedule and, rather than offering them a role and backpedaling, we tell them right off the bat it won't work out.

Use this method. Trust us. You don't want to cast someone blindly without seeing their work schedule, no matter how good they are. Filmmaking is a community-based process and one person's shitty schedule can put everyone's lives into jeopardy.

Jim Mickle: I met Nick working on a student film for a friend. Nick was the lead actor. We hit it off and I cast him in my student film and then started talking about screenplays together. It all happened very organically.

On *Mulberry Street* we wrote a lot of parts around good character actors we knew, so a lot of the casting was happening while the script came together. On *Stake Land* I got to work with a casting director named Sig De-Miguel, and we cast a lot from meetings with great local actors and auditioning for the side roles. The meetings were much more informative than auditioning because it's a chance to discuss the role and the story and the tone and also get a feel for what type of people they are. Especially on lower budgets, it's great to see if you click with somebody and if they're up for the indie mentality.

In the case of Kelly McGillis, I had somehow never seen *Top Gun*, but I grew up near Amish country and had seen *Witness* many times. When her name came for up for Sister in *Stake Land*, I thought she'd be perfect but never thought in a million years she'd be interested. She hadn't done a movie in almost ten years, and didn't seem into the horror genre. But it turned out that she lived 20 miles from where I grew up, and, where we were shooting, I wrote her a letter and Sig talked to her manager, and the next day she took the part. Turns out she never read the letter and she took the part because she could drive to set every morning.

Damon Packard: I can't think of anything "weird" offhand. I look [for actors] in every way possible. Years ago, prior to the internet age, it was posting breakdowns in publications like *Dramalogue* and *Backstage West*. Now it's all via online sites like *lacasting.com* and others. The process is still the same: you're poring through hundreds and hundreds of candidates. In my case, thousands. Maybe one in 500 has an interesting quality worth contacting. Maybe one in 5,000 is available and willing given the circumstances and/or minimal pay. It's extremely difficult (if not impossible) to find uniquely talented actors, especially in the micro-budget independent world. But that's just my experience. It's always a Scarlett O' Hara search for me and practicality always wins in the end. In my experience the casting gods always find the right people, even under the most unusual conditions. The film I'm doing now, for example, has multiple actresses playing Foxfur, which isn't the way I planned it. But given the no-budget, more "experimental" circumstances of the version I'm doing, it works well and seems to make sense (and was the ONLY way to shoot it).

Amanda Mullins as the sorceress in Damon Packard's *Foxfur*

Not that (as usual) anyone will be able to make sense of it. But again, I attribute this to budget constraints. If I had the money I could make a perfectly sensible linear film.

Brad Paulson: In the beginning, we went through the free casting sites — we even had a few cats help us with the process. Lately, though, we've just been picking people we know and avoiding the casting process entirely. There are a number of stories about actors that have been a pain in the ass to work with. Some are an absolute joy and others are a nightmare. Some are great on one movie and a thorn in your side on another. It's really one giant crapshoot. You never know what you're going to get in L.A. There are many bizarre stories we have about actors.

One time we had an actor who was a drug addict. More actors would turn out to be drug addicts in the future, but that's beside the point. This is just one of the stories. About this particular addict, I didn't know he had a drug problem at the time. My small-town upbringing has been responsible for quite a bit of my naïveté. However, I believe it's also kept me grounded and from crossing over into the dark side that so many people find themselves in when they move here. I just thought he was naturally charismatic and funny. However, on the first day of filming, he got real shitty real fast. Where was his naturally entertaining demeanor? I was just too naïve to know what was really going on. He wasn't getting paid, so he instantly diva'd out and demanded to be driven around to pick up painkillers before we started shooting. I must have driven him to ten locations before I realized that maybe he was looking for something a little stronger that just painkillers. Either that or he just had a whole lot of pain he needed to kill and a very short time to do it in. Then, 20 minutes after we picked up his painkillers he was somewhat less of a dick. Everything was okay until we went out of town, although even on his best behavior he remained a smug, condescending ass. He was under the impression we were going to be in city limits, but we were about

30 minutes outside of where he wanted to be. He instantly freaked. We were going to be gone for three days and he was not going to be anywhere near civilization. What followed was only what I could imagine a full-blown exorcism to be. There was definitely a demon inside this man. We had to pour a bottle of whiskey down his throat just to get him to be quiet. He passed out and we finally had peace for the first night. We had no idea how long the weekend ahead of us was about to be.

Each following day got progressively worse, until we realized our actor was going through serious withdrawal. He looked like living hell. Too bad we weren't making a zombie movie because we would have been won an Oscar for make-up. The thing is, he was the lead actor, so things got very difficult. My AD had to feed him hot tea just to keep him from passing out and dying. We, to this day, compare it to Ed Wood tending to Bela Lugosi, except this guy wasn't nearly as cool as Lugosi. When I drove him back he was so anxious to get inside his house, I thought he was going to jump out of the car. He told me he needed to get home as soon as possible because his mother was arriving and he needed to clean the house to impress her. Yeah, right. More like clean all the sobriety out of his veins. And then, after the movie came out the son of a bitch extorted money out of us. We were too naïve at the time to know any better, so we let him do it. Needless to say, we'll never be using him again.

Jose Prendes: If they aren't "names," it is always based on if they are good at what they do and if they are willing to work for food. With my "name" actors, meaning someone with a recognizable face and a fan following, it was always whether they were available and if I could pay them enough while not breaking the bank.

On *Monster Man*, I approached Tom Savini at a horror convention and asked him if he'd be up for playing a part. He was hesitant, until I offered him $400, and then he jumped at the chance. We filmed the scene in my hotel room, and it took, like, 30 minutes. That's just how it happens in the micro world. But he was great and fun to work with.

Paul Scrabo: I was fortunate to be acquainted with several actors already living on the East Coast, including, thankfully, Debbie Rochon and Mike Thomas. They had already made their mark in the indie film world as solid performers.

I was looking forward to shooting a scene featuring Mike Thomas, Nathan Sears and John Zacherle (Zacherley, the Cool Ghoul). It was written as fast-talking banter that required a lot of energy. Zach's role was to punctuate the scene here and there, taking advantage of his natural timing and talent for comedy. He could only be with us for one day, but we ended up using that time on Zach's major scene — the musical number. So now Zach is gone and we still have to do that three person scene. It was obvious that we had to move up Conrad Brooks's participation a notch. Now, Conrad is a cult/B-movie legend and that's why he's in the film, but his acting style is "let

me do my own thing" rather than [adhering to] strict dialogue. So the night before, we give him the "good news," that his part just got bigger and he freezes, takes a breath and says "Paul, I'm putting myself in your hands." I laugh and say "Don't worry" and leave the room and immediately start to worry. I pass Trent Haaga, who is done for the day and hunched over his laptop working on a script for a future film. Trent's a good actor, a good, fast writer and a great listener, having heard what just happened. Without looking up, he says, "A buddy of mine worked with Conrad. He said that if you get him first thing early in the morning, he comes through fine."

While having my morning coffee, I see that producer Rich Scrivani is already outside with the cast, and George Ann Muller hits me with the tripod she's carrying. "Let's go." This scene is designed as one master shot, and I figure if we just keep doing it over and over until we're all totally sick of it, something has to be usable. Take one — Conrad's perfect. I'm not

The *Demon Divas*: Debbie Rochon (Nemain), Lilith Stabs (Babd), Brinke Stevens (Morrigan), Amy Lynn Best (Lamia), and Robyn Griggs (Masha).

sure. Let's go again. Take two — Conrad couldn't be better. Three takes and he's great in all of them.

Now, it's worth mentioning again that you must have real actors in your production, because as I think many of your interviewees may agree, you do not have time to really direct — you are too busy "putting out fires"! You have to direct the budget and the scene, and then, hopefully, you'll have time to discuss the

scene with your cast, but you can't always count on it. My four leads, Debbie Rochon, Mike Thomas, Trent Haaga and Nathan Sears were always ready to go, and improved what I had on paper, on many occasions. Debbie helped with continuity all the time, and what a bonus that was.

Eric Shapiro: For *Rule of Three*, we put out a casting call for SAG performers. It's a good idea to get union talent if you can, because they have a lot of experience on sets and are great with memorizing their lines and not blowing takes. My initial encounter with Lee Schall, who stars in *Rule of Three* and *Mail Order*, was very strange. He came in for his *Rule of Three* audition holding what appeared to be a toolbox, and his first words to us [producers Rhoda Jordan and Cerris Morgan-Moyer were also there] were, "I've done this before, right?" We didn't know what he meant. We thought he was crazy, and were expecting him to open the toolbox and start

Top: Brutal sociopath Russ (Rodney Eastman, left) reflects on how his behavior has impacted Jon (Ben Siegler). *Bottom:* Eric Shapiro (center) gives direction to (left to right) Ben Siegler, Cerris Morgan-Moyer, Rhoda Jordan, and Rodney Eastman.

beating us to death with a hammer. Turned out he meant the psycho character he eventually played in the film had raped women in the past, which was indicated in the text. He froze us for a moment, though, and we never found out what was in the box.

Anthony Straeger: My system for crew and cast is identical. I often use people that have worked with me, that know how I operate. In *Call of the Hunter* the cast comprised of Don McCorkindale, Katrin Riedel Kelly, Angelique Fernandez and Michael Instone, all of whom had worked with me on different projects, such as shorts, corporate and events and shows. The other three — Sarah Paul, Julia Curle and Jonathan Hansler — auditioned after answering the call via our advert.

As an actor I have often wondered why so many production companies use the same actors and crew. But the fact of the matter is, when it gets down to it, I am guilty of the same thing. The theory about casting (which I guess a number of directors will also adhere to) is that you cast by trust. Don, Katrin, Mike and Angelique are people I had worked with over a number of years. They are professional and experienced. The rest of my cast — Sarah Paul, Julia Curle and Jonathan Hansler — had to audition.

I was looking for good team players that could work under pressure for 12 days straight and keep a smile on their face and their energy up ... and they all were.

As to weird stories... Hmmm... There have been some odd people down the line and some people I have auditioned have been so totally incapable of delivering anything, but other than that the only bad story I have concerns an actor I was working with on a theatre tour. One night after the show we went out for a few drinks and a few drinks became more drinks and then he started chatting up this woman, who was, well — I wouldn't have!!! Anyway, he was completely hammered when he took her to his apartment. He went to bed with her, but must have passed out without delivering. He woke up the following morning lying on his back with his wallet gone and a nicely piled turd on his chest. Not so much weird as nasty!

Marc Trottier: I get actors by picking up the phone and saying, "Hey, I wrote this part for you ... wanna do it?" (That's one benefit of being an actor with acting friends.) Or I call up actors that I don't really know, and tell them about the project and the role, send them the script, tell them that there's no money involved and convince them to join the team. Usually actors are looking to add stuff to their demo reels anyway, so as long as you're giving them something good to use, then they're more inclined to say "yes." I've never had anybody say "no." As a matter of fact, people often say, "Let me know next time you're filming something, I want to be in it." It's always fun to see people wanting to film things simply for the love of filming.

A funny/weird story was that I asked an actor (Morgan Kelly) to play the boyfriend of my girlfriend at the time (Annie Julian) in *Darkness Waits*, and he agreed. There was a scene where they were supposed to get hot and heavy before being killed by the psychopath in the movie, and he turns to me and says,

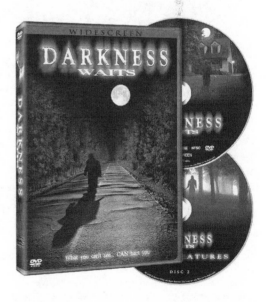

DVD packaging for *Darkness Waits*, directed by Marc Trottier

"Come on man, I can't make out with your girlfriend," and everybody starts laughing. So in that scene, they're leaning against a railing that leads upstairs, and the killer chokes Annie from behind with a leather belt. I was playing the role of the killer that night, as I did most nights (almost all the scenes with the costumed killer were played by me). So I was holding the belt that was wrapped around her neck through the railing, and I told her that I wasn't going to pull on the belt, and that I wanted her to gauge how much pressure she needed to push against the belt to make it look convincing. Well, she pushed hard ... and she ended up choking herself unconscious! So when she was supposed to die, she got really heavy ... and I ended up holding her body weight up with this belt around her neck before I realized that she wasn't acting! No one else realized in time, so I had to stretch my arms through the railing as far as I could go to try and let her down onto the tiles without

hurting her, while I was saying, "She's out!" Then I ran down the stairs and got to her, and before long she regained consciousness and asked, "What's going on?" I explained what had happened and that she was okay. She was up and ready to go again, right after. I think everyone was a little freaked out, but I was used to that because of my experience with chokeholds in grappling martial arts. I think Morgan thought that I had killed her. Fun fact: We actually used that take in the movie.

Mike Watt: I hate auditions. We've conducted only a couple in 14 years and they're miserable for all involved. Nobody is relaxed, including us judges, and it's always difficult to judge a performance based on a couple of cold readings. We have, on occasion, "stolen" actors from other people's auditions, however. There's less tension, at least on our end, if we're not shopping for something at the moment, but adding headshots to our wish list, so to speak. We very much prefer approaching other

Shooting the *Resurrection Game* opening sequence in the Munhall Cemetery, ca. September 2000. Left to right: Dan Franklin (zombie), Bill Homan (producer/co-star), Gina Preciado (Ms. Hill), Mark Dobrowolski (assistant camera), Bill Hahner (cemetery scene director of photography), Mike Watt, and Brian Kohr (sound engineer). Photograph by Amy Lynn Best.

filmmakers and saying, "I really liked so-and-so in your movie. How are they to work with?" Ninety-nine percent of the time, you'll get an honest answer; you then meet with the actor and discover they're perfect for the role.

One thing we've done consistently over the years has been to try people out in small parts or as featured extras, see how they are on camera, off camera and how they get along with people. On *The Resurrection Game*, Charlie Fleming and Tim Gross started out as background zombies and became not only good friends but proved to be such fun actors to work with that their roles started expanding. Charlie wound up as a major character in TRG, and he and Tim both starred in *Severe Injuries*.

The same can be said of many members of our family — Stacy Bartlebaugh-Gmys, Alyssa Herron, Sofiya Smirnova, Nikki McCrae — all started in small roles in projects and proved themselves to be fun and talented and we'd bring them back again and again. Every film company develops a family in this way.

For *Razor Days*, we searched for the third lead almost as long as the script had been in development. We approached a number of union actresses for the part and the problem was never money, but scheduling. Since Amy and I are big believers in kismet, we chalked all of these "failures" up to the universe telling us we hadn't found the perfect actress. Finally, we sat down to watch the rough edit of Eric Thornett's period horror movie *Sweet and Vicious*, starring Bette Cassett, an actress he had been telling us for years, but one we hadn't met. Within the first scene, Bette proved she was capable of conveying great subtlety and subtext with only facial expressions, and it was a real slap-to-the-head moment for us. Here was our perfect actress right in front of us, if only we'd set aside the time to watch the movie earlier.

Finally, the best audition process is the horror convention, particularly the ones with a more "relaxed" atmosphere where you can hang out with the celebrities and talent. The characters you love on screen are usually far removed from the people who play them, so meeting them first-hand is essential, particularly if you're dealing with SAG actors. You'll be spending a lot of money on their participation, you'd better be sure you like who you're working with. Someone who is "an amazing actor" but requires more attention than a newborn isn't someone you need to bother with. The world is filled with "amazing" actors and actresses who aren't pains in the ass. Unless that "name" is guaranteed to sell your movie (which isn't a guarantee at all anymore), find someone you like who can do the job.

But through conventions we've become close friends with some very recognizable and wonderful people. The two names that always spring to mind, and always will, are Debbie Rochon and Jasi Cotton Lanier. Not only are these two ladies amazing friends but their talents know no bounds. They were both essential to our getting taken seriously in the industry without asking for anything in return, doing us great favors at the beginning of our careers. And we met them both at conventions. Facebook and email are terrific, but nothing beats a face-to-face meeting.

Working with name pros, even if they are close friends, can still be intimidating. And since no one really teaches "How to Direct 101 and Not Feel Like a Loser or a Tyrant," it's tough, at first, to work with people whose résumés are longer than the average roll of wall paper. I'm not ashamed to say that the first times I worked with Brinke Stevens, for instance, was a nerve-wracking experience for me. The same was true directing Debbie for the first time on *The Resurrection Game*, even in a small cameo. The real nightmare blow to my confidence came on *Razor Days*, where I not only had to direct Amy through some very nasty emotional scenes, but also Bette (whom I'd never worked with before), Debbie in the largest capacity since we'd known each other, and Jeff Monahan, who'd been directed by John Sayles, George Romero and Dario Argento. That's when I really had to follow John

Huston's advice: "The secret to directing is hiring the right actors and then getting the hell out of their way."

I'm trying to think, but I can't recall too many *weird* experiences. In five features and 13 years we've had only one no-show — someone recommended by a friend at the last minute who was in touch with us up until 20 minutes before her call time. Then she vanished off the face of the earth for two weeks. We managed another Hail Mary pass to replace her at the zero hour. Eventually she called our mutual friend to assure her she was still alive, but we never really got the whole story as to why she bailed.

On one film, we had an actress volunteer some nudity that wasn't called for in the script. Since that's usually a good selling point, we accepted. When it came time to do the scene — actually, many hours before — she accused us doing some sort of bait-and-switch on her. I pointed to the scene in the script and showed her where it remained unchanged "X Character is clothed," and reminded her that the nudity was her idea. It was nerves and cold feet on her part, but we resented being accused of "tricking" her into it. She isn't Coco and this wasn't *Fame* and the scene was fine the way it was.

Other than that, everyone's been perfectly professional and certifiably batshit crazy in their own special ways.

Ritch Yarber: After making films for over ten years now, I tend to rely a lot on actors that I have previously worked with or have auditioned in the past. I keep people in my memory bank and when a part comes around that is perfect for them, they get the first call. Beyond that, I have always gone to North Coast Central Casting in Cleveland to hold casting calls for my projects. The organization is headed by Ray Szuch, who teaches martial arts during the day and facilitates an acting/stunt school in the evenings. He provides many wonderful services and opportunities for independent filmmakers and artists in the Cleveland area. Through North Coast Central

Casting, I have always been able to find the best actors/actresses for my needs. We have also held auditions at local conventions, but the results have been less than stellar, with too many out-of-town actors trying out. Out of town means scheduling problems, or worse, having to put up money for a place for them to stay. There are usually enough talented people from the area to find what we need, but we have paid hotel fees on occasion to bring in just the right person for a role.

There are so many actors/actresses trying to break into films that most of them will go to great lengths to impress even a micro-budget filmmaker like me. They will give everything in their performances, even more than you may want. Our lead actor in *Murder Machine!*, E. Ray Goodwin, is one of these actors. He totally locked into the role of the ultimate killer. So much so, that he actually would creep out some of the other actors when he was in costume. He literally became the character. In one scene, the character is fighting a jail cell full of local thugs that he has been incarcerated with. He has killed all of them except for the leader. The gag was that he actually does a martial-arts punch to the thug's chest and tears his heart out and eats it as the victim looks on in shock. We used a bloody pig's heart from a local butcher shop for the prop. It had been frozen and thawed and then actually frozen and thawed again as the date changed unexpectedly that we were going to do the shoot. Goodwin rips the heart out of the dummy and proceeds to start eating it with a demonic look in his eyes. Everyone was so in awe of what was happening in front of us that we forgot to yell "Cut!" He quickly gulped the whole heart down. Realizing that Goodwin had just eaten something potentially dangerous, I quickly ran to him and apologized for not stopping the scene. I guess I figured that he would stop when he put the smelly lump of meat to his lips. Goodwin said that it didn't taste bad at all and that he really didn't think that it was a real heart, but rather something that we came up with in the prop

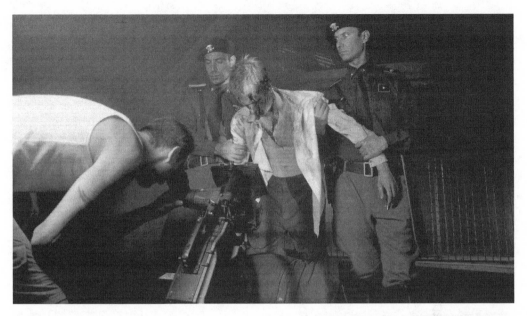

Shooting a jail scene for *Wrath of the Crows* with actors Michael Segal, John Game and Matteo Tosi. Photograph courtesy Marija Obradovic.

department that was edible. The scene is in the movie and really looks nasty and vicious. Goodwin never got ill.

Ivan Zuccon: I usually use my instinct to choose the actors. Sometimes I make auditions, sometimes I don't, depending on my instinct. I love actors. I love working with them and I have a great respect for them. It's true that sometimes they behave in a strange way; they're eccentric people, able to influence your job. But I think this is an interesting and amusing side of working on movies. I like my set to be heterogeneous. I think variety can be very stimulating.

Locations: Where You Live and Where You Shoot

The main benefit of being an independent filmmaker is that you can do it anywhere, as long as you have access to what you need to get your movie done. When I lived in New York City it was like having a large movie set at my disposal. Any exterior I shot had production value. Also, everything was within subway or taxi distance, so that saved on travel. Many actor's apartments were used, if they were available. For a few of my films I had access to an entire empty floor of a building where I worked. It was convenient and cheap — I just had to slip the freight elevator 20 bucks and I had all day to shoot. Wires were ripped out of the walls and it had the post-apocalyptic look I needed. In fact, years later, the company that makes the Jarvik Heart took over this same space.

It was also relatively easy to find crew and actors in the Big Apple. There was talent. When I moved back to my home state of Michigan and did a feature, I found it a bit more challenging. There are very few film/video production professionals in this entire state, so there was little support. While I could handle most of the technical end of production, I had a much smaller acting pool to choose from. Also, finding suitable locations and figuring out the logistics of travel was more work. In fact, the talent pool and crew choices were so lackluster it put a damper on making the low-budget genre movies entirely. These films were, for the same budgets, so much less than what I was doing in New York City.

One of the things that irritated me in Michigan, at the time, was the government passing film-incentive tax breaks, which lured out-of-state production companies to shoot their movies here. They'd get up to 40 percent of their budgets paid for. These were films like *Gran Torino* and *Vanishing on 7th Street*. While this may have helped the catering companies and allowed a few hundred locals to be "extras," these companies brought in all their crews. Yet acquaintances never failed to tell me how lucky I was that they were now making Hollywood movies in Michigan. Why? This had absolutely nothing to do with me or my films. The incentive was only for out-of-state companies and budgets over $100,000. Untold hours were spent explaining these facts to non-film people, who typically answered, "You never know, they may need a director." On the flip side, even non-experienced production assistants and unknown actors wanted the "Hollywood cash" when working on a micro-budget production.

Not surprisingly, this was about the time I switched to the documentaries. I could do 90 percent of the work myself, from shooting to editing. When I began producing/directing these non-fiction features I made sure that the majority of them could be shot in the Metro-Detroit area. A few were health related and one was on a psychic Capuchin Monk. I also traveled to New York City at least twice during the year for freelance-editing work, so I could also videotape there without adding any further expense to my productions. This added more production value to the projects and made the programs wider in scope, which helped with the national television broadcasts.

While I honestly had no intention of becoming a "documentary director/producer" this past decade, I found that this type of production suited where I was living much better than making horror features did. Wherever you are based, use your locale to your film's advantage.

The Filmmakers were asked:
Does where you live have an impact on getting your films made? And, if so, why is this?

Glenn Andreiev: I'm lucky. Long Island is next door to New York City, which has endless resources for a filmmaker — trained professionals, equipment and prop-rental houses. I also live near The Cinema Arts Centre, a privately run movie theatre with an enormous audience turnout. They often play the works of local independent filmmakers. Seeing your film with a big audience is so important and fun. It would be great if this were available to filmmakers all throughout the country.

John Borowski: I suppose if you live in New York or L.A. you will be under constant scrutiny while shooting your film. Other cities, including Chicago, seem to more laid back about filming. Once your film is complete and you search for distribution, it does not matter if you live in the Antarctic. When completing my second film, *Albert Fish*, I lived in Los Angeles and I mailed my film to distributors in the U.S. and around the world. Ironically, I decided to have my first distributor, Facets Video in Chicago, distribute *Albert Fish* as they did such a great job distributing my first film.

Keith Crocker: I live in a suburb of New York called Long Island. I'm about 40 minutes from Manhattan, which is convenient when it comes to casting my films, as many of my actors and actresses come from New York City. Lots of acting hopefuls are there. You really have your pick of the lot. Long Island itself is very eclectic; you have farms far out east, yet you also have an airport. We have the Hamp-

tons and Montauk, both of which offer summer retreats for the very wealthy and Hollywood types, but also have lots of local folks who are extremely organic and border on inbreeding. I'm from Nassau County, which once had a taste of country to it, but has since become overpopulated, and now really functions as an extension of Queens, New York. We have some historic landmarks, but lots of fantastic places have been torn down. Very little regard is given to historical preservation. There is wilderness if I need it, and there are suburbs. With *Blitzkrieg* I lucked out because we have the remains of the Suffolk Psychiatric Center, which was built in the late 1800s, and now sits in decay. Once I saw that place, I knew right away that it would serve as the perfect bombed-out prisoner of war camp I needed for the film. *Bloody Ape* benefited from the Long Island locals because it was small-town set, and Long Island was still small townish when I shot it (beginning in '92). The areas I shot *Bloody Ape* in look quite different today. They've been given a face-lift. Honestly, with the type of film I like to make, I'd be better off living in Europe!

Richard Cunningham: I think sometimes it can have more impact on what happens to a small-budget movie after it's made.

I grew up in rural upstate New York. There wasn't a film department in my high school, or anyone really to approach for guidance, let alone funding. I remember in middle school my friends and I went around to houses once, like kids for charity, except we were asking random houses for money for our movie production. Later on, we just got jobs and invested in our own movies. The problem was, I still wasn't expanding the film's promotion beyond a local audience, or even hitting my target audience.

Currently, with the advances of digital video and post-production software, and also with the development of the internet and social media, people can make a quality film and promote it effectively, wherever their backdrop. Film festivals attest to that, I think. They play all over the country, and beyond that, the globe now; and these little indie films from just about anywhere, made on shoestring budgets with blood and sweat and love and dedication, play in festivals around this country all the time.

In 2010, the Tribeca Film Festival launched an online festival featuring a portion of their official selections. It was a great chance for some of the lower-profile features and shorts to gain more exposure. In 2011, Tribeca featured *Year Zero* online, and by having my short streaming through the festival's website, *Year Zero* could now seen by anyone in the country, as well as by theatergoers in the New York City region. I think, if this trend picks up — and I suspect it will — film festivals soon will not only offer recognition for good low-budget filmmakers, but greater chances of exposure to the masses: the filmmaker's best challenge, no matter where they live.

Maurice Devereaux: Well, if you're talking about an indie film, not so much. You can make them anywhere. But the drawbacks would be, if you're in a small town, your choice of quality actors and crew will be limited. The upside will be that it will be easier to get people to work for free or let you use locations, as they haven't been corrupted by many expensive film shoots and it's still exotic and exciting. Cities that have lots of film shoots, everything is overpriced and people are jaded.

Donald Farmer: I've filmed all over the world, though its obviously easier to film in the general area you're living. I was living in South Florida when I did *Demon Queen*, so it was a no-brainer to shoot in Miami. That was the city with the biggest talent pool for casting, and it has the best variety of locations within a concentrated area. But since my cam-

Keeping out the zombies: a still from *Year Zero*

eraman and equipment was coming down from Nashville for three days only, this put the pressure on me to shoot everything in a very concentrated time frame. When I made my Super 8mm movies like *The Summoned*, I shot them at a leisurely pace over months, never attempting more than one scene a day. Then, after a ten-year layoff from filmmaking, my first day on *Demon Queen* I have a schedule to shoot at least a dozen scenes over three or four different locations! At least I didn't repeat that situation the next year on *Cannibal Hookers*. I got a cameraman who lived in the same town as me, and we spread the schedule out over several months, just getting together to film on weekends. The trouble with this type of schedule, though, is that some actors may become unavailable if you count on their participation for months at a time. Our male lead on *Cannibal Hookers* shot about 75 percent of his role before he broke his leg in a motorcycle crash. This required me to complete rewrite the film's ending and add two detectives as last-minute heroes.

Even though I live in Tennessee, I've shot most of my movies in Georgia. That's where I found the investors for *Compelling Evidence*, *Deadly Run*, *Vicious Kiss*, *Demolition Highway*, *The Strike*, *Blood and Honor*, *Battle for Glory* and *Chainsaw Cheerleaders*. And, nine times out of ten, investors tend to want a movie shot where they live. At least the ones I found want to be able to come on location every day. And if they have a nice house we can film in for free, so much the better. On *Compelling Evidence* I actually convinced my producer to pay $1,200 a day to rent a $4 million Italian-style villa for us to film all Brigitte Nielsen's scenes in. When you're lighting and setting up shots, who wouldn't prefer a house with big, ornate rooms and ridiculously high ceilings. Instant production value!

Finally, if you're going somewhere exotic on vacation, why not shoot exteriors there you can use for a future movie? I did that one better when I took a vacation to Russia one year. I whipped up enough script for a 15-minute movie and made it an episode of my anthology film *Red Lips: Bloodlust*. I had a friend in Russia help me find local actors, then we filmed at some of the most iconic places in St. Petersburg, like the summer palace of Catherine the Great, with sweeping staircases lined with life-size gold statues, and the huge courtyard of the Hermitage Museum. I didn't have a camera crew in Russia, so I rented a camera before the trip and shot everything myself. But when I went to Paris to film *An Erotic Vampire in Paris*, I hired a French production crew so I could concentrate on directing. I think I set a personal record there for doing the most different locations per day. I made a wish list of great spots around the city like Notre Dame Cathedral, Père Lachaise Cemetery, the ferris wheel at Place de la Concorde, et cetera, and was determined to get them all in.

Jeff Forsyth: I think where I live has a positive impact on getting my projects made. I live in Syracuse, New York. It's a small city and filmmaking is happening here, but not on a big-budget scale. When I approach people about being part of a project or using their location, they are more apt to be say yes because this request is outside of the norm and is fun for them.

Richard W. Haines: Since most of my cast and crew live in New York City, that's where most of my features take place. All they have to do is take a subway or cab to our location. The Big Apple is also very photogenic and recognized throughout the world. However, I have secured locations in other parts of the Tri-State area (New York, New Jersey, Connecticut). I try to limit these shoots since it increases transportation costs to get everyone there on time.

William Hopkins: If you live in a city like New York, as I do, where every third person is an aspiring filmmaker and the cost of just existing is higher than everywhere else, you have to expect that the expense and difficulty of making an indie film is going to be that much greater. But being able to say your film was made in New York City and being able to use the city as a backdrop can certainly add commercial value to your project. So there is that benefit. Permits and insurance are an additional expense you have to worry about if you're shooting in public places. We shot the majority of *Sleepless Nights* and all of *Demon Resurrection* on private property in Long Island, where there's a greater variety of locales — everything from modern office buildings to undeveloped woodlands — and things were a little less expensive. Being in Long Island meant our transportation expenses were higher, but it still wasn't anywhere near as expensive as it would've been if we had shot in New York City. And the locations we were able to find in Long Island were pretty spectacular, which added to our film's production value.

Steve Hudgins: It's going to cost you about ten times as much, if not more, to shoot a movie in L.A. or New York. You shoot it anywhere else, especially smaller-type towns as opposed to big cities, and you're going to save yourself a fortune.

Rolfe Kanefsky: Well, this is actually a tricky question. I'm from New York and made my first two films there. Then I moved to Los Angeles and have been making films in Hollywood for the past 20 years. There are advantages in shooting in L.A. You can find many talented actors, crew, and have easy access to equipment. On the downside, you need permits for everything, and it can get very expensive. Plus, there are no film funds in California, so there's very little government/loans support. When I made *Nightmare Man*, it was impossible to shoot that film with the locations we needed in L.A. We had to go to Big Bear, two hours away, and put up the entire cast and crew. Surprisingly, that was actually cheaper to do than dealing with all the union rules.

The advantage, if you're not in L.A., is you can get a lot of favors and places to shoot for free. Many small towns and communities find movie-making exciting (oh, how little they

know) and want to help and support you. That's not the case in Hollywood, since it is such a business. So, it's sometimes easier to shoot anywhere else.

If you are making a movie outside of your town/state, then you have to worry about travel and living situations. Putting people up in motels/hotels can get pricey. You can fly in your main talent and key crew members but then you have to find local hire. That's cheaper, but you may not find the greatest actors or crew people locally. Professionals versus wannabes is the big difference and can affect the final result of your movie. I worked with a lot of people who thought it would be fun to work on a movie, only to realize that it's a lot more work and pressure than they thought it would be, and quit. Again, plan everything and have backup plans. I worked with a producer who told me, "When directing a film make sure you have Plan A, B, C, and D ready. And then be prepared to use Plan E."

Now, I'll also answer this question in terms of finding funding for your picture. If you are trying to raise money from investors from California and you live in Ohio, you will probably need to travel to California. Out of sight, out of mind. You must be in the investor's face and ready to take a meeting. It's always hard finding that money, but trying to do it long-distance is near impossible. That's one of the reasons why many people move to L.A. Because that's where the major studios are. But if you're doing a low-budget independent, you're not going to be getting your funding from studios. You have to find a private investor and convince them why you and your project are a good investment and, for that, you need to meet face to face with a well-written proposal that you can pitch like a pro.

Brett Kelly: I'm in Ottawa, Canada. We don't have a big infrastructure of a film industry here. There are indie filmmakers and occasionally some [made-for-television movies] will come here to film, but that's about it. As a result, permits aren't a big deal here and you can often get permission to shoot in residences and businesses quite easily. Actors here are starved for opportunities, so I'm happy to provide them. A bigger town, like nearby Toronto or Montreal, is full of jaded film folk that we don't have.

Chris LaMartina: Baltimore, Maryland, my hometown, has a great pool of talent, cultural energy, and support. There are countless filmmakers here that also produce micro-budget content and there is a great community atmosphere. We work on each other's projects, attend each other's premieres, and provide a network to make sure we're not hiring jerks/potential headaches.

We've been very lucky to live in a city where everyone is excited to help and not rude enough to ask poor filmmakers for big paychecks. We rarely pay actors (although I sincerely wish I was in a position to do so); we hardly ever rent locations; and we consistently find folks who go out of their way to be involved. Now, this is not the case for every production, but Jimmy and I make sure every person who works on our films feels valued. The most important words to come out of a directors mouth are "thank you." You'll bust your ass for someone you believe in and who respects you.

The budgetary restrictions must be combated with genuine passion and goodwill. We couldn't make the films we make in Hollywood or a bigger production town. Favors are phoned-in constantly and, because of this, your reputation is paramount. No bridges are worth burning.

Jim Mickle: I live in New York City, and *Mulberry Street* is a complete product of living there and shooting in a real apartment. Much of that movie's success is due to its authenticity. Half of *Stake Land* was shot in my dad's backyard, where I grew up in Berks County, Pennsylvania. The other half was shot in upstate New York, where I have a cabin and spend a good deal of time. The locations play a major part in that movie.

When you're working with low budgets, it can save money and add a lot of production value if you can use areas you know well. In both cases we were able to involve locals and friends to help out and be in the movie as well, so it's a huge advantage to be outside the bubble and making movies at home. That's one of the things that separate my films from mainstream genre films. And it's fun.

Damon Packard: From what I hear it's easier to keep a dedicated group together, willing to work for no pay, outside of California. But I don't know for sure. People tell me location shooting is much easier outside of Los Angeles, as it's easier to obtain permission or simply film without hassle (free of charge) in many other places, but it depends. The locations I'm usually interested in are very difficult or impossible to get access to without massive amounts of money.

Brad Paulson: The best thing about living in Los Angeles is the talent pool here is so huge. There's a lot of actors here that will work for meals, copy and credit, either to build their résumé or because they're financially stable, have the free time and really enjoy acting. In small towns you don't have a lot of options. L.A. houses a lot of the great actors as well as a lot of shitty ones. The trick is learning to differentiate between the two. However, any director worth half their salt will be able to do this. L.A. is also home to a lot of flakes and bullshit artists, but as long as you can avoid this, you can pull off some good things here. If you're in a small town, on the other hand, you can get all kinds of amazing locations for free. And you don't have to deal with noise, either. With L.A. you have to deal with that bullshit constantly. You can't go anywhere here for peace and quiet. There's always planes flying overhead, dogs barking, cars driving by, screaming kids, domestic arguments, you name it. And if you're guerrilla shooting there is also the risk of getting shut down and/or fined. On the other hand, L.A. is a town so many people are used to the idea of filming in, you can actually get quite a bit done here as well. In *Evil Ever After* we were doing a scene where an actor got their heart ripped out in the back parking lot of my apartment and people kept walking by pretending nothing strange was going on. Not only that, one neighbor of ours who I'd never met before brought their kid over to come talk to us and joke around. The kid probably thought it was cool that we were ripping someone's heart out in the parking lot for a horror movie. I don't know if I want to run into that kid again when he grows up.

Jose Prendes: I think where you live does indeed impact your film career. I used to live in Miami, Florida, that's where I made my first two films, and I didn't exactly break out of the box with them. Now I live in Los Angeles and have made so many contacts and can call in so many favors from great, talented people that I know my next [project] will be bigger and better, and will probably get a lot more attention. That's not to say that someone from Kansas or Nevada can't break out with an indie hit, but if you look closely, all the movies people are talking about started from L.A. I recommend you move on out here to Hollywood and swim with the sharks. If you're realistic about your goals, things can happen.

Paul Scrabo: I think you can produce a film anywhere. You should be realistic. Does that important three-minute dialogue sequence HAVE to be shot in Times Square? Do you have the permits and insurance?

Eric Shapiro: I've been in Los Angeles for 11 years, and aside from having great access to a huge pool of SAG actors, which is important, I exist with the awareness that I can make films anywhere. This becomes more true every day, what with other states having tax incentives and California taxing the business out of its own borders.

Anthony Straeger: Hmmm! Interesting! If you had asked if being of a specific race, gender, physical ability have an impact I would have answered with a resounding YES.

There are funding bodies all over the country (U.K./U.S.). The fact that it is cheaper to make a film now more so than ever before,

there is an old saying in a writing class: write about what you know. So whether you are Miss Suburbia, Mr. Hicksville — everything lies on your doorstep: friends, acquaintances, and locations.

Some advice I like to give first is, as a filmmaker/director, don't take it personally. Second, if you can't stand the heat, get out of the kitchen. Finally, you have got to give it everything until you don't want to give any more. This business attracts lots of "wannabes," but keeping yourself motivated is difficult when your rent is six months behind.

So, to the nub of the question and taking into consideration the above, where you live will never have an impact on getting your film made. You will have the impact as to whether you get your film made.

Marc Trottier: Up to now, I've primarily lived in Montreal and Toronto, where it gets mad cold during the winter months. So unless you're filming indoors or in a studio, it gets really difficult and uncomfortable to film outside during that time (especially if you have a low budget). I'm not sure if I answered this question correctly, but for me, weather/temperature definitely play a role in filming.

Mike Watt: Living in and outside of Pittsburgh, locations are usually easy to come by, depending on what our needs are. Offices, homes, interiors, exteriors, full haunted attractions — all have been gotten through polite, casual meetings and location agreements (which always include a clause on damage, which is covered by our insurance). Friends of ours who shoot primarily in New York and New Jersey, often tell us how they spent $500 for two hours of shooting at some lavish location. Farther down or west of those places, people are as likely to volunteer their property as they are to give permission. This falls under the "it never hurts to ask" department. We usually approach an owner [by saying], "Your house/farm/national landmark is gorgeous and we'd love to shoot here. Would you be okay with that, and how can we make that happen?"

Always credit people correctly. Actors, crew, extras and anyone who helped you in any way, shape or form. It's the absolute least you can do, and it makes people more amenable to you returning. (Or, in the case of the owners of Laurel Caverns in Uniontown, Pennsylvania, willing to come find you when you're hopelessly lost half a mile beneath the ground).

Ritch Yarber: Living in Cleveland has a double-edge in its impact on getting my films made. It is not the greatest place to try and break into filmmaking on any level since it is not a hotbed of opportunity. That being said, it makes it much easier and affordable to get my films made as there are so many people wanting to get their talents noticed but cannot take on the challenges of moving to the East or West Coast to "give it a go." So much great talent is at my fingertips for little or no cost. People are looking for a venue that is local and convenient to show their work. They cannot afford to take the big gamble. My films give them that chance. This is lucky for me since I, too, am in that same boat. I have three children, a wife and a handicapped father who count on me for their livelihood. I have worked at the same job for 26 years. I cannot afford to leave and "take my shot" at Hollywood. I have to try and create my opportunity from here. That makes me even more passionate and dedicated, since I understand what

these people are hoping to achieve, and I try and make it happen ... for all of us.

Cleveland has been getting some notice lately by the big studios, since Ohio is offering great incentives on making films in this state. The bad news for local filmmakers is that locations that were previously pretty open for use in independent productions are starting to tighten up. Everybody wants to get their share of the money pie, so it doesn't matter if you are local or a big studio, everybody thinks that films mean money to be made, thus, less freebies. It is another shot in the heart for microbudget independents.

Ivan Zuccon: I like telling stories about my country, and that's why I locate my movies here in Italy, near my home. I think a director should tell stories about what he knows best, because the cultural background helps in strengthening the storytelling.

Making movies is like a drug. Shooting movies turns your life upside-down (for better or for worse), and your life starts hinging on the shooting of the movie. Once you finish shooting, you immediately begin to think about the next film, and so on. There is no way out. It 's like a curse. The important thing is to impose a limit on yourself. If things start working to your advantage and what you do gets a good response, great. Otherwise, you should quit.

The Filmmakers were asked:
How do you secure locations?

Glenn Andreiev: The best thing to do is to tell the location owner you will mention their place of business in your press release (never say "news articles about us shooting will mention your place of business" because you have no power what the newspapers will edit out from your press release). This worked well for me when I needed to film in a hotel room for *The Deed to Hell*. I let the manager know

what I was doing, and how I can get them local press. He gave us two rooms for free, and let us hit their breakfast buffet. If the manager sees you sneak in lights, camera, and, especially, a woman, he'll think there's a porno shoot and toss you out.

John Borowski: When seeking locations, I usually work with the local film office if the location needed is a substantial location. By substantial I mean a large set that cannot afford to be built. For *Carl Panzram*, I worked with the Chicago Film Office to secure a jail location. I was surprised to find out that Michael Mann filmed *Public Enemies* at the same jail. Liability insurance is needed when filming on any location. I recommend buying into a group insurance as it is more economical and you are covered for liability insurance for an entire year. When filming *Albert Fish* in L.A., I rented out a studio where porn films were filmed. Not only did I get a great deal, but I had the run of the studio, including their standing sets and the area around the exterior of the studio. If the location needed is not substantial, I usually utilize the guerrilla filmmaking technique of trying not to attract attention and being as quick as possible. For *Albert Fish*, I needed an empty apartment set. I knew many apartments in L.A. were left open by the realtor for renters to enter and check out the apartment. There was an empty apartment two doors down from where I lived so I took the actor, one light, and my camera and tripod there and filmed as quickly as possible and left. No one ever knew we were there.

Keith Crocker: I don't secure locations, I steal them. Just about every location I have in my films is begged, borrowed or stolen. I don't believe in securing permits — it takes time and money. I simply hit and run. Let me give you an example. For *Blitzkrieg*, I used a closed-down psychiatric institute to double for a bombed-out prisoner of war camp. When I approached the first security officer about getting permission to shoot on the site, he said that "if he caught us trying to shoot without proper permission he'd confiscate all our equipment and not give it back." Okay, I tried to get permission from higher-ups, especially since my alma mater owned the property, but they (the school) kept telling me they no longer owned the property but were obligated to guard it. Anyhow, I start seeking out another location [when] I meet a guy who wants to act for us, and — surprise — he turns out to be a former guard from the school. He tells me that

the old head of guards was fired and now they have a guy there who doesn't give a shit. We buy that guy a box of donuts, and he simply says, "Don't destroy anything." So, we shot there three or four times. At one point we had about 35 war re-enactors crawling all over the property, and not once did we get thrown out. The Lord works in mysterious ways.

Richard Cunningham: Ha. I don't usually. I started guerrilla filmmaking when I was young, I guess. I asked permission to film on a location if the property's owner was around, but sometimes there was trespassing done in the name of the film. I also shot a no-budget mockumentary/horror film called *America the Mental* that has all kinds of beautiful New York City locations, scenes that were often captured in one take, if you follow me. Of course, I'm not recommending this.

I've gone through the proper channels for locations, as well. In New York City the governor has an Office of Films that processes permit applications. I've also worked with local municipal offices for permission to film in public; you can directly approach a business, like a café or bar. Many [owners] are willing to accommodate a low-budget film without charge, if you don't cause them inconvenience or take too long getting the scene down.

Maurice Devereaux: If you have no money for a location scout, you look around for what you need (online, drive around, ask friends), then find the owner and negotiate a price. This part is not rocket science. Try to find places with easy access by public transportation, available parking and low-noise levels. Also make sure if ever you rent someplace, that you don't need to re-rent it for extra time, as they now have you in a vice hold and can overcharge you if they feel like being greedy, since they know you need to shoot there. Once, on *End of the Line*, I rented an empty warehouse for one month for $1200. Then, while shooting, my production designer met an old acquaintance on the street. She lived in a loft across the street, I needed an apartment for a small scene in the film, and her place was perfect. Unfortunately, she worked in the film industry and was greedy — she wanted $500 for a day of shooting. Since it was so close by, it made sense to still go there. But, three weeks later, I needed an extra day at the warehouse. Well, the owner said sure, that will be $1500. I almost choked! "We paid $1200 for a month! What the hell?" Well, what happened was, the girl next door who I rented the loft from, KNEW and told the owner of the warehouse what we paid for her place, so now he had me by the balls. Since we had already shot there and needed it for continuity, I was fucked and had to pay.

Donald Farmer: There's about as many ways to secure a location as there are locations. Sometimes we shoot in a cast member's house. Sometimes we may shoot in MY house, as I've done on *Scream Dream* and *Deadly Memories*. Other times I'll get double duty from the motel where our cast and crew is staying. If a room's already on the production tab, why not knock off a few bedroom or shower scenes there? The opening scene of *Demon Queen* was shot in some Ft. Lauderdale motel. All the nude scenes for *Vampire Cop* and *Deadly Memories* were done at motels, too. When I needed a quick shot in *Compelling Evidence* of Lynn Lowry answering a late-night phone call, I didn't rent some studio for a three-minute scene — I shot it in Lynn's room at the Atlanta Holiday Inn. Another case of double duty on *Compelling Evidence* was when we needed a movie theatre to film a screening of our lead character's new action movie. An Atlanta production company providing our camera gear happened to have a screening room, so we filmed it there. It was a little trickier getting permission to shoot in a real TV studio for some of Dana Plato's scenes, but the local FOX affiliate eventually gave us the okay. When I needed a nightclub for the musical scenes in *Scream Dream*, I told a local club owner how our movie would be great advertising for his place. He agreed, and we used it for both that movie and *Savage Vengeance*.

The biggest location was the mansion we rented as the home of Brigitte Nielsen's character. For that I checked with the Georgia Film Commission for their list of Atlanta estates available for location rentals. I toured through some jaw-dropping homes that had been featured in *Driving Miss Daisy* and *Boxing Helena* before picking the place that was supposed to be the home of Brigitte Nielsen's character.

I've shot a couple of times in New York City and always hear stories about how it's impossible to shoot there without expensive filming permits. But I shot right in the heart of Times Square for *Red Lips: Bloodlust*, with no problem. A policeman even walked right by us at one point and just ignored us. Then on *An Erotic Vampire in Paris* we pretty much filmed where we pleased, never asking for permission, including inside Notre Dame Cathedral. Our French crew recommended some other good locations, and all the interior scenes were filmed at the Paris home of our cinematographer's father-in-law.

Jeff Forsyth: I have been very fortunate with locations. I have lived in or around Syracuse, New York, all my life and even when I was not working on a project certain locations speak to me and I remember them. Through so many wonderful people I have met in my life I have been able to shoot in some wonderful places. Plus, I am not completely ashamed to say that I have shot rather quickly in some places that I probably shouldn't.

Richard W. Haines: The locations I use for my features are secured in advance of writing the script, as I mentioned before. There's no point in writing a scene at a place that would be too expensive to film, at considering my budgetary limitations. Sometimes I'm able to get a building for free by offering services to them. For example, I've shot scenes at Technicolor Career Institute by using the students there as extras or production assistants. That gave them a credit and reference, so it worked out to everyone's advantage. Some complex locations, like the Gothic Castle, have to be rented.

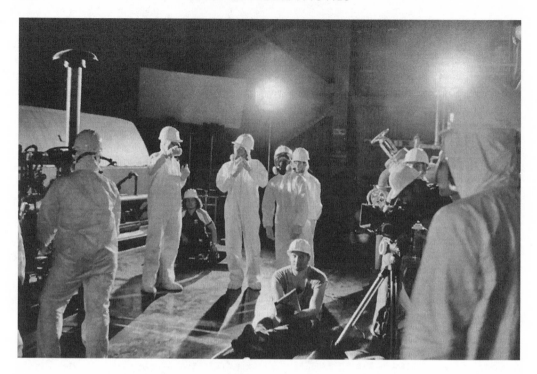

On the power plant set of *Space Avenger*

William Hopkins: On both films, the producers and myself put out the word to all our friends and associates about the type of locations we would be needing. *Sleepless Nights* was a far more challenging experience, since the script required several rather difficult locations, like an abandoned warehouse and a midtown–Manhattan skyscraper. Those aren't easy things to find when you have a budget of less than $100,000. We never did find the skyscraper, so we had to fake it using various substitutes. And as the production dragged on, we kept losing access to locations after we had begun to shoot scenes in them, so with both the skyscraper scenes and the abandoned warehouse scenes we ended up shooting in several different places and cobbling it all together in the editing. The scenes that take place on the roof of the skyscraper were actually shot on roofs in Manhattan, Queens, Brooklyn and the Bronx. And the abandoned warehouse scenes were done on locations in New Jersey, Queens and the Bronx. That all the stuff cut together properly was a small miracle in itself.

With *Demon Resurrection*, I simplified the shoot by writing a script that could be done in and around one house. But finding that house turned out to be a real trick. It had to be an old house — our story wouldn't work in a more modern building. And it had to be remote — the story wouldn't work in a house on a block with 20 other houses. And it had to be a fairly big place, since the action of the script was spread out over several different rooms of the house and the yard outside.

We were just a week or two away from abandoning the project because we couldn't find an acceptable place, when a friend of Frank's put him in touch with the owner of a beautiful piece of property way out on the furthest reaches of Long Island. It meant a good part of each day was spent in travel back and forth, but the location was ideal. It was big and old, with plenty of rooms and a slightly run-down look. It had plenty of exposed wood and big rafters running overhead, which was perfect for our purposes. And it was surrounded by several acres of woodland and situated right near a cliff looking out over Long Island Sound. It really added enormously to the look and feel of the film, almost as if it had been designed for us. In a way, the house became a character in the film, which is just what I was hoping for when I wrote the script.

Steve Hudgins: We ask. You'd be surprised how many people are happy to let you use their location for a movie if you ask nicely. Having a good amount of experience under your belt, along with a good reputation, goes a long way as well.

Rolfe Kanefsky: Usually, you just have to pay for them unless it's the producer's house. I've shot a lot of scenes at producers homes. If you're doing a real small production, you may be able to keep a low profile and "steal locations," like parks or streets, or fronts of stores. I did a lot of that on *Pretty Cool Too!* There's a montage when the main character is using the power of his cell phone to seduce/control people he meets. He goes to the park, a Goth store, and the beach. We shot all of these scenes on the same day with a four-person crew and a few actors. Nobody stopped us. We were in and out without anybody really noticing.

But if you're shooting in a house and are going to be there for a while, you need permits, permission from other homes in the area, signs that say you're filming, and usually a payment to the owner of the house. A great location can add a lot of production value to your project, so sometimes it's worth it. On *Jacqueline Hyde*, we found an amazing house that almost becomes a character in the movie. The people who owned the house were magicians and had never had a movie shoot in their mansion. We got them down to a thousand dollars a day, which was more than we wanted to spend. In fact, it doubled our cost. So, to make it work, we cut down the number of days at that location from six to four. But it was so worth it. Luckily, we didn't have to pay the strip club because Gabriella Hall, the star/producer, knew the guy who owned it. We just had to shoot after two o'clock in the

morning when they closed and be out before they opened the next night. We also used Gabriella's house that we dressed to be many different places. The Beverly Hills office we shot at night in a real office. It was $3,000 for one night, which I paid for myself. However, the outside of the office was actually a building in the valley that always keeps its lobby lights on. Paul Deng, my director of photography on that film, turned us on to that, and one night we just went there and stole all the exteriors. The funny thing is that the company that ended up buying our film and selling it to Warner Bros., had their offices inside that building. Small world, huh?

So, if you're smart you can get a lot of locations for free and pay for the ones that are really worth it. *Jacqueline Hyde* was shot in ten days for under $100,000, but it looks a lot bigger and a lot more expensive. I believe our locations had a lot to do with that.

The same can be said for the main house in *The Hazing* and the three different homes that made up the main house in *There's Nothing Out There*. Personally, I love shooting in actual locations versus building sets. It is sometimes limiting but a real place feels like a real place and that shows on screen.

Brett Kelly: Always get written permission from the owner. That's the whole trick.

Chris LaMartina: Micro-budget filmmakers have a tendency of setting films in one central location and it's often somewhere easy/safe to shoot in (e.g., a summer house full of perky teenage girls). It's cheaper to use this motif, but we've tried to veer away from that because it is so common. We, like most artists, want to stand out. An interesting location can really add to the atmosphere and eeriness of a horror flick.

Find interesting locations that you already have access to ... you'll be shocked at what you can use just because of a business owner's enthusiasm. Using this philosophy, we've shot in nursing homes, antique shops, and even funeral parlors. If you can't get away with using them for free, figure out a favor trade. For

On the set of *President's Day,* director Chris LaMartina checks the audio levels of screams while Director of Photography Joe Davidson captures Evil Lincoln chopping up actress Carolyn Wasilewski. Photograph by Jimmy George.

Grave Mistakes, we shot expensive-looking mansion scenes at a local bed and breakfast, and in return, I was asked to do a video tour of their business. We shot our slasher comedy, *President's Day*, at a small private high school because we agreed to install exit lights in every hall and make a small donation to the "Principal's fund."

Think within your means, but get ready to rely on your charisma to seal the deal. A great attitude and friendly smile can go a long way. People want to get involved generally, but they have to trust you first.

Jim Mickle: I've secured them with location managers and good producers who are willing to do the legwork to develop and maintain respectful relationships. Lots of places in *Stake Land* were written for specifically, but for other locations our producer, Brent Kunkle, took on the role of location manager, moving to the area for about six weeks of prep and getting to know the area and making contacts locally. When we needed

certain places, people would often offer up their place or another that they knew of.

On *Mulberry Street* we had written in three or four main apartments in the script and had gotten permission from many of Nick's neighbors to use their place for some time to shoot. But the day before principal photography, they all backed out, so we improvised and shot the whole thing in Nick's one-bedroom apartment. He and the art team redecorated for each location, painting walls, taking out cabinets, and building fake doors to play as four different apartments. It worked seamlessly.

The best advice is to be incredibly respectful of locations. I've worked on crews that abuse locations, and I've had my own place torn apart for other people's shoots and it sucks. Treat it like it's your own.

Damon Packard: In my case it's often not a budgetary consideration, so it's a situation where you hope and pray that nobody tosses you off a location in the first five minutes. I've been very lucky in that regard. But I have also been thrown off hundreds of locations. One should always have backup locations, if possible.

Brad Paulson: In the good old days we'd guerrilla most of the locations and plan on being out of there before the cops arrived. Or we used to get locations for free. But times have changed and so have the owners. So we've been scaling back to shoot in places we absolutely know we can get, not just ones we think we can get. From now on, I'm going to do what's easiest for me. I've had my fun with guerrilla filmmaking and will still do it from time to time, but I'll only do it if it's something I can pull off quick enough before anyone arrives to shut us down.

Jose Prendes: Well, with no budget you shoot at your house, or you get your friends to hook you up with a sweet location. In the case of *Corpses Are Forever*, I filmed in a massive warehouse studio and had to rent it out for the duration, which was costly. But if you want to shoot somewhere, then go shoot there. That's easier said than done in Los Angeles, because the cops are savvy to the ways of indie moviemakers, but securing a location can be done fairly easily ... and usually for free.

Paul Scrabo: I haven't had much practical experience with that. We did a bit of "run and gun" here and there, and that's never pleasant By the way, a few months after we wrapped up shooting at the house used for the main location, a tree fell on it. It's since been largely rebuilt and now it can be a new location for our next film!

Eric Shapiro: When you're going beyond residential locations — which friends and family are great for supplying — it's a lot like casting. If it's a hotel, like we used for *Rule of Three*, it's a good idea to talk to the management and get a feel for their disposition. If somebody seems like they're gonna drive you crazy for three weeks, run. If you're dealing with reasonable people, it's a matter of negotiating costs and time frames. On *Mail Order*, we shot in Sante La Brea, a great restaurant that's now closed. I told the manager we couldn't pay much, but that we'd buy the cast and crew dinner from the restaurant. He was sold.

Anthony Straeger: In terms of securing

Call of the Hunter location—Cleve House Ivybridge—shooting the night transition shot.

locations I can definitely say that I've never used a location scout or a locations bureau. Whatever script I have done, once it is broken down and I have a fairly good idea of what locations I am looking for, I either contact friends and associates to see whether they might know of such a location, or I do some internet research, looking at areas that are in the best and most convenient location.

Working as an independent filmmaker, you are continually pulling favors, and I personally have had some great locations for nothing. I'm fairly sure that people can sense that you haven't got a shed load of money to hand to them for their location, and as my budgets are often limited, I think that I have been lucky with the people I have met. If a company or individual wants too much for a location, it's simply not plausible, and I look elsewhere. If it's close and it's free, the foibles of the venue can often be worked around.

Marc Trottier: Finding locations is kind of the same as finding actors. You're filming stuff in your parents' basement or your friend's pool, or you're sneaking onto private property to get certain shots (don't get shot trying to get your shot!). I filmed a short film where we robbed a convenience store (in the film — don't actually rob a convenience store to get money to film). We knew the girl behind the counter and she was bored, so we did it on the spot. Another time during the filming of *Darkness Waits*, we went into a hospital (which we used as the entrance to our mental institution), and we asked the receptionist to hand my character a clipboard to sign before leaving ... and she agreed.

You need to come up with creative ways to film in certain locations that would otherwise cost money, like pretending to be a security guard, or a construction worker to divert traffic ... or sometimes just by asking nicely.

Mike Watt: The easiest thing to do, for us, has been to ask. Many of our movies have actually been written around the location, such as the "Bathory House" in *A Feast of Flesh*, which was owned by our friends and

"stable" actors, Stacy Bartlebaugh-Gmys and Ron Gmys. The only requirements were that we limit the blood use to one specific room of the house and that we not track shit in from outside. We had them sign a location release form and chipped in for their utilities (which they hadn't asked for, but we felt it was only right to do so). Thus, we had a gorgeous Victorian house to utilize for our little ode to Hammer.

In the case of the working haunted attraction, the Hundred Acres Manor, which inspired *Splatter Movie: The Director's Cut*, we knew one of the head employees and, through him, we met the location's owners. They required that we provide them with proof of insurance, which turned out to be much easier and cheaper to obtain than you'd expect, which has now become standard operating procedure for us. Debbie Rochon's on-set accident, resulting in partially severed fingers and leaving her nearly bankrupt thanks to amateur filmmakers lacking the simple policy, served as a wake-up call for all professional independent filmmakers. In fact, if you can't afford what usually amounts to a couple hundred dollars for a million-dollar policy, you have no right to ask your actors or crew to risk even the smallest amount of hazard.

For *Demon Divas and the Lanes of Damnation*, the idea to use King Lanes bowling alley was pitched to us by the owners and their daughter. We renewed our insurance policy and paid for all food and beverages provided by the business's kitchen staff. Since we were shooting during an off-period (as we did with the Hundred Acres Manor) near the end of summer as they geared up for league-play, there was no demand for any sort of rent. In fact, owners Bob and Sandy Hall actually provided the majority of our cast with sleeping accommodations at their home and came aboard as associate producers.

Utilizing the Laurel Caverns for *Razor Days* came about through a series of coincidences. Amy and I had covered the shooting of a segment of *George A. Romero Presents Deadtime*

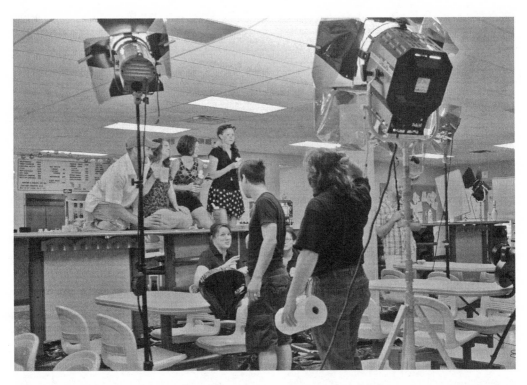

Shooting *Demon Divas* in King Lanes, Kittanning, Pennsylvania: Top, left to right: Michael Barton (Cal), Rachelle Williams (Frankie), Tabatha Carlson (Becki), Tara Cooper (Infinity). Seated: Nikki McCrae (Lisa), Sofiya Smirnova (Taffy). Standing: Hugo Bissonett (camera, DiggerFilms), Mike Watt (director), Steve Villeneuve (Camera, DiggerFilms)

Stories for *Fangoria*. The film's writer, co-producer and co-director, Jeff Monahan, put us in touch with the landmark's proprietors and we arranged a very reasonable agreement that allowed us to shoot uninterrupted for a weekend, again, under the stipulation that we provide proof of insurance. The insurance didn't make us physically comfortable a quarter-mile beneath the Earth during a snow-melting spring, but it covered anyone who might have slipped on the limestone paths, walked into a stalactite, et cetera.

So the long and short of things has always been: Ask first; it rarely hurts. Especially if you don't live in a "Hollywood" town where proprietors and property owners are used to being compensated by movie crews. Most people find the filmmaking process to be fascinating and love to be on set. As long as you and your crew don't act like entitled jerks, the person-to-person negotiations are usually very smooth.

Obtain liability insurance for personnel, at the very least. For additional fees you can get your equipment covered as well, but, normally, your gear is already covered by homeowner's insurance (if you're a homeowner, obviously). But under no circumstances should you risk the health and livelihood of your cast and crew in order to save a few hundred dollars. Most of these people are your friends and family. How would you feel if someone was injured to any degree under your watch? The old "we make everyone sign a waiver that says any injury is their responsibility" is a callous and cowardly attitude to have.

Don't be a jerk. It's not your property, and even if you're paying a fee to be there, that doesn't give you ownership. You and your crew are guests of someone else and they don't have to let you be there. Maintain a good relationship with the owners, agree to their restrictions and utilize the location the best way you can in the movie. To that end, have a location agreement signed by both you and the proprietor. It's always best to have things in writing, and it covers all parties. Remember, people are usually fascinated by the filmmaking process until they realize just how tedious it really is. Some people may tire of having everyone around, even after a few hours, and I've known a number of "handshake" agreements fall apart simply because the proprietor of the business lost interest midway through the first day's shoot. You can easily download a boilerplate agreement whose terms you can modify to indicate how long you'll be at the location, times that you will arrive and leave, et cetera. One slip of paper keeps everyone honest.

Ritch Yarber: We secure locations by basically explaining what we are about and what we are trying to do. Luckily, so far, we have never had to pay for the use of a location. A lot of people are excited about being a part of a film and are eager for us to use their locations. Some are less than eager, but, begrudgingly agree under specific conditions and times. For *Murder Machine!* we shot for four straight weekends at an old horse barn in Oberlin, Ohio. Since the place was a working ranch during the day, we could only shoot at night, which was great for us since the scenes took place at night. The owner was a friend of one of the wives of one of our actors. He said that we could do whatever we wanted in the barn and use whatever we needed for the shoot. Problem was, he worked nights, leaving his wife in charge of the barn at night. She was never very happy to see us. It put a whole new level of pressure on us to get the shots we needed under the disapproving eye of the wife. We had to shut down production several times during the night as she fed the animals and "tended" to things in the barn. We had to wrap by daylight and ensure that everything was cleaned up and that we were gone when

the customers started to arrive for their riding lessons. When you are getting free access to a location, you have to suck it up and do whatever has to be done to get your shots.

TwistedSpine.com Films has a policy that we are sticklers about when using a location. We always leave a location as clean or cleaner than it was when we arrived. Our reputation for this policy helps us continue to secure locations that we could never afford to pay for. With this policy in mind, I recently worked on another local filmmaker's project as part of the crew. We were shooting at Burke Lakefront Airport, in downtown Cleveland, Ohio. Someone removing garbage from the craft-services area of the shoot had left a trail of liquid out the door and all the way down the concourse of the airport. It was on a weekend and the place was practically empty. I was the last crew member at the location. I was assigned to clean up the remaining craft-services area and secure the location as I left. There was no mop to be found anywhere I looked in the whole airport. I was forced to clean the entire concourse on my hands and knees, with a roll of paper towels and one old rag. I was tired and sore when I left that day, but I remembered that this policy had enabled me to get many great locations for my films and that, even though this was not my project, my reputation and opportunities were earned because I always operate to a higher standard. When you are trying to make movies for no money, your reputation can be just as important as money when securing great locations that will add fantastic production value to your works.

We have never written up a contract for terms to use a certain location. Other filmmakers that I know have had horror stories about verbal agreements that suddenly change in the middle of the shoot. Please keep this in mind when committing to a location. People are fickle.

Ivan Zuccon: It's hard to find a location for free. When we find a location that is good for the film, we look for the owner and we ask him how much money he wants for the rent. Of course, we explain him that we are making a low-budget movie and we do not have a lot of money to spend. Because when they hear "making a movie" they believe we are Hollywood and start asking for tons of dollars. Usually we use this trick: we tell them we are making a student film. This often works, and we secure a location for a cheap price. But no one gives you anything for free here.

Special Effects

There are two types of special effects. The first are the ones you do during the actual production, like make-up or blood effects. The second are those done in post-production, like explosions or computer animation. With both, I tried getting professional effects people, primarily because I wasn't able to do those effects myself. With the first film, *Vampires & Other Stereotypes*, I had the services of a professional effects company out of New Jersey. They were the same outfit that did Rolfe Kanefsky's *There's Nothing Out There* a few years before. On my film they did everything from the vampire fangs to full-head demon prosthetics to giant rats. However, with my next film, the anthology *Twisted Tales*, I did the majority of the make-up effects myself, as they were so much simpler to execute. I also needed a break from time-consuming special effects. That was the main thing I learned from doing an effects-laden feature — those effects take hours of preparation.

Blood and gore are fairly easy on a low budget. On a zombie short I did for an anthology called *Goregoyles* I created most of the special effects to see if I could do that myself. Intestines were made from uncooked links of sausage, blood from Karo syrup and food coloring. Even the Fulci-like zombies were modified from generic rubber masks, doctored with liquid latex and moss. In fact, I was more pleased with the effects in that short movie than anything else in the entire production. One of the worst experiences I had with effects, which haunts me to this day, were the werewolf costumes in *Rage of the Werewolf*. I had been impressed with the effects artist's portfolio and [demo] reel, so he was hired to create two full-bodied lycanthrope outfits. He had several months do to this. But as the date of the production neared he said he was having problems meeting the deadline. If I canceled the dates of the production and postponed them, I knew the movie would not get made. Everything was coordinated and locked in, from locations to actors. So I told the guy to mail me what he had finished and I'd use what he had. What came in the mail the next day looked like two cheap gorilla suits and unpainted latex masks. There was no sleep to be had that night, as the co-producer and I "fixed" them. But what to do with these giant Muppet-looking werewolves? I treated it as if I were shooting a 1960s *Godzilla* film.

The first digital effects I needed were on the *Alien Agenda* movies in the mid–'90s. This was a trilogy of features that revolved around two different types of aliens overtaking the Earth. The needed effects were done by several different people, to expedite the post-production. Again, many different filmmakers were involved and they were responsible for many of their own effects. However, certain effects and props needed to be consistent, such as the "look" of the aliens, so all that had to be coordinated. With the sequel series, *The Alien Conspiracy*, I had one person create most of the miniatures, such as the flying saucers, and another person digitally manipulate them into the various scenes, such as flying over the Twin Towers.

Although there's been great advancement in digital effects I recommended that you keep your effects to a minimum. Today's audiences expect a lot and there's no way you can measure up to *Avatar* on a minuscule budget. In fact, watch nearly any movie made for the Syfy Channel and you can see lousy computer effects.

What I've learned from 20 years of production is that if you aren't able to realize the effects in your script then you probably should do a rewrite.

The Filmmakers were asked:
How do you handle special effects?

Glenn Andreiev: Try not to go over your head. On a $15,000 film you're not pulling off the "bullet time" effects from *The Matrix*. It's easy to make do with what you already have. In *Mad Wolf*, for gunshots to a tree, we drilled holes into a tree and put firecrackers in them. During post-production in *Silver Night*, we saw this shot of a vampire woman running to catch a victim. We wanted to turn that into a special effect. The shot was done with a steady camera on a tripod, and we did five takes of her running off. I simply superimposed all five takes of her running together so it looks like she pulls apart into five ghostly figures. We sped up the image and added a weird scream. The shot came out pretty good.

John Borowski: Photoshop and After Effects are amazing programs. They are almost limitless in what can be created and manipulated for special effects. I edit my films on a Mac in Final Cut Pro and create all of the effects in Photoshop and After Effects. There are many tutorials available on the internet that guide you through the making of certain special effects. Sound is very important as you can utilize sound to complement and enhance the special effect. When filming *H.H. Holmes*, a fake hole in a wall was created to serve as a chute opening where Holmes would dump a body from the third floor down to the basement of his "castle." The set was built in my apartment, so the chute was fake. But the illusion was complemented by the sound of a body falling three stories and then landing at the bottom.

Keith Crocker: I let other folks handle special effects. Back in the old days, right up to *Bloody Ape*, I also did the make-up effects myself. Every once in a while I'd get a "guest" make-up artist, like Nathan Schiff, another Long Island-based filmmaker, who handled Herschel Gordon Lewis–style effects very well. On the *Bloody Ape*, George Reis, Larry Koster and I called ourselves the Cinefear Effects Troupe, and we handled all the special make-up effects ourselves. But when *Blitzkrieg* came, I had John Farley, who had been working on other Long Island–produced horror film effects. Nothing pleases me more than having a make-up effects person; I'm sick and tired of handling and cleaning up stage blood. I don't miss doing effects at all. I never really liked it. And, again, you don't want to wear too many hats.

Richard Cunningham: With my first productions, *Lycian* and *Arcadium*, the story had a fictional medieval backdrop. Some of the visuals we accomplished by brute force, like building a village set that spanned more than half an acre of land. For that we were carrying fallen trees from the surrounding woods to form building frames, transporting rocks to make functional fire pits, carving and painting Styrofoam to make fake rock walls. For the castle scenes in the movie, I contacted an actual castle in Tarrytown, New York, that operates as a hotel, and they allowed us to shoot on their property. CGI ultimately became necessary to capture the grandeur of a capital city referenced in the script, and to fill the sets

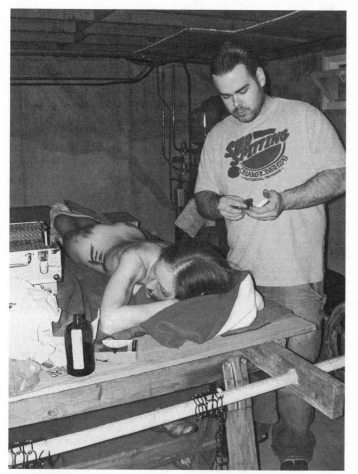

with more extras than had originally shown up. That task fell on my production partners, who accomplished it by pain-staking rotoscoping techniques with Final Cut Pro.

With *America the Mental*, we were doing minimal effects, but because the film was shot impromptu, we usually had but one take to get the shot right. These effects involved blood spatter or other violence, and required some trickery of camera framing and/or actor concealment, so that the effect could be accomplished seamlessly during long shots without inserts dedicated to featuring the effect itself. I suspect, for this reason, that stage experience would be especially useful knowledge when filming a movie in that documentary-like style.

Top: **John Farley applies make-up to Tatyana Kot so she will appear battered and bruised in** *Blltzkrieg.* *Bottom:* **Another disturbing scene from** *Year Zero.*

With *Year Zero*, my production partner set me up with the programs, and I took on the challenges of special effects myself. To give the animated film its particular look, I photographed objects and brought them into Adobe Photoshop, where I added a filter that converted the still images into line drawings. I then extracted the subject, creating an individual layer, coloring it in and shading it, and eventually adding it to a composite image.

From there I used Adobe After Effects, separating each layer within a sequence to mimic perspective when employing the movement of the program's virtual camera and lighting features. I used something called a "Puppet Tool" in After Effects to manipulate the still images into animation, with a few other techniques, like stop-motion, but that was often a complicated and awkward process. As I had no crew, I was taking photographs of myself, using the camera's timer, and a guitar case as a stand-in.

For the opening titles of the short film, I wanted to begin with a shot of a single cell dividing exponentially, and that required me to look into several After Effects filters, but I managed to find one for free that accomplished the effect. I even used an old GIF animator for a sequence. Whatever got the job done.

Maurice Devereaux: I don't [do special effects]... I get someone who does that for a living. I was lucky to be friends with Oscar-nominated special make-up F/X artist Adrien Morot, who is a tremendous artist; he worked on all my films at a discount rate (or, in the case of *End of the Line*, for free in exchange for a percentage of the film). But special F/X are very time-con-suming on set, so beware and schedule your shoot accordingly.

Donald Farmer: I like to leave special effects to the experts. As I mentioned, I was my own effects man on *The Summoned*, rigging one of my friends with a firecracker, but I don't need to repeat that experience. I've mentioned how I hired Rick Gonzales for the make-up effects on *Demon Queen* right after he'd assisted Tom Savini on *Day of the Dead*. I used Rick again on *Scream Dream*, *Savage Vengeance*, *Vicious Kiss* and *Vampire Cop*. For that last one Rick did a vampire's death scene that Joe Bob Briggs described as "ten seconds of a drug dealer's face turning into Silly Putty and getting fried off in the sun." Actually, it was more like 90 seconds — I liked to milk Rick's effects for all the screen time they were worth!

Donald Farmer poses with Jackey Little (in demon make-up) on the set of *Scream Dream*.

For *Cannibal Hookers* I found an effects guy named Brian Sipe who had absolutely no film experience but was making these huge animatronic dinosaurs for museums out of his garage. I came by his house one day, saw a huge robotic Tyrannosaurus head he'd made and hired him on the spot. Now Brian is one of the top effects guys in the industry, with credits on *Hannibal, Star Trek, Van Helsing, Terminator Salvation* and *The Curious Case of Benjamin Button*. But his IMDb page still lists *Cannibal Hookers* as his first feature credit.

Another effects man I've used is Bob Shelly, who runs a full-blown studio and weapons museum in Atlanta with his son B.J Shelly. Bob's done everything from Jim Wynorski's *Return of the Swamp Thing*, creating gunshot squibs for Robert Rodriguez in *Desperado*, rigging rain effects in *The Notebook*, and running various pyrotechnic and gunshot effects in *Zombieland*. When you hire Bob you can usually film on his studio lot as part of the package, which is very useful for doing car stunts and explosions without having to get permits and blocking off public streets. We filmed a big chunk of *Vampire Cop* on Bob's lot, then came back a few years later for a motorcycle-crash scene in *Vicious Kiss*. Bob and B.J. both work on *Demolition Highway*, doing the extra bloody squibs I requested, along with bike stunts and a laundry list of other effects, big and small. My favorite of Bob's work for me is the front and back squib he created for actress Doris Ragsdale in *Compelling Evidence*. Doris is supposed to get blasted through the forehead, with blood flying out the back of her head. Bob made a filament cord/button effect for her forehead that reveals a pre-made bloody wound. Then he taped a protective metal plate on the back of her head with a small explosive charge rigged beneath a condom full of movie blood. For the effect to work, one man detonates the charge at the exact instant another guy yanks the filament cord. This pulls a buried button from her forehead and reveals the make-up, just as a spray of blood come out the back of her head. I'd first seen an effect like this in *Taxi Driver*, then again in *Dawn of the Dead*, so I wanted it in one of my own movies. And, with Bob in charge, everything worked perfectly on the first try.

Chainsaw Cheerleaders was the first time I wanted to go the CGI route and was referred to a guy could do both CGI animation and traditional make-up effects. Joey Pruitt had just done a movie for Lionsgate called *Side Show*, where he created some disturbingly realistic CGI snakes, so I had him do one better on *Chainsaw Cheerleaders*. Joey designed and animated a CGI mutant snake that could rape Debbie Rochon, slither through her body, and burst out of her neck in a blast of CGI blood. Naturally, I featured this effect front and center in the preview trailer.

Jeff Forsyth: On the first film I handled all the make-up, props, design work and digital effects myself. I believe in the idea that knowledge is power. If I didn't know how to do something I either read about or asked someone how to do it. Originally, all the UFOs in *Children of the Sky* were models, which was rather fun to construct and photograph. By the time post was finished on that film I entered the world of CGI. I love being able to do all my work myself. I don't really want to do *all* of it but I like being learned enough about special effects to guide people to what I'm looking for.

Richard W. Haines: My features that require special effects or squibs and explosions are handled by hiring F/X Artists and pyrotechnicians. Amodio Giordano and Ralph Cordero did the gore effects for *Splatter University*. John Bisson and Ralph Cirello created them for *Space Avenger*. Brian Spears handled them for my latest movie, *What Really Frightens You*. In all cases they utilized latex rubber techniques, which involved making molds of monsters, aliens or the actors. I prefer those type of effects. I'm not a big fan of digital monsters, which look artificial and cartoonish to me. CGI are astronomically expensive compared to the latex monster effects. Wilfred Caban and Neal Ruddy were among the pyrotechni-

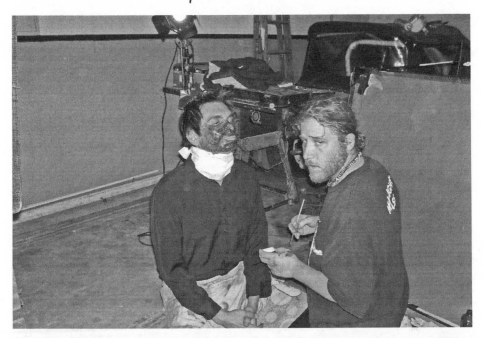

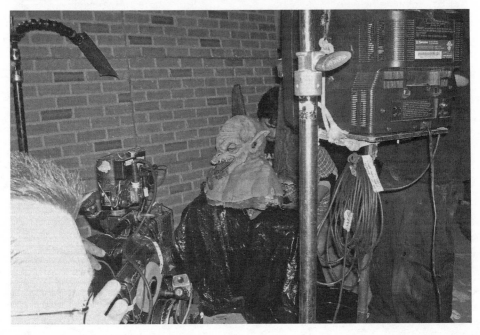

Top: **Brian Spears works on an effect for *What Really Frightens You?* (2007). *Bottom:* Filming a** **gargoyle creature for *What Really Frightens You?***

cians I used for blood squibs and explosions. I like to shoot as many of the effects shots in advance of principal photography, since they take a long time on set. It's a reverse of the usual method of shooting wide-shots first and then close-ups. I prefer to shoot the special effects close-ups during pre-production, then match them to wide shots on location later. It also gives me the option of re-shooting the effects if they don't come out the first time.

William Hopkins: With both of my films we hired professional make-up artists to do beauty make-up and hair styling for the cast and to supply things like vampire fangs and some gore effects. With *Demon Resurrection*, I did the zombie costumes, with Frank and Ed assisting, and I did the monster baby, which was a puppet shot in front of a blue screen and inserted in the shots with the actors. All the optical work and a number of more elaborate gore shots were done by me in post, things like Steven's neck being ripped out and Marcy's belly being ripped open on the shards of broken glass. I tweaked a number of the gore effects we had done on the set in the computer in post.

Just about every shot in *Demon Resurrection* had some optical work in it — the addition of smoke or the supernatural glow around the zombies or the breaking glass shots — and all of that was in addition to the actual editing of the film, the scoring of the film, the shooting of additional effects shots and color correction, looping, et cetera. Since all of that was being done by just one person, the post-production period stretched on for well over a year.

I think the special effects work in my first film, *Sleepless Nights*, was a little spotty, though I recently spruced up the film for re-release and fixed some of the weaker effects. But I'm very happy with the effects work in *Demon Resurrection*. I think the zombies look quite good, and some of the gore scenes, like Marcy's belly ripping and the monster baby's birth, always get very strong reactions from audiences.

Steve Hudgins: It's nice to have a knowledgeable effects member on board. But if you don't have access to such a person you need to remember that we live in an information age and you can find all kinds of "how to" tutorials on the internet, which allows you to go the "do it yourself" route, if need be. You can also learn a lot by watching some of the "making of" specials that are on many DVDs nowa-

Creature shop for *Demon Resurrection*

days. You'd be surprised at how simple many great special effects are to do.

Rolfe Kanefsky: Very carefully. They're delicate, you know. But seriously, effects, especially in horror movies, are very important. If they look cheesy and cheap, they can destroy your whole movie. I have done a lot of horror flicks and have never had enough money to really do great effects, but I try my best and hire the best people I can.

When I started making films and shorts as a teenager, I did my own effects. Fake blood, earthworms, et cetera. In college, I found a friend who created a monster hand for a short called *Peek-A-Boo*. The result was so-so.

When my first professional film came along, since I was in New York, I looked for some local effects places. We needed many effects for *There's Nothing Out There*, including the star creature, and found Scott Hart and his company, Imagifects Studios. He had worked on some low-budget stuff, including *The Basement*, a film that just recently came out for the first time. He made our creature and head molds. It was 1989 and everything was done practically except for the opening credits and a few electrical sparks at the end.

Then I moved to L.A. and my next directing assignment was on a series of sexy comedies designed for late-night cable. Nudity was the most important aspect in these films, but since I wrote the scripts I tried to put in some special-effect gags in as well, like someone's tongue suddenly growing three feet long and a woman getting so aroused that her nipples suddenly jump to attention underneath her leotard. Well, there was a young effects man working his way up in the Corman ranks at the time, and he ended up doing all my effects. His name was and is Robert Hall and he's now a big effects guy as well as a director himself.

A few years later, I had a few bigger budgets (almost million-dollar projects) and for *Tomorrow by Midnight* and *The Hazing*, the effects job went to SOTA effects. Then, my budgets went down again and I worked with Jeff Farley on *Jacqueline Hyde* and *Nightmare*

Man. If you don't have a lot of money, you can still do amazing things, if you're creative. Like I've said, sometimes the most effective things are the things you think you see but don't. Lighting can trick the eye and the right camera angle can give the impression that you saw something horrible when, in actuality, it was your imagination making it more than it really was.

Again, talk with friends and find out who is good or who may think your movie is cool enough to want to do it, even without a lot of money. Now that CGI has taken over, there are a lot of very talented effects guys out there looking for work.

It also helps to know how to shoot the effects. I have impressed many special effects departments by telling them that when the effect is ready, I want to shoot the close-up of it first so I get it looking its best. I can't tell you how happy they are to hear that. Most of the time, directors shoot the master wide shots first and work their way into the close-ups. By the time they get there, the effect has to be cleaned up and reset and loses some of it glamour. Telling them that I know it's better to shoot effects first puts them at ease, since they know their hard work will be shot correctly. You'll really get them on your side if you do this. It also helps to know what you want. Give them some creative freedom, but know what you're looking for. Many directors have vague ideas but don't know what they like until they see it. That trial-and-error process drives effects guys crazy. Plan and discuss everything. Find out what can and cannot be done with the time and money at hand. Figure out simple ways around certain gags and decide which ones you really, really want. It's better to have five to ten really good effects than 20 poorly executed ones.

Brett Kelly: I always hire experts in their field. A director should be good at directing. Find other people who are equally good at what they do. I usually budget half a day's shoot for an elaborate blood or make-up effect — they always take longer than you think—and things WILL go wrong. Plan ahead and budget the time, and it should all be good.

Chris LaMartina: Early on, we did a lot of the effects ourselves, but after your camera buttons start sticking with Karo syrup you question the practicability of that dynamic.

For *Book of Lore* we hired a fellow named Darren A. Mosher, who was killing time (no pun intended) in Baltimore before a big move to New Zealand, where he got a job with WETA.

For *President's Day* and *Witch's Brew*, we used graduates of the Tom Savini effects school. Kaleigh Brown did *President's Day* solo and then we used her, Jason Koch, and John Laveck for *Witch's Brew*.

There are plenty of make-up school graduates, just like film school kids, who want to get in on projects so they can remain active within their craft. They understand limited resources, but are positive artist types who will give you their all for low numbers.

Jim Mickle: For make-up, I worked with Adam Morrow on *Mulberry Street*. We had gone to NYU together and I heard he was working a day job and still doing effects whenever he could. We gave him a big chunk of our very tiny budget to design and create the effects, and he wound up leaving his job and working on our effects full-time for many months.

On *Stake Land*, we worked with Brian Spears, who is a part of Glass Eye Pix's frequent roster. He and his partner, Pete Gerner, are very good at being flexible and doing whatever it takes to pull off ambitious ideas. They recycle a lot of gags (a lot of our vampire teeth were also in Glass Eye's *I Sell the Dead*, worn by the same actors, in fact). A lot of heads and body parts were put together, like Mister Potato Heads to create many different looking dead bodies. Brian also played two of our key vampires, which made casting and effects pre-production very easy.

For digital effects and compositing, I've done my own for both films. My day job requires a lot of After Effects and animation, so I've gotten very comfortable with compositing and 2-D/3-D work. It's also incredibly helpful to be able to mock up effects shots during the editing process so they can go hand in hand, instead of farming it all out to different departments and trying to keep many people on the same page. There's an excellent website called Video Copilot (www.videocopilot.net) that teaches After Effects through entertaining and informative tutorials, from beginners to advanced. They also have a lot of great products, like lens-flare plug-ins and stock-action footage, elements like blood spatters and shattered glass. Highly recommended for doing genre films on a budget.

Damon Packard: Well, again, that's determined by budgetary constraints. You do what you can.

Brad Paulson: If it's horror, we can do a lot of those ourselves and they usually turn out better than if we have someone come in and do them for us. If it requires make-up, though, make-up artists are aplenty here in Hollywood and they're very hungry for work. That's another perk of living here. A good one who knows how to do gore is pretty much impossible to get for free, so I'd recommend learning the basic carnage effects yourself. The one gold mine that I found when doing effects was the Mexican supermarkets. In L.A. they're an absolute gold mine if you're looking for authentic gore. They're the only places that carry strings of sausages that look close enough to human intestines. In Montana we used to go to slaughterhouses to get our gore supplies. They would get us leftover parts, but were upset for some reason when we asked if they had any extra eyeballs lying around.

Jose Prendes: Short answer: I don't. I let the special-effects guys do it. Long answer: On *Monster Man* I was the F/X guy and I used ground beef as brains and Alka-Seltzer as disintegrating alien goo. That's why I leave the bloody work to the blood experts.

Paul Scrabo: Most of our film was designed with minimal physical or digital effects in mind, with the exception of the last section:

The Perfect Woman, the science-fiction tale co-written by Brinke Stevens.

Originally, our hero enters a cave and finds a hidden alien craft, where a group of sexy space babes are monitoring the behavior of earth men, hoping to find the perfect man to take back to their planet. Flying saucers and an alien city of beautiful women were also featured in the story. Not having the money or time to present this as any kind of state-of-the-art digital-effects extravaganza, we thought it best to go the old-fashioned way. George Ann Muller created a city out of assorted flower vases turned upside-down, and built an interior of a flying saucer out of Owens-Corning insulation, the natural pink color matching perfectly the motif of the female planet. Co-writer Brinke Stevens changed the opening scene from a cave to a spaceship interior, where Queen Exotica can be "teleported" to earth. We used a leftover Fourth of July sparkler for that effect. And here's what I never expected. The Syracuse B-Movie Film Festival nominated the film for "Best Digital Effects"!

Digital-effects technology can also be used to correct mistakes that, years ago, you may have been stuck with. Two scenes in our film revealed a boom mike, and it was relatively easy to paint it out.

Eric Shapiro: Never heard of 'em! (laughs). As of yet, I haven't had the opportunity. I'm generally interested in behavior and psychology, and don't necessarily foresee doing an effects-driven film, but never say never.

Anthony Straeger: Realistically — I don't — not my bag! There are a number of departments to do that, from a make-up special effect — e.g., vampire teeth, lenses blood etc, action effects (like a hanging or car crash or a Visual Special effect or CGI Effect), all need a specialist.

For standard make-up effects you have to get luck to get someone like we had on *Call of the Hunter* Sally Alcott made less than $1,000 dollars go a long way in blood, guts and gore.

From the action side, Martin Shenton produced a hanging, which was very important

in the film. But, for the sake of a few moments in the film, it took a great deal of preparation time. Being hung from an actor's point of view is a very scary business ... you could die. So you require someone who understands all the health and safety issues and has all the necessary equipment to keep an actor as comfortable and safe as is possible.

If you are looking for visual effects, you have three options for people you might employ: Someone new who might like your project and is in the process of learning *Nuke* (A video effects program) or something like that and will do it for free [for the love of it]. Someone who will do it relatively cheaply as they are not a novice and realize how long it takes to work on any project. Someone who is at the top of their craft and will deliver, but for this you have to pay. We had some green-screen work on call of the Hunter along with a decapitation, and Nick Tregenza of TrigFX did a really good job at producing exactly what we needed.

The special effects in a film can also be a big eater of cash, so you have to be inventive with little money and work out a clever way around any problem.

Marc Trottier: I didn't have special effects in my films in the beginning, only because I didn't have any resources to do so. But then I taught myself how to use Adobe After Effects, and now I can pretty much do anything I want. There are a lot of great tutorials on the net that teach you how to do everything your heart desires. One amazing site for learning and for purchasing great products and plug-ins is: www.VideoCopilot.net. (I have no affiliation with this website.)

I combined a few different tutorials that you can find on that site, and I created a short film called *Urban Saber*, which you can see on YouTube.

Mike Watt: This is one area in which we've always been incredibly lucky. When we first formed Happy Cloud Pictures, partner Bill Homan had graduated from the Art Institute with a degree in special practical effects. He hand-picked and trained make-up assistants for our numerous zombie make-ups and gags and created a very efficient team. I was also fortunate to meet another AIT student, Don Bumgarner, who became an indispensable unit of the family over the years.

Our main fortune came from the opening of the Douglas School of Education and the Tom Savini School of Make-Up and Special Effects. The head of this department is Jerry Gergley (*Buffy the Vampire Slayer*, *Babylon 5*) and happened to be one of Don's and Bill's instructors at the Art Institute. With this relationship already established, along with getting to know other instructors, particularly Eric Molinaris, we have managed to employ hand-picked students for all of our make-up and special-effects needs, usually in exchange for credit, food and gas money. When Eric served as our lead, he used the shoots as teaching opportunities as well. Many "kids" whose first set experience came on one of our movies have gone on to work with KNB, Stan Winston, Optic Nerve and Precinct 13.

The nice thing about the indie horror industry is that relationships beget relationships. Through Jerry and Tom Savini, Pittsburgh's hometown gore god, we met Greg Nicotero, Robert Kurtzman, Al Tuskes and Gino Crognale, all of whom have been there for us on numerous occasions with advice, techniques and tricks. Gino and Jerry both lent assistance on *Razor Days*, charging us far, far less than their talents were actually worth. And, again, the "don't be a Jerk" rule always works in your favor.

The best thing about working with pros and students of pros is that they have terrific "bedside manners." I've never worked with an effects artist who didn't talk the subject through the processes being applied to them. When Bill made a face cast of me, and when Jerry created Amy's, they kept up a stream of reassuring (and usually hilarious) chatter to subvert any claustrophobic or other concerns we'd have while having our faces encased in alginate.

Above all, effects guys know how to improvise. They understand low budgets and they also understand time and space constraints. Don has applied make-up on actors while we recorded voice-over dialogue, and there wasn't a noise on the track. When gags fail for whatever reason (and it happens on every set, regardless of the artist's experience) there are always two or three backup plans on hand.

When choosing an artist, ask to see samples of their work. They usually have a portfolio on hand or, nowadays, on their phones. Get to know them through a face-to-face meeting, talk to other people they've worked with. Some guys who seem like awesome guys may have different set personas, or vice versa. If you like their work and they seem to "get" the project, trust them to do their jobs. If they're pros at heart (again, regardless of experience) they'll be at the ready with anything, for touch-ups, "last looks," et cetera.

Ritch Yarber: I have a pretty good background in special effects and make-up. When I was younger, I wanted to be the next Tom Savini, my idol. I took courses in college at Cleveland State University, acted and did make-up as part of The Legion of Terror, a noted local haunted house organization and experimented with techniques discovered in books that I collected. I have established myself as a person with know-how. However, I have come to understand that I really do not want to be a professional effects person. I only did it to take part in the rest of the acting and filmmaking that I enjoy. I do special effects on my films if I have to, otherwise I hand those jobs off to people that come to us and express interest in pursuing this discipline as a professional and that are seeking experience. Currently, our special effects are supervised by Ernie Smith, a local filmmaker and talented effects artist. Our CGI work is handled by Andy Tubbesing, a great artist that we hooked up with at one of our open-to-the-public meetings we advertised on a local bulletin board.

Ivan Zuccon: I lean on high-level professionals: this is obviously a cost in terms of time and money, but that's how it works if you want to do a good job.

Music

Music is important — if your film needs music. However, it's probably one of the last things you'll deal with in terms of production when you are making an ultra-low budget production.

A few years ago I had a "producer," the son of a famous Hollywood actress, ask me advice on how to make a low-budget independent movie. He confided in me that the first thing he did was pay someone $5,000 upfront for music. He didn't even have the actors cast or a frame of the film shot. Then he complained how he didn't have as large a budget for his actors. When I asked him, "Why did you get your music already?," he was surprised and sputtered, "You have to have music!" Throughout the years I've repeatedly heard filmmakers say, "I already have the soundtrack," before they even wrote the script for the movie. How is this a good plan?

With all of my genre films music was thought of after the fact. I figured I'd find music that "fit" after I made the movie. It was a budgetary and time consideration. Plus, there was nothing in the content of the films that needed to have exact music cues. Of course there was instrumental music for when characters were talking, but also I could use entire songs if it was a montage scene it was going over. My first two vampire films had original scores, while others, like *Twisted Tales* and *Rage of the Werewolf,* used already-existing tunes. I put an advertisement out for music and received hundreds of responses. I did not need to own the music — I just needed their permission to use their original music in my movie(s). More often than not they did not

ask for payment — they used the publicity of the movie to sell their own CDs, which worked out for them.

However, when I switched over and did documentaries, I needed music for the specific tone of each project. The purpose of the music was to create a "feel," whether to signify sorrow or happiness. In many of these cases, I finished the documentary, sent it to the musician, and they had a few months to compose the tracks I needed for certain sections. I gave them specific "examples" of the type of music I needed and they emulated that.

One band I've consistently used the past decade is Seasons of the Wolf. Their songs are in *The Alien Conspiracy* movies and my most recent documentary, *The Life of Death* (2011). It's an example where the visuals and audio fit quite well, though both were done independently of each other. Below, writer/composer/guitarist Barry D. Waddell (a.k.a. "Skully") answers a few questions about his involvement in the world of low-budget, independent productions.

Interview with Barry D. Waddell

What is your background as a musician?

First off to give away my age — hahaha!— I started practicing guitar when I was 12 years old and had my first band together playing originals at age 14 in 1974.

I never really got into playing cover material. I only listened to it and practiced along with it to learn all those cool riffs. I played bars with one cover band called The Dirt Bags from '79 to '82. And even then we would throw in several originals I wrote. I was in several different bands until age 24. I learned to play drums and bass just so I could be in bands that needed those positions filled. This was good training for my future role as a music producer. I ended up being lead singer and songwriter in a progressive hard rock band, Equinox, from 1984 to 1988. That is where I got the nickname "Skully." Once that band fell apart the engineer/keyboard player Dennis Ristow and I started Seasons of the Wolf. At first just the two of us composed original instrumental music inspired from soundtrack music. Established artists such as Tangerine Dream, were a big influence on us as, was the soundtrack music from horror and sci-fi filmmakers such as Carpenter, Romero, Argento, King and so many others. Still, having a full heavy metal band together and putting out albums is what we really wanted — and so SOTW was formed. My younger brother, Wesley Waddell, just out of high school, joined as singer and lyricist. Together we wrote hundreds of songs. We found a small local studio (Tric Tracks) and started recording the first full-length cassette tape releases from 1989 to 1991. Fully packaged, we released them locally. We set up some live shows with the full SOTW presentation. It was very apparent that SOTW was not an average bar band. After a couple years we found ourselves working with [Allman Brothers Engineer] Bud Snyder co-producing our first international album. We learned a lot from that situation.

In 1995 we built our own recording studio, Level-D-Green, a large rehearsal stage, and formed our own independent label, Earth Mother Music. This allowed us to write, practice, record, produce, design, promote, and have control of everything from start to finish. I set up writer and publishing membership with ASCAP and a studio partnership with Discmakers, of which EMM is now a platinum member. And so this allowed me the leverage to negotiate licensing deals to re-release product on several interested European labels.

With our music being spread out in the underground over several releases we ended up making a lot of friends and, of course, eventually SOTW music coming into contact with and being used by several independent filmmakers. So the music part came around full circle to what Dennis and I originally started. Over the years Dennis and I have recorded and produced several other bands in our studio and we even opened up our rehearsal stage for other bands to rent for practice. And that is the short version of my background in music. The devil is in the details.

What makes you interested in doing music for movies? How different is this from doing music for your band, Seasons of the Wolf?

Well ... because Dennis and I originally compose a lot of soundtrack-sounding music that ends up being intro's or outro sections for SOTW songs, it already fits the mold. There is a difference, sometimes, especially if just instrumental music is what is required for a film. For SOTW it is more about "the song" and the presentation of the song lyrics and how it fits into SOTW conceptually. Of course what ends up happening is a lot of sections of SOTW music and lyrics fit quite naturally into the dark sci-fi ambiance of horror and sci-fi film landscape. As for the interest part — I just love film, especially anything that makes the hair raise on your arm or makes your mind think "what if?"

It is fun creating the background sounds that will add impact to film. Chase scenes, kill scenes, sleeping scenes, lovemaking, party time, getting ready for battle, the actual battle, blowing up things, crash landings and such. Every kind of scene requires a "backing sonic feel" to boost the impact to the audience without them knowing it. In film and TV — sound-beds are almost subliminal.

I had read once that there was no soundtrack in the John Carpenter film *Halloween* when it was first presented to a movie house for major distribution. And they said it was cheesy and not scary at all. They said, "Make whatever changes you need and bring it back." So, John Carpenter came up with the music theme on keyboards — added the soundtrack behind the scenes. He did not change anything about the film. When it was presented the second time they said it was fantastic — it was scary as hell. And the rest is history. Music makes a very big difference in the impact of film. Take the film *Jaws*, for instance. Sometimes it does not require much detail or complicated music. Just the right few simple notes set to the scene can make a person jump right out of their seat. And that is interesting and damn fun.

You've done music used in several independent horror and sci-fi movies. Was this music you had already created or was this music made specifically for the movies?

When we have first contact with filmmakers we send full albums of SOTW music. They use whatever sections of music that suits their needs. Sometimes full songs with vocals were used and sometimes they ask if we can give them just a instrumental version. Sometimes they will use the instrumental version during the main theme of the soundtrack and then, at the end credits, use the full song with vocal track, if it is fitting lyrically. We have also composed and recorded music specifically catered to a film for main theme. In that case we are usually provided with some footage already filmed in pre-production and sometimes a tip sheet where the filmmaker might point out what type of sonic feel they have for a particular scene. For instance, if they want something very eerie or something very bombastic, or slow, fast, simple, complicated, wacky, and such. It is always a good thing if the filmmaker has descriptive ideas to help when we are customizing music for their film.

If an independent filmmaker is looking for music for their low-budget film, how do you recommend they contact musicians?

Well, of course, the best way these days is initial contact through Facebook or email. But definitely a phone call to discuss details and get to know each other once you have the number. It is necessary to make the music artist feel the "contact" to be serious and legitimate. Dealing in the independent low-budget or no-budget world, as we all know, there are a people who do not follow up. Hot smoke blowers we call them. So, definitely if you are "actually" doing a film and you want "actual musicians" that are really doing music, then it is always best to get that contact solidified and the air of interest, trust and admiration going. The payoff can be very good in ways of cross-promotion once the project is fulfilled. We are all mostly doing it for the same reasons, to create entertainment with hopes of making it a career and feel fulfilled at the end of the day.

The Filmmakers were asked:
What about music? Do you usually have someone compose a score or is it music that already exists?

Glenn Andreiev: Up until *Every Move You Make* I used the music created by a friend, Nicholas D. Kent, who has a great ear for film music and applies his unique tastes to a film score. For my Revolutionary War thriller, *Mad Wolf*, he said he was creating "Hitchcock on a Harpsichord." The first 80 percent of *The Deed to Hell* has almost no music score, except incidental music playing on radios and televisions in the background. The final 20 percent, which takes place in Hell, has constant music. These were previously created scores by an excellent group called The Devil Music Ensemble. For *The Make-Believers* I went to a website that offers well-orchestrated, license-free classical music pieces. Each piece is about $35 and it's worth every penny.

John Borowski: Music is the most important element in a film, second to the image. It seems like a bold statement, and I am not saying that sound effects are not important. Music creates the emotion for the characters and sets the mood of the film. I work with film composers because I have been a fan of film music ever since I began listening to and collecting film soundtracks when I was a teenager.

Keith Crocker: In the past, for the 16mm films, I tended to use classical music, mostly material in the public domain. For *Bloody Ape* we featured some public domain music, but the bulk of the score was synth music supplied by a guy named Frank Perri. For *Blitzkrieg*, editor Steve Gocinski dug up tons of interesting public domain music, but the main gist of the score was from K.C. Allen, a friend of mine who's been playing in various underground rock bands since the late '60s. We went with no synth. Instead, he used his guitar, both electrically and acoustic, and accentuated the action on the screen. Plus, he gave me some great mood pieces that really set the scene for some of the most dramatic parts of the film. My dream would be to have a full band or orchestra for my next film, but the budgets just don't allow for such things at this time.

Richard Cunningham: I've taken a few approaches to music in my films. In the first homemade movies I made as practice in my mid-teens, we just blatantly lifted scores from blockbuster movies. But I was in high school and the movies were only showing in the local library, or there was no admission cost. I don't think anyone cared about the copyright issue back then, but I certainly don't recommend it. My first effort into making a completely original film was at 19 with *Lycian*, and the other producers and I decided to hire a professional composer, which constituted more than half the film's budget. For my next film, one of those same producers decided to compose the score, so he conducted a collection of musicians to record the music, cutting the costs of the score down drastically.

With *America the Mental* we used a handful of local bands that contributed some really great music to the soundtrack. That still seems like a good symbiotic approach, if you're looking for good free songs to help drive a film.

I'm also a multi-instrumentalist with passable recording capabilities, so for *Year Zero* I decided I'd try composing the music myself. I used a 2001 Acid Music program, in which I engineered and mixed the audio tracks and rendered them into MP3 or AIFF files, ultimately adding them to the video edit in Final Cut Pro.

Nowadays, built-in programs (like Garage Band) make it easier than ever, with features like drum/instrument loops and effects that make it possible for someone with their own instruments, or band, to produce their own soundtrack for a film.

If this all seems too much, simply Googling "royalty-free music" brings up a vast library of legal songs and scores with which to fill your movie. This works for sound effects as well; there are a number of quality sound effects offered for free online at sites like freesound.org. It all just takes a bit of searching and weeding out the bad examples.

Maurice Devereaux: Yes, I always worked with a music composer. My last three films were composed by Martin Gauthier, who is terrific. Music is so important — choosing what kind and where and when to put it and when not to put it is a very creative process and can greatly affect the quality of the film. The time I spent working with Martin on the scores of *Lady*, *Slashers* and *End* are among my happiest and most fulfilling artistic moments.

Donald Farmer: I've handled music both of these ways. My co-producer on *Demon Queen* was friends with a girl singing in various Nashville hotel lounges and gave me her demo tape. I loved the song "Angel Fire"— especially that it would be free — and used it under the opening credits of *Demon Queen*, and again for a scene in *Cannibal Hookers*. For *Scream Dream* I wanted a title song, so the band hired for our nightclub scenes volunteered to write one. They ended up delivering that and two other original songs we had Melissa Moore lip-sync in the movie. When the songs were written we all went to a budget-priced Nashville recording studio for one night so the band could record finished versions of all three tunes.

For *Deadly Memories* we had a larger-than-usual budget and applied some of it to the film's soundtrack. My executive producer was friends with Gene Sisk, the keyboard player for Kenny Rogers, and asked if he would be game for composing a full movie score. Gene was doing a U.S. tour with Kenny at the time, but said this would give him something to do during downtime on the tour. We gave him a DVD of the movie's rough cut he could play on his laptop while he composed the score and Gene got to work. Before long Kenny Rogers was looking over Gene's shoulder during those long trips on the tour bus. Now *Deadly Memories* has some fairly lurid scenes, constant gore, torture and a screaming nude Tina Krause being spray-painted blue. I was wondering how the straight-laced Rogers might react to all this. Apparently pretty well, according to Gene. He reported, "Kenny says to tell ya'll he likes your movie!"

Jeff Forsyth: I like original compositions. I always seek out a composer.

Richard W. Haines: I always hired aspiring composers for my movies and I've lucked out in that I've found some talented people that created very innovative tracks that enhanced the narratives. Among them were Andrew Nixon, Seth Wright, Gary Shreiner and Richard Fiocca.

After I finish editing I put in temp tracks from other movies to indicate the type of music I want. Then, the composer creates their own unique score using the temp tracks as a general reference.

William Hopkins: To avoid any rights complications, I only use music in my films that is specifically created for them. With *Sleepless Nights* we hired a couple of very talented composers to create music for the film. They supplied me with extended cues, chunks of music that I could cut up and drop in wherever I felt it was needed. The resulting score has a reasonably lush, romantic sound that works well for the kind of gothic melodrama *Sleepless Nights* is.

On *Demon Resurrection*, I felt a more minimalist approach was called for and I had a hard time finding someone who could give me what I wanted. I didn't want the small indie film we were creating to be crushed under a heavy, symphonic score. It wasn't a film that needed the Hollywood sound. What I wanted was a score comprised of ambient sounds more than composed music. I wanted the music to blend in with the natural sounds of the environment we were shooting in. After several failed attempts with different composers and after a fair amount of money had been spent, I decided to give it a try myself. I recorded several hours of stuff and then took the best bits and cut it together to make the final score. I doubt anyone will walk away from *Demon Resurrection* humming the music, but I think it's reasonably effective and more in keeping with the mood and the style I was going for.

Steve Hudgins: We've gone both routes with this. There's a lot of royalty-free music available out there and there's also a lot of musicians looking for any kind of exposure they can get that may be willing to record some original music for you, often just for a credit in the film.

Rolfe Kanefsky: With all of my films up to last year, I've always had original scores written. I love music and think it is one of the most important aspects to any movie. That said, I think *Dog Day Afternoon*, *The Birds* and *The China Syndrome* work wonderfully without any score. However, I love Jerry Goldsmith and you just can't beat a full orchestra. I've never had enough money to hire a composer with an orchestra, but I have worked with a great composer. From 1996 through the present almost all of my films have been scored by Christopher Farrell, who has done amazing things while working with very little budgets. The great thing about Chris is that I've worked in many different genres, from comedies to thrillers to horror to erotica, and have needed scores and songs in just about every variety of music there is. Chris has come through every single time. I met Chris through a filmmaker friend of mine, Jay Woelfel, who is also a composer. In fact, he brought Chris in to help with a score he was doing for me. It was a parody of James Bond called *Rod Steele 0014: You Only Live Until You Die*. Jay wrote the theme song and he and Chris collaborated on the musical score, nailing that John Barry feel brilliantly. It's funny, effective and done straight enough to actually sound like a real Bond score. After that Chris has done every one of my films except for *Corpses* because York had their own composer and wouldn't let me hire Chris. But, from *Rod Steele*, Chris and Jay did *Misadventures of an Invisible Man*, *Alien Files* and *Tomorrow by Midnight*. Then Jay got busy with his own directing career and Chris continued working with me on *The Hazing*, *Jacqueline Hyde*, *Pretty Cool 1 & 2*, *Nightmare Man*, *1 in the Gun* and the list goes on.

My latest film is a full-out musical called *Emmanuelle in Wonderland*. The problem was that we had NO money for music, let alone a full score and 12 all-singing, all-dancing musical numbers. But I was determined to do a musical. I've always loved them and with the success of *Glee* there was no better time. So I called a composer friend of mine, Ron Zwang, who has done many songs for me in the past. I asked, "What songs do you have prerecorded that I could use for free? I was sent around 24 songs that Ron and Ron's music partner, Rick Novak, had created. I then picked out my 12 favorite songs and wrote the script around the music so it would come out organically from

the characters. It was a tricky task that turned out wonderfully (pun intended). However, the score had to be composed by using a friends' stock music library. Luckily, it was an amazing library, and I knew exactly what I needed and how to use it. I've had to do this multiple times this past year because the producer decided it was cheaper to buy a library of music than hire someone to write original scores. So this is the first time I've taken stock music and reinvented it for my movies. I know this happens a lot and if you have a good ear and really know how to use it, it can work very well.

My preference is always to have a new score written for the film. It gives the movie a voice that is all-important. John Carpenter is famous for saying that *Halloween* was not effective at all until he wrote the score. It makes the movie. The same could be said for thousands of films. Every film should have its own feel and every musical score should reflect that. I have said it before but if you want to temp your "suspense/horror movie" with a great piece of music, use Track 5 from Jerry Goldsmith's *Psycho II*. It always, always works, and watch how it elevates your film in the process.

Brett Kelly: I usually find a composer who is interested in working on an indie or low-budget movie. There are many of them. I have a ton of them contact me out of the blue all the time. If the musician is registered with a publishing company (like ASCAP), they get paid if and when your movie appears on TV. It's a gamble, as many movies don't make it to TV, but if they do, it's a paycheck for a registered composer. They may take the chance. I have also used stock music from various websites. It's a great way to score a film for next to nothing.

Chris LaMartina: Using the *auteur* motif, I really enjoy scoring my own films. I've scored four out of my five features. Since I play guitar/bass/drums/keys, I find it very liberating to write to my own sensibilities as both an editor and as a screenwriter. The score is always okayed with my co-producer, Jimmy

George, but we've had only a few disagreements about music.

In addition, we use some local bands for other soundtrack bits. Sometimes I'll produce a music video in exchange for a song use, but most bands are just excited to be included in the production of a horror flick and don't require the extra effort.

Jim Mickle: I've had a composer for each film and both experiences were great. I find it can be initially hard to make the transition to working on music, because everything up to then has been creative but concrete and mostly focusing on visual language. Music has its own language and abstract thought process, so working with a composer is about finding that language and a shorthand for expressing thoughts about the music.

I tend to use temp music when I cut. There are a lot of pros and cons to temp music, and it's very easy to get married to temp music when you're watching rough cuts all day. Ultimately I find it very helpful for finding the right tone for the music and it's a good chance to try and fail and get a feel for what works. Some composers don't mind this, but some would rather start with a blank slate and not be influenced by anything.

I've also used pre-existing source music in both films, but in the first one I overdid it and clung to many songs that added up in license fees. Not the best idea for low-budget filmmaking, but I had built a lot of scenes around specific cues. In *Stake Land*, because it was in a way Depression-era film, we tried to use old public domain songs and keep the licensed cues to a few very specific moments.

Damon Packard: Again, budgetary constraints. Unless I had a $50 million budget I probably would not be able to find or afford a composer good enough to satisfy my tastes. Unless I got darn lucky, it would be a tough and frustrating search.

Brad Paulson: Usually we'll have someone do a score and then pick up some other music to throw in there as well. I love good scores. Just look at the those old Carpenter movies and how great the scores are. There are a couple of great people we've worked with that have done our music: Seasons of the Wolf and Tony Longworth, for example. Seasons did an incredible score for us on *The Bloodstained Bride*. Longworth has been a great friend and my go-to guy for music for a soundtrack. He's exceeded every expectation I've had. Another guy, Russel Holsapple, who did the music and vocals on the song parodies for *Reservoir Drunks*, did an amazing job for us as well. These artists are all incredibly talented. If you find good ones like the above mentioned, let them know how much you appreciate them and take care of them however you can. Good, loyal artists that are a joy to collaborate with are very difficult to find and are extremely valuable.

Jose Prendes: Music is so important to a film. It is the movie's heartbeat and you have to make sure you get it right. I had my pal Eddie Castineira compose some guitar riffs for *Monster Man* and I did the composing on my little Casio keyboard for *Corpses are Forever*. But I think for the next one I want a seasoned pro to take a crack at it. My dream would be to have John Carpenter compose one of my films, because I'm not only a fan of his films, but of his soundtracks, which are phenomenal and memorable. I use music that exists if it fits, but things are different for every movie and every tone.

Paul Scrabo: There are several original tracks composed for *Dr. Horror*, but the mini-movies contained within the film were an ideal container for stock music.

Eric Shapiro: My dear friend Bilvox, who's a very talented musician, did the original scores for *Mail Order* and *Rule of Three*. In both cases, he brought a legitimate metabolism to the movie that defined its essence, weight, and character. I would like to go Scorsese-style at some point and use pop songs, since I think that technique cuts really deep into the viewer's mind, but right now it's way too expensive. Learning how to develop a score with Bilvox has been invaluable; I've had to generate a whole new language, asking for adjustments and explaining what I want.

Anthony Straeger: For me it's a combination of both original score and music already in existence.

I think it's important to have an original score to underpin the whole film; it's like an audible grading, as you would do with the final look of the film. There are so many really great composers out there, either fresh from college or already established. They all tend to have solid websites so you can go through the type of work they do and the way they work. Since setting up Quid in Shrapnel Productions, I have been inundated by musicians looking for opportunities.

Dan S. Elliott did the score for *Call of the Hunter*. He really listened to the thoughts I had on music and asked for examples and made instrument suggestions in order to get the texture of the music right. He maintained some really interesting and clever themes and I was totally delighted with the speed and way he worked with me. So the importance of having the score was underlined in the fact that (I believe) the original score works in total sync with the pictures — marvelous.

I found the music for the soundtrack by looking for artists and bands that fit with my personality and the personality of the movie. I'm a big music fan, but not a lover of chart music. I hunt down new and exciting bands and artists not only for personal pleasure, but also with a view to using their songs and material in any of my projects. I found a wonderful selection of artists/bands from around the world who excel in their type of music and was pleased to say that only one artist actually didn't want to include their music in *Call of the Hunter*.

One of my hopes is that viewers of the movie will take the time to also look at the music section of our website and check out the music we have used and enjoy these artists for not only what they have contributed to the movie, but [to hear] more of their material. Most of the bands are unsigned or with small independent labels. There really is some great music out there.

Marc Trottier: Up until *Darkness Waits*, my buddies Sacha and Youri Pommepuy helped me create all the music for our projects. They're great at coming up with fun original stuff, and we work so well together that it's almost like we speak a different language all our own. You can see a bunch of behind-the-scenes stuff for *Darkness Waits* on YouTube, including the Pommepuy brothers and myself in action.

Since I discovered www.VideoCopilot.net, I picked up Designer Sound FX (which has royalty free sound effects & audio elements), and Pro Scores (which has orchestral music tracks and epic musical elements), which I use for all my current projects.

Mike Watt: Again, fortunately, I grew up around artistic people, so finding musicians was rarely a problem. For our first film, I discovered that I worked with Paul McCollough, who scored Tom Savini's *Night of the Living Dead* remake and retained the rights to his score. He offered a number of pieces from that film, both used and unused, for *The Resurrection Game*. When it came time to finalize the film — ten years later — Paul's electronic score was rounded out by contributions from pianist Mike Shiley (who we'd gotten to know through the convention circuits) and legendary Scooter McCrae (director of *Shatter Dead*), who experiments with different sounds and harmonies to suit [a given] mood. While we picked and chose finished songs from Paul and Mike, Scooter filled in the gaps and composed directly to the picture, which made it easier for him to find the "voices" for each scene.

We have friends in bands that have contributed music as well. Jim Steinhoff and Hotel 9 scored *Severe Injuries* with hard '80s guitar riffs, which suited that film. World-renowned composer Mars of Deadhouse Music offered to score *Demon Divas* for a very reasonable price. This was the first time I'd ever had to finish a picture lock for a composer, as I'd been previously used to cutting to music, but Mars somehow read my mind and found equivalents to my temp music tracks, though I hadn't provided them.

Again: network! It's easier than ever now, with Facebook, YouTube, conventions, clubs, to find anyone and anything you need. I've found that most artists — regardless of medium — want to feel like working artists, so make sure you set aside something for their hard work. Shamefully, I've gotten entire scores for a mere $50. Most artists will work with your budget. You can always start a Kickstarter campaign to raise a hundred or two for your starving artists and their services.

Ritch Yarber: We have mostly used music by local bands. It is great for both of us since we get it for free and they get the visibility and publicity of being in a movie. We always try and promote the bands that help us out by being sure to mention them whenever we can in connection with the film. I usually always also include music from one of my favorite local bands, *The Lowlies.* I work with one of the members of the band and he always writes special tunes for me to use as I request. We

have found it increasingly harder to find just the right music to create atmosphere in scenes, thus, we are committed to using composers to customize the music for our next projects. Another step forward for us as we continue to improve our efforts and increase our quality. We have found that there are just as many great composers as there are actors and crew that are looking for showcase opportunities. Several award-winning composers from the 2011 Indie Gathering International Film Festival have expressed interest in working on our projects after meeting us and finding out how our films are made and what our goals are. We are extremely excited about the prospect of adding this new tool to our arsenal.

Ivan Zuccon: It depends on the project. I've been working both with composers and using pre-existing music. I personally prefer the second choice, as long as it's excellent-quality music. This allows me to put the music in the movie while I'm editing it, without having to wait for the composer to write it and synchronizing it while he's watching the movie. It's a question of time optimization — this way is faster and you save money.

How Long Does It Take to Make a Movie?

Some features I have worked on have taken as little as four months to shoot and edit while others took nearly a full year to complete. It always depended upon whatever else was going on in my life during that time that would interrupt the filmmaking process. For example, right after I shot my first film, *Vampires & Other Stereotypes*, I shot and edited the anthology *Twisted Tales*, primarily because I needed a break from that particular film. Then, I went back, with more enthusiasm, and completed that first movie. Generally, the shooting would be done within a month and the post-production would take four or five times that long, as it's simply a much more time-consuming process. This is especially true if you are doing everything by yourself. Add to that doing post-production visual effects, or waiting for a film score, and time flies by.

The documentaries I directed/produced, however, took much longer than the genre movies. At the quickest, it was nine months' time. At the longest, the most recent one, *The Life of Death*, took two and a half years. This was primarily because the first one was intended for PBS — and I had to complete it first before I could even approach underwriters for funding. With the latter, it was much more of a personal project and I was in no rush. Half of it was shot in Michigan, the other half in New York City. I went to New York City twice a year for other video production work (I edited the New York Fashion Week shows!) and just piggybacked my production on this, to save on expenses.

Yet, however long it takes you to complete your film make sure that you're able to maintain your excitement and keep the momentum so that you don't get weary of your project before it's done.

The Filmmakers were Asked:
On average, how long does it take you to make a film? Talk about your first film and also about one of your more recent ones.

Glenn Andreiev: *Vampire's Embrace* took a few years. I only had the money to shoot, and edit a 16mm work-print in 1988. Other producers came in at that point and really gave it polish, but it took them nearly four years to finish it, in between their paying gigs. I wrote *The Deed to Hell* in the summer of 2007 and showed in April 2008.

John Borowski: On average it takes me about three to four years to make one of my documentary films. If I had a proper budget I am certain I could complete them in a year.

150

Sometimes taking years pays off, as during the process of making the film I am usually contacted by people interested in assisting in the making of the film. I have been contacted by descendants of the serial killers H.H. Holmes, Albert Fish, and Carl Panzram, who are usually interested in the film and fascinated to learn their family history. My first film, *H.H. Holmes*, took three years to create a final cut and about another year to complete the post-production and DVD authoring. I self-released *H.H. Holmes* on DVD before I chose Facets Video as the North American DVD distributor. My third film, *Carl Panzram*, took about five years to create as the scope was massive: *Panzram* was in numerous jails and prisons as well as traveling around the world.

Keith Crocker: Because of the fact that I'm a working-class filmmaker, which means that you balance your film work with making enough money to cover your life expenses, you split your time between working and making the film. The cast and crew are usually in the same position. This tends to force us to shoot on weeknights and weekends. The first feature I made, *Bloody Ape*, was shot in a year and three months. Because my films tend to be epic in their scope, the time frame doesn't really do much damage to continuity. It does much more damage to filmmakers' nerves to carry on this way. I promised with *Blitzkrieg* the shooting time would be shorter, but guess what? It wasn't. *Blitzkrieg* ended up taking one year and a half to make, and one of the reasons was that we lost a month of shooting due to a personal emergency with the film's main star. That, and the fact that I had to fire an actress and bring Keith Matturro in to do re-writes and fill in now-discarded material just made that film drag on. But, again, the story is told in flashback and takes place within a several-year period, that really helped knock out major continuity issues. I keep promising myself that the next film will be shot in a month. If budgets remain the same that will be a miracle.

Richard Cunningham: Usually longer than I assume it will in the beginning.

I was finalizing the script to *Lycian* in 1999, and IMDb is telling me that film wasn't released until 2004, which sounds about right. The scale of the movie and the way that we funded it out-of-pocket made for a long production period. I also moved out to California in the middle of production — quickly learning that you shouldn't transplant yourself to California unless you have either a well-thought-out plan or a solid prospect for a job.

Arcadium and *ShE* each took about year. Because of the shooting style of *America the Mental* we shot it relatively quickly (three months). Editing took about seven months, because of computer setbacks. But still, churning out a movie within a year felt good to do.

It was over two years with *Year Zero*. I started photographing test shots in October of 2008 and, aside from some later revisions before its world premiere, I had the 24-minute animated film completed in the winter of 2010. That film came with some notable challenges, the most daunting of which was teaching myself how to illustrate and animate digitally. In fact, I considered the project overall an experiment, because I didn't have much experience with that end of production at all, and with it I was suddenly forced to confront the entire process. In the past, I had mostly acted as a writer/producer/actor until *America the Mental*, when I first took up a camera, and then assisted with some of the editing — but I never learned Final Cut myself. So I had to mature as an artist quickly, as well as learn how to manipulate a bunch of computer programs and formats.

That learning by trial and error development really contributed to the animation style and unique look of the film, but I was forced to go back to the beginning several times over to revise the sequences, because my skill with these tools were still progressing as I was making the film. I was also working on a computer that was prone to crashing (teaching me effectively to routinely save my project).

It took me about a year to photograph all the actors and props used in the film, though that was interrupted for several months when I took work as a stand-in on a television show called *Royal Pains*, during its first season. Though the rigorous schedule slowed production of *Year Zero* to whatever free time I had during the weekends, it also afforded me a new set-up: a Mac Mini and a good-sized screen for taking on animating and editing. I spent the next seven months animating, consistently working on it anywhere from 12 to 18 hours a day. This concentrated effort, I think, actually helped with the storytelling, because there was a strong theme of isolation driving *Year Zero*, and sitting in front of the computer each day, waiting hours and hours for a three-second animated sequence to render, I was able to tap into that disconnect from the outside world somewhat.

The real cost of going cheap comes in either quality or time—I realized at the end of that production.

Maurice Devereaux: If were talking number of shooting days, *Blood Symbol* was about 60 days, spread over six years to complete. We started by shooting weekends, when we had money for film. Then, at one point, we did four weeks full time and ran out of money again. Then I started editing what I had, all the while trying to find money to finish the shoot and the film. Of course, the actors changed in appearance throughout the movie. Since we were shooting in Super 8mm, we had many technical difficulties. Once we had shot for two days, then two weeks later we were eagerly awaiting to see our rushes (yes, it took that long for Super 8), but when we watched the reel, instead of images of my shoot, it was images of Timmy's sixth birthday party. So we go back to the lab to tell them about the mix-up, and they say, "Here's a new cartridge." I say, "No, I want to get MY reel back." They said, "Sorry, nothing I can do." Since the lab handled Super 8 reels from across Canada it was too complicated for them to try and find my reel, so Timmy I still have your sixth birthday film in a box somewhere in my closet and someone somewhere in Canada got

this strange reel of low-budget Super 8 horror rushes!"

Lady of the Lake took 30 days to shoot, but the shoot was split 15 days in 1993, then I ran out of money. Five years later I did another 15 days and finished the film. Not recommended.

Slashers was shot in 25 days and the whole production from casting to end of post-production was done in an insanely quick four months! It's a complicated story. I had sold the rights to my script to a producer, who then pre-sold the rights to a distribution company. Then the producer went bankrupt, and a completion bond company came to me and said I had to deliver the complete film in one month to the distributor to honor the original contract. But no actor was cast yet, no pre-production work was done, nothing. I said, "Are you guys insane?" and they said, "Either you do it in one month or we'll replace you as director, as we need to deliver this film." I refused and they tried to find someone else, but couldn't. So they then backed down and offered me a four-month [extension]. As I did not want to lose the chance to do my film, I accepted. They were supposed to give me a $250,000 budget to do the entire film, but, of course, two weeks into the shoot the completion bond company went bankrupt as well, and I ended up putting back all my salary as producer, editor, director and writer of the film back into the production. I also put in another $25,000 of my own money to finish the film. Needless to say, I never made a dime on the film, as it was caught in a legal mess. It's a miracle it was even released, as the rights are all over the place.

End of the Line took 21 days to shoot and 18 months from pre-production to finished film.

Donald Farmer: Well, *Demon Queen* was a five-day shoot. Three days with the Tennessee crew shooting in Miami and Ft. Lauderdale, one day in Nashville for the video store scenes and, finally, one in Miami shooting additional bits and pieces on half-inch VHS. But several of my movies have been shot on very loose schedules, usually getting together on weekends over a period of months. *Cannibal Hookers* was shot over probably a four to five month period this way, but probably no more than 20 shooting days all together. *Dorm of the Dead* is another project shot over a period of several months. I flew to Los Angeles to do all the scenes with Tiffany Shepis in about three days, but the Nashville shooting with the rest of the cast dragged on for several weekends.

Whenever possible, it's obviously better to shoot everything in a concentrated period, like the tight two-week shoots for *Compelling Evidence*, *Vicious Kiss* and *Demolition*. Two weeks really is pushing it when you're shooting a script with lots of locations and scenes like those movies had — I ended up having to really rush some scenes to get everything in. *Deadly Run* had a nicer four-week shoot, without the pressure of doing so many setups in one day. And *No Justice* was six weeks [in production], but it had the added complication of a 30-person crew. And it seems the larger the crew, the slower everything moves! That's why I like to use the smallest crew possible, like we had on *Deadly Run* and *The Strike*. Probably never more than five crew members on those movies, but they were shot on film and we moved very quickly.

The longest schedule I ever had for a film shoot was 14 weeks for the back-to-back Civil War movies *Blood and Honor* and *Battle for Glory*. But that was a special circumstance where we had an elderly producer who couldn't handle more than seven or eight hours on set a day. And since he wanted to be on set ALL the time, we had ridiculously short shooting days, and those movies took forever to finish. But we were all getting paid weekly salaries, regardless of how much we accomplished, so knocking off after eight hours was a treat after some of the 20-hour days I've done on other movies.

The first time I used High Def was on *An Erotic Vampire in Paris*, and my two-person French crew whizzed through shots as quickly as I could give directions. Doing everything handheld on that picture made it go even faster still — we shot the full script in three days, with one more day in New Jersey for second-unit interiors. With film you're slowed down by checking the focus, checking the gate, reloading the camera, et cetera, but there's none of that with High Def.

Jeff Forsyth: The first one took about three years, and that was two years longer than I wanted it to be. Since I have started a family, that number has more than doubled.

Richard W. Haines: Most movies take about three to five years, from writing the script to the actual release date. All of my shoots are about a month long, although in every movie I ended up going back into production to do pickups and additional scenes. My shortest shoot was *Splatter University*, which took two weeks, although we did additional filming a year later to expand the running time, which was too short.

My later productions were a lot smoother than my first one. The trick in filmmaking is trouble shooting. No matter how carefully you plan a production, many things go wrong. It rains on the day of your exteriors, you run out of time on set, an actor gets sick and has to be rescheduled or you lose a location, which are things beyond your control. During my first movie I wasn't prepared for these circumstances, which made it very difficult. For example, we were given permission to shoot for two weeks at Mercy College, in New York. At the last minute they limited us to one week, so we had to work around the clock to get it done. My F/X artists, Amodio Giordano and Ralph Cordero, slept on sleeping bags in the classroom so they didn't have to return home and lose preparation time. We were so late in finishing our crew was still mopping stage blood and guts from the floor while students arrived for their classes.

Over the years I've learned to compensate for these problems and have emergency rain-date locations lined up. I try to finish the wide shots with extras first and save the close-ups for last since they can be faked in another location by painting a stage flat to replicate the wall color of the original location. Close-up lenses have a shallow depth of field. Only the person's face is in focus and the background is blurry. That makes it easier to simulate the background. I've done this on several films.

William Hopkins: Both of my films took a fair amount of time to complete. Because of budget problems on *Sleepless Nights* the production had to shut down for several months while additional funding was found. Then we continued to shoot a few days a month for the next year or so. It was a terrible way to do things and the film suffered as a result, but we got it done and learned some valuable lessons.

On *Demon Resurrection* the entire shoot was completed in the scheduled time of 21 days. But because I was handling all the post-production work, and there was a huge amount of work to be done, we didn't end up with a finished film till over a year later. Farming out the work to others really wasn't an option, since we had no money to pay anyone. On my next film I'm going to try to avoid being so ambitious with the effects work so I'll be able to complete the film faster. I think all the work and time put into *Demon Resurrection* made it a better film, but I'd rather not have my next film take so long to complete. It's hard to keep everyone's enthusiasm level up when a production drags on for years.

Steve Hudgins: Writing a script and re-writing it and revising it to the point where it's ready to be shot usually takes three to six months. Of course, a lot of the re-writes and revisions can be taking place while other pre-production duties are being done. Once we start shooting, we do most of our shooting on weekends and normally take six to eight weeks to wrap shooting. Post-production normally takes six months or so.

Our first movie, which I look at as a training film, took six months to shoot as things were not as organized as they needed to be. But you live and you learn and we run a much more oiled and smooth machine now.

Rolfe Kanefsky: Well, the average from the coming up with an idea, writing a script and then getting that script produced can take anywhere from a month to a lifetime. I've written so many scripts, I know many of them will never be made, which is a shame because some of them are very good.

In terms of a movie getting made once the money is in place, I'd say usually a month or two of prep. I've been working on an average of 15 days for production and then about three to four months of post. Selling is a whole other story. That can take years. But from start of pre-production to a final "answer print," let's say — in my case — five to six months total.

My first professional film, *There's Nothing Out There*, was written when I was almost 18 years old and still in high school. When I was 19, in college, my parents decided to try to help me produce the movie. We spent a good six months trying to raise the money from various sources. Finally, my mother, who was in the jewelry business, knew another woman whose husband was in the construction business and had some friends with money. They came on board and invested between $20,000–30,000 into the film. That was all the money we could raise. But my father had made a promise to himself years ago that if he ever got any money to produce a movie, he would not give it back. So, my parents made a major sacrifice and mortgaged their home! This is the advantage of having supportive parents and being an only child. They put up the rest of the financing and we went into prep in the summer of 1989. We cast in New York City with a casting director named Bill Williams and found all of our actors through him, except for the lead who plays Mike, the horror buff who has seen every horror film on video and knows the rules of how to survive a horror movie. He was played by my high school buddy Craig Peck. We had a nice three weeks of rehearsal and then shot the movie in August. It was a 24-day shoot and, to this day, it is still the longest production schedule I've ever had. The shooting was finished in early September just before college started up again. Craig had to get back to USC, but I was able to take off the fall semester to finish working on the film.

There's Nothing Out There was shot on Super 16 and actually edited on a Steenbeck, the old film editing system. Now, it's pretty much obsolete. My father had been an editor for 30-something years and owned a post-production company, Valkhn Film and Video, based on Broadway in New York. Again, this was very helpful, for we knew once the film was shot it would be finished professionally. The problem was that because there was so little money, a lot of people worked deferred and gave favors. So, some of our optical effects took a long time to get completed because they had to work around other paying jobs. The film was completed in 1990 and screened for the first time about a year after production had ended. But that was also the time that the entire horror genre collapsed. Horror wasn't selling and I went on the big roller-coaster ride of trying to sell the movie. At that time, the film festivals were very different than they are today. You could actually submit a low-budget horror/comedy and get into festivals without knowing anyone. We premiered the film at the IFP (Independent Film Project) in New York City and it exploded, becoming the most talked-about film of the festival. This got us a lawyer and film rep. We had some important screenings, but the studios didn't understand the movie. It was a horror film and a comedy that talked about horror films. "Too funny to be scary and too scary to be funny" was the response.

However, every time we played the film, the critics loved it and the audiences went crazy. At that point I knew that if someone made a film like this with a decent budget and some name actors, it would make a fortune. My theory was proven correct in 1996 with the release of Wes Craven's *Scream*. But that's also another story.

Anyway, we did wind up getting the film released for a week in January 1992 in New York City and then midnight showings in Los Angeles. This was accomplished by four-walling the film. We actually paid and partnered with the theaters to play the movie, spending our own money on prints and advertising. We didn't make money, but the positive reviews and good word-of-mouth led to a sale. We sold the picture to Prism Entertainment (no longer in business) and they released it on video and laser disc (through Image Entertainment) in the winter of 1992. We also made a cable sale and the film played on HBO/Cinemax the following year. So, the first draft was written in 1987, film was shoot in 1989 and sold and distributed in 1992. In short, it took four to six years depending on how you do the math.

My parents said they would never produce a film again ... but 15 years later we did. In 2005, I made *Nightmare Man*, which had a 15-day production schedule, a similar budget, and the film went through a similar experience. This time the film was edited on the Avid and we didn't have to make film prints ... at first. We four-walled a theater in Los Angeles this time and got a similar reaction. Horror fans seemed to dig it and we got mixed reviews, but few very positive ones. We hired a producer's rep to sell the film and got the same response from the buyers: horror was dead. There was a glut on the market and nobody wanted it, despite the good reviews and the word of mouth. Very frustrating. It seemed like nothing had changed. After a year of trying to sell the film, I went down to Comicon in San Diego just to get away. Walking around I noticed After Dark had a booth there. A year ago, they had started a festival called "Horrorfest: 8 Films to Die For," where they picked up eight horror films and released them in 500 theaters nationwide for a week before Lions Gate put them out on DVD and SyFy Channel plays them on cable. For all the low-budget independent horror filmmakers out there, this was like a potential golden ticket. So, I went up to them and asked how they select films. They go to the major festivals like Sundance and Toronto and have a deal with Lions Gate.

But they were willing to look at my film so I gave them a copy of *Nightmare Man* with a copy of our press release. I told my friends what I did and most of them thought I was crazy, saying After Dark is looking for big, slick films, not my little supernatural slasher movie. Even Tiffany Shepis, the lead of the film, thought I was out of my mind. But if you don't try, you can never succeed. Two weeks later I got a call from After Dark. They lost my film. They still had the press kit and wanted to know if I was trying to sell them a script or what. I explained that it's a press kit to a completed movie. They then asked me to send them another copy, which I did. At least someone was following up, which is more than what you usually get in this business.

Two days later, our producer's rep quits, saying that horror is dead right now and we should try to sell the film as a thriller, but she can't do anything with it. Sorry. Bye. So, I call MTI Home Video, a domestic distribution company based in Miami. They had released a few of my previous films, like *The Hazing*, *Pretty Cool Too*, and *The Alien Files*. They liked me and they loved Tiffany Shepis. But even they turned the film down, saying that "horror is a tough sale right now, blah, blah, blah..." I'm telling you this is a tough business. The next day I emailed After Dark Films just to see if they received the new DVD copy I sent them. Ten minutes later I got an email.

Sara Finder [the program director] had watched it, enjoyed it and was showing it to other people in the company. She said she would get back to me soon. I'm happy to hear it, and I go out to lunch with a friend. An hour later, my cell phone rings. After Dark loved the film and wanted it for their Horror-fest 2007 line-up! No MG [money guarantee] but a two-week run at 350 theaters, with a $10 million advertising budget! A minute ago it looked like my film was going to sit on a shelf unreleased, and now [it was getting] theatrical play. Pretty amazing. We took the deal.

There were a few catches. We had to now make a film answer print and remix the audio for Dolby Digital. After Dark doesn't pay for this. Total cost: $50,000 dollars. Ouch! I asked, "Has anyone ever gotten into After Dark and then turned it down because they couldn't afford to make the print and remix the movie?" "Not that we're aware of," was the answer. Well, we did it and the film got released and it sold big-time on DVD. Unfortunately, because of the eight different films and advertising budget, even though I found out *Nightmare Man* alone made almost $6 million, all the films were still in the red (which means, no profit for the filmmakers). That's where that MG clause comes into effect. So, a film that cost us now $250,000 and made six million did not make any profit and to this day we have not seen a penny. This is [one of] the dangers of distribution. The kicker is that, last year, After Dark started their "After Dark Originals," where they are producing their own horror films. Hmmm... I wonder where that money came from? Welcome to Hollywood.

But it was great exposure, and my film was everywhere. So, again, if we do the math, we shot the film in 2005 and it came out in 2007. Only three years this time. A little better. Too bad we can never afford to do it again. But that hasn't stopped me from making movies. I just don't use my own or my parents' money.

Since *Nightmare Man* my films have been work for hire. Although I still write, direct, and care about everything I do. In fact, I'm very proud of one of my most recent flicks, a modern film noir entitled *1 in the Gun* starring Steven Man (an actor and producer who put up his own money to make this one), Katherine Randolph, Steven Bauer, Robert Davi, and James Russo. MTI Home Video released it on November 8, 2011, and I heard they did really well with it. Only time will tell if I ever see any backend money on this one. Can't count on it. Word of advice: Never count on it.

Brett Kelly: My first movie was shot on weekends whenever I could afford it. It took about a year to shoot and a few months to post, using rental houses to edit before the days of home-editing systems. Nowadays, I shoot on six 13-day schedules, depending on the budget. I'd love to shoot more days, but it's hard to afford to pay crews their day rates and take longer. The more days, the costlier the movie. If money was no object and I could guarantee that actors would stick around forever, I'd love to shoot at a more leisurely pace. My last two movies were six-day shoots at the time of this interview. The post usually takes a few months.

Chris LaMartina: It generally takes a year to finish a feature for us. Sometimes it takes longer and sometimes it's less.

Dead Teenagers, my uber-cheap first feature, was an anthology that took roughly two years to complete, because I shot it during breaks at college, and I was still getting used to shooting longer narratives.

President's Day, my fourth feature, was shot in 19 days, and edited/scored in about two months. From script to screen, it was about nine months' total. All the while, I was working a full-time job at the mayor's office in Baltimore, doing video work.

Witch's Brew was a 30-day schedule, and it was intense. The film contains over 40 speaking roles, a dozen locations, and over 60 practical make-up effects. The process of syncing up audio and transcoding the 7D footage took forever, in addition to some digital effects (magical zaps and whatnot). Adding post-production, *Witch's Brew* took about 17 months from screenplay to screener DVDs. It was exhausting, but it was a larger film that deserved the extra attention.

Jim Mickle: Both of my films have taken about 18 months from script to a finished film. In both cases the film premiered about a year after the actual shoot.

Damon Packard: Often it takes FAR too long, months become years because weeks and months go by with virtually nothing accomplished. Why? What else? Paralyzed by penniless pockets.

Brad Paulson: About a year. A good four months to write, five months to edit and three

months to film. Lately it's taken longer, though, since I've recently acquired an XBOX 360. Movies that were supposed to be finished in a month have now taken years because of that damn thing. However, the older I'm getting and the harder it is to get favors and the more everything is costing right now, the more I'm moving to simpler battle plans for movies. The last two films I did: *Suicide Poet* and *Paranormal Inactivity*, reflected this as well. *Paranormal* only took about two weeks to film, on and off, and they were very easy days. A couple hours at a time. Not one day did we go over five hours. The rest of the time, we sat around bullshitting about comic books with the male lead in the movie. It was a very low-stress project and a nice change of pace.

Jose Prendes: On average, about two month or so. *Monster Man* was shot sort of off-and-on. We shot all through October, with a few pick-up shots before and after. With *Corpses Are Forever*, I shot the black-and-white sequences in a 14-day period, and then the color portion half a year later, in about 18 days. I like to shoot fast and loose, keep things organic, which actors appreciate, so I prefer a short shoot schedule. I thrive on the vicious chaos of filmmaking.

Paul Scrabo: I did not have any deadline. I think *Dr. Horror* took about two years from concept to the first showing. That's too long. I did not have a complete editing system at home, so I had to schedule time at outside places. I am my own editor and it's my favorite part of the process. The manic part, the shooting of the film, is over, and post-production can be a more leisurely part.

Eric Shapiro: *Rule of Three*'s shooting schedule was insane. I think our longest day consisted of covering 11 pages of script. That's absurd. Five pages is far more reasonable. *Mail Order* was 15 pages and we did it in three days — five pages a day. *Rule of Three* took 12 days, with miscellaneous page counts, most of them extremely demanding.

Anthony Straeger: This question sort of comes back to things we have said earlier. The length of time it takes to make a film is directly related to the budget you have and type of film you are making.

So how long did it take to make *Call of the Hunter*? From start to finish was a total of 18 months. The idea for the story began in February, and the script was completed by the end of June. During that time I put together the essential components of the budget and began to look for interest in funding it. Thanks in the main to John Slocombe we had the pre- and production money in place by the end of August.

Pre-production began in September, for a total of six weeks. This included script revisions, location scouting, budget refining, casting and crewing up. We had originally planned to shoot at the beginning of September, but due to either cast or crew commitments we finally went into production on Friday, October 17, 2008. We shot for 12 days, which included traveling time to a remote place called Ivybridge, in Devon, over 200 miles from London.

Post-production took exactly one year to complete. One of the main reasons being that the second half of the funding came in dribs and drabs. In addition, I was doing the editing and had to fit that around surviving.

Delivery was made to RSquared, our agreed U.S. distributor, and was launched on November 19, 2009. The U.K. launch didn't happen until September 2009. So, overall, it took a considerable amount of time to realize. Despite this, the learning curve for the whole period has taught me that:

1. You can never rush things
2. IF you haven't got the finances, you cannot complete.

For my latest project, *Blue Green Yellow Dead*, we will have six to 12 weeks of pre-production and a four-to-six week production schedule, depending on whether it is shot in 2-D or 3-D. As we intend to make this a bigger production, and it will not be set in motion unless all the finances are in place, I would anticipate a 13- to 26-six week post-production schedule, once again depending on technical requirements. Realistically, we would like it to complete in a six-month turnaround period.

So, what's the difference? *Call of the Hunter*'s budget was $45,000 and *Blue Green Yellow Dead*'s budget is $500,000. [It's that] simple.

Marc Trottier: It all depends on the type of film you're making and if there are many visual effects involved. It also depends on whether or not you re-edit your film three times and continue to add shots over a period of seven years ... in that case, it'll take at least seven years to finish.

I've never purposely filmed a feature film yet, so I can't give any numbers on that subject.

On average, my short films usually take three to four weeks to make. The first couple of shorts that I made took about a day to film, a few days to edit on the VCR, then I'd throw a single music track on it from a CD and copy it to a VHS tape. It would be about four to five minutes long, with no [special] effects, no color correction and no titles. *Urban Saber* is about two and a half minutes long, which we filmed in one night as well ... but then I spent about three weeks doing digital effects (including titles and color correction), one night for video editing (not much to do) and another week or so doing the sound and music mix (with already-existing music). After that's all done, I spent another few nights making the DVD menu with already-existing music.

So, as technology gets better and makes things easier, people's expectations also become greater and it takes much more effort to keep them impressed.

Mike Watt: *The Resurrection Game* took two years to shoot and another eight to complete. *Demon Divas* was filmed in seven days and edited in three months. *Razor Days* was shot in 11, with the last day occurring seven months after principal wrap and real life has gotten in the way of any significant editing.

A 90-second movie took us six hours over

the span of two separate days and should have been edited in 45 minutes were it not for some severe technical issues due to limitations I didn't know I had.

Really, it takes as long as it takes.

Ritch Yarber: In general, once the script is finalized, completion of the film takes at least a year from start to finish. TwistedSpine.com Films is a group of working-class people that come together to create a film as a possible doorway to their dream jobs of working in professional movies. This means that every project is subject to work schedules, personal obligations, availability of locations, et cetera. Coincidentally, each of our last two films took exactly 26 weekend-only shoots apiece to complete. The rest of the time was [spent on] editing, music and all the rest.

The first movie that I made, *Transylvania Police: Monster Squad*, took about six months to create. I knew from the start that I would be working with friends and co-workers instead of knowledgeable actors, so I purposely chose to forego a strictly scripted format and just created a very loose outline of what was supposed to happen in the movie. Since my idea was to mimic the television show *Cops*, I felt that this improvisational approach would work nicely and give kind of the same feel. We would start the scene and just follow whatever happened with our one camera and see what developed. This was the first of many hard-learned lessons to come. Editing this hodge-podge footage into an entertaining and somewhat intelligent story was rough, to say the least. I later realized that, although the show *Cops* was not scripted, the events depicted unfolded naturally and told the story. Our scenes depended on certain plot points to be hit to propel the story along. With untrained improvisational actors, these plot points often were totally missed or took way too long to develop, leading to boring or inane gaps. With a lot of hard work, our first-time editor Matt Ford was able to carve a decent *Cops* knockoff

out of some really crazy footage. This was our first wake-up call as to the value of a well-planned script. We were fortunate to be able to get notorious B-movie icon Conrad Brooks to host the film. This would unexpectedly pay off in the future. Our actors doubled as the "crew" in this initial effort that cost about $600 to produce.

Our latest film, *Murder Machine!* cost a little over $5,000 to produce. Cast and crew totaled about 50 people. Shooting occurred over a period of 26 weekends, utilizing two cameras, monitors, microphones, lighting packages, special effects, wardrobe, stunts, weapons, vehicles, locations, et cetera — a stunning comparison to our first film that featured about five guys running around with a consumer grade Hi-8 camera and no microphone! Having evolved through a ten-year film school of hard knocks, our latest venture went smoothly, due to our well-planned script and dedicated preproduction efforts. Of course, our micro-budget efforts were dealt a series of setbacks after principal photography was completed due to computers and their inexplicable tendency to crash. This added two years to the time it took to put the finishing touches on the product as we had to wait until we could come up with new equipment that could handle the job. Our luck was so bad that even an attempt to edit the film with equipment owned by the Cleveland Museum of Art resulted in another computer crash and another start from scratch. Luckily, perseverance pays off, and the film has not only quickly made its budget back, but has been making its way into film festivals, with great reviews.

Ivan Zuccon: It usually takes from four to five weeks to shoot and a couple of months for post-production. In the past I used to shoot movies in three weeks, but I don't want to do that again. I think the right amount of time to spend on set is six to eight weeks, but in low-budget movies this is very difficult to do.

The Filmmakers were asked:
Is it easier or more difficult making movies now, as compared to your first movie?

Glenn Andreiev: When I did *Vampire's Embrace* the expensive-to-rent cameras had to be constantly cleaned. You really needed to know what you were doing when threading film in a 16mm camera. It's so much easier now. You pay less attention to the physical mechanics of the movie camera and more attention to your film. Broadcast-quality cameras are now easily available, as is the editing software. I edited my last four films from my coffee table.

John Borowski: Being an independent filmmaker never gets easier. It is easier in the sense that the more films you make, the more popular your name and work becomes. I have been contacted by people around the world, [who are] interested in my work or willing to provide assistance. When I was searching for someone to create the fake tattoos for *Carl Panzram*, I reached out and was contacted by many people who wanted a rate that was too expensive for my budget. I was contacted by Matthew Aaron, who was a fan of my work, and he agreed to work on the tattoos. The added bonus for Matthew was that he fit into Henry Lesser's jail-guard costume, so Matthew was also in the film as the guard who beats up and tortures Panzram. So money is not always the best motivator. Find people that are excited about working on your films.

Keith Crocker: This is one of those double-sided answers. Certainly the technology has become so much easier and consolidated; with digital video, the camera can do so many jobs [whereas] with film you need so many separate pieces of equipment. On the other hand, folks just seemed so much easier going years ago — now it seems that every actor or crew person has the ego of dinosaur proportions; I find that the bullshit level has increased dramatically. There are more and more story-tellers and outright liars than there ever were. On top of all of this, because of how easy and accessible the equipment is, everyone is a filmmaker. They [all think they are] Orson Welles just waiting be discovered. And what they do is flood the market with a sea of shit, which means those of us doing this for years and years on end have to work so much harder and be so much more creative to make sure our product shines heads and tails above them. For instance, my attempt at being different involves re-inventing Retro. With *Bloody Ape*, the anti-hero is a gorilla, played by a man in an ape suit. Ape suits made for the easiest monsters in the 1930s and '40s. The film, at times, plays out like a slasher film, only with the ape playing the slasher. And the plot itself is a re-working of *The Devil Bat* (1941) and *Phantom of the Rue Morgue* (1954). *Blitzkrieg*, while being hailed as "Nazisploitation," is actually just a reworking of *Stalag 17* (1953) with elements of *Mark of the Devil* (1970) added to it, to spice up the proceedings. The one area I excel in is making period pieces on a dime; no one wants to be bothered [with] ever trying to do this. The worst type of film you could make now is a slasher film or a zombie movie — they've been done to death and there is no place to take them.

In fact, thinking outside the horror genre is really the way to go. These days documentaries do really well; there are plenty of outlets for them and they are a great genre to stick with. Horror, in many ways, should have been buried years ago.

Richard Cunningham: That definitely depends on the movie and how much I'm responsible for on it. My last film was easily the most difficult film I've done [since] I was there for every bit of its development.

But, in general, it's much easier for a filmmaker now to produce a professional-grade film than it was ten years ago. The software used to make films has not only drastically improved, but has become more affordable and user-friendly, as the technology has become more mainstream. High definition is a staple in camcorders already, offering even a beginner filmmaker an image with quality resolution.

Also, the internet now offers a vast amount of knowledge on how to make movies and you easily can go on YouTube to learn how to properly work with complicated equipment and software, usually from a 15-year-old know-it-all who has grown up with computers.

Maurice Devereaux: As I mentioned earlier, technically it is much easier today (digital cameras and computer editing and CGI effects), but now financial realities have set in and the cruel business side of filmmaking have made it almost impossible for me to make a new film. As I know now that barring being a miracle "lottery winner" (*Blair Witch, Paranormal Activity, Open Water*) you will NOT make any money if you finance your own film. The various sales agents, distributors, and producer's reps are mostly all scumbags and will rip you off in a million ingenious ways, and you will not get paid. And, even if you're lucky enough to find a few good people, the amount they will pay is now so small (because of DVD piracy, et cetera) that unless you make your films for almost no money, you will LOSE whatever money is invested.

Donald Farmer: For the reasons I just described, High Def cameras have made it easier than ever to shoot your film. And nonlinear editing clearing beats working on a 35mm flatbed system or building your edit from the head of a three-quarter or one-inch master tape. Everything today is easier. I really don't see a downside to the today's cameras and editing software.

Jeff Forsyth: Technologically it is MUCH easier [now]. Now you can actually stay on par, quality-wise, with Hollywood. I would have to say it is easier in every aspect. Social networking sites have opened filmmakers up

to people that can assist them that they would [otherwise] never have met.

Richard W. Haines: Making movies is never, ever easy. It's like managing a military campaign. It's always challenging, and since I try to expand my filmmaking techniques, each production offers new problems to solve. For example, when I decided to print *Space Avenger* in real three-strip Technicolor in China, back in the '80s, I had the Chinese lab technicians on the set giving me advice on how color was rendered in that process. Chris Condon was the technical advisor on *Run for Cover*, explaining to the crew how his Stereo-Vision 3-D lenses worked. We needed a sharp depth of field for the system, which meant a lot of light to generate higher F-stops.

We had no advisors simulating the film noir look for *Unsavory Characters*. Cinematographer Brendan Flynt and I watched old RKO movies to analyze the lighting design. For that feature we shot part of it in black and white, which had its own set of issues. The stock had a different thickness than color film, which made the camera noisy, so we had to blimp it differently. Tom Agnello examined old Hammer movies to try to replicate that look for *What Really Frightens You.* He developed a method of cross fading the lighting transitions from normal color to the Gothic appearance.

It's been my experience that when you challenge people by trying something different, they'll respond positively and have some fun figuring out how to create the visuals. Most crew members are used to working on low-budget movies with poor technical specs, so my pictures gave them an opportunity to be more creative than usual. I never believed that budgetary limitations were an excuse for bad photography or sound.

William Hopkins: With the equipment and software that's available now it's certainly easier to make a movie that is comparable in image quality to studio productions. The High Definition cameras are a great advance over the equipment we used on *Sleepless Nights* and *Demon Resurrection.* With the Standard Definition equipment, it was a challenge just to make the image look acceptable, to make it look something like film. With the cameras that are available now, it seems even an inexperienced user can get a startlingly good image. But, even with Standard Definition equipment, we certainly had it easier when we were making our films than indie filmmakers who were working back before digital video became available. I can't imagine how difficult it must've been for filmmakers on tiny budgets to have had to contend with all the difficulties that shooting on film creates. I love the look of film and would love to be able to afford to shoot on it. But the productions I've done so far wouldn't have been possible if we hadn't been using digital video equipment.

Steve Hudgins: It's easier, as we learned from a lot of the mistakes we made on the first movie. The main thing being that we are much more organized in every aspect of the process now. And, as is the case with most things in life, the more you do it, the better you get at it.

Rolfe Kanefsky: Well, with the economy the way it is, it's getting more and more difficult. You are now expected to do everything yourself, including editing and mixing your films out of your own home. Producers are trying to lower the budgets more and more. You really can't do a film cheap enough. They don't want to pay for anything. Making any movie is a challenge, but when they want you to shoot it in five or six days for $25,000 total, it should be impossible. Unfortunately, it isn't because stupid people like myself will kill themselves to make the film and make sure it's good. Miracles are performed every day in this low-to-no-budget arena. I know some filmmakers who have made really impressive feature films for $10,000 or less! You should not be able to do this. The fact that it's happening is why it's very hard to make a living in this business. A year ago, I wrote and directed seven feature films just to pay my bills. It's crazy.

Yes, the technology has made it easier and much more affordable. You can do a lot with a very limited crew and budget, but this is what everyone expects now. I made a film called *Pretty Cool Too*, right after *Nightmare Man* was shot. In fact, we stopped post on *Nightmare Man* so I could shoot this teen comedy in 12 days just before Christmas for $25,000, not including post. I told the producer that this was an experiment and I could not guarantee that the final result would be any good. Well, somehow, we pulled it off, going only $500 over budget, got the film released, and I'm sure someone made money off it. Being able to make something like that is a double-edged sword, because now that you've done it, they expect you to do it again and again and for less and less money and time.

But unless you pull off something like the success of *Blair Witch Project* or *Paranormal Activity*, you aren't going to impress anyone in the studio system. Instead of them being amazed at what you did for pennies, they say it doesn't look like a $100 million film. We want directors who can make $100 million films and the only way we know if they can is if they're already made one. I was told years ago that the studios would rather hire a guy who made a slick music video or commercial than someone who has directed ten B-movies for Roger Corman. In the old days, those directors did get into the studios and became James Cameron, Johnathan Demme, Ron Howard, Joe Dante, et cetera. Today, these guys wouldn't be given the time of day because everyone's making movies and it's all about the bottom line. This is the sad-but-true nature of the business. However, that doesn't stop some young directors from winning the lottery and having that lucky breakout hit. So, we all just keep trying because you never know.

Brett Kelly: It's easier now, as I have a lot of old tricks to fall back on. However, every single movie provides a ton of challenges. I have yet to make a single film that didn't challenge me in some way, be it dealing with people, budgets, weather, locations or any one of a million variables.

Chris LaMartina: Making movies is never easy, so I hate to use that word, but it's definitely easier than it was. By the same token, with every project, we raise our standards, so technically it did get more difficult (mostly because we were challenging ourselves).

I couldn't have made *Witch's Brew* at 19. Hell, I couldn't have made it at 23. Every feature was a learning experience. They were baby steps to bigger productions, each subsequent movie providing valuable lessons.

Completing a 90-minute movie is a monumental task and I give kudos to any individual who pulls it off ... no matter how bad it may be. So many things can go wrong on a film set, so I say "bravo" to anyone with the gusto to make it to the finish line.

Jim Mickle: It's hard to say if it's any easier now. Since my first film we hit the economic crisis and that's made it a lot harder for many people to get films (or anything, for that matter) financed. But having made two successful genre films on a budget, many more opportunities have come along, just not necessarily great ones. Time will tell if the next one is any easier, but in general, the process of making movies is never, ever easy.

Damon Packard: I would say it's easier now because of the tools. That isn't necessarily a good thing. The field is FAR too over-saturated now. In many ways the production process is more difficult, because people's lives are so much busier and more frantic. Getting people together on the same day, for example, and committed to a full shoot is extremely difficult, sometimes simply impossible. But it all comes down to the same thing every time. Money.

Brad Paulson: It's a little bit of both. It's more difficult because most of the favors have run out. All the people we had hooking us up are either making their own movies now, have given up and gotten real jobs, or came to their senses and moved out of the madhouse that is Los Angeles. On the other hand, we know a lot more as well and don't expect to get rich tomorrow. We're just doing it because we love it. And we're much smarter about the way we do things now. In the old days, it was a crapshoot. But now we have a much better sense of what works and what doesn't.

Jose Prendes: It is always difficult to make movies. I hear people saying how difficult filmmaking has become and how they wish it was like the good old days. Well, guess what guys, it was always tough. I read Charlie Chaplin's autobiography and he was complaining how hard it was to make movies back in the silent era! And that was even when he was a known commodity! I made my first movie in a bubble, so that was fairly easy, because I was the god of that movie. Anything out of that bubble, where I have to deal with producers, distributors, marketing strategies, test screenings, script notes, et cetera, would be much more difficult.

Paul Scrabo: I know my next project will be easier, whatever it is, because I'd be smarter! I actually outsmarted myself while shooting *Dr. Horror* because I was, in a way, too efficient. I knew how each scene would be edited, how many close-ups, et cetera, so I cut down on coverage. I just shot what I absolutely needed.

We previewed the film to good response, but I could see the scenes that could benefit from trimming. I graduated from "every frame is important!" to "I have a chance to make this a better movie." But I could only fix so much, due to not having extra footage to re-adjust those longer scenes. I won't make that mistake again.

Eric Shapiro: It's much easier. It's a strange art form in the sense that you can approach it in a real simple, primitive way — with very few angles and no camera movement, and get a legitimate result. Much of Clint Eastwood's work is extremely basic, and he creates a sense of beauty from the simplicity. At the opposite end, you have your Scorseses and Kubricks and Oliver Stones, where the demands on the visual side are incredibly intense. Once I got the basic, simple-coverage approach down, I didn't find it very hard. It's physically hard because the days are long and you're in nonstop conversation with people, but, aesthetically, it's a very navigable form. I'd say writing is 1,000 times harder.

Anthony Straeger: This is where the immortal line, "If I knew then, what I know now!" comes into play. You can't beat knowledge or hindsight. The film game is filled with things you cannot know until you have been through it. The whole process of making *Call of the Hunter* as a first feature was a big learning curve. Previously, I have made two documentary films and about 12 shorts and with every single one I have learnt something new — that is the beauty of it all. Since completing the movie and distribution has been placed, I have learnt even more about internet marketing, video-on-demand, pre-sales, distribution rights and have learnt loads about the way my distributors have gone about business and the way I would do it the next time around.

I think one of the best pieces of advice that can be given is, step back and think. Sometimes the train rolls and you can't stop it and you can't keep a tight control of it. But, somehow, you need time to think and give yourself time to breathe.

Is it easier? I think bigger names than myself would say the answer would always be NO! New problems occur, each film is an individual and it has its own personal needs that will never compare directly to something you have made previously. I find problem solving and problems interesting. I am quite practical, but sometimes the whole thing can get so big you just find yourself faced by a mountain.

Marc Trottier: Nowadays, it's easier than ever to make a movie because technology is advancing so fast ... cameras are getting better and cheaper everyday. Even young children can (and do) make feature films because of the equipment that's available today. I know for a fact that if I had access to a video camera when I was a kid, I would've made all sorts of fun little short films. Cameras just weren't as common or easy to come by as they are today. Hell, I could technically film a 1080p HD feature film on my cell phone today if I wanted to! In the future, that'll be normal ... but, right now, the fact that there're apps for color correction and editing available on a phone — and that the cameras are as good as they are — is just incredible! It's going to be really fun to see what kind of new technology comes out, and how it will become even easier to make movies in the years to come. Cameras implanted in our eyes, anyone? You'll just walk around looking at stuff, and then come home at the end of the day and say, "movie's finished"! No biggie.

As I mentioned before, I began my career editing on a VCR. I had figured out that if I paused the VCR at the point I wanted to add the next shot. I had to move it back 14 frames before hitting the record button, to have it start where I wanted it. It was ridiculous! But I was making movies, and that's all that mattered. With digital editing today, you can cut, paste and move things around with ease ... and if you don't like the way it looks, you can just change it around or modify things on the spot. Back in the day, I had to instantly re-watch every cut that I made on the VCR to make sure it looked okay ... and if I missed something the first time or changed my mind later, it was too late and I just had to live with it ... or redo the entire thing!

I look at technology today and I say, "*Jetsons!*" Ok, so it's more like I yell, "*Jetsons!*" But it's funny how the stuff we have now will look ancient in ten or 15 years.

Mike Watt: There's no easy way to answer that because every film brings with it its own truckload of challenges, many of them hiding in the wheel wells. To paraphrase Neil Gaiman, "You never learn how to make movies; you only learn how to make the movie you're making." To which I'll add, "Usually by the last day of production."

As the "Second Wave" of independents in the '90s (the First Wave being the Ritters, Lindenmuths, Bonks, Bookwalters and McCraes), we got into the business too late to take advantage of the home-video boom and haven't yet figured out if there's money to be made in Video On Demand. Making a movie is always going to boil down to writing a script, scrounging the budget, casting, shooting, editing, scoring and finishing. That's what a movie consists of and what it will always consist of, whether you have a cast of thousands or a team of yourself and a couple of hand puppets. What you do afterward is always going to be the biggest hurdle: finding the audience and all that goes with that.

Ritch Yarber: It is much more difficult making movies now since the expectations of the production are much different than when we first started. After working and learning for over a decade what it takes to make successful and entertaining micro-budgeted independent films, you never want to go backwards. Although the amount of money that we have available has not increased that much, we are constantly looking to push our standards to a higher level. This means the scripts, pre-production, casting — everything — has to be tighter and more demanding. With people lending their time and talents to your production, you are obligated to do your part to make sure everything is in place and ready to go. We have managed to develop a small following for our brand of film and we have to work hard to keep our reputation intact. In my mind, TwistedSpine.com Films stands for one thing, quality entertainment, thus our logo: "Your premiere micro-budget film experience." We pull out all the stops to make that logo mean what we say.

Ivan Zuccon: Not much has changed, compared to the past. The problem is not making movies, but distributing them. Distribution is the real obstacle. Finding honest and reliable distributors is the real trouble nowadays.

Publicity, Promotion and Distribution

If you self-produced a project you'll most likely have to self-publicize and promote that project. No one is going to be more enthusiastic than you are about your movie. Even if you get an eventual distributor who will get it out to renters and retailers, you still have to obtain promotional quotes and some publicity to get those distributors on board.

When I first started making the genre movies there were dozens of print magazines, from *Samhain* and *The Darkside* in England, to *Independent Video*, *Draculina* and *Fangoria* in the States. In the early '90s this was the only route you had. You would have to physically snail-mail VHS tapes to reviewers, along with slide photos and any other printed material. Nowadays, there are a thousand genre websites for every print magazine that ceased publication. You can send the entire movie and photos to reviewers digitally, either directly or on a shared download site. So, in a certain regard, it's much more inexpensive to garner publicity nowadays.

If you decide to sell and market the film yourself, there are many avenues to do this, from independent film sites to megastore sites, like Amazon.com. You also have to create your own website for the movie and maintain that, do all the duplication and fulfilling of orders. It can be a full-time job, and expenses can run high. While you may have dozens of positive reviews and links to your site for ordering, this still doesn't guarantee that you'll sell any copies.

Then there are distributors who will promise you the world — and they'll want "worldwide rights" as well. Just recently I had a dis-tributor interested in my recent documentary. He called me and told me how much he like the documentary, then asked if I ever did anything else (obviously he didn't read any of the info I sent him). I spoke with him for over a half of an hour, after which point he said he'd email me over his usual contract so I could look it over. The one thing that stood out was his wanting "worldwide rights" and that my share would be 40 percent, minus his expenses. But there was no cap on the expenses, so if I gave him the movie he could continually say that the expenses were more than my share. I emailed him back, telling him my concern about this. The next day he called back, saying he understood my concern but that he couldn't change this (he couldn't give me an answer, basically). Then, he proceeded to ask me a legal question about something related to his distribution business. After 15 minutes, when he said, "Since you're a lawyer..." I stopped him and said, "Uh, I think you're confusing with me with someone else." He explained that he got me confused with someone else he spoke with the day before but that he liked my film and wanted to talk to me about it. But I already talked to him about it, at length. So it's not a good sign when the distributor can't get his shit straight. Least to say, I'm not signing away my rights with him.

I always recommend to filmmakers that they try to license their movie out and to get money up front. The terms are usually for three to five years. You simply have to supply a master copy and photos so they can make up the box artwork. However, if the distributor does not pay a license fee up front, and promises residuals, this almost always means there's not going to be any money whatsoever. You see, many of these sorts of distributors work it into their contract that they can subtract their expenses for your residual percentage. If you *do* get a contract and are not sure what it says, get someone who can decipher it.

So do you need to publicize and market your movie? Yes, you do. But how much work depends entirely on how your movie is going to be distributed.

One filmmaker who has a great deal of experience in self distribution is director Tim Ritter, who is probably best known for the *Truth or Dare* movies.

Dare to Self-Distribute! (by Tim Ritter)

Once your movie is completed, what do you do with it next? How do you generate money from it? Is it possible to make your budget back? Can a distributor help? These are the kinds of questions you should ask yourself *before* starting any new project. You should have some kind of rough plan in mind for getting your movie out to the public when you finish it and actually start promoting it *while you create it*. No matter what kind of movie you've made, you've spent money on it (probably your own) and you'll be looking for a way to recoup some of that investment. You also want to get the project out there and have people see it.

I've been involved with both commercial distribution and self-distribution of my own movies for over 25 years now and it's a constantly evolving challenge. To answer the biggest question right off the bat — do you need a distributor? No, you don't, at least not right away. There are many affordable things you can do to get your movie into the public eye and generating revenue.

It all started out pretty simply in the early 1980s: make a movie, dub off Beta or VHS copies, create some passable artwork, slap it in a hard-shell case, and drive around to local mom-and-pop video stores to sell each copy individually. It was fun meeting the store owners and interacting with them, especially with a movie made right in their own back yard. Kind of a slam-dunk sell! Through the local video stores, you could connect with independent rackjobbers in vans that would buy copies to sell to mom-and-pop stores hundreds of miles away and even to other rackjobbers operating in different states. So things worked out quite nicely ... for a while.

Of course, this scenario got a little more complicated when the mom-and-pop stores went out of business or were bought out by the corporate chain stores. Gone was the interaction with the local proprietor. You had to submit your movie to a "committee" or a "chain buyer" to see if they were interested in picking up your flick. One of the biggest problems was getting a buyer to actually *watch* your movie, with literally hundreds of moviemakers and distributors continually inundating them with titles every week. It was so easy to get lost in the shuffle, and many good movies never got decent distribution because of this. Many times, even if your movie got noticed by a corporate buyer, the chains would inexplicably pass on your project after months of negotiating, or make crazy demands like asking you to change your box art (at great expense) or edit out scenes that might be "too strong" for their customers. And even if you got a deal where they finally agreed to pick up a few thousand copies ... the price you ended up getting per unit was so low that you barely broke even on the costs of delivering the packaged goods (not to mention shipping!).

As videotape renting evolved into DVD selling in the late 1990s, there was a brief period where if your title was with the right small distributor and part of a package deal, you could get into the big box retail stores simply because there was great demand for new titles at low price points. Profits were pretty slim in this era (again) and we all found out the hard way about corporate stores and their return policies. Store terms allowed them six months ... or a year ... to pay for product and there was a very unfriendly clause in the agreement, one that read, "If the merchandise doesn't sell, we get to return it all (without payment of any sort) and *you owe us shipping*!" Needless to say, we all went through a rough patch here because the small distributor (or moviemaker) was forced to take all the risk, not the big corporate stores that could afford it.

As the 21st century rolled in, Hollywood started offering its hit catalog titles at lower and lower price points (yep, those $3 and $5 DVD movie bins) and once again ... the small, independent guys were pretty much thrown onto the train tracks again. The average consumer would much rather buy a slick Hollywood production over the latest shot-on-video "trashterpiece" by someone like yours truly.

As the independent moviemaker dealt with these blows, the proliferation of bit torrent downloading added further insult to injury. Suddenly everything you had ever released was posted on the 'net and available as an absolutely FREE download to anyone who really wanted it! (As I watched my catalog DVD sales plummet, I noticed the number of downloads on my titles listed on bit torrent sites were sometimes 10,000 or more! That would've translated into a heaping load of nice DVD sales.)

With foreign markets drying up for small video projects, Netflix offered a brief respite for independent movies when they first started up (and continue to do so, though to a much lesser degree). At first, they'd buy a respectable amount of DVDs to rent out by mail in those snazzy red envelopes, and later, pay a decent fee to put your title in their streaming program. But the streaming model, while gaining decent exposure to some smaller movies like my own Truth or Dare series, has had one major downfall — it's devalued ALL movies in the eyes of the consumer. When you pay $8 a month for a smorgasbord of endless movies to watch as many times as you want

with the click of a button, you begin to see the single title $5 DVD bins as being *way over-priced*! Hence, we've entered the era of 20-movie DVD packs (for $5!) and quadruple blockbuster studio packs for $3. While Hollywood might be able to eek out a meager profit by sheer volume of sales ... the indie moviemaker and distributor just cannot compete. These days, the whole business of streaming is turning into a studio-dictated moneymaking machine ... with the independents scrambling for crumbs that fall off the table.

So how does the small guy (or gal) with a finished movie and very little 'net and advertising money compete? Well, the first thing is, you dare to do it yourself— you self-distribute. It's almost like going back ... to the future. This is the approach I'm taking with my latest shot-on-HD movie, *Deadly Dares—Truth or Dare 4*. You might end up signing with a distributor way down the pike, but in order to get the ball rolling and get your movie exposure, income, and larger distribution interest, you just have to get out there with your product and HUSTLE, using little fragments and bits of knowledge from nearly *every era of distribution* that I've just outlined.

First, you should keep your budget as low as possible and pick a project that has an instant potential audience or niche market. For me, it was a no-brainer to pick my latest production as the fourth movie in my fairly successful direct-to-video *Truth or Dare* series. There's an audience that has seen the first three movies and Netflix Streaming ran the original movie for three years straight when they introduced their streaming services, capturing interest from thousands of new viewers. So if you have access to a small franchise name (or can get one affordably), this can help you gain some instant market recognition. I also kept my ENTIRE budget in the under–$5,000 range, and that may have been a little bit too high, upon reflection.

It's still sound advice to stick to exploitation, horror, or science-fiction–themed movies at this level because these are the type of projects that, if you make them right, will usually find an audience. There are websites that heavily promote independent genre projects, conventions celebrating these types of movies year round all over the U.S., and it's easier to book your movie in independent theaters if you have an exploitable angle accompanied by an outlandish poster of some sort.

When you begin pre-production, this is the time to start promoting your movie, especially on all the FREE social websites where you interact with family, friends, and acquaintances. Have some snazzy artwork created to plaster everywhere and start posting short video teasers that spotlight storyboards, special effects, casting, and anything that might intrigue people. Be careful not to give away all of your project's secrets, but at the same time you have to get people talking about it. This can be a fine line to walk! As you cast the movie, post interviews with some of the actors and actresses taking on various roles. It never hurts to hire a "scream queen" or a "cult actor" to essay a part for a day or two. With *Deadly Dares* I was able to wrangle both rising scream queen Jessica Cameron and original *Jackass* television star Mike Holman into playing important characters in the movie.

While you film, start a 'net presence for your movie on the free social sites. Post random "behind the scenes" teasers and still photos to entice interest. The term teaser is key in all this — you're TEASING people with brief, informative snippets of your work-in-progress, hoping they'll want to see more and that good word-of-mouth will follow. The videos should be no more than two to three minutes in length — people clicking around on the 'net have limited attention spans and an infinite number of viewing choices. You can also release this info to the various websites that cover independent movies and provide them with links to your pictures and videos. This can help expand the potential audience that will hopefully be waiting to see your finished movie. In the "old days," all this pro-

Deadly Dares poster #1

motion was done with print articles in various trade and genre magazines — and you can still send press materials and photos (via email) to the remaining print magazines, but, unfortunately, most of them primarily cover studio fare these days.

When your movie is completed (even a rough first cut), get it listed on IMDb.com and put some poster art and photos up. This costs under $50, and once you're signed up IMDb will also send you weekly information on film festivals going on all over the world where you can possibly show your movie. It's never been easier to pick and choose film fests that might be good exposure for your project. Critical acclaim can help, and distributors play close attention to the fests. You want to be careful not to break the bank here, though, because there are festival entrance fees in the low and high range, and you won't always be accepted.

While entering your movie into film fests

and hoping a big distributor makes one of those "offers you just can't refuse," you can also start booking it in small, independent theaters across the U.S. For starters, just look around locally (or in the closest big city) and you're likely to find an indie theater or two. Most all of them are set up to project DVD or Blu-ray — and the resulting quality on the silver screen is usually quite excellent! Making posters has never been easier- take the artwork you've been hyping on the 'net and blow it up to poster size at your local Walmart photo department. You'll spend under $50 for high quality one-sheet sized posters that you can take (or send) to each theatrical showing. Hype the movie in local press and news, set up midnight screenings, and start letting people pay to see your work! Take video of the events and post it on your websites.

Like the mom-and-pop video stores of yesteryear, independent theater owners are more than happy to talk with you and give you lists

***Deadly Dares* poster #2**

of other similar theaters across the country. Then it's simply a matter of making some inquiries, sending out press kits and copies of the movie, and getting it booked. Of course, not every theater will show your movie, so it's trial and error, but definitely it's worth pursuing. You'll be able to legitimately say that your project has had a limited theatrical release while making a few extra bucks on the side. Usually the theater owners will split ticket sales 50/50, but you won't get any of the snack-bar residuals — that's where they make their real money!

Be sure to make 8.5" × 11" photo paper lobby cards (pictures from the best scenes of your movie featuring the title logo and cast and crew info) and mini-posters for all theatrical showings. These are a great way to promote the movie, and you can give them away or sell them (with or without autographs) at various venues. With *Deadly Dares*, we did nine separate poster designs and half-a-dozen lobby cards to have a variety of eye-catching material to offer. Fans seem to really enjoy simple novelties like this, along with T-shirts, hats, and bracelets. I've noticed that many times, you'll make more money from merchandising tie-ins than off the movie itself. This is similar to the music business, where an artist's latest album is usually a loss leader for concert ticket sales and merchandise.

Everything you do and offer at theatrical showings also applies to the sci-fi and horror convention circuit, where you can show your movie in a large viewing room to fans. Also invite the cast and crew to assist you in selling DVD copies and autographing all of your merchandise at a table for the entire weekend. The best thing about conventions is that everyone attending is a potential customer because they are ALL diehard fans of the type of movie that you (hopefully) made! Many moviemakers do extremely well at these events, and here is where you can offer "limited edition" VHS (!) copies of your movie (which are now collected by the same sort of retro fans who enjoy vinyl records) and "special edition"

DVD-Rs available exclusively at these shows. I am doing this with *Deadly Dares*, beginning with a polished rough cut subtitled *The Underground Bootleg Edition* (available exclusively on VHS tape with a choice of covers), which will be followed up by a DVD-R release and then a completely different HD cut (featuring extra bells and whistles, like alternate takes and all-new Virtual FX) suitable for streaming, pay-per-view, and Blu-ray. Each edition has to contain different "extras," like bonus video footage, trailers, alternate endings, and interviews. It's all about maximizing the sales potential of your project as many different times and ways that you can. Yes, remarketing and repackaging like Hollywood has done so well.

Being an avid movie soundtrack collector, I decided to produce the music score for *Deadly Dares*, featuring composer Toshi Hiroaki's compositions interspersed with dialogue cues from the movie. As a young newbie horror fan, nothing was more exciting to me than reading about an upcoming genre movie like *Maniac, Phantasm* or *Escape from New York* in *Fangoria* magazine, then running out to purchase the vinyl soundtrack score at a local record shop. Listening to that music ... re-reading the articles and staring at the pictures ... and letting my imagination soar ... were all part of the experience leading up to finally *seeing* the movie. I thought about that part of my early fandom and decided it might be fun to try recreating that excitement for others — using today's technologies — especially the technologies that have been traditionally causing more harm than good. So we uploaded the *Deadly Dares* soundtrack (along with some exclusive CD artwork) as a free bit torrent download and promoted it heavily on various websites. It didn't take long for fans to discover this "freebie" and start enjoying the music. This strategy worked out extremely well. People got something for free and were suddenly talking about the movie, anticipating when they'd get a chance to view it or buy a copy.

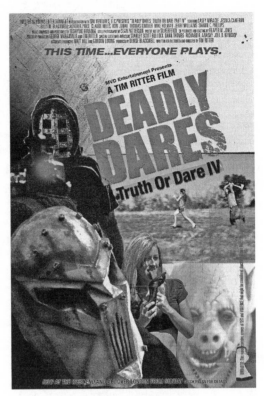

Deadly Dares poster #3

By this point you'll have a variety of different trailers posted on the 'net to hype your movie, and maybe even entire scenes that don't give away too much of your story. With *Deadly Dares*, the plotline intentionally dealt with an odd assortment of crazy characters posting wild video dares on the 'net, so I played that up by posting some of these "dares" onto video sharing sites, cutting away at the moment when some outrageous or violent event would take place. Right at that "money shot" crescendo, I inserted a title card with the movie's name in huge letters while the action continued to be *heard* on the audio track only. The idea was to entice people into wanting to see more, to seek the movie out to see what visuals we had been forced to conceal! I tried to censor myself and keep things at a PG-13 level, but this still didn't stop a couple of my videos from being banned from top video-sharing sites. It wasn't a big issue, though, because I simply re-posted the clips on different sites and hyped the fact that they were BANNED elsewhere, gaining even more viewers and additional word-of-mouth.

As you continue to hype your movie on the 'net, a time will come when you want to sell physical DVD copies to customers. These days, most people buy their movies and books through Amazon.com, and you can get your movie listed on Amazon through Createspace (an Amazon affiliate). Once you send them a DVD-R master and get your artwork set up, they will make copies on demand, avoiding that distribution nightmare of having unsold product returned. They will also print out the insert sleeve, package everything, ship it out and wire you a fair portion of the sale! Yes, it's that simple — you retain all creative rights and can cancel the deal at any time. Your only job will be to continue HYPING the movie up to generate additional sales. You can also concurrently get your movie listed on Amazon's streaming rental section and share in those proceeds each time someone pays for a view. These are things that used to require at least a small distributor to accomplish, but today it's simpler than ever to get your product out in the marketplace all by yourself. Even though selling your movie relies entirely on modern technology and giant corporations, it's very much like the old days, when you had to make and sell your tapes, one at a time. The difference is now a big company is manufacturing your discs and a potential *global* audience is just a click away! The real work continues to be promoting your movie and getting potential viewers to rent or purchase it in an overcrowded marketplace. That's why, if you do well over time, you'll probably consider signing the rights over to a distributor and letting them take it to the next level. That's part of the goal of self-distribution: being able to prove that you have a marketable product. But if that doesn't happen, at least you got your movie released and seen.

Amazon and Createspace are by no means the only high-profile places to hawk your movie on the 'net. In addition to Netflix and YouTube, there are countless new companies with which you can negotiate deals if your product meets their criteria. Sometimes you might need an agent, but most times you won't. Many video-hosting sites will share revenue with you from advertisements that they place below your movie as it streams. So if you continually get an escalating number of viewers, you will make back some cash. Again, it's trial and error as you explore new cyberworld opportunities.

Even though the 'net is oversaturated with tons of seemingly useless information and millions of video clips that are competing for viewers, it still remains the best and most affordable way to garner attention and get your movie hyped internationally. You just have to be clever, spend a lot of time gambling with different ideas, and never stop thinking out of the box. Here are the rules: *there are no rules.*

The Filmmakers were asked:
How do you tackle the publicity of your films? What is the best way to go about this, from your perspective?

Glenn Andreiev: The simple "local guy makes movie" is just not news anymore. You need a unique angle, something that in one sentence of explanation will get the public going "Oh, no way!," or maybe even cause debates. We hired Bernard Goetz, New York's famous subway vigilante from the 1980s, to be in our film *Every Move You Make*. Well, this got us on CNN, *The View*, *Court TV* and in the *New York Daily News*. Also, when you shoot a movie, have a stills photographer on the set. The publicity outfits require good stills.

John Borowski: Grass-roots marketing is the most cost-effective method of publicity for the independent filmmaker. I recommend the following: Create a website for your film (and for yourself as a filmmaker). Even if it is just one page, it is better to have some web presence than none. You can always add on to the site. Create a blog. Create an email list of people interested in your films. Basically, utilize every tool that you can online to promote your work for free or cheap. Send your films to reviewers. It is free publicity. I would not recommend paying for ads as I tried this once and found that it was a waste of money. My key to being a worldwide renowned filmmaker is that I pretty much have done everything myself. People appreciate the personal touch and human contact. Sparzanza, a Swedish heavy metal band, contacted me and asked to use Tony Jay's audio from *Albert Fish* in one of their songs. I approved, since they would mention my name and the film in their CD booklet. It is this type of cross-promotion that helps independents help each other.

Keith Crocker: Back in the old days, I did everything through mail order. I'd take ads in the horror magazines, specifically target an audience who was into what I was selling, and that's how I handled sales pre-internet. Giving review copies to the mag you were taking the ad in always generated publicity, and you just hoped you got some glowing reviews. The ads were lots of fun to make in those days; everything was done by hand, cut and paste — they sort of resembled the old Paragon Video boxes, with additional blood and gore added by colored-pen ink! Those were the good old days. I was very lucky, because after inventing a distribution arm called *Cinefear Video*, I not only sold my product but I was also able to sell 16mm films that were quite rare and had been transferred to VHS tape by either myself or one of my projectionist friends. Hence, I was able to supplement a living as a mail-order

video business. A small art house label called Vanguard Video (now a big art house label), acted as a sub distributor for *The Bloody Ape*. The film's official date of release was 1997, though the film had been shot in '93. Anyhow, Vanguard handled it until DVD started to become all the rage. Then the distribution rights reverted back to me. Anyhow, for *Blitzkrieg*, the job got even easier. I became partners in a DVD distribution business called Wildeye Releasing. The other half is run by a fellow named Rob Hauschild. Rob has been working in advertising just about all his life, and he really does know how to sell things. Rob does a lot of work with publicity on the internet, he's really inventive with his artwork and copy, and comes from the same tradition of trying to reinvent the past, as I do. Rob went bonzo on the *Blitzkrieg* campaign. His headline "A new era of Nazi terror" can't be beat, also his decision to forgo using painted artwork for the DVD cover and instead use the image of a nude, booted and machine-gun–wielding Tatyana Kot makes this film a popular sell to this day. He did the same thing for the DVD release of *Bloody Ape* with "400 Pounds of Fury Hungry for Female Flesh." Honestly, you can't beat it. He also re-cut the original *Bloody Ape* trailer, added some different sound effects, et cetera, and we had a brand new sales gimmick for an old film. He made up posters to be signed and given away at our New York premiere. He even made up lobby card sets to be given out as door prizes. I came up with the idea of giving out a vomit bag during the New York showings, old-school gimmicks like this go over like gangbusters.

Richard Cunningham: When I was younger, I would either call up or go to local newspapers in person, and talk about my film to an editor or reporter for either the arts and entertainment or the local section. It worked more times than not, and if it didn't result in a cover story it was always a generous article featuring film stills, and it was promotion that was reaching a wide area of subscribers.

With *Year Zero* I started publicity much

earlier in the production stage. I still had work to do on the final edit when I released the first two trailers online. Having little clout in the social media environment, which I was just entering into, I suspected that the earlier I began getting the word out, the more anticipation I can build up for it. Because *Year Zero* is a zombie apocalypse film, the genre gave me the opportunity to present it to a very large and enthusiastic crowd. I had a clear idea of my target audience, so I sent press kits to various horror/zombie fan sites. Those websites helped to generate the initial buzz surrounding my short, posting the trailers on their websites and backing the movie with positive comments.

These same websites helped *Year Zero* gain exposure when it premiered at Tribeca. The festival itself helped *Year Zero* with publicity, getting me articles and interviews in local New York City news. In general, I've found larger film festivals have a press consultant on staff, who is there to either present you with advice or actual press coverage. However, if you're not in the feature category, you can generally assume there will be less of a push with your film, especially in larger festivals. Smaller film festivals may feature you more, but they also don't attract the same level of press. It's always best to be pro-active with publicity so you're not lost in the shuffle, also because you might not get many good opportunities for it.

For *Year Zero* and a multimedia book called *Dead Land*, that I'm also developing, each has its own Facebook and Twitter accounts. For *Year Zero*, I've experimented some [by] using these outlets. With Twitter, aside from posting information, reviews and articles of the film, trailers and clips, I created a side character of the *Year Zero* story; the fictional character tweeted about surviving daily in a post-apocalyptic zombie-ridden New York City, presented in the same general tone as the film. On Facebook I started a weekly competition for which I was drawing a zombified celebrity, and whoever was the first to guess the identity correctly, could assign the following week's

celebrity victim. I also adapted the film into a webcomic and posted it online for free, to draw further attention to the film with online comic book fans.

In the promotion world right now there's something of a gold rush going on with social media. A lot of independent filmmakers that had to rely on festivals or press, or expensive theatrical showings for exposure, now have the capability themselves of both promoting and selling their films on the internet, through either a movie's official website or via a number of VOD services available that can print DVDs on demand or download a digital version to the consumer.

The venture in social media is not an easy one. It can quickly turn into time-consuming, continuous contributions to gain notice in a highly competitive fast-paced medium, but it may be one of the best options available for an unknown filmmaker to target a specific audience.

Maurice Devereaux: If you manage to get into a big festival this will help a lot. Contact various film websites that talk about similar movies. Have a website and trailer for the film online.

Donald Farmer: When your new film is completed, you've got two choices to promote it. Hire a publicist or do it yourself. And since most of us don't have the budget to hire a well-oiled publicity firm, it's pretty essential for filmmakers to know a few basics about self-promotion. If I've got a new horror movie I want the world to know about, first I'll email a press release to the major horror websites, then do the same to the main genre magazines. I'll usually upload the trailer or clips to You Tube, then include a link in my press releases. It's also good to alert some of the online genre radio shows and offer a couple of your actors as guests.

But don't be shy about approaching mainstream magazines and newspapers. When I was doing *Cannibal Hookers*, I got a nice article in *L.A. Weekly*, then *Variety* ran a half-page with my Canadian distributor, where he talked almost exclusively about my movie. *Chainsaw Cheerleaders* got mentioned on both Playboy.com and in the *New York Post*, plus I plugged it on a VH1 reality show I did (with a viewership of two million plus). But my best publicity coup was for *Dorm of the Dead*. Jackey Hall was starring and told me her friend Andrea was a regular on *The Howard Stern Show*, where she was known as "Miss Howard Stern." Jackey promised that giving Andrea even a small part in *Dorm of the Dead* would guarantee major coverage on the *Stern* show, and she was right. After we wrapped Andrea's scenes, a *Stern* producer contacted me to request video clips for Howard to show on his TV show. Then he invited Andrea to his New York studio and basically plugged my movie for a solid hour. Howard even gave me a quote we plastered over the DVD box and the movie's trailer. His audience perfectly dovetailed with mine, so I'd call that a match made in P.R. heaven.

Jeff Forsyth: The only publicity I have used so far has been internet based. For the newer projects I'm researching the idea of viral campaigns. I'm still learning about all the possibilities there are out there for getting your project seen. Although I have been at this "part-time" for years, there is still so much to learn.

Richard W. Haines: That's a difficult question to answer now since I'm still exploring new methods to promote my movies. Internet exploitation is still relatively new and everyone is examining the best method of reaching consumers.

In the past I hired publicists to help. They placed ads in *Variety* and other trade magazines, but that might not be the most effective way today, considering how the markets have changed. Publicists were useful for theatrical bookings, but many filmmakers are bypassing that now and releasing their pictures on DVD and internet downloads directly without theatrical exhibition.

William Hopkins: *Sleepless Nights* was originally released on home video by a small DVD distributor that specialized in low-budget fare. As I understand it, they had standing arrangements with big rental chains like Blockbuster, who would buy pretty much whatever product they put out, so there was little incentive to do any advertising of the film to the general public. It was only advertised in trade publications to rental chains and retailers. The trailer and key art they created were slick enough but weren't enough, apparently, to make the DVD a particularly strong renter or seller. Still, sales and rentals were good enough for the distributor to make back their expenses and make a small profit. The producers of the film might've considered spending some money advertising the DVD while it was still available in stores, but I doubt that would have had much effect on sales or rentals, so it probably would've been a case of throwing good money after bad. In the end I think there's probably a very limited market for low-budget films like *Sleepless Nights*, and the original distributor probably made as much from the film as could be made. No additional amount of advertising would've helped much.

By the time we completed *Demon Resurrection*, the DVD business had changed considerably. Blockbuster and other rental and retail chains were on the verge of bankruptcy and were closing stores and buying less and less new product. In addition, file sharing and piracy online had increased, further diminishing the DVD market, especially for low-budget entries like ours. So, while the internet gives us a greater ability to do inexpensive advertising for our film, the chances of making any great amount of money from DVD sales has diminished greatly.

So, what is the best way to publicize an indie film like ours? It seems these days you need a website and a Facebook page and maybe a Twitter account just to be in the game. But what will actually work to sell your DVD or streaming video? I'm not sure yet. I'm going to keep working on that and I'll let you know when I find out.

Steve Hudgins: It's great to have a publicist or someone handling those duties for you, which is definitely the way to go if you can do that. However, for a lot of filmmakers, that is not an option, so you have to publicize yourself the best way you can. It's very wise to get a website that you can refer people to or, at the very least, a social network page, like Facebook. A combination of the two is even better. That's a good starting point.

Rolfe Kanefsky: Well, here's where a lot has changed since I started making films in 1989. Back with my first film, the web was barely around. Everything cost money. To open a film in New York, you had to do radio advertising and newspaper ads. They cost lots of money. Television spots were out of the question because of the cost. We would hold screenings for critics and hoped they show up, enjoy the film and write a good review. Festivals were easier to get into back then and you could get some places like *Variety* or *Hollywood Reporter* to review the film there. All of this was to create enough buzz to find distribution and sell your movie. Today, all of this is still possibly but much harder. The advantage now is the internet. Between Twitter and Facebook and Myspace and personal websites, links to genre sites, et cetera, you can spread the word a lot easier. You still need to send out screeners and hopefully show your film on the big screen, but with digital and Blu-ray screening rooms available that's a lot more affordable as well. I'll give you a "that-was-then, this-is-now" approach. With *There's Nothing Out There*, we blew the film up from Super 16 to 35mm and held a cast and crew screening. We then submitted the film to many festivals, both domestic and abroad. This led to following the film around and collecting reviews, hiring a PR rep to organize critic and agent screenings. This was good and costly but didn't get enough attention, so we decided to open the film in New York and Los Angles ourselves with the theater chains. We held an advance screening in Santa Monica and invited dozens of studio people and agents before we began our midnight run. Guess what? Not one showed up. So, we had a private screening for about five critics. Kevin Thomas of the *L.A. Times* gave my film a rave review, calling the film "fast, funny, and a fine calling card for Hollywood." The following Monday, the phone never stopped ringing. Every studio wanted to see the film RIGHT NOW. They wanted us to send prints over to them. This is what one great review in the *Times* meant back then. Of course, they didn't end up picking up the film or grabbing me as a director because they were confused by the combination of comedy and horror and there were no stars in the movie. However, the word was out and eventually we did get the film released. When it hit video and cable, we sent out hundreds of postcards, letting people know. It took a lot of work back then to do something like this and we weren't a huge success.

Cut to 2006; *Nightmare Man* is ready to screen. First, we set up a Hollywood screening for some friends and reviewers of horror websites and magazines to see if they would help spread the word. Without distribution, they wouldn't. So, we went to *Fangoria's Weekend of Horrors* and took a booth and had a panel. We also screened the film that weekend. The response was great and a writer for *Jane Magazine* was doing an article on Tiffany Shepis. He saw the film and had a blast, giving us a great review in his article on Tiffany in *Jane*. Good start, so my parents and I decided to try the four-walling thing again. We contacted the theater chain that had released *There's Nothing Out There* way back when and got them to book it for a week in August. Again, they helped us screen a digital copy for critics. Again, we got a very good review in the *L.A. Times*. "A for effort in B grade Man" the headline declared. This time the phone didn't ring off the hook. Great reviews don't impress the studios anymore because everyone is a critic now, thanks to the internet. They want to see box-office gross. In the middle of summer, without much advertising, it didn't make much money. We did take out a small ad in some papers, did a ticket giveaways on the net, started a web page for the film, but there is so much competition out there now it's hard to stand out. Not that you shouldn't try. Use the 'net and every resource you have. Send out hundreds of protected screeners that read, "For Screening Purposes only," so people can't steal it. They will anyway, but protect yourself as best you can. Adam Green did a tremendous job with this for *Hatchet*. He started the *Hatchet* army and it paid off in a successful career. Eli Roth is also a master of self-promotion.

Anyway, with all of the great reviews, week-long theatrical run, producer's rep, great artwork and trailer designed by the Ant Farm, one of the biggest ad companies in Hollywood, it still didn't do much for us for *Nightmare Man*. We had a great poster, cool trailer, good reviews and still could not sell the film until I stumbled upon *After Dark* at Comicon. So, it's tricky but you must pursue every avenue you can think of. You never know what path might work. You have to stick with it and never give up. Remember, nobody cares as much about your film as the filmmaker ... and it helps to have a little luck.

But getting back to the question. Once you have a finished film, make sure it is finished before you show it to any potential buyers! It needs to look and sound great, because if you do get anyone important to watch it, they will only watch it once. Everyone says they know how to judge a rough cut, but they don't! Finish your film properly and don't rush it. You only get one shot at impressing the powers that be.

Then come in with a campaign. You need good artwork (maybe the most important thing if you don't have any name actors in your film). You also need a trailer to put up on YouTube and on the website for your movie (get your domain name before you even make the film so nobody steals it out from under you). Have an electronic press kit ready with behind the scenes, interviews, bloopers... All of this will be good for your eventual DVD/Blu-ray release. Make lots and lots of DVD screeners. This is very easy to do nowadays. Buy 100 blank DVDs and burn away. And then there are tons of ways to advertise on the net. Clips, links, banners — hit all your friends and all their friends. This is now common practice. Have frame grabs or stills ready to send out to genre sites. The cooler pictures you have to accompany your articles and press releases, the better coverage you'll get. And even though it will cost you money, submit to as many festivals that target who you think your film will appeal to. Have press kits ready to go with the screeners. Withoutabox is a fast and easy way to submit to literally thousands of festivals. Make sure you have some advertising money available, because this is going to cost you. Just submitting to 15–20 festival will run you $1 or two thousand dollars. Try to have a good trailer. Don't do it yourself. Hire a professional. It has to be slick and grab peoples' attention, just like the poster. If you don't grab their interest, they'll never even watch your film. The festival game has become a real scam, but you still have to do it.

Publicizing and marketing is a long, tiresome process. There are companies that can help, but if you have little money you have to do it yourself and be prepared for at least a year's worth of hard work. You never know what will pay off, so try everything. You have to be aggressive, determined and stay in people's faces to make your film stand out from all the others.

Brett Kelly: I always send out a press release when I start production to drum up some early buzz. Usually I don't spend a lot of time publicizing a film if it's signed for distribution. I leave that to the marketing people. Locally, I usually try to get a theatrical screening of some sort and send releases to local press so that I can have some press clippings to send along with my screeners that I send to potential distributors.

Chris LaMartina: A strong "high concept" story is necessary to mounting a successful publicity campaign. I'm sorry to tell you, but your existential rants on love in the mod-

Producer Jimmy George (left) and writer-director Chris LaMartina stand outside of the Charles Theatre in Baltimore for the *Witch's Brew* world premiere. Photograph by Charles Zimmerman.

ern world will not sell as many tickets as a splatter flick about a killer Easter Bunny.

Once a film is completed, we send out screeners to various websites that review horror films. Over the years, we've compiled a nice database of reviewers/sites that are friendly to micro-budget flicks, and we send those folks screener discs first.

These reviews will start the buzz going and will often lead to more coverage on third-party sites. After some decent press, we compile the nicest reviews into a list of sound bite–style blurbs and, then, throw them into a press kit of movie facts, a synopsis, and a flashy-DVD box. These packages are sent to distributors who have the potential to release the film commercially. We sell to distributors so we can focus on our next project. Speaking personally, I feel that we are the storytellers, not the salespeople.

However, it's important to fine-tune your distribution options before you drop hundreds of bucks on mailing out press kits. Miramax is not going to license your $300 Camcorder epic, but a smaller horror distributor just might. Do your research. Ask around with other DIY filmmakers. It will save you a lot of money and time.

Jim Mickle: Publicists can be miracles for low-budget films without big stars. For *Mulberry Street* we hired a publicist for the Tribeca Film Festival and they really helped to capitalize on press opportunities, setting up press screenings, scheduling interviews and playing up the recent rat outbreaks in downtown Manhattan at the time, which coincided with our little rat creature movie. That made a big difference for getting interest in the film and was the beginning of a wave of grass-roots affection for the movie that built and ultimately led to a distribution deal.

On *Stake Land* the distributor hired a publicist during the shoot and kept awareness on the project even before we started shooting. By the time the film was released there was a lot of press for it already.

If you're going to be at a festival that has any size or influence, it definitely helps to hire a publicist to help get buzz for the film. It can get lost in the crowd very easily.

Damon Packard: You're lucky to get *any* publicity. Some are better at making that happen than others. I've always said, "Control the circles of reality and you control the world." It has nothing to do with how "good" or "bad" something is, or "talent." It's all subject to interpretation. You can influence those things on the masses.

Brad Paulson: I think the best way to go about it is to have someone do publicity for you. This is something we've been doing a lot of lately. If you do this you look far less low budget than someone who no one has heard of that is trying to get their movie out there. There's just too many movies floating around right now. My usual plan of attack is to hit up all my favorite websites, send them a screener, build up some good reviews, then send that to distributors.

Jose Prendes: If you want your movie to succeed, then you have to make sure that EVERYONE knows about it. How do you do that? Well, you start pumping out info about it from the minute you get started. Casting news, teaser posters, production diaries, whatever! Get the word out and start building buzz before you even have a product. Social networking is one thing, but you have to go out and make a big splash, or your film will disappear on the video store shelves (if you are lucky enough to be distributed). I know from experience, and if I had to do it all over again, I would milk the shit out of my movies. You have to be Barnum & Bailey if you want to be Spielberg. Just look at Lloyd Kaufman. He may not be Spielberg, but people know him and his films.

Paul Scrabo: Publicity must be one of the items in your budget, and it's easy to forget this. I was so relieved (and worn-out) when *Dr. Horror* was completed that I neglected to publicize the film as much as I should have.

Eric Shapiro: The best way is to try to access good festivals that have built-in press awareness. Once you get into one of those, you can find out what publications are covering it and make sure they're aware of your film. If you don't find yourself in that kind of environment, it's all about directly contacting as many websites as possible and other publications that are interested in your subject matter, then sending out review copies, offering to do interviews, pooling the results onto IMDb and your own website, and trying to generate a sense of "chatter" so your work is relevant and on many people's radars.

Anthony Straeger: Tackling the publicity side of the film was also a learning curve for me, especially as I realized very early on that *Call of the Hunter* wasn't "genre specific" and didn't fit easily into a box or category. It wasn't a slasher, exploitation flick, zombie, vampire, ghost, or a comedy. What it was a well-written story with good characters. It was a bit of horror, suspense and humor all rolled into one.

One mistake I made in getting the film out there was that feeling I needed to prove I was working hard on the film for my private/friend investors. So I jumped pretty quickly into getting a distributor. What they made me do was put together important things like a press pack that included production notes, cast and crew details, production stills, et cetera. This proved really useful when I started looking at trying to get the film into festivals. These days you are tied with the festival circuit because it is mainly run through Withoutabox in association with IMBd and Amazon. That being the case you need to have all the information to hand in order to promote and publicize in festivals. One problem of jumping into a distribution deal is that it restricts you from getting into certain festivals. Getting a distributor for any film is really easy — getting a really good distribution deal is very hard.

One more point about festivals is to set

some money aside. Festivals are now big business and with companies like Withoutabox running it, it's $50 dollars an entry — that's not acceptance. It doesn't take a mathematician to work out the figures.

The best way to go about publicizing your film is not to rush to get it out there. That will not help you or the movie. You need to produce a whole list of things, such as a press pack for festivals. The website has to be good and you need help making it a site that will sell your product, not just show it. I think *Call of the Hunter* has a good website, but it is not a very good monetizing site and would do the next movie very differently. You have to have good stills and a great synopsis. You need to look at your social media, i.e., Facebook and Twitter, and you need everyone involved in the movie to be enthusiastic about promoting it.

Also, look for publications that may be sympathetic to your type of movie so that you can send them a copy of your film for a review. You can get some good reviews when promoting your film. If you have money then maybe a few chosen adverts in the right place will also help. Every member of your cast should contact their local home radio station and get an interview. One of the best audiences you can get to is a radio audience. It might be people at home, stuck in their car or in the work place, but millions of people are engaged with the radio. The internet is over flooded.

To reiterate, handling the publicity takes time and thought. You need to get into festivals, you need to get reviews, you need to get people to comment on your product. I have attempted to get entry into as many festivals as possible and have now renegotiated our distribution of the film in order to try and put the post-production knowledge I have gained over the last year or so into action. I think it is better to sell territories individually rather than that lovely phrase: worldwide rights in all media — hands tied.

Marc Trottier: I think a good way to get publicity is to get your film into festivals, which will in turn promote your movie. Cre-

ating a website is always a good idea as well. Make sure that there's a trailer available for people to watch. I never entered *Darkness Waits* into any festivals, but you can check out the website www.DarknessWaits.com and watch the trailer on YouTube.

Another example of "get your stuff out there," is my short film *Resolute*. After I made it, it sat on the shelf for four years until I decided to submit it to its first film festival, where it was publicly acclaimed and nominated best film at the Actra Montreal Short Film Festival. It was so well received that they changed the festival's judging rules for the following year, to make sure that there could be no manipulation for audience voting from other participating filmmakers. Moral of the story: It's fine to make things for fun ... but make sure people get to see it.

Mike Watt: The best way to achieve publicity with your film is to hire a full-time publicist who will spend every waking moment booking reviews, interviews, magazine, trade and internet coverage. Since we're forced to live in reality, that has never been an option.

I have spent some time as a publicist over the years and I know just what a Herculean task it is to sell anything in this economy, so the odds are really against you and your movie from the start. I can usually stack the reviewer deck in my favor at the beginning, but after that, it's really the word-of-mouth machine that will get your movie seen. The level playing field for independents consists of the horror convention market and your own website. Amazon has made it easier to list your movie on their service and you can even provide a VOD version if you want, but unless people know it's there, Amazon won't do you terribly much good. Retail stores always treated independent films like bags of flaming dogshit on their porch, and today, with fewer retail stores in existence, that prejudice has gotten worse, not better.

And Netflix? Once a bastion for indie movies, it has virtually turned its back on the micro-budget cinema, thanks to years of over saturation from small distributors, pressure from the Hollywood studios to release only their product at certain times, and, of course, the illiterate rat bastard publicly educated mouth-breathers who pride themselves on only posting the most negative hyperbole they can. Follow a couple of Netflix or IMDb "customer reviewers" some time — you'll find a dozen that have listed every movie they've ever seen as "the *worst movie I've ever seen.*" Netflix, the company, doesn't usually pay much attention to those reviews, but their shareholders do. So, once again, screw the indie rabble.

Even the IMDb has made it more difficult to get your film listed, requiring major coverage from websites or film festivals first. The star chamber judges at Wikipedia are even harder to circumnavigate. So, in the world of self-promotion, you have to be creative. Judging from those I know whose movies have done fairly well, their marketing campaign seems to rely heavily on YouTube clips and 24/7 Facebook posting. Magazine ads don't seem to do anything anymore (I once traded a couple thousand words of journalism for a full-page ad for *The Resurrection Game* in one of the major genre mags and netted a grand total of zero sales).

Film festival awards will help a movie in the long run; even those festivals run in someone's basement, because very few people bother to check a festival's credentials. The problem is that the bigger ones charge entry fees that can border on outrageous (I want to get my movie into your fest! I'm not applying to Harvard!) and often you're going to pay for a rejection due to a fest-runner's best friend vomiting a movie the weekend before and taking an available spot. But if they're free, or within your budget, enter your movie into as many festivals as possible. Get it to play everywhere. Because here is where the internet is on your side. Even the snarkiest blogger at least *lists* the movies playing at this fest or that. The more people that see your movie listed, the more potential sales you have before you.

Ritch Yarber: Unfortunately, micro-budget filmmaking does not lend itself to leaving much money for publicity once the film is complete. I think that it is important to explore every option to get the word out about your film. Taking the finished product directly to your target audience is the approach I use. Conventions, film festivals, the internet, social networking, word-of-mouth, begging, or anything else you can come up with, is a viable method for getting publicity. The main idea is to get the movie seen by the people that it was made to entertain. If the product is good, eventually things will take wing by themselves and the whole effort gets a lot easier. Trying to shove a bad product down this same chute will be a whole different story ... rejection will be quick and brick walls will be found. Successful publicity is made much easier by having a great product to promote.

With firsthand knowledge of how hard it is for independent films to get screening opportunities and publicity, TwistedSpine.com Films has twice held The TwistedSpine.com Micro Film Fest, a film festival dedicated to independent films made for $10,000 or less. Selected films from around the world were screened at our two-day festivals, and no admissions fees were charged to view these films. The idea was to get asses in the seats to view some great independent films. The festivals were a great success and we hope to present another event in the near future.

Ivan Zuccon: Promoting your film is vital. The truth is that you should always include the cost of publicity and promotion in a movie's budget. In independent cinema you often have no money for promotion, so you use new media to spread the news about the movie. I learned by experience that one of the best ways to launch a film is to work with actors who have a strong fan base. Working with Tiffany Shepis and Debbie Rochon helped promote the movie a lot, not to mention the fact that they both are incredibly talented actresses.

The Filmmakers were asked:

How have you handled distribution? What are some of the horror stories you've encountered? To your knowledge, has anyone made money from streaming yet?

Glenn Andreiev: *Vampire's Embrace* got video distribution, but it was a nightmare quest. Most distributors wanted me to go back and shoot extra nude scenes, so we filmed these soft-core scenes that really didn't fit into the film. The nude stand-ins looked nothing like the original actors. I heard of one person who made money from online distribution. I've become friendly with the man behind YouTube's highly popular *Annoying Orange* series. It's a series of simple, funny, and clever short one to two-minute-long videos of a screechy-voiced orange who picks on other fruits and vegetables in the kitchen. Okay, they are not feature films, but the little shorts — to me — qualify as films, and he's been quite successful with them.

John Borowski: Be very, very cautious when working with sales reps and distributors. I was sent many contracts when making my first film. I asked for changes to one of the contracts from a distributor and they refused, telling me that I was "asking for too many changes." The problem was that the changes would benefit me and not the distributor. Just because you are a filmmaker, do not expect respect from distributors, because you will not receive it. They are in business as well and they want the best deal for themselves, which is understandable. But if the contract is not acceptable to you or seems fishy, move on. Ask other filmmakers if they have done business with the distributor. The distribution waters are filled with many sharks. Foreign is very difficult, as there is no way for you to check on the accuracy of their reporting. Many times the sharks feed on first-time filmmakers and promise them the world, but once the contract is signed, then you never hear from them again and you never receive a penny from them. I

have learned this from my own personal horrific experience of dealing with a worldwide sales rep. No matter what happens, you must have an advance because sometimes the advance is all you will ever receive. Streaming is such a new method of distribution that everyone is trying to figure out how to transition. The good part is there is no up-front money being spent on replicating and shipping DVDs, since a master dub (usually Digibeta) is the only thing needed for digitization of your film for streaming. Get your film streaming on the internet; there are many sites that can stream your film for a nominal monthly fee, and you receive the residuals from viewers.

Keith Crocker: Okay, I pretty much answered most of this question in the previous question's answer. As far as the horrors of distribution goes, it's always the same, the concept of the middleman who is not needed. In other words, though Wildeye Releasing is a distributor of DVD titles, we need a third company, in this case, MVD (Music Video Distributors) in order for our titles to be carried in stores like FYE (For Your Entertainment), J&R Music World, et cetera. I had found this out years ago. I was trying to peddle one of my many titles that I sell through Cinefear to Tower Records. The guy at Tower kept asking me, "Who's the distributor?" I kept saying "I'm the distributor," but he didn't want to hear that. He wanted to hear names like Baker & Taylor and Koch Media. Unless you have a catalog with a hundred titles in it, they don't want to hear from you. I found out the hard way that the only way to make money in this business is to have bulk. At Wildeye, we are starting anew; we don't have a hundred titles to offer, hence the reason we need a sub-distributor, such as MVD. Luckily, they are a good, honest company, but like anything, too many hands spoil the soup. It seems, at times, like there is no money to be made in this business. The real money was in theatrical distribution and the early days of video and cable. DVD became sell through very, very quickly; it had none of the shelf life like VHS did. Streaming online is utter nonsense, fucking pennies; you have to be kidding me with that. Then add that all the fans have become socialist and want all entertainment for free. With the deluge of illegal downloading, making money in this business went from bad to worse. Abandon hope all ye who enter here!

Richard Cunningham: I've never actually handled distribution. In fact, for a long time I was shooting myself in the foot by producing films out-of-pocket, with great passion and sacrifice, and then failing miserably to effectively promote the film and enter it into festivals.

I do think though that online streaming is the way of the future for distribution of low-budget independent films. There are already several sites that offer filmmakers distribution and advertising services at a fee. The music industry was assimilated into the internet, so I can't see any reason people won't be purchasing the majority of their movies online in another five years.

Maurice Devereaux: For *Blood Symbol* I was so happy to have someone pay to help finish the film that I gave all my rights away (even if I spent about $27,000 of my own money). They then sold it to a U.S. company for peanuts. *Lady of the Lake* cost me $125,000. I sold the U.S. rights for $10,000. But then I, unfortunately, signed with a sales agent to handle foreign sales — they then sold it to a dozen countries for $39,900, coincidently, just under the amount they were allotted for expenses, which was $40,000. So, in the 12 years they have had the rights to the film, I made $0. Later I found out this a very standard practice by devious sales agents and their crafty accounting. They basically sell a bunch of films together to various distributors and just cross loop the amounts to all the films they have the rights to (and are allotted expenses for to promote, etc.), so they always have nothing to pay out. It's legal robbery. So, let's say a distributor really wants your film and is willing to spend $25,000 for it. The sales agent will throw in the deal four other films for next to nothing, but then will divide the amounts between each film, always ensuring that they will each be under their recoverable expenses amount. That way, films that would not have sold anything will sell the total amount of the recoverable expenses — but nothing more. So they pocket all the money and the filmmakers get nothing.

Most indie filmmakers are not business savvy and all the ones I've met, have ALL been screwed ... all of them. Here's another anecdote: I had also tried to get my film *Lady of the Lake* on Pay-TV in Canada. I sent a tape to the biggest Pay-TV channel but they refused it ("not good enough," they said). Then I met and signed a deal with a distribution company, who, in exchange for 15 percent, promised me they would get it sold to Pay-TV. Since I had already been refused, I thought I had nothing to lose. Well, lo and behold, three weeks later the distributor sold the film for $75,000 to the same Pay-TV channel I had initially contacted and it played in heavy rotations for over two years (over 90 times, which is strange for a film that "wasn't good enough" before), but the distributor never paid my share (85 percent) and went bankrupt. I never got a dime.

Why did the Pay-TV channel take my film from the other guy and not me directly? Well, the distributor probably packaged it with other films he had that the station wanted. And who knows, maybe he had a "relationship" built over the years of brown envelope "kick backs." Who knows? All I know is that my film played for two years on TV and I didn't make a dime.

So, because of all these middlemen ripping me off, I decided in 2007 to rent a booth at the AFM (American Film Market in L.A.) for *End of the Line* with a filmmaker friend to sell our films directly to foreign buyers. It was pricey ($10,000), but still a better option than dealing with sales agents who would rob us blind again (my filmmaker friend had similar nightmare stories with his films). At the AFM we both made a few sales, but, unfortunately, the market prices have dropped too much for international sales for this to be cost-effective now. Sales agents handle a lot of films and have not invested in the films themselves, so they can still coast for a while. But for us indie producer/directors, the game has gotten a lot harder. Also, for my U.S. DVD deal, a huge U.S. video rental chain had requested 6,000 DVDs for a rent-sharing deal. It was risky, but they were a huge, well-known, respectable company, and this could really be a profitable deal. So, instead of paying the regular $5 a copy (yes that's how much goes back per copy the distributor, minus his percentage, and the cost of shipping and fabrication, which leaves about $1.83 per DVD coming back to the producer), we could make much more. But, of course, they went bankrupt as well owing us a LOT of money. Also for *End of the Line* I finally managed to sell the film directly to Pay-TV, this time for $90,000. They paid one-third on signature and the rest was supposed to be given in installments six months later. They also went bankrupt and defaulted on the rest of the money.

But in the strange workings of Corporate America (and Canada) they reopened for business, under the same name, weeks later (with just a change of ownership for legal mumbo jumbo). Once again, the little guy gets shafted. Having been on the bad end of many business frauds, I am a big Michael Moore fan! There is real need to change laws in both Canada and America to prevent white-collar criminals from continuously raping the workingman in every field (not just the movie business).

On a different note, for my film *Slashers*, the U.S. release was a great DVD, uncensored 16:9 (widescreen) enhanced edition, but for Canada the company released a 4:3 completely censored edition that not only cut out all the gore, but replaced the many gores shots in the opening credits with spoilers on how each character would die later in the film — which is a live show! It was an absolute insult. And, to be even more ridiculous, the jump to a scene menu was kept from the U.S. edition and featured little clips with the all the CENSORED GORE! As well as the "Making of" that featured the gore NOT in the actual film, too. The reason is that they did not want to pay to have the film rated in each province (the film was unrated in the U.S.) so they asked the U.S. company to deliver an R-rated copy (which then gives an auto rating equivalent in Canada), so the U.S. distributor took out all the gore shots to be sure to get an automatic R (and not have to resubmit and pay more than once).

I contacted the Canadian distributor and pleaded with them to not release this butchered version. I even offered to PAY to have the film re-rated in each province. They told me to fuck off! They had the rights and I could not do anything. I was so ashamed I actually replaced all the copies at my local video store (at my own cost) with the U.S. uncensored version.

There's not any amount that you could make a living from, from internet streaming. The internet is still in its infancy as a money generator for filmmakers. Right now, it has hurt filmmakers more then benefited them.

Donald Farmer: The hard part in distribution is getting deals which pay the same rates as in the "video boom" days of the '80s. Back then it wasn't uncommon for producers to grab six home video figure deals for a 16mm or 35mm feature. These days you have to be more inventive with distribution, and more producers seem to be getting into self-distribution. Should you give your movie to a company that won't cover your budget but gets you in stores nationwide? Or would you rather sell fewer copies through self-distribution but actually make some money?

Three popular routes for self-distribution these days are: (1) place full-page ads in magazines like *Fangoria*, *Rue Morgue* or *Horror Hound*; (2) purchase booths at the major horror conventions; and (3) make online sales available through the Amazon store, eBay et cetera. Duplication is dirt-cheap, so lots of producers are opting to go this way and maintain more control. Besides, turning your movie over to a distributor can have plenty of pitfalls. They reserve the right to change your title, like when MTI Video retitled my film *Fighting Chance* as *The Strike* or E.I. Video retitled *Vampire of Notre Dame* to the embarrassing *An Erotic Vampire in Paris*. And with Blockbuster, Hollywood Video and others closing shop, there's fewer and fewer stores that will even stock low-budget titles. Now Redbox seems to be taking over, but everything may be completely online in a few more years.

Jeff Forsyth: I have not handled distribution myself, although I would like to learn. I've heard several horror stories of filmmakers receiving checks for about $14 several years later for a distributed project. I haven't delved into the streaming issue yet myself, and I need to research it. Eventually I would like to get to the point where, when I make a low-budget genre film, I sell it outright. That way I know what I have and I can divorce myself from the way it is handled after.

Richard W. Haines: As any director will tell you, distribution is the most difficult part of the filmmaking process. Over the years cinema has been classified as a producer's medium and a director's medium, but the reality is that it's a distributor's business. They decide when, or if, your movie will be available to the public, under what terms and who receives profits.

I guess it's better to discuss "collected revenue" rather than distribution itself. Collected revenue refers to the money a filmmaker actually receives as opposed to what the picture grosses in theaters or how many DVD units were sold. That all depends on what kind of deal you've negotiated.

I will say that, in general, many distributors play the "expense game." While the profit split may sound reasonable on the surface, they deduct their marketing expenses off the top. That's where it gets dicey because many exaggerate their expenses to the point where it seems as if it exceeds revenue. If that was the case they would be out of business.

In the past I've seen all kinds of questionable expenses in the statements they sent me. One gimmick in the past was for the distributor to place an ad for five pictures they were representing in *Variety*, which is very expensive. Rather than pro-rate that cost between the five films, they write off the entire ad expense against each movie. In other words, they're recouping more than they've spent.

There were ways around this. The best option was to get an advance in excess of your budget, which enables you to recoup your negative cost and show a profit. That's the most difficult type of deal to secure, especially today. Another method was to cap distribution expenses to limit the off-the-top deductions. A third was to give the distributor a higher percentage that included their marketing costs. It's better to receive 25 percent of a deal than 50 percent after expenses, which may not generate any revenue to the filmmaker if those costs are padded. Other worries are when your movie is packaged with lesser titles. In that event you'll only get a quarter of a four-picture deal, even though your film was worth more individually. It's advisable to separate domestic and foreign markets so you have two ways of generating income from separate distributors or sales agents.

I've negotiated all kinds of deals with my seven features. I've gotten advances that put me in the black and profited on deals where expenses were capped or recouped from the distributor's share. Other times I wasn't as lucky. I sold *Run for Cover* to a Pakistan distributor, but his check bounced. Every once in a while an indie movie becomes a "sleeper hit," but the odds are against that type of windfall, so it's wise to work out one of the options I mentioned.

Some filmmakers are using the DIY option, which means "do it yourself." It's very difficult but not impossible to distribute your own movies. I've done it on and off in the past, depending on the production. For example, I booked *Space Avenger* myself by calling up every cinema I could get a contact number on until one chain agreed to play a seven-theater run in the Washington, D.C., area. It's a non-stop hustle, but if you don't believe in your product no one else will.

In terms of advice I would tell aspiring filmmakers to keep a reserve fund for an entertainment attorney in case you need legal assistance to collect on a deal.

William Hopkins: As I mentioned, my first film, *Sleepless Nights*, was originally released through a small DVD distributor. That arrangement ended some time ago and a recut, remastered version of the film is now being distributed through Amazon.com on DVD and video on demand.

Demon Resurrection is being distributed on DVD by the producer and is available on Amazon.com and a number of other web retailers. The film can also be streamed on the official web page and on its Facebook page.

Whether or not streaming will ever come to represent any significant revenue source for small films like mine remains to be seen. But, for now, it's really the only way to go. Nobody seems to be making a great deal of money with product like this in any format right now. But we're going to keep trying different approaches and we're hoping to have a breakthrough eventually.

Steve Hudgins: We do self-distribution and keep any agreements we make with distributors, sales agents, et cetera, on a strict non-exclusive-rights level. If you're not signing your rights away, you don't have as much to worry about. But, still, you have to be careful when dealing with distributors or sales agents. Some of them are shady and won't pay you after they've sold your movies. You definitely should research their reputation before you decide to deal with them or not. It's not difficult to find some of their other clients and get the lowdown on their experiences with them. As far as streaming goes, it's in its infancy right now. Yes, I know people who have made money from streaming. I don't know anyone who has made a whole ton off of it yet, but some have done pretty well with it. Everyone is still trying to figure that particular medium out.

Rolfe Kanefsky: Well, distribution is the subject that very few people talk about. Everyone discusses how hard it is to make the movie, but once it's finished, selling it can be twice as hard. Like I said, I've gone as far as putting my films into theaters myself, but since I don't own my own distribution company, I have had to sell my film to others to get them into stores and on cable. I have often gone to the AFM (American Film Market) in Santa Monica, California. This used to be a great place for independent filmmakers and companies to find distribution for their films, both domestically and internationally. It now occurs once a year, usually the first week in November. When you're selling a film, there are many avenues to get it released. In the U.S., you have DVD, VOD, cable, television sales, and, now, internet streaming. Then you have the same for all the foreign markets. This could be a lot of territories and money. You can try to do it yourself, but buyers buy from people and companies they know. That's why you need a foreign sales agent to get your film out to them. Domestically, you hire a producer's rep or try to do it yourself.

A lot of companies want worldwide rights to your film. In the old days, a company would give you money to handle your film. Those days are mostly gone. It is very hard to get any kind of advance now when it comes to a rep. Because of that, you want to try to keep the domestic and international deals separate, so if you're not happy with your sales person, the whole film isn't locked up with one company. Now, it's easier to go with one company and let them handle the world, but if they don't come through, you might see your film sitting on a shelf (meaning unreleased) for years and years. So now, I'll give you an honest rundown of who has handled/distributed my films and how happy/unhappy I am about the results. The following is the stuff nobody talks about in this business, but I believe knowledge is power, so here goes:

There's Nothing Out There was sold to Prism Entertainment in 1992. They paid $75,000 just for domestic video. We then had a rep get the film to HBO, who also bought the film. I can't remember how much they paid. I'm guessing $50,000. Internationally, it was first handled by a company called Trident Releasing (now gone). They did very few sales, but had the film for five years. When we got it back, I gave the film to Alain Siritzky for a year and he actually sold to some important territories, like Japan. We made some money from that, maybe $25,000. After Prism went out of business and we got the rights back, we sold it domestically to Image for it's tenth anniversary on DVD. I was very happy with the DVD, but the money was very little. Seven years later, we got the rights back again, and through a filmmaker friend/connection, Ramzi Abed, got Troma Entertainment to pick it up. Troma had actually wanted the film when we first made it. They can get your film out there, but don't expect to see any money. However, for it's 20th anniversary, I thought Troma was a perfect fit, and we did a great two-disc special edition on DVD, in 2011, with the hope of one day going to Blu-ray. So far, we have not seen any money from this release, but it's out there and its cult reputation continues to grow.

My Family Treasure—a family film — was given to Arrow Entertainment, a company based out of New York. I don't think the producers saw much money from them. I believe Arrow is out of business now.

Rod Steele 0014: Now, this is a case where the producer is also his own foreign sales agent, which is very smart. Alain Siritzky has been doing this for years and he does very, very well, selling mostly erotic films. He produced the original *Emmanuelle* back in 1973. It made a fortune and established his name as a top producer/seller of well-produced, high-class erotica. I have made a bunch of movies for him in this genre since 1996. In the past he pre-sold his films even before he produced them. Those days are mostly gone, but he has a lot of foreign territories that still pay nicely for his product. So, internationally, these films are covered. The problem has been in the domestic market. Alain has a sales rep named David Gil, who has a good relationship with HBO and has bought many of his films to them. The current going price for HBO/Cinemax and their VOD channels for a late-night erotic flick is $75,000 and they usually have a two-year window to exploit the film as much as they want. So, it's a flat buyout deal. He does not see any more money unless they renew the deal after the allotted window. However, they do not take video/DVD/Blu-ray.

In the past, Alain had deals with Roger Corman, who released many of Siritzky's films on DVD, like the *Emmanuelle in Space* series, *Justine, Rod Steele* and *Misadventures of the Invisible Man*. But then Roger folded his video label and gave all of Alain's films back ,so Siritzky currently has all domestic DVD/Blu-ray rights to about 80 feature-length films. Having all domestic rights to this many films could mean a lot of money, but Alain doesn't trust many of the companies. He's tried to release some of the titles years ago with Image Entertainment and he didn't make any money. Peach Video (an adult label) picked up a few of "Emmanuelle's Private Collection." I believe they paid a little and grabbed the title *Emmanuelle vs. Dracula*.

The funny thing was that, whenever Alain gave or sold one of his films outright to a distribution company, the title did very well. But when Alain had a piece of the title, the movie was always in the red and never made any money for him. This is a common practice in Hollywood [known as] "keeping two sets of books." Of course, I've never had any backend to these films, so it doesn't matter to me.

Anyway, after doing a few of these sexy late-night comedies for Alain, I convinced him to produce a dark comedy thriller entitled *Tomorrow by Midnight*. With this project he had foreign partners, so when it was finished, his French partner got the film to Capitol Entertainment, a British company run by three women. They loved the film and were given all worldwide rights (remember my warning about giving one company all rights). Well, to put it nicely, they dropped the ball. I went to the Cannes Film Festival the year they premiered the film at the market (which happens alongside of the festival), and it was a mess. They got busier with higher profile movies and pretty much walked away from the film. When I went to their offices and asked about my movie, the people working there weren't even aware they were handling it. Without going into all of the unfortunate details, a big lawsuit resulted, with the producers suing each other over the movie. It got ugly, and the real crime is, *Tomorrow by Midnight* is a good film. In fact, it is still the film I am most proud of. Anyway, when a company can't sell a film, they naturally blame the film. It's never their fault.

So, this wonderful independent film starring Carol Kane, Alexis Arquette, and featuring Jorge Garcia (years before *Lost* made him a star), sat on a shelf in distribution hell. Capitol claimed that the film didn't work, so nobody was buying and they stopped selling.

That's when I stepped in and started submitting the film myself to festivals. I got it into a few, including "*MethodFest*," a festival that used to be in Pasadena, California, that supported "outstanding acting in independent films." Some important critics reviewed films in this festival, but we got in late. So, I personally sent a screener to Kevin Thomas of the *L.A. Times*, since he was such a supporter of my first film, *There's Nothing Out There*. He wrote back and said he couldn't promise he would review it, but he'd try his best. His plate was full. A week or so later he called me personally. He had watched the film, loved it, and gave it a rave review. In fact, he said it would

be a crime if this film wasn't seen. So, I proved that the film was good and it was the sales company that just didn't know how to sell it. I got *Tomorrow* into a few more festivals where it even won [for] Best Feature!

Meanwhile, the lawsuit ended with both producers winning ten dollars from each other, since they sued and counter-sued. At that point, I tried to get Alain Siritzky to take the film back from Capitol so at least we could try to release the film in the States. Well, Capitol said they would give the film back, but they had spent $40,000 on marketing costs, and, since the film sold so poorly, they wanted Alain to pay the difference and cover their expenses. He refused, saying that we can't keep throwing good money after bad. So, my film was dead in the water, being handled by a company who didn't want it anymore but wouldn't give it back without being paid for failing to do their job.

Frustrated, I refused to give up. I started going online and Googled the movie every now and then to see if there were any reviews, foreign sales, et cetera. One day, I stumbled upon a review in German for a film called *After Midnight*. Looking at the names, I realized that it was *Tomorrow by Midnight*, retitled for Germany. I had the review translated. It was a rave and I asked Alain if he ever heard of *After Midnight*. He hadn't. I told him that it was *Tomorrow by Midnight*. He was happy to hear that. I then asked him (remembering the paperwork because of the lawsuit), "Isn't there a minimum guarantee for selling Germany?"

Let me explain this. When you give a company rights to sell your film, you can put some clauses in the contract to protect yourself. The major international markets are Japan, Germany, England, France, maybe Italy and Spain. With these markets, Alain had a clause based on the going rate for sales at the time was "X" amount of dollars. Let's say $75,000 for Germany. (This was back in 2000, so prices have changed.) If the sales company had an offer for Germany that was below $75,000, they would have to get permission from the producer before they could sell the film. This is a good clause to have so your sales agent just doesn't give your movie away in a package deal for a couple thousand dollars. So, that's basically how it works.

Back to the story. I reminded Alain about the minimum and asked him to find out what Capitol had sold Germany for. He did, and guess what? It was way below the minimum guarantee — which means they breached their contract, selling the film for less money without getting permission. And that means Alain could sue. So, they quickly gave us back the film to avoid a lawsuit and waved their "expenses." And there you go. All that work that I had to do to salvage my film and I don't even have a back-end deal, so I'll never see money, whether the film is released or not. But every film is your baby and until it sees the light of distribution, it's hard to walk away.

So, Alain Sirizky now owns free and clear all domestic rights to *Tomorrow by Midnight* and has still not made a deal to release the film because he doesn't want anyone else making money off this movie if he hasn't. One day I still hope the film is released here. It has never been on cable, VOD, DVD, Blu-ray, and, personally speaking, it's my best movie.

Well, after that "great" experience, I made a teen comedy called *Pretty Cool*, also produced by Alain. This was a good commercial comedy in the *American Pie* and *Porky's* tradition. Alain, not wanting to be in the same boat with *Tomorrow by Midnight*, decided to hedge his bets. He would produce *Pretty Cool*, but I also had to shoot a more erotic version for foreign markets called *Emmanuelle Pie*. I did, and he sold that version in Europe immediately. He didn't even want to finish *Pretty Cool*, so my father stepped in and deferred all the postproduction costs to edit and mix the movie. Domestically, we screened the film a few times in Los Angeles, didn't find any takers and the film sat on the shelf, unreleased for five years. This is when I went through a bit of a depression.

I had made two 35mm features that were both good and both unreleased because the producer didn't know how to sell a non-erotic movie. And if the films don't come out, they don't really exist. I didn't know what to do. Luckily, I finally got *Pretty Cool* released in the States on DVD through MTI Home Video and that came about because of my next film.

The Hazing: I wrote and directed this film for a different first-time producer, Tom Seidman. He raised the money through his father and some wealthy friends. It had a small but healthy budget of $750,000. It also marked my return to horror/comedy. But before we even shot this film, Tom hired a producer's rep company called Lantern Lane to handle the film domestically. When the film was finished, we had a screening and then they sent out a lot of DVDs. This is now 2003. The film was well received, but the offers were low. Blockbuster wanted the film, but was only offering something like $25,000, so Lantern Lane sold the film to MTI for no advance, but MTI is one of the few fairly honest companies out there. MTI sold the film to Blockbuster for a lot more money and Tom Seidman did get some of his cost back. With foreign there were a few companies that wanted the film. Mainline Releasing made the highest offer of $75,000, and they took the film to sell overseas. They didn't do a good job on this title, which they changed to *Dead Scared* because people in Europe don't know what "hazing" means.

But MTI did do well and, because of this relationship, when they asked me if I had any other films I said yes, and convinced Alain to sell them *Pretty Cool*. So, even though it took five years, *Pretty Cool* saw the light of day in America in its proper R-rated form.

After *The Hazing*, I was hired by York Entertainment to write and direct a zombie comedy, called *Corpses*. Again, this was a production company that also sells their own product. Despite endless problems and the worst experience I ever had making a movie, it turned out to be one of their better films. But Tanya

York, the head of the company, had no idea what to do with the film. Just after we made it, a film called *Shaun of the Dead* came out through Universal. I loved that film and without knowing it had been trying to make something like that with *Corpses*. Anyway, after the film was finished and York was trying to sell the film at the AFM, I went into their booth to see how things were going. She was very unhappy. She couldn't sell a zombie comedy. There was no market for it. I brought up *Shaun of the Dead*, which was currently a smash-hit in theaters. She had never heard of it. This is a good example of having the wrong person selling your movie.

This brings up another issue worth discussing. Try to find the right salesperson for your movie. Sometimes the best sales company is not the best for your film. When *The Blair Witch Project* screened at Sundance, most of the buyers passed on it. They didn't understand it, which is good because, if New Line had picked up the film, it might have sat unreleased for years, been thrown out on DVD with no fanfare and *The Blair Witch Project* would not have become what it became. Same goes with Warner Bros., who owned the rights to *Slumdog Millionaire* but didn't like the film. They were about to go straight to video with it before the producers stepped in, showed it around town and got Fox Searchlight to take it, where it ended up making over 100 million dollars and winning the Academy Award for Best Picture.

So, be careful who you get into bed with. Make sure the people selling your film are really excited about it and give it their all. It doesn't guarantee good things will happen, but you're going to be with this company for awhile, so you want to be on the same page.

Well, after *Corpses*, I was frustrated with bad producers and decided to start producing myself with a friend, Gabriella Hall. We made *Jacqueline Hyde* together. Gabriella found a producer's rep who got the film to a company called Polychrome Entertainment, who had an output deal with Warner Home Video. It

was only for domestic and was a good advance. They paid $100,000, which at the time was very good for a no-name sexy horror film. We took the deal especially excited that Warner Bros. would be releasing it. Internationally, we gave it to a company called Shoreline. They did not give any advance and didn't do very well with sales, either. We never saw another dime from Polychrome; eventually, they went out of business with multiple lawsuits, having to declare Chapter 11. Again, there are a lot of crooks in this business. Now, Shoreline didn't do a great job for us, but that's not to say that they can't do a good job for others. It has a lot to do with timing and luck. I know some people who have had good experiences with companies and others that have had very bad experiences with the same company. Unfortunately, ALL of the companies I've worked with for foreign sales have been bad experiences thus far.

Next came *Nightmare Man*. You know what happened domestically so I won't go into that again. For foreign we tried American World Pictures, run by Mark Lester. He had handled my friend Jay Woelfel's film *Ghost Lake* and they had done a good job with it. Decent domestic sales through Think Entertainment (not in business anymore) and good foreign sales. They created a wonderful poster for the movie. So, based on his experience, we gave Mark Lester a shot. They put together a terrible poster and a bad trailer, which was really a crime because The Ant Farm had done a great poster and trailer for us that they refused to use. Unfortunately, this is standard for most companies. They will always do their own campaign, if for no other reason than to charge you the $40–70,000 for expenses. But the worst part was with such bad artwork and bad trailer, you know the film won't sell well ... and it didn't. So, once again claiming horror movies weren't selling well, American World sold [to] a few territories and, to this day, we only received about $20,000 for Japan and one or two other territories.

Pretty Cool Too came next. Now, this is an

interesting story. As I had said, *Pretty Cool* had sat unreleased for close to five years. I then got MTI to take it. The movie had shipped 10–15,000 units. Not great. However, a year later, MTI told Alain (the producer) that the stores that got it were doing great with the title and nobody knew why. It had become a modest hit on video and it was all word-of-mouth. *Pretty Cool* was a cute throwback to the '80s with a good attractive cast, some funny slapstick, nice nudity, and a surprisingly wholesome romance. I was very proud of the film from day one and very upset when it never came out. Finally, the audience I made it for got to see it and they liked it. Upon hearing this, Alain suggested we make a sequel and literally a month after we had that meeting with MTI, we were shooting *Pretty Cool Too*! Alain made his own foreign deals like before and gave domestic rights to MTI again. This one got into more stores and I think did pretty well. At one point, MTI said they would be interested in a *Pretty Cool 3*, but Alain had not made enough from either film to make it worth his while. However, I have written the script and would love to make it someday. Anyone interested?

So, then came *1 in the Gun*, which was originally called *One in the Good*. Once again, MTI took domestic rights and changed the title from "One" to "1," because it comes up first in lists on VOD. Smart marketing ploy there. Numbers come before letters, so 1 is number 1. As of this writing, I hear the film is doing great, having been bought by Redbox (27,500 units) and Blockbuster (10,000 unit or so). I think the producer (who isn't me this time) will make their money back and do pretty well. Unfortunately, international once again has stalled. This time, we went with Artists View Entertainment, a company who we heard great things about and has worked with MTI on a lot of films. But, for reasons still unknown to us, they have not been able to sell the film abroad, which they were very confident they would have been able to. We are currently looking for a different interna-

tional salesperson, but maybe they will still surprise us. Here's hoping.

And that leads to *Emmanuelle in Paris* and a new Rod Steele adventure called *Today Is Yesterday Tomorrow*. Both produced by Alain Siritzky again, these are R-rated comedies. One is a musical fairy tale with nudity. I'm calling it "Naked Glee meets Disney on Acid ... For Children of all ages ... Over 18." The other is my follow-up after 15 years (!) to Rod Steele, [the first in] my James Bond parody franchise. Siritzky is letting us run with *Wonderland*, and we've been submitting it to film festivals. It premiered at the Queens World Film Festival in New York in March of 2012. As of this writing, distribution is up in the air for both these films right now but I'm hopeful.

So, there you go. All the companies that I've dealt with for the last 20-something years. It never gets any easier, but if you work really hard you can probably get your film out one way or another.

As for the second part of the question, I have not had much experience with "streaming." My only internet experience was with a short film I made, called *Mood Boobs*. It was an 18-minute short starring Tiffany Shepis and Shaina Fewell. We shot it in 2005, just before *Nightmare Man*, and sold the film online. We did not stream, but instead shipped DVDs. It took a while, but we made a little money from it. The problem is that once the film is out there in any form, people will illegally download it, putting it on sites for free. I've spent a lot of time trying to get my movies taken down. *Mood Boobs* was doing really well with orders at $23 apiece until it started getting pirated. Then the sales just stopped. This is the risk of streaming, and people are still trying to figure out how to put an end to this. Currently, I don't think there's a good solution, so you have to be careful.

Brett Kelly: I've been very lucky and am sort of an oddball in the biz, in that all of my features, except one (a teen comedy), have been distributed internationally as of the time of this interview. I've been fortunate in that I

Brett Kelly with the publicity poster for his newest film, *My Fair Zombie*.

send screeners to potential companies, and someone contacts me to say that they want to release the film.

I've got a friend who paid a supposed sales agent to rep his film. He gave them $2,000 up front and they did the minimal amount of legwork possible. Sales agents get paid from the sale of your movie and should not need money up front. In the end, his film got signed to a tiny company and he hasn't got a prayer of seeing a return on his 2k.

Chris LaMartina: Distribution sucks. It's *always* sucked, but it's been especially bad lately. Digital downloads and streaming are not there yet. DVD sales are over saturated in content and dwindling in revenue. Even the shittiest no-budget flicks are popping up on torrent sites and there's not much any of us can do about it.

Recently, a friend compared the time we live in now to the time between the drive-in days and the VHS boom, where there was no real

outlet for exploitation content. I agree with the comparison, generally. I do believe streaming and VOD will figure themselves out ... but as for now, we can just tell stories for as cheaply as possible and hope they return their investments.

We've gotten burned plenty of times by shady companies. I've read dozens of inconsistent royalty statements where it's painfully obvious a distributor was making money when I wasn't. These aren't big bucks, but when you make a flick for a couple thousand dollars ... you *think* you should easily make that back.

Book of Lore, my second feature, got held hostage for two years by a distributor who was using it as part of a package deal with a dozen other titles. Empty promises were made. Lies flew fast and furious. Finally, we hired a lawyer and got the rights back. It was a fairly easy task, because of all the breaches of contract that the original distributor wreaked upon our deal.

We eventually signed the film over to the awesome gang at Pop Cinema, who consistently prove to me that they are the most honest game in town. The only bummer was that *Book of Lore* came out YEARS after being complete. This is all too common for indies. Distribution takes forever, and, in a climate where camera formats go out of date in six months, your movie has to be released as soon as possible so it looks fresh.

I've had plenty of comrades take the self-distribution route. It's admirable, but very difficult. You have complete creative control, but there are many downsides as well. You have to put in long hours and be willing to spend real money on promotion (magazine ads, web banners, horror film conventions). I've considered it many times, but at the end of the day, I'd rather be making movies and not selling them. Once you become your own distributor, you find most of your time will be spent marketing an old title instead of producing a new one.

Jim Mickle: For *Mulberry Street* we hired a producer's rep who helped navigate the festival/distributor/market stage of the film and they wound up getting a sale with Lionsgate. Lionsgate partnered with After Dark Films to release the film through the Horrorfest 8 Films to Die For label.

On *Stake Land*, the company that financed the film is also a distributor, so they held onto the rights and released it themselves, partnering with IFC for a limited theatrical release.

It can a very stressful looking for distribution, and a lot of people can get involved. It's hard to know what the right decisions are. Producer's reps can make a difference, but if the film doesn't work, they can't do anything to get people interested. In the case of *Mulberry Street*, most distributors passed on the film after the SXSW premiere, but then, after a lot of great reviews and buzz came out of several European festivals and the hometown crowd got to enjoy it at Tribeca, a deal finally happened.

I've heard of sales reps ripping people off or charging very high fees for doing very little work. But I've heard of people with amazing films who never get distribution, because the filmmakers decide to do everyone themselves and don't trust a sales rep. I've had good experiences so far, but it's up to each film to find the best way to get distributed.

Damon Packard: Virtually everyone I know has had trouble getting a fair distribution deal if they get ANY kind of distribution. And, as far as money for streaming, I don't know. Unless you are Netflix I don't see how, but I suppose there are others. Everything is so easily and readily available for free I don't see how — but I imagine people are doing it.

Brad Paulson: We've been corn-holed royally through distribution. *The BloodStained Bride* got out to quite a few of the big chains and had several thousand copies floating around. This doesn't even include the deals the distributor made with foreign territories. And, sadly, after all this, we've only made a couple hundred dollars. It's just too easy for

these assholes to hide money. I mean, look at how Peter Jackson had to sue New Line Cinema over *Lord of the Rings* because they claimed they didn't make any money. Some people, unfortunately, have absolutely no shame over taking all the profits over someone's hard work and not paying back the artists that brought them that great wealth in the first place.

As far as whether anyone's made money through streaming, I haven't run into that yet. I don't usually run into people with money. This would be a nice thing to change.

Jose Prendes: When I had *Monster Man* out there, people were telling me that you never make money with your first movie. It's true. I made some, but I didn't recoup my budget, which was barely anything anyway.

With *Corpses Are Forever*, my second film shot on 35mm and with an all-star cast of horror's best and brightest, I was hoping to make some money, but I ended up making less ... even though it got a wider release than *Monster Man*. One company wanted to take on *Corpses* for free and said they had a ton of places to sell it to, but when I asked for details, they got pissed at me for enquiring and I hung up on them. Another time, I got a voicemail from Lionsgate, concerning *Corpses*. I excitedly called them back, only to find out that the guy had forgotten he had already watched it and passed on it. That was the most disheartening phone call of my career. Distribution is tricky, but if you just want to get your movie out and don't expect big bucks, it is actually fairly easy to land.

I'm not sure about the streaming side of things, so I can't comment on that.

Paul Scrabo: Our movie is self-distributed through Scrabo.com and Amazon. I never considered even showing it to a distributor. For my DVD cover art, I hired a friend who is a professional artist.

Eric Shapiro: We were fortunate to have a good distributor, Big Screen Entertainment Group, license *Rule of Three*. They released it on DVD and got Netflix to license it, and it's being seen daily at a level that we once only dreamed of. It's heartening to know that many people out there are interested in watching a strange film with unknown talent. The horror stories are rampant. The worst one I've heard applies to my pal Hal Masonberg, who directed a film called *The Plague* (2006), which was seized from him in post-production and recut in its entirety before release. That experience pulverized him; he had no control, and has never, to my knowledge, even watched the final cut.

In answer to the last question: yes, there is serious revenue in streaming.

Anthony Straeger: How have I handled distribution? Well, in the beginning, very badly. As I mentioned, I jumped into signing a distribution deal far too quickly.

In the United States there are a million and one distributors with a roster of films on their books as long as your arm. They will make you pay for everything they do and then take 50 percent of the rest. You end up with very little, whilst they at least make something on your movie.

I have not handled the distribution of *Call of the Hunter* at all right. I have to take blame for rushing into the process because I thought that gave us kudos —*wrong*. Patience is a virtue, something I lack at times. But if you have spent so much time on your script and then production and the problems of post-production to come out with a product YOU think is great, then why the hell would you give away your rights? My advice is to submit to festivals, especially the important ones where you have a chance of negotiating a better distribution deal. You have to find the right target audience for your movie, and that involves patience.

There is, of course, an exception to this, and that is when a distributor offers to partly fund your movie in exchange for their territorial rights. Generally, this will be about 20 percent, and you will have had to secure the other 80 percent before they will consider.

What I have learnt is that you need to plan your strategy from the moment you have the final draft of your script, which includes:

1. How are you pitching the script?
2. What genre is your target market?
3. Financing. You have to calculate and recalculate what you have and will spend so that you get value for your money and that every cent ends up on the screen.
4. Take your product and aim it in the right direction of the market and festival circuit in order to stand the best chance you can at getting not only distribution, but maximizing the number of people that can and will see it. You will make or break your film on how you handle the distribution.

As far as streaming is concerned, and as to whether anyone has made any real money out of it, I seriously doubt it. I seem to pick up a few bucks here and there. The documentary I streamed has made about a hundred and fifty dollars in two years. I certainly won't get off the bread line with that!

Marc Trottier: I've only ever attempted to get distribution for one title, which was *Darkness Waits*. I ended up letting www.ScreamKings.com distribute my film, because I had lengthy conversations with them and I felt that I could trust them.

I don't know anyone who has made money streaming yet ... but I'd like to give it a try when it becomes available to me. YouTube now does rentals (but only currently available in the U.S.), so as soon as Canadian filmmakers can take advantage of this feature, I'll be sure to give it a try. I'd also like to look into using iTunes, if possible.

Even if I get *Darkness Waits* available for digital downloading for $1 or $2, I think I'd be happy. Hell, if the only way for people to see my movie was to give it to them for free, I think I'd do it at this point. Sometimes you do things for money ... and sometimes you work so hard on something that money becomes unimportant. What's the point of making something if nobody gets to see it?

I think the days of walking into a store and

renting a movie are coming to an end. All the Blockbusters in Canada are closing, in part because of a shift to digital downloads. Currently, Netflix is kicking video store's asses, and I think that's the way of the future.

Mike Watt: Again, we've been lucky enough to have avoided horror stories, thanks to many friends in the business. I know too many people who had to sue (if they could) distributors to get their royalties and/or rights back. Or filmmakers whose film was picked up and stuck on a shelf. Or they were screwed out of any profit, even when the movie made an ultra-rare fortune.

The majority of distributors we've dealt with were ones with whom we already had personal or professional relationships. Often our biggest complaint has been lack of advertising, particularly when an arm of the company will take out a full-page ad on something that (in our opinion) is garbage, while our (amazing and commercial) movie is left behind or relegated to a slug-line.

It's nearly impossible to get an independently made movie into retail stores any more, and with Redbox and Netflix continually throttled by the mainstream studios, forcing them to limit or even eliminate the number of indies they pick up. Because of this, we came to the conclusion that we cannot get into stores, without anyone's help. We've recently taken to paying for our own run of a DVD (which often means paying for authoring and design as well) and then making an agreement with a pro distributor to wholesale the units for us. This has been a beneficial arrangement for both parties. They don't have to pay for any of the manufacturing and we don't have to beat down doors to [sell] the product. Marketing is usually split down the middle and the wholesaler takes a much, much smaller bite than a distributor who had to handle the product from start to finish.

The internet has leveled the playing field very little, because *everyone* relies on word-of-mouth. While the studios can afford to dominate a top website with advertising, they're still largely at the mercy of the consumer. Since indies have a lower overhead, it's not unheard-of to break even or even turn a modest profit just selling DVDs from websites or at conventions. It may take longer, but an indie has less to lose.

And, no, I know of no one who has made any money off of streaming or VOD. In fact, many of the companies who have approached us for our content wanted us to pay up front for conversion, or "set up" fees, or whatever, in return for a 50/50 split after expenses (their expenses, not ours, even though it would seem that we're covering all costs). I'm sure there are legitimate outfits out there, but whenever I see, "Get your content to stream on Comcast," I file it with all the email for penis enlargements and Nigerian money laundering.

Ritch Yarber: We are currently testing the waters to gain distribution for our last two features, *The Deep Dark Woods: No Witnesses* and *Murder Machine!* Interestingly enough, although TwistedSpine.com Films was formed to develop and showcase the talents of people hoping to gain entry into the world of professional filmmaking, we have never had the salesman-type person in our group. We would take our finished films around to screenings, conventions and film festivals for our intended audiences, and eventually make the film's budget back through in-person and internet sales. Then, we'd re-invest the money into our next movie, totally ignoring and neglecting the distribution process. Our lone film currently with a distribution deal is *Transylvania Police: Monster Squad,* our first film. This came about as I happened to meet Steve Kaplan, the head of Alpha Home Entertainment, at a horror convention. During our conversation he found out that I had a film that featured Conrad Brooks. He was looking for a product to pair with another Conrad Brooks's film. He watched the film and quickly acquired the rights from me. Bada boom!! We have our first movie in distribution! Money comes in on a regular basis! Hey [I thought to myself], I like this! This was about nine years after the film was completed. It was just sitting on the shelf.

We are getting great interest from distributors for our last two feature films. The problem is that the companies want to obtain all of the rights to the films and pay nothing up front. All of our potential earnings are projected at 20 percent of future sales after this, that and other things are paid for. When we sell our own movies we make 100 percent of the profit. It just takes more effort on our part to get the product in front of the buying public. Thanks to some sage advice from a veteran independent filmmaker, we are marketing the films ourselves and keeping all of the profits from our work. Both films have already made back their production costs and are doing nicely for us. Unless a distribution company comes to us with a deal that knocks our socks off, we will continue with this style of marketing our films. We are also developing a new grass-roots marketing strategy that we hope will soon prove itself to be an innovative way for independent films to get a form of distribution that will enable the filmmaker to keep most of the profits from their works.

I have heard a few horror stories from fellow filmmakers concerning their experiences with distribution companies, particularly ones that deal in acquiring small-budget films. Charging for duplication and packaging costs, dishonest revenue reporting, lack of any real marketing for the film — the tales run the gamut, none good. The control and returns that marketing your product yourself gives is well worth the effort. Why not? Nobody knows your film like you do. Exploit this knowledge and enjoy the profits.

There are so many options for your film online. Streaming, pay per view, et cetera. More ideas are coming down the pike everyday, but, so far, to my knowledge, filmmakers are not making any noticeable profit from these venues. However, I do believe that the internet will eventually prove itself as a valuable tool for independent filmmakers, as more and more people turn there for their entertainment resources.

Ivan Zuccon: I don't deal with distribution personally. I sell movie rights and leave it all up to the distributor. If you're lucky, everything works. But never choose a distributor thoughtlessly: if you do, not only will you not see a single penny, but your movie may never come out and you won't be able to do anything about it because you'll have already sold the rights.

The world of distribution is changing; streaming is taking the place of home video. This is the future, and the future is now. I'm sure big studios are already making money with movie streaming; it's going to be hard for small, independent productions to enter the business without being absorbed.

Being an Independent Filmmaker

I've worked professionally in the film/video business longer than I've been making my own movies (by several years). During that time I have met hundreds of people who say they were writing a script or trying to get funding for their movie. Years would go by and they'd be in stasis. "Why aren't you making your movie?" I'd ask. The answers varied from, "Oh, I'm trying to get the money" to "Oh, my wife just had her first baby." Or, better yet, "If I can't get the money I need then it's not worth doing." Well, only about 4 percent of these people actually made a feature-length movie in 20 years.

The main reason I am an independent writer/director/producer is that I have a low-bullshit tolerance. I've always wanted to make movies, no matter what. My first movie, *Vampires & Other Stereotypes*, had the biggest budget and probably the best production value, but when that wasn't realistic for the next one I made due with what I had available. Only $2,000 to make an apocalyptic werewolf movie? Sure, why not? It was fun and adventurous finding creative ways to get these projects completed and distributed. Fortunately, it worked so well for so any years.

While a movie is always made for an audience, I envisioned that audience to be a fan just like me. If I was going to spend months or years on a project I had to love that project. I wasn't out to "make a quick buck" (as if that's even possible with micro-budget films...). I made enough money working at a production house in New York City. What I was going to do was make something that was specific to me, whether it be a vampire movie influenced by

Producer/director Kevin Lindenmuth (left) and Tom Sullivan, effects artist of *The Evil Dead*, who was interviewed for the documentary *The Life of Death* (2011).

197

a childhood of watching the original *Dark Shadows* (*Addicted to Murder 1–3*) or a documentary about death (me dealing with the impending death of my maternal grandmother). I was always going to do the best job I could on it, considering the circumstances and budget in which it was made. I like all of my films and there's not anything I would change in any of them. They are what they are.

Years ago, when I first started making documentaries, a moviemaker friend who had only seen my horror movies said that he could recognize that I had made it. It had the same pacing and the same types of shots. Basically, my style translated to a different genre, which I thought was interesting.

How do I want to be remembered? On one hand it doesn't matter to me if the films exist in some future time. Some people get hung up on this; they are downright paranoid that if their film vanishes a hundred years from now that all semblance of them will vanish as well. Who cares? They'll already be dead and probably not care at that point. But if someone *does* remember me, the filmmaker, I hope they recount that I was serious about the whole independent thing, that I did not tread lightly in the matter.

The Filmmakers were asked:
How would you best describe your work?
How do you want it to be remembered?

Glenn Andreiev: That I made genre films (thrillers, horror films) differently.

John Borowski: Someone once called my films "holistic works of art," and I feel that is the best description. My films are true crime docudramas based on serial killers from the early 20th century. They are created with meticulous research and precise filming and editing, to create a film that will have the audience holding their breath from the first frame to the last. My intention is to make timeless films that can be watched hundreds of years from now and still be as powerful as when they were initially released.

Keith Crocker: I come from a family of whom many members have worked in the social work field. I view my films as an extension of that same type of work. My films are therapeutic, almost like a real good enema. They clean you out, unscrew your head, set it straight and screw it back on for you. My films are designed to help people. They are steeped deeply in justice, activism, morality, and yet they are also very critical of society, have lots of dark humor in them and each film has a different effect on just about every type of member that constitutes my audience. You either love them or hate them. A real polarizing effect is achieved by my films, dividing audiences every time.

Richard Cunningham: Wide-ranging, maybe; I've tried to diversify the genre and style of my films and scripts. Engaging stories and characters. I guess I'd like to be remembered as a prolific artist, one who's contributed to and in some way innovated storytelling in an age when books and films and video games are all forming closer and more symbiotic relationships. But I also like to think that my real contribution to film is still ahead of me. I have a lot of material yet to produce before I can hope to reach that lofty of a goal. It's a continual process of learning and improving, sharpening skills and gaining new perspectives.

Maurice Devereaux: What I aimed for was to make entertaining horror films with strong female lead characters (something I always found lacking in mainstream films), but the only film I've made that I can truly recommend is *End of the Line*. For all its low-budget weaknesses, I do believe it's still smarter, scarier and more original then 90 percent of all Hollywood horror films made in the last 20 years. *Blood Symbol* and *Lady of the Lake* aren't worth anyone's time. There are some good scenes in both, but overall they are very amateurish. *Slashers* is pretty funny, but only Z-movie aficionados, who can forgive all its low budget flaws, will get a kick out of it.

I want to be remembered as someone who tried and gave 100 percent of all he had to his films and accomplished miracles with no money. And I hope one day some hotshot in Hollywood will look at *Slashers* and *End of the Line* and see that, with proper budgets, stars and marketing, these could be successful films and PAY ME for the remake rights (I'm too jaded to believe I would be offered the chance to direct them myself).

Donald Farmer: How do I want to be remembered? I tend to agree with Woody Allen when he said, "I don't want to achieve immortality through my work. I want to achieve it through not dying."

I'm probably more satisfied with my written work, the issues of *The Splatter Times* and my magazine articles, than with any movies I've made. With writing I'm not so handicapped by a low or nonexistent budget. More money wouldn't have made *The Splatter Times* any better or worse. But a bigger budget would definitely have helped my movies, so I'll almost always be dissatisfied when I watch them. I wish all of my 16mm movies were 35mm. I wish all my two-week shooting schedules had been tripled. I wish I could have had bigger names, better effects — pretty much better everything.

Jeff Forsyth: I really do not know how I would describe my work. My style is not fully developed. I have several genres I would like to explore. It's hard to pin something like that down. I would like to be remembered by friends and family, mostly, but as a filmmaker I would like to be remembered as someone with passion and as someone who never gave up.

Richard W. Haines: I think my "life imitates art" trilogy represents my best work so far. Each film is about a writer whose real-life experiences influence his work. The trilogy began with *Space Avenger*, which chronicled the adventures of a comic-book artist whose fictional alien terrorists turn out to be real. The picture featured real three-strip Technicolor from China, which is where we made the release prints. The vibrant primary colors simulated the look of a cartoon panel. I donated a print to George Eastman House archives as an example of the process and kept two copies for myself as a reference. The next film in the series was *Unsavory Characters*. A pulp-fiction writer picks up a femme fatale at a bar, and she seduces him into murder. He uses his ordeal to finish the novel he's completing. I shot the scenes from the book in black and white, simulating the look of '40s film noir mysteries. My last movie, *What Really Frightens You?*, is about a monster-fanzine author who asks the title question to a group of New Yorkers. After the article is published, their primal fears come true. We used a bizarre lighting design for the hallucination scenes and expanded the sound field from front channels to the surround tracks, giving audiences a visual and audio cue that something gory is about to happen.

I also think my technicolor movies book is a useful history of the process for film buffs interested in color cinematography.

William Hopkins: My films are meant to be escapist entertainment. On the budgets we're working with, we can't hope to produce product as slick as the stuff the major studios put out. But every once in awhile I'll hear from someone who has watched one of my films and they'll tell me how much they enjoyed escaping into the odd little world we were able to create. That makes it all worthwhile for me. It would be nice to be able to make money on the films we've made so far, if only to be able to make more films in the future. But, if in the years ahead, my films are looked back on as enjoyable, reasonably intelligent escapist fare that didn't walk in lockstep with everything else being put out at the time, I'd be happy.

Steve Hudgins: I'd like the films to be remembered for original horror, told in fresh and interesting ways. I'd like to be remembered as one of the top horror/thriller filmmakers out there, offering something new to the genre!

Rolfe Kanefsky: Well, right from the beginning I've always used "A Rolfe Kanefsky Flick." I did this because I think the whole "A Film By..." or "A Picture" ... is a little egotistic. It takes a lot of people to make a movie and even though the director is the one who usually gets the credit if it's good or the blame if it's bad, I never liked that possessive title. But I was told way back when that if a director does not take that title it means that he/she is not proud of the film or something went wrong. Well, I was and still am very proud of most of my films, so I decided to use "Flick." Spike Lee had already coined the phase "A Spike Lee Joint" so when I made *There's Nothing Out There* in the late '80s, I decided to use "Flick" and have used it ever since.

And I think the word "flick" is a good one to describe my films. In my opinion, a flick is a fun, somewhat lighthearted movie that you can sit back and enjoy. It's not trying to change the world, but is something you can have fun watching. I have always been most comfortable with comedy, and you'll find a sense of humor in everything I do. I can't help it, and what's the matter with lightening the mood every now and then? But, being a filmmaker who also likes to challenge myself, I constantly work in different genres since I love all movies. So, I've dabbled in horror, suspense, thrillers, film noir, musicals, dark comedies, and, at times, drama. I love directors like Alfred Hitchcock, who focused mostly on thrillers, but I also respect the hell out of directors like Richard Attenborough. I mean, who would ever guess the same man who directed *Gandhi* also directed *A Chorus Line* and *Magic*? A good director can do any genre and put his mark on

it, even if it's a invisible mark. That's impressive.

I hope my films are fun to watch. Sometimes scary, sometimes exciting, sometimes funny. I like to work in multiple genres and then twist them up. I always put a little quirky feel to my movies and have surprised many of my producers with the final results. I think a good film should keep you guessing a bit. You should not be able to predict the ending five minutes into the film, or, at least, it should surprise you in how it gets there. I've always said a good movie should be designed like a good mystery. The ending should be one where you don't really see it coming, but, when it happens, it all makes sense and you can go back and see how all the pieces fit together.

As for how I want my films remembered, I think I'd be happy if they were just remembered. I'm delighted that *There's Nothing Out There* has stood the test of time. The film is over 20 years old and on, the last release from Troma, received probably the best reviews I've ever gotten. People like this movie and continue to like this movie despite the whole "*Scream*" debate. It holds up. If all my films held up this well, I'd be very happy. I hope some of my films that were dismissed would be re-examined again, because I think people tend to overlook movies that have sexual content. They immediately write them off as "sex films," and I've tried very hard to reinvent the genre a little bit. I have never made a movie that didn't have my mark on it. Since I've written everything I've directed, each film and every character is a part of me in one way or another. My movies are personal, and each one does have something to say about the human condition. I've gotten knocked for this in the past. In college I learned that all films say something, whether you want them to or not. So, I decided then, "Well, if people are going to put meanings into my film, I might as well put them in myself." I try not to hit people over the head with the messages, but they are there if you look for them. I'm proud of that, but in the long run I just hope that people find my films entertaining and a good way to spend 90 minutes.

Brett Kelly: Jeez, I don't know. I prefer the title "genre filmmaker" to "B-movie maker." I guess history will be the judge. Hahaha. I like to make films about fantastic (in the classical sense of the word) subjects: monsters, aliens, robots, creatures, et cetera. I'd like them to be remembered as fun. I'm not trying to enlighten the world with a message. I just want to make people smile.

Chris LaMartina: Generally, we produce horror-comedies. There have been variations in tone, here and there. Some more atmospheric or darker than others. My recent features have been more "high concept" (highly marketable content ... able to be pitched in a single sentence). I'm a huge fan of ensemble films and my work reflects that. I enjoy crafting a sense of community through mingling story lines and characters. Coming out of a premiere screening and overhearing audience members discuss their favorite character is extremely rewarding.

I'm drawn to inject humor in my films because I see horror flicks as basic escapism. Even when I am alluding to real-world anxiety in a narrative, I try not to bum out the audience — the world is depressing enough. I'd prefer not to rent a movie and mope around for 90 minutes. I want to meet some characters I believe are decent folks and see them excel against the horrible odds on screen.

For a long time (and still, I guess) the most important thing for me was just to get a film distributed. I wanted to make sure that one day a young horror geek could stumble upon one of my flicks in a thrift store or bargain bin. That's what matters to me: having an audience find my films through self-discovery, just like when I sought out crazy low-budget horror flicks in my youth. It's a legacy of subversive culture that I'm honored to be an even remote footnote in. If I die tomorrow, at least those stories will be around forever. Telling stories keeps me going.

Jim Mickle: I make dark genre films with a heart and an emphasis on character. I like to think I'm helping to elevate the horror genre above what most people expect from it.

Damon Packard: I don't feel my best work has ever been realized because I've never had the money to realize it.

Brad Paulson: I make entertaining microcinema that transcends budget. I want to be remembered as someone who was always trying to do something different and never lost the edge of what it felt like to not only exist on the fringes but also to make movies on the fringes. I don't want to be a work-for-hire guy who just makes standard shit you forget about a week after you watch it. I really want to make something people can get behind. I would really love to make a living at making movies someday. Until then I'll be known as that weird but really nice kid in school who made movies that showcased the unique. I'd like to get people away from the CW crowd and all those people with horrible taste watching *Twilight* and reality shows and make them realize there are other people on this planet who are far more interesting than these douchey-looking Fabios who dominate TV and movies nowadays and, dammit, they deserve a look. I'd really like to be the guy who spreads that joy of that which is different to the mainstream. I'd also like to be known as one of the nicest guys in indie cinema. There are way too many assholes making movies out there.

Jose Prendes: Oliver Stone said, "When you look at a movie, you look at the director's thought process." This is very true, and you can quickly tell a shitty director from one who gave a shit. I consider my films to be an interpretation of the world through my eyes. I want the audience to see the story through my eyes, and that's why I love to operate the camera — because I can frame it the way I want to frame it and shoot it the way I want the audience to see it and experience it.

My first two films were formative, they were a learning process, and I don't think I've actually hit upon any of my major themes, so I

Writer/director Jose Prendes

can't describe my work based on my previous cinema. I will say that the themes of alienation and vengeance runs through most of my screenplays, so I see a real gritty viciousness in my material and the way I interpret the world that will become more evident in my later films (of which I hope there will be many).

In the end, I guess I just want to be remembered as one of the guys who really had fun with the medium. Everyone wants to be the next big thing, and I want that too, I'm not going to lie. I'm too driven to say, "I want a backseat to the big show." I want to make it big. We all do. But I don't want to do it alone. I want to be remembered as a good man who made movies like no one else and really brought something different to the world of cinema. It's a pretentious answer, but, then again, how the hell do you answer that question any other way?

Paul Scrabo: Since my only full-length feature so far has been *Dr. Horror's Erotic House of Idiots* and it's been described by a reviewer as "the first family-friendly erotic horror movie," I'll have to be satisfied with that!

Truthfully, I'm really not ready to be remembered yet, let alone any movies I've done!

Eric Shapiro: To date, my thing has been taking well-known pop genres and placing psychologically complex characters into them. With *Rule of Three*, that was Rhoda Jordan's achievement; she wrote a series of six-dimensional characters. The behavior in that film is very resonant. So the idea is, you come for the genre — which is something of a mystery-thriller — and you stay for the characters, who are stranger and deeper than you might have expected. I approached *Mail Order* the same way. It's adapted from a Jack Ketchum story, which means realistic psychology is part of the package, and instead of focusing on the gore and sadism, I tried to focus on what the characters' minds were like. I don't care if I'm remembered or not; I frankly just want to work actively in this medium while I'm here!

Anthony Straeger: I would best describe my work as something that I would not necessarily choose. That sounds odd, I know. What I love most in film, as a consumer, is not exactly what I produce as a filmmaker! As a punter, I love out-and-out gore and action, and anything that moves at a rapid pace. I have a low-attention span and need to see things coming at me at a rate of knots.

What I produce tends to be psychological thriller-based work. I like to describe my work as tight, lean and to the point. I hate having something over explained to me or drawn out. So I hope that, when people look at my work [they never say], "That was a waste of two hours of my life." What I want them to say is, "Wow, that passed quickly!"

I'm not sure that "professional" is a word that would be expected here. But I like to conduct myself in a way that makes people want to work with me again. Everyone who worked under extreme pressure on *Call of the Hunter* said the following: "I had a great time and you made hard work a joy." That works for me.

I would like to be remembered as someone who cares about what he's doing, but not at the expense of the people involved. I'd like to be remembered as a man that did what he said he would do.

Marc Trottier: Even though I'm a huge fan of the horror genre, I've tackled different genres and I think my work is very diverse.

I still have a couple of feature film ideas that I'd like to make. I believe one of them is a great idea, which has some very graphic content with an amazing twist, that would be huge.

But this film would require a lot of visual effects, and I think it would cost a lot of money to make. I almost feel like I'd need to make an impressive lower-budget movie to convince investors to fund this film. But I would love to get my idea from paper to movie screen and see people's reactions to it.

As long as I'm making movies that I like to make, and people are entertained, then I can't ask for anything else.

Mike Watt: "What kind of films do you make?" is actually the toughest question I'm asked. The short answer is usually the best — "horror" — but I don't think that tells the whole story of what our body of work is about. Without getting (more) pretentious, we tend to make hybrid movies, (blank)/horror movies, where the horror is just the jumping-off point for the story we want to tell. *Resurrection Game* we refer to as a "zombie-noir"; *Severe Injuries* was a horror-comedy that I feel lovingly beats up on the slasher genre; *A Feast of Flesh* was intended to be an unabashed sell-out movie about, as Amy wanted, "lesbian vampires in a brothel," but it became something very different with no clear-cut heroes or villains. *Splatter Movie* is probably our weirdest film, because it explores how horror movies are made and why, and keeps drifting in and out of reality. It's been referred to as "near-brilliant" and "not as smart as it thinks it is" — both of which I'm satisfied with. *Demon Divas* is an almost-pure '80s horror-comedy, but we still sneak in some satire. *Razor Days* is more a psychological thriller than a horror film, but it has horrific elements.

Again, we rarely draw from actual horror films as inspiration, though that genre is one of our first loves. *Splatter Movie* takes as much from *Performance* as it does any slasher movie. I also drew from what I thought *Inland Empire* was about before I'd seen it (and did a decent job pre-ripping off David Lynch, considering I'd only caught it from beginning to end about three months ago). *Razor Days* started off as a "*Chainsaw Massacre*" entry but became visually and thematically transformed by *Badlands* and *Persona*. Hell, *The Resurrection Game* is more *L.A. Confidential* than it is *Dawn of the Dead*. Horror is always the blanket we wrap around the stories we want to tell.

I hope that if we manage to leave any footprints at all that we're remembered for making offbeat, intelligent and largely original movies that give you something to talk about at the end. I would not want our stuff to be considered "disposable," by any means. Regardless, you can tell we always gave a shit about what we were making and that we were having fun playing with expectations.

Ritch Yarber: I describe my work as entertainment with a touch of quirkiness. I want my works to be remembered as purely fun entertainment that took the audience to a comfortable place for a few hours and that featured characters and stories that are reflected on fondly long after the initial viewing is over.

Ivan Zuccon: I don't want to be remembered; I want my films to be. My work as a director is in the service of the movie. My presumption is to be an author. I always try to impose my point of view, and, in the end, my point of view becomes the movie itself. It's like being a son to parents — the child is the only thing that matters. The parents' life, interests and needs take second place.

The Filmmakers were asked:
What is your favorite film that you have made and why— and what is your least favorite and why?

Glenn Andreiev: Let's end this one on a positive note. I'll name the worst ones first. For the worst, the tie is between *Vampire's Embrace* and *Silver Night*. Both were unpleasant productions. The first — looking back on it — was a very character-driven script. It was my first film and I wasn't quite yet an "actor's director," but more of a mechanical filmmaker. It was like giving an avant-garde filmmaker a soap opera episode to direct. I think that if I did *Vampire's Embrace* now, it would be so much better. Also, it was my first feature, so I was a nervous kid shooting that one. On the second "worst" film, *Silver Night*, there was serious hostility on the set. Both films got distribution, and I watched the distributed copies of both films just once, and that's going to be it!

My favorite is *Sharp & Sudden*. It's a comic paranoid nightmare that I think was nailed just right. The leads were so pleasant and were inventing funny stuff all throughout the film. The cast, crew (including my co-producer Vernon Gravdal, who whipped up the greatest, wildest no-budget stuff on the film), the location owners and the police, who let us use two police cars, were all so nice, they were all like out of a nursery rhyme!

John Borowski: *Albert Fish* is probably my favorite, even though there is a shot or two I would have liked to re-shoot. *Carl Panzram* is probably my least favorite because his story is on such a large scale, yet my budget was minuscule in comparison. I wish I could have shot reenactments, such as when he killed the six Africans and fed them to crocodiles, but that scene alone would have equaled my entire budget for the film!

Keith Crocker: I love both my features, *Bloody Ape* and *Blitzkrieg!*, because they are both very different films. *Bloody Ape* is very crude and very Punk in its attitude (and Punk is a word I hate to use, as I never had an appreciation for Punk music or culture). But *Bloody Ape* is just that, Punk! *Blitzkrieg!* is much more me stretching cinematic muscle, taking my time and trying to combine some fantastic imagery, interwoven with important dialog. Both films are loaded with production mistakes, which, in the same breath, makes me dislike them. They are fun to watch for a retrospective showing, but honestly, I have no

desire to dig out and watch my own films. We are always aware of the mistakes we made and would love to repair them, but that is something I would never do, as my mistakes speak volumes for me, as well as my triumphs. So it all makes for a nice little road map to me.

Richard Cunningham: My favorite would have to be *Year Zero*, because I was so intimately attached to every aspect of the film, and probably also because it's the most recent. They're all a little hard to watch for me after a while, but I think that's a sign of progress, that my early work is no longer on par with my current standards, and though I'm less confident in my older material, those are the projects that helped train me for my next film.

Maurice Devereaux: My favorite film is my short, *PMS Survival Tips* (on YouTube), because it is perfect for what it wanted to be (and only cost me $1,000).

End of the Line is my favorite feature and the closest I have gotten to making a "real" movie that is watchable. My least favorite is *Blood Symbol*, as it is the worst, but I have to say that all of them are my children and I still love them, warts and all.

Donald Farmer: I suppose the one movie of mine I'm most satisfied with is *An Erotic Vampire in Paris* because it came out the closest to my original conception and has the production value of all those Paris locations. Plus, Misty Mundae is at her best, so I'm happy with that one. In most of my other movies there are always individual scenes I like, such as the first sorority house scene in *Cannibal Hookers*, Mal Arnold's chainsaw death in *Vampire Cop*, Melissa Moore's demon transformation in *Scream Dream*, and Tiffany Shepis's zombie attack in *Dorm of the Dead*. But my goal is always to make a movie that works for me, from beginning to end. Ultimately, *I'm* the audience I want to please. My least favorite would be my kiddie movie, *Space Kid*. That was strictly a job for hire and I had zero personal interest in making it. Fred Olen Ray and Jim Wynorski have both made successful kiddie movies, but it's not for me.

Dave Meyers, Tatyana Kot and photographer Jim Knusch get ready to shoot the infamous castration scene in *Blitzkrieg: Escape from Stalag 69.*

Jeff Forsyth: The films I've worked on are kind of like my children. I love them all differently. I think that *Children of the Sky* is much more adult script. Much more serious. And *C.A.I.N.* is a bit more "fun." So in some ways I like *Children of the Sky* a little better, despite the limitations of the technical equipment I had.

Richard W. Haines: As I previously men-

tioned, I think my "life imitates art" trilogy are my favorite movies. My least favorite would be *The Class of Nuke 'Em High*, which was a work for hire that I didn't have creative control over. My original screenplay was much better than the altered version used during the shoot. For example, at the climax the mutant fetus shouted "Mommy" before allowing the teenaged couple to escape and blowing up the school. The creature was their offspring, which gave the story a Freudian twist. It was cut out by the producers, making it a campy monster on-the-loose picture. The movie has a cult following, but it's not the film I wanted to make. If you compare my subsequent feature, *Space Avenger*, you can see the difference in filmmaking styles. The experience inspired me to create my own company, New Wave Film Distribution, Inc., after its release.

William Hopkins: Having only made two films so far, that's an easy question to answer. While I have a certain fondness for *Sleepless Nights*, it clearly has many faults that will prevent it from ever being embraced by a wide audience. Even in its newly refurbished version, it's rather talky and slow, has some weak performances and a generally cheap look and feel. It has its strengths as well — the story is solid and the film has a certain creepy atmosphere, but it's only ever likely to appeal to fairly small audience.

Demon Resurrection, on the other hand, is a pretty solid piece of work, I think. We were able to tell a pretty involving, exciting story on a budget that was actually quite a bit smaller than the budget we had on *Sleepless Nights*. The film touches all the exploitation film bases, with plenty of sex and gore, and still manages to present a story that's intelligent, well structured and satisfying overall. So *Demon Resurrection* would certainly be my favorite of the two films I've made so far, though I hoping to top them both with my next film.

Steve Hudgins: *Hell Is Full* is probably my favorite movie we've done. The zombie genre was in dire need of something different and I think we accomplished that with a very original screenplay. *Maniac on the Loose* is right up there as well. It was the first movie we did under the Big Biting Pig Productions banner and definitely the one with the most twists and turns! It will always be one of my favorites. I expect our next movie, *Spirit Stalkers*, to be a great one. Anyone who enjoys shows like *Ghost Hunters* or *Ghost Adventures* is going to love *Spirit Stalkers*!

My least favorite is the first movie we did, which was called *The 3rd Floor*. Again, I look at it as a training film. The production values are very rough, but the amount I learned doing that movie was invaluable.

Rolfe Kanefsky: Well, I have to say my favorite is *Tomorrow by Midnight*, the film that still to this day hasn't been released in America. Isn't that always the case? It's my most personal film, it's about four college students who take a video store hostage for the night. I've described it as *Clerks* meets *Dog Day Afternoon* or *Breakfast Club* with guns. It was the only film that I had enough time and money to do it properly and the final result is almost exactly the way I imagined it, so it's closest to my original vision. It was well planned, and well executed, with a fine cast, a good DP and the proper support. That's what makes what happened to the film all the more tragic. It was also, in many ways, the most challenging. *Tomorrow by Midnight* and *1 in the Gun* are my most serious features that still have humor but also a lot of drama. Comedy comes easy for me, but to have six people sitting in a room and just talking for almost ten minutes about the world and their lives without the use of fancy camera moves or even any music and still hold the audience's attention is an accomplishment I'm very proud of. It was a tight script and the cast supplied great performances. *TBM* should have been the film that opened some doors in Hollywood and put me on the map but, because of bad timing and really bad selling, or non-selling as the case may be, that didn't happen. But if anyone wants to come over to my apartment in North Hollywood and watch it, I'd be more than happy to show it to you. It may not be my most commercial film. That's probably *The Hazing*, but *Tomorrow by Midnight* is my favorite.

My least favorite films are probably the ones I took my name off of, but I guess that's a given. So, if I disqualify those, I have to go with *Corpses* as both writer and director, and as just the writer, *Blonde and Blonder*, because these two are the furthest removed from my original vision. *Corpses* was a nightmare experience from beginning to end, with lack of money, a very bad producer, and a real lack of professional crew members. The only saving grace was the cast and meeting a talented script supervisor, Esther Goodstein, who ended up becoming a good friend and my producer of choice over the next couple of years. The film was sabotaged from day one and never recovered. I'm amazed the final result resembles a movie at all.

Blonde and Blonder was a script I wrote ten years before it was produced. I had hoped to the direct it, but once it became Canadian content and since I'm not Canadian, I was out of the picture. It was a funny script, destroyed by terrible rewrites, two actresses who were either too old or too uninterested to be in it, and another bunch of horrible producers who really shouldn't be in the business. I've said *Blonde and Blonder* suffered from too many crooks in the kitchen. It is not worth watching. *Corpses*, with the right amount of alcohol and the knowledge that it's a "zomedy," is almost fun. *Blonde and Blonder* is not, and, of course, this is the most-seen movie of my career. I just want to say one thing for the record. I was able to keep my name on the film despite the producers' best efforts to remove it because I was not Canadian and they need enough Canadians on the project to qualify for a tax break. Unfortunately, the real director of the film was not that lucky. His name was removed and replaced by the producer, who was Canadian and who took the director credit. The true director of *Blonde and Blonder* was Bob Clark, director of such classic Canadian movies, such as the original *Black Christmas*, *Porky's*, *A Christmas Story*, and many others.

You see, Bob Clark had been living in Beverly Hills for a number of years, so they claimed that his residency expired, so he directed the film with the producer's name on the slate as he tried to prove that he did still have residency so he could keep his name on the picture. If the writer and the director are not Canadian, the film does not qualify for the tax break, and this film was all about the tax break. I met Bob Clark on the last day of shooting. He was a very nice man and a personal idol of mine. His *Black Christmas* is a true groundbreaking slasher film and inspired many moments of my own in *The Hazing* and *Nightmare Man*. *Porky's* is one of the great teen-sex comedies of all time, and my *Pretty Cool* and *Pretty Cool Too!* owe a hell of a lot to it. And, of course, *A Christmas Story* is one the most beloved holiday films of all time. So, what is his reward for a career of 40+ years of making amazing movies? He and his son are killed during post-production on *Blonde* in a car accident, at which point the producers remove his name from the film, giving him a slight "dedication" at the end so they can get their tax break. As they say, the show must go on ... especially if the problem goes away by dying! Lesson to be learned: money rules the film business. Friendships and loyalty can't be counted on. Sad, but true.

Brett Kelly: I think my two favorites (as of this writing) are *Kingdom of the Vampire* and *Hell at My Heels*. They convey my sense of humor and they also look exactly the way I envisioned them. At the moment, my least favorite is *Attack of the Giant Leeches*. I had a lot of crew [members] drop out at the last minute and rather than put the project off till I could find replacements, I shot it myself. I felt pressured and rushed due to the lack of crew and the changing of the seasons. No fault of the writer, crew or actors, I just think I dropped the ball and should have waited. My total crew was three people, if memory serves. It was also a mistake to do a remake — I should have used the source as inspiration and come up with my own story.

Chris LaMartina: *Book of Lore* is the most personal, but it still has a million sophomoric mistakes in it. It holds a special place in my heart, but I can't call it my favorite. Instead, it's a tie between *President's Day* and *Witch's Brew*. I love the characters and direction in *Witch's Brew*, but also love the political in-jokes and tone of *President's Day*. It's like picking a favorite kid ... you can't do it.

On the flip side, my least favorite is *Grave Mistakes*, because we basically shot it to stay busy. We'd wrapped up *Book of Lore* and didn't have a producible feature script waiting. So, we began shooting shorts, with the goal of finishing an anthology. It was a good learning experience (writing shorter stories for effectiveness), but in the end, I felt like I didn't put in the extra effort. Not necessarily a rush job, but it seemed like we weren't challenging ourselves enough. If the film you're making seems too easy, you might be in trouble.

Jim Mickle: That's like asking who your favorite child is! I cringe at my student films, but I love them, for all their warts and for what I learned from them.

Damon Packard: I have a lot of problems with *Reflections of Evil*, because it was the one and only time I had the money to make a feature. It makes me cringe now for various reasons. I'm glad I made it, but there were some bad editorial decisions and I should have spread the money out and made two films. But I had no interest in plunging into another film after completing *Reflections*, it took a couple of years.

Brad Paulson: To date, *The Bloodstained Bride* is my favorite because I love the script on that movie and think that all the actors, with the exception of myself, did a stellar job. It's just a great all-around micro-version of a Hollywood movie with an edgy indie sensibility they'd never be able to bring to it. There are flaws with that movie, of course, but I think overall it's a very solid piece. My least favorite is *Paranormal Inactivity*, not because I think it's a bad movie, not by any means. I'm actually very happy with it, and our actors were amazing. But it was so easy I don't feel like I earned it. Blood, sweat and tears weren't poured into that movie and that makes me feel like I don't have as much of a personal connection with it. However, I feel like it's better in many ways than the movies I've worked much harder on and wanted to pull my hair out over.

Jose Prendes: *The Monster Man* is my favorite, by far. It may not be the slickest or most expensive, but I had the best time, and the best memories, making that movie. I spent $11,000 on that movie and it was worth every penny, even if I didn't make my money back. The main reason was that I got to work with all of my friends. Everyone pitched in with music, to camera work, to acting, to stunt doubles, to carrying crafty, and everything in between. Plus, I got to work with the hilarious Conrad Brooks and Denice Duff, who I had been a fan of since her *Subspecies* days, which made the experience very surreal. I look back on this movie and I smile. I wish every movie experience could be like this. Everything pretty much went off without a hitch and I got to share the experience with my pals.

Corpses Are Forever would be my least favorite. Now, I love it for what it is. But this $200,000 35mm project not only made me broke for a few years, but it severely winded me. I was dealing with a big crew and big cast (Debbie Rochon, Brinke Stevens, Richard Lynch, Felissa Rose, and others), and I was not only the writer/director, but the main star and the only producer on it. I was so burnt out by the end of this movie that I almost gave up filmmaking and didn't even want to watch another movie again in my life!

But when you have a passion, a need for something, it calls to you, and that's when I was sure that making movies was what I *had* to do, and not what I wanted to do. Also budget and time [limitations] killed me, and I wish I could have spent at least a few more days adding some more oomph to the picture, and fixing some very obvious mistakes that no one on set brought to my attention. But it was a learning experience and I am grateful for that.

Paul Scrabo: Certainly a love/hate relationship with *Dr. Horror's Erotic House of Idiots*. I was ignorant of all the capabilities of the camera for the first few days and the result is some footage that could have been better looking. At least the film was shot pretty much in sequence, so you can actually see the visual quality improve as it progresses!

If I had held off production till the next year, there would have been a wider range of affordable HD cameras to use, but the timing is never perfect — you just have to start making your film. A few years later, Mike Thomas, without whose participation *Dr. Horror* could not have even been made, passed away. And Debbie, Trent and Nate have gone on to greater accomplishments and it would have been tougher to get if we waited. And Zacherley is not as spry as he used to be. It's a miracle; you've captured time, and it was one of the greatest experiences of my life.

Eric Shapiro: I have to punt on the question, since my body of work is so tiny. For some reason, though, I generally come away proud of my work. That doesn't mean I think it's perfect, but that I do my best to capture an emotion, and if it's in the final piece, I'll always feel a strong connection to it. I can't go back and watch my work that comfortably, so I understand artists who are hard on themselves, but, in general, I love my stuff.

Anthony Straeger: This is a short answer, as I haven't made a thousand and one films and I don't consider my documentary work in the same way as I do my movie making. The choice is limited. But, for the sake of the question, I will group all of the work I have done.

I have made just one feature-length film and that is *Call of the Hunter*. I am proud of what we achieved in the making of this film. I've gained a huge amount of experience on so many levels. But the main thing is, I really believe it is a great low-budget British independent movie. I believe we have told a very interesting story in a very fascinating way. It will remain a favorite of mine, no matter what I do in the future, because I didn't go into it blind. But, despite all of my knowledge, I learnt so much. At every level we had a new challenge and at every moment in the development someone came onboard and did something surprising. It was incredibly hard work for all involved and was completely rewarding for everyone concerned. Everyone had a great time making it. In conclusion, the product itself shows that we made good of every cent we had, and that can be seen on screen. It also gave some new industry people, like Chris Reading and Sally Alcott, a good baptism into the business.

My least-favorite film I have made is a documentary called *A Day in the Life of Felix*. It's not a bad documentary and has been well received, but it deals with a subject I find disturbing and, as such, felt uncomfortable with. I could not have an opinion because it was important to stay neutral and let the audience decide what is afoot and how they feel about it. It deals with a very rare muscle disease and the problems of integrating a child into normal society. It might sound like I am being shallow here, especially as it was and is a subject that should be discussed; it's just not something I would have preferred to do.

I can't really qualify my shorts as favorites or not. They are the backbone of your education in filmmaking and, as such, each one has merits, one way or another. The main thing is, at the end of each one I could step back and ask, "What did I get out of doing that and what did I learn"?

Marc Trottier: Wow, you know, I'm going to have to give the same answer for both ... and that would be *Darkness Waits*.

It was my least-favorite movie to make because I've never been so stressed by something in my entire life. We had a lot of trouble with our microphones and with the audio during filming. We had renovations and changes going on at different locations that needed to be shot from different angles to hide these changes. We had a dirty lens that almost ruined a scene. Also, during post-production, everything that could go wrong did go wrong. I had a corrupt file that resulted in losing about 15 minutes of edited footage. I had to re-edit the entire film and redo almost all of the music when I decided to put the two short films together. I had someone try to scam me, which left me wondering if I was going to lose half of the film (which, luckily, I didn't ... or I would be writing this from prison right now if I had). I had technical difficulties when trying to get the color correction done at a professional studio. And, finally, I had my hard drive stop working, with no possibility of recovery, which contained everything (with no backup). For about a year after completion, whenever I would discuss the movie I would get this uncontrollable facial tick with one of my eyes! I'm having heart palpitations right now just by writing these words.

Ok, I'm all right now.

Surprisingly, after all that ... *Darkness Waits* was also my favorite film that I made, because I have so many fun memories from the entire process. I had so many laughs and good times during filming, and so much fun during sound recording and music mixing with my buddies. It was such a long adventure that took up so much of my life that I have nostalgic memories all the time about moments that I'd love to relive again.

Mike Watt: That's a tougher question because there are elements of all of them that I'm immensely proud of, but only see the flaws on the whole. I can sit through *Severe Injuries* more easily than the others, because it's shorter and tighter, with most of the cheesiness [being] the intended goal. Plus, I like that we have two very likable psychopaths as main characters. But I don't think I have a most or least favorite. Who is your favorite child? It's not really a fair question, because every one is an aspect of who we are as people and as a creative family.

Ritch Yarber: My favorite film that I have made is *The Deep Dark Woods*. The reason is, we approached the project with a crazy goal, making a feature-length movie in one day. I wrote the script featuring the character of The Ranger, a psychotic park ranger who killed to protect the "Law of the Woods." I cast Michael Perzel, a fellow TwistedSpine.com member, as the lead, which proved to be per-

fect in every way. At the casting call, we informed the auditioning actors of our goal and what our expectations would be of them. We got great actors who were firmly committed to helping us reach our goal. We started shooting the first scene at daybreak inside a car and ended with the sun going down on the final scene, just as planned. It was a long, tiresome, crazy day, but, we went home with a deep satisfaction and a knowledge that, from that point on, we were going to be a filmmaking force to be noticed. We could set goals and make them happen. Looking back, certainly things could've been improved with more time, but this was the maturity point for our group. Our next two films went on to win awards at film festivals and help establish our reputation for quality films on a micro-budget, all because of the confidence we got from successfully producing *The Deep Dark Woods* on our terms.

My least-favorite film that I have produced is a short, *The Tricky Treat*. Not because it is bad, but because it represents, in my mind, the one failure of TwistedSpine.com Films. *The Tricky Treat* was supposed to be one story in a projected anthology movie that our group decided to produce around the theme of Halloween. I am not a fan of doing short films, but the group convinced me that an anthology film would be fun to do. Reluctantly, I agreed to participate, and wrote and directed the short. Other members of our group were going to write and produce their tales to add to the film. They never were developed or filmed. The anthology idea was scrapped and the short that I produced quickly gathered dust on the shelf. Recently, I was able to shoot some additional footage and retrofit the short to fit the theme of another local filmmaker's movie, *Welcome to Cretinville: Legend of the Melonheads*, produced by Brian Lawlor of Laugh-at-the-Law Productions. The short looks great in this film and I am glad that it is getting used, but it still reminds me of the time when I let the ball get dropped. I am not a fan of that.

Mike Trivisonno (left, actor), Ritch Yarber (writer/director), and Michael Perzel (producer) at The 2011 Indie Gathering International Film Festival, during which *Murder Machine!* won for Best Thriller and People's Choice.

Ivan Zuccon: I am very proud of all my films since 2003, from *The Shunned House* on. My favorite is always the last one, of course, so it's *Wrath of the Crows*, because it's the freshest in my memory and the richest in recent events. Making a movie is like taking a wild ride. A strong bond is created among the people involved and when the shooting ends it's very hard to go back to your everyday life. It's like getting jet lag — you feel dizzy and empty for a while after the end of the shooting.

The film I like the least is *Unknown Beyond*

(2001). It's true that you learn from your mistakes and, for this reason, it is a very important film for me. I had to make it in order to make the mistakes I would have never repeated in the future. It's visually powerful, sometimes visionary, and has interesting insights, but the plot is muddled and often stumbles. It's all my fault, but I had to make all these errors in order to understand what direction to take in making movies. The films that followed are very consistent and I can say I'm proud of all of them.

Working on Other People's Independent Films

If you're not ready to take the plunge into making your own movie and want to gain experience, a way to do this is working on other people's films as a crew person. I think the best way to gain experience, such as with shooting and lighting, is to work as a production assistant on some professional video or film productions, where there's an actual budget and you have a specific role to fill. In this way, you gain technical knowledge and know what it's like to work on a professional production. I recommend you start with a "real" production company that works in the "real world." This can be anything from television to commercials to corporate videos. The skills you learn are basic and will be applied to your own productions.

Another way is to work on someone else's independent feature. However, keep in mind that these particular filmmakers may offer absolutely nothing in terms of the actual filmmaking. You may be more knowledgeable in many regards. You may end up working with idiots who will offer only frustration.

Last year I was having the itch to work on a new horror feature. When I was contacted by someone, with money for a budget and who wanted to produce a monster movie, I was interested, to say the least, and it would be a novelty not having to worry about coming up with the financing. Working on movies was something this guy always wanted to do but had gotten sidetracked with his real-estate business. He had a story/outline for a script, and lots of enthusiasm. He knew nothing

about filmmaking and needed me to do everything from writing the screenplay to coordinating the production to casting the actors and, ultimately, directing the movie. After we worked out the details and what I was getting paid, I was on board.

To put it mildly, this project went horribly awry and made me perfectly happy to just work on my own projects from now on. These are examples of what NOT to do on an independent film:

Dudley Does It

In 2010, nearly a decade after I directed my last genre feature, it looked as if I had landed a Michigan producer. I had been producing/directing/shooting documentaries that were later broadcast on PBS, but I was itching to do a narrative fiction feature. What this would be exactly I didn't know. This potential producer said he had lists of great ideas and wanted to develop one of these into a script. This was Dudley, the Producer.

This, of course, began with an email, which I automatically take with a grain of salt. If I had a nickel for every would-be producer who wanted to hire me to direct their movie I'd be set for life. This turned into a phone conversation that escalated into a meeting about a week later. He even paid for lunch, which constitutes a big spender in Michigan. He had found out about me through some how-to internet videos I was paid to do some years before. Again, it was one of those things I did for money, though I did put in all my two cents' worth about making independent low-budget movies. And Dudley had purchased my first two books. So he seemed serious about the endeavor.

He explained to me how he'd written comic books in the '80s, then got sidetracked with jobs and ended up in real estate. A big point was made that he wrote a story that was featured in the very same comic book as the very first "Crow" story and that he knew Jim O'Barr, the creator of that character. As soon as he told me this he whipped out the very same issue and handed it to me to read. Really? I went through it in about ten minutes and did my best to hide my true reaction. It was awful and derivative. I guess the point is that he always wanted to make movies and didn't want to wait any longer. It was a mid-life crisis — only he wasn't going for the affair — he was going for the film. The most surprising thing, though, was when he told me how old he was — only three years older than me, and I thought he was in his late fifties. Then he added that he had three children in the past ten years, and that explained the rapid aging.

The one thing that convinced me to do this is that he was sincere. He really wanted to make an independent movie. This was his dream. I understood that. It's what I had always wanted to do when I was a kid — grow up and make movies, though it's debatable if I ever actually grew up. He also seemed to take in what I was talking about — and if he had watched all those how-to videos and read the books he knew this wasn't going to be a "Hollywood Production." Well, you know what they say about "assume"...

I got through the basics — what he thought his budget was, and how, exactly, he wanted me involved. This was $50,000, and with me as the scriptwriter/director. He also wanted to shoot it by the end of the year, which was six months away, so this would be quick. He had written down a 20-page outline of a horror tale entitled "The Pharmacy" (terrible title!), which was about a golem-like creature that kills for revenge. It took me two days to read through the stereotypical, basic story, but it was something I could do and change it around enough to make interesting. The main reason I was interested is that he planned on releasing a comic book around the same time, which would be written and drawn by Vince Locke, who had done the *Deadworld* series and was the artist on *A History of Violence*. We'd both be basing our scripts on the same source material — this 20-page outline, though it would be up to us what we did with it. I thought that was a great idea. Most important, it would be something different.

I also asked if he had access to video equipment, as he wanted to shoot this in high definition. I did not have a HD camera. His answer: "Oh, I'm going to buy a camera and lights." In fact, what he said he was going to do was then rent it out as a "camera package" to film students and make his money back on it quickly.

"Have you ever rented anything out before?" I asked.

"No, but you just do it."

It was a bit more complicated than that, I knew, as I had worked at video-rental places when I was right out of college. A bit more complicated ... but one thing at a time. I wanted to do his movie before I ran his rental empire. Anyway, if he was buying the equipment, that was $10,000 of the budget right there.

What Dudley needed from me was a detailed budget breakdown and what I would charge. So I went with the amount he told me he had and worked backwards from that, working in my fee for my work naturally. This was six months' work, full-time. Because it was such a low budget, I was the writer, director, shooter and editor. It's not that I necessarily wanted to do everything, it's just that I knew I could. And the number-one rule of making a low-budget movie is to have as few crew people as possible working on it, in order to get it done. The first movie I had done, *Vampires & Other Stereotypes*, had over 30 people working on it and it really slowed things down and took about a month longer than I thought it would to shoot. It turned out about half as well as I wanted it to be. Five years later I did *Addicted to Murder*, with just me and a sound-person, and that went right on schedule. That turned out almost exactly as I envisioned it.

Dudley agreed to everything I said and assured me that my getting paid would not be an issue. I wanted him to sign a detailed contract, which listed everything we had discussed, and he said he had to show it to his lawyer. In the meantime he paid me the deposit for the script — and within two months I had the entire thing completed, exactly when I said I would. There were certain things he was hung up on, like having the main female character dress like a school girl (it was some fetish he had that I'm not even going to go on about here...) and another scene in which it looks like a guy eats another guy's eyeball. I didn't see the relevance of that to the scene, but I put it back in. These were little things, little hang ups. No problem.

The script was finished within two months and he paid me on time. Then, I asked about that agreement.

"Oh, I'm having my lawyer look at that," he said. "He's busy."

Okay. Dudley wanted to go on to the next step, which was scouting locations and finding a make-up person. The city of Detroit would be the backdrop against which the story took place. He said he'd met someone at some Detroit filmmakers' meeting, who had a loft space in a building downtown, which he thought could be used for the majority of the locations which took place around an old warehouse. I went with him since I needed to see this in order to plan further. What should have been an hour drive took two, as Dudley's GPS was not working. Once we got to the building he could not remember the guy's loft number or even the floor. Another hour went by, with Dudley calling on his cell phone every ten minutes. While we were "waiting," we wandered around the place.

The building was cavernous and barren, and it would take a lot of props to make it useful for our purposes. I mentioned this.

"Oh," he waved, "we can just put a green screen up and CGI all of the props in."

I tried to explain that was probably more work than actually getting the physical props.

"No, they do it all the time in Hollywood movies. I met a guy in Detroit who works for an ad agency and I saw his reel. He'll be great to do all this."

"Did you talk to him about this and find out what his rate is?"

"Oh, no, but I have his reel. I'm sure he'll work on it, though."

Oh, here we go...

I knew that if someone was working at a commercial agency they were getting paid real rates, which was far above our budget. I didn't even bring this up to Dudley, since this was outside his experience. I had to remind myself that this was going to be Filmmaking 101 for this "producer" and I'd have to treat it as such if I wanted this project to work out. Besides, I was too busy scouting the location. Later, I would have to go through my list of special-effects people who were willing to work on "budget" films.

When we finally heard back from Dave, the owner of the loft, and went up to the fourth floor, I saw that he was doing a great impression of an effeminate homeless man. I think he had just awakened. His loft was huge and ramshackle, and I wasn't quite sure what he did, though there was a studio green screen on one side of it, and a lot of backdrops and props. He explained, in a faint lisp, that he did a show (with producers and directors) that was on local cable. "Independent filmmaker" and "movies" came up quite a bit, but I never heard of him. When we went out for lunch, because Dudley slyly whispered to me that "once they agree to go to lunch with you, you've got them to work on your project." I just think the guy was hungry since it looked as if he hadn't eaten in days. We were also joined by a woman artist who shared his loft, this bald chick in a denim outfit. She was a local artist who kept on name-dropping other artists I've never heard of. And she had nothing at all to do with the movie we were making, as far as I could tell. The lunch went on for two hours and nothing was accomplished. Dudley didn't bring up the fact that we were interested in shooting there, and, as producer, this was his job. On the hour-long drive back to the suburbs I asked him about this.

"Yes, we're definitely going to shoot some of the movie there."

"Do you need me to send you a location release so you can schedule all of this?"

"That's a good idea."

"You should probably do it soon."

Twenty minutes later, he asked, "Do you think Dave and that woman are an item?"

Was he really that clueless? "I think they are both gay," I said.

His eyes widened in surprise. "What makes you think that?"

"I lived in New York and worked with the fashion industry. I knew a lot of gay people. I can tell."

"No, I think they're a couple."

I let him think that, since the alternative was clearly too upsetting for him.

After this "meeting," during which nothing was accomplished, I was anxious to get home. But Dudley informed me that he had to take some photos of some buildings in the area. What was this? I wanted to know.

"I'm helping a friend of mine with locations for a movie he's working on and told him I'd take some photos of some rundown buildings," he explained.

Well, there was a plethora of ruins in downtown Detroit, for sure. "Who is this guy?" I asked, already semi-knowing the answer.

"It's Jim O'Barr, the guy who created The Crow."

Of course it was. I think this guy was the only minor celebrity Dudley knew.

In the following weeks, I went on a few more "scouts." One was in his home town, about 40 minutes from where I lived. He wanted to redecorate the street to look like a street in Detroit. It could be done, but that would be a lot of trouble. "I can get all my friends as extras," he assured me. "And I can charge them to be in the movie." I didn't say anything because I didn't want to encourage what would be a mess. In the back of my mind I thought this was something else I had to add to my workload.

Around the same time Dudley said he may have found a make-up person, a guy named Hills, and wanted me to meet with him. The meeting was at this odd restaurant that was a combination bar and family center. One half was the "adult" section, and the rest consisted of games, pool tables and pinball machines. Dudley explained that this was his favorite place and that he frequently brought his family here. This time of day is was empty. Of course, I was the first one there and waited a half hour for my producer to show up, unfashionably late. We sat at the booth and waited ten minutes before I asked where the make-up guy was.

"Oh, I have to call him. He lives close by, so he said to call him when we got here."

Fantastic. The meeting was already an hour behind schedule.

Surprisingly, when he did show up, he seemed to know his business and had an impressive portfolio. The thing I liked the best is that he has a grasp of the low budget — he was accustomed to making something out of nothing, which is exactly what we needed. Later that night Dudley asked what I thought, and I said he'd work out. He shrugged. "I need to see his work," meaning he had to see it in person. So another meeting was scheduled at the guy's apartment, where we could see some of his props. This confirmed what I already knew — that the guy could more than do the job — and we left after 20 minutes, since I told Dudley I had an appointment I couldn't get out of. I just didn't want to waste any more time.

Dudley was excited and wanted to shoot a trailer for the movie.

"But we haven't even shot the movie yet," I said. "It's sort of backwards to make a trailer for something that doesn't exist." Actually, I thought this would jinx things. Every time I've seen a pre-trailer, the movie never actualized. Worse, it was the sign of an amateur filmmaker. It was something I did not want to do.

"We can use it to get investors," Dudley explained.

Hmmmm. He had already told me that he had the entire budget for the movie set aside. Why would he need investors? "I thought we were all set with the budget?" I said.

"If we get more money, we can do more," was his reply. "And I can use the trailer for promotion at the convention next weekend."

"What convention?" I said, somewhat alarmed.

"I rented a table at Detroit Comic Fair. I'm having flyers printed up and I want to show a scene from the movie." (Perhaps he should have mentioned this to me.)

"Well, this is going to take away some time from pre-production, at least ten hours."

"That's fine, that's fine. This is more important," he smiled, not having a clue.

So by the end of the week it was arranged that I'd go to the make-up guy's apartment, he'd have the mockup of the film's monster ready to go and we'd shoot a sort of generic scene. We shot in the garage of a friend of his, since we needed a dark space. I must say that the mask and hand prosthetics he made were better than I thought they'd be. The creature was basically a golem, made from a human corpse combined with automotive parts (Hey, we were shooting near the Motor City). The scene would be the monster walking in from a foggy/smoky darkness, looking at the camera, raising its hooked hand and walking by. All of one minute.

It took about an hour to set everything up. Of course, Dudley was nowhere to be seen. The make-up guy was concerned, but I told him that he was always at least a half-hour late, and that we should shoot the scene. As we had no other person to play the monster, the make-up guy donned the outfit. We shot several takes before Dudley showed up and a half-hour went by as he ooed and ahed over the monster. "We can use this scene in the movie!" he exclaimed. This wasn't even the finished monster and this "scene" wasn't even in the script. Hopefully he'd forget this grand idea.

Dudley wanted to shoot the monster killing someone and I reminded him that we didn't have another person in order to do this. I asked if he wanted to get all bloody. He was taken aback: "These are good clothes!" he said defensively. That answered that.

We did five more takes, although I already had what I needed to put together the video. I had to go.

"Send the video to me as soon as you get back," Dudley said.

"Don't you want it edited?"

"Yes, you are going to edit a trailer."

Although I had already told him how long this would take, I repeated, yet again, "This is going to take me a few hours and then another hour or so to load up to the internet. So probably around 10 P.M. tonight."

"You can't do it sooner?"

Maybe I could have, an hour, if he hadn't been an hour late... "That's the soonest," I stated. And that was quick. Everything was done on schedule.

With that over, this was now preproduction time. The script was broken down into scenes, locations and special effects needed and, of course, the most important thing of all — the actors. While the planning was happening I put ads for actors on a few Michigan actors sites and also on Backstage, which is the way to do it. The one thing I couldn't do yet was schedule the actual shoot of the movie until we had locations. Dudley told me, "I'll take care of it — don't worry about it."

Okay.

There was a whole slew of places he talked about shooting. I told him he'd have to get them to sign location-release forms, and also see if they wanted any money.

"Okay."

Weeks later, when I'd ask "Is that location secure?" he would say "Yes." I was relieved that this wasn't yet another job I'd have to do. However, when another month went by and I asked to see these locations, he said he hadn't spoken with the owners.

"I thought you said you secured everything... I've asked you this many times."

"Yes, we talked about this."

"I kept on asking you if you had secured the locations and you said you had." Perhaps I wasn't making myself understood, although I had sent him specific instructions on how to go about this. So I wrote an detailed email, again defining that "securing means you have it locked in, that we have permission to shoot there on specific times and days." The reply was this: "No, I don't have that. I thought you meant that we already talked about it."

Oh, my head...

As it was now fall, there was no way it would be possible to start the movie any sooner then February. I assumed I would have to help on locations, but the more immediate task was to start searching for actors. On October 4, the casting info was on several actor websites. Hundreds of emails came in, which translates to dozens of hours of downloading their résumés/head shots and sorting through them. I told Dudley that we would have to have auditions in three weeks, at the latest. His job was to find a place where we could have the auditions, just a room where people could wait outside. I had done this many times when I lived in New York City, and it would be only $50 to rent a space for that amount of time. Every other day I emailed or called to see if he had secured an audition space. The reply was always the same: "I have a call out to a hotel I stayed at a while ago — they'll give me a good rate on a conference room." Wasn't this simply a matter of calling them up and reserving the room for a specific day?

And what about crew? This was something I mentioned from the very beginning, as it was the backbone of the actual production. While I'd be doing the directing, shooting and edit-

ing, we did need some extra hands, at least five other people who could work the entire film shoot, for two weeks. Another meeting was held at Dudley's favorite bar/restaurant. I showed up, along with a 20-year-old guy who revealed that he was Dudley's neighbor from down the street, as well as the make-up effects guy. Why was he here? He had nothing to do with crew decisions. But Dudley wanted his input, nonetheless. Dudley was excited about the idea of getting all interns who maybe even paid a fee, to learn on set so they'd be future workers. No, no, no, no. It was going to be a challenge enough to shoot the movie with a small, tightly functioning crew who knew what to do. This wasn't film school and I had no interest in worrying about students while I was trying to get a movie done. This was bullshit.

I suggested we contact local colleges and put ads for film students. They'd at least know their way around. And put an ad on the production websites. Something ELSE I'd have to do as "ghost producer."

"We need an assistant director and a script supervisor," Dudley intoned.

Yes, if we were shooting a million-dollar movie. In this case those two titles were absorbed into "low-budget director."

"No, we just need production assistants and some gaffers — a few guys who know how to set up lights."

Dudley looked around at the two other people, then at me. He was frowning. "Kevin, we need to do this professionally."

Seriously? Two hours later I left the meeting with nothing accomplished. I had offered to search for crew but the producer insisted, "I'll take care of it."

I needed 30-hour days...

What I could work on was the actor situation. I contacted several genre actors I had already worked with who would be perfect for a few of the roles. I knew they would do this. Dudley wasn't sure they could act, although he'd seen them in the movies I had done, and demanded video auditions. Ron Ford, who was up for the main role as the pharmacist, emailed the YouTube link the next day and it was great — exactly what I had in mind for the role. However, when I told my friend, the "Scream Queen" actress that he wanted to see an audition tape and explained if it was up to me she'd have the part — I was just humoring the "novice producer," her reaction was this:

No, I have thought about it and I certainly understand someone wanting to see an audition, but, I mean, I just starred in Tom Savini's movie and he didn't ask me to do this. I wouldn't mind, but I don't know how to do lighting and don't want to send something that looks like crap out to anyone.

So I want to thank you SO MUCH for all the trouble you have gone to, Kevin. I really appreciate it a lot!! THANK YOU. But I won't be videotaping an audition for him.

Happy holidays I hope to see you soon!!! Debbie

I completely understood that she didn't want to waste her time. Hell, I didn't want to be wasting *my* time. I relayed this info to Dudley and he thought it was for the best that she declined, stating that she wouldn't be right anyway. A few days later he brought up the bright idea of "flying to Philadelphia and videotaping her audition." He explained that he knew someone who had a plane and that we could get aerial footage along the way.

"Uh, how much will this cost?" I asked.

"A few thousand dollars," he replied.

"Shouldn't we just put that money into the production? She already said she wasn't interested in the part. And why would you fly to Philadelphia? She lives in New York City."

"Oh." Oh.

The audition space room was set for two months later, a week after Thanksgiving, for two days, a Saturday and a Sunday. He expected a huge turnout. I told him that my concern was that too much time had passed from the time of the original actor posting and that the actors may not even remember the posting they had responded to. It took two days to email all of the actors and send them an "audition to do list," which told them to bring a résumé/headshot and prepare a three-minute monologue of their choice and that they may also be reading a short scene or two from the script. Auditions were from 9 A.M. to 6 P.M., and they should show up during that time.

I emailed Dudley to make sure everything was on schedule. I also emailed him explicit instructions of how to behave during the audition, such as sitting down and paying attention to them when they were performing, asking relevant questions, not spending more than five minutes per actor. I did this because he was a yapper and I could envision him talking endlessly about "his movie" with anyone who walked in. I asked him to confirm that he received all the info. When there was no reply I called his phone and left a message. He did not call me back.

Saturday morning was a severe snowstorm and what would normally be a half-hour drive took an hour and a half. I left early, planning for this, and arrived at 8 A.M., dragging my camera and tripod as we'd be taping the auditions. I went up to the lobby check in counter. "Hi," I said to the clerk," can you tell me which conference room is reserved for the auditions? It should be under 'Dudley Howard.'"

The woman typed on the computer, frowned and looked up at me, saying, "No one has reserved any conference room today."

Uh-oh. "Are you *sure* there aren't any auditions here today?"

"I don't know anything about any auditions. And neither of the conference rooms are scheduled today."

I quickly dialed Dudley and was promptly sent to voicemail. I left three frantic messages in 15 minutes. Meanwhile, actors started showing up early, so I directed them to sit down in the front lobby. I called Dudley again. Dudley stumbled in, appearing sleepy.

"So, are we all set?" he asked, a questioning look on his face.

"The hotel doesn't know anything about the auditions, and they say the conference room hasn't been booked." I stared at him.

"Oh, I'm just getting a hotel room. We can do it up there."

Oh, no. One of the things you never, ever do when having auditions is to have them in a hotel room. Unless you're doing a porn, that is. It's simply unprofessional and makes the actors uneasy, with good reason.

"I really think we should do it in the conference room," I insisted. "I mean, the actors are all waiting here in the lobby..."

"It's too expensive. We'll do it in the room."

I shook my head and walked away. I really had to take a crap now. When I came back out of the restroom he was getting his door card to the room. "So, where's the room?"

"It's up on the third floor."

No, no, no. "Do they happen to have a room on the first floor here?" He wasn't understanding. "If we have it on the third floor, how are we going to coordinate the actors? You're going to have to keep on running up and down the stairs to get them."

"That's a great idea. I'll see if I can switch the room."

He did. However, there was a king-sized bed, along with a just-as-large hot tub. I must have stared at it for a full minute. Then, I moved out the desk, put it in front of the bed and the hot tub, to sort of downplay it, then set up the camera and tripod in front of the desk. Hopefully, this wouldn't be too much of an issue.

While I was doing this setup, Dudley had disappeared. There was something he had to get in his car. When he came back he had a new HD camera and tripod. "Do you want to try out the new camera?" he asked.

I looked at my setup and then back to him. We needed to start seeing actors in minutes. Why didn't he mention this when he first walked in? "No, there's not enough time," I said sternly.

"That's a shame, I wanted to try out the new camera. The auditions will look better in HD." The disappointment was palpable.

"Seriously, it doesn't matter, we're just using the video to view their performances." Who cared if it was in HD? The only two people who would see this were me and Dudley.

It began. There was a very sparse turnout. I thought it was because of the horrendous weather blowing outside the window — two feet of snow expected by the end of the day. But when an actor mentioned that they weren't sure that the auditions were happening, I asked why.

"There's a post on the actor's website that says the audition was canceled. Someone called the hotel and they said there were no auditions."

Someone must had phoned the front desk earlier, and since Dudley didn't communicate with the hotel, they answered as best as they could. So this actor or actress relayed this misinformation on the website. The website itself, "Midwest Actor's Resource" printed the hearsay. And people obviously listened. I was expecting over 200 people to show up, but only 50 actors were taped that first day. Weeks of work — *poof!*

While I did most of the talking with the actors, answered questions and videotaped their bits, Dudley sat at the desk, typing furiously at his computer, not paying any attention to the performances. He'd get up in the middle of a monologue or scene, read, go into the bathroom or walk out the door, down the hallway. There was no rhyme or reason other than that his ADD was acting up. Then, at five o'clock his wife and three children showed up, bearing bags and swimsuits. He neglected to tell me that they'd be coming because they wanted to use the hotel pool. This was not cool, nor was it professional. I was still mortified we'd been doing this in a hotel room all day.

The post was taken down that night, but the harm was done. About 30 actors showed up the following day. I turned to Dudley and said, "I think we're going to have to do this again."

"Why? I think we found some great people?"

What the fuck was he talking about? He

hadn't even witnessed half of the auditions; he was either internet surfing or talking on his phone.

I assured all of the actors that we'd let them know our decisions within two weeks, by January 7, and I reminded Dudley about this. He and I had talked about this ahead of time, so I thought we were on the same page. As it turned out, we were on different chapters ... in different books. In different languages.

"Yeah," he beamed. "This went well."

I wasn't going to argue. "Okay. Well, I'm heading out of here. I'll make a copy of the auditions on DVD and mail it to you in a few days." I did all of this, along with my recommendations, the three best actors for each part. Over the next week I spoke with my producer a few times, though he had very different ideas for the lead characters. Basically, what determined the actresses for him was breast size rather than talent.

"Well, let me know if we need to do more auditions — we'll have to adjust everything."

"Oh, no, we're fine," he insisted, clearly pleased in his ignorance.

The two-week deadline was nearing and he would not give me the list of actors to contact. All contact stopped. Another week went by, during which he did not reply to at least one email and phone call every day. I emailed the make-up guy and he said he was supposed to meet with the producer the following week.

Maybe Dudley had either decided he was going to do things his way, and ditched me, or he ran out of money. The only thing I could do was guess, as there was no contact. A month later I tossed in the towel. I wasted enough time and energy on this no-go project. As email wasn't working I mailed him a letter saying, "Best of luck, hope it turns out exactly like you want." After all, I had gotten paid for all my work. It's just that the work did not culminate in anything. There was nothing left to do.

In April, three months later, I was emailed by the make-up guy, who asked if I was in contact with Dudley. He was frantic because he had put his own money — $500 — into all of the make-up supplies he had purchased and wanted to be reimbursed. Of course, Dudley was not returning phone calls or emails. I was curious: "When did you last hear from Dudley?"

"It was the end of January. He said he was having some money problems." Of course he was.

"Well, I haven't heard from him since December 12th. I emailed and called over a dozen times. He never told me he had run out of money, and he wasn't able to do the movie. There was no contact whatsoever, just silence." The make-up guy asked me if I wanted to buy the props, that maybe I could do the movie. "No, he hired me to write the script, it's his property. I was just a hired hand."

One year later I was still receiving résumés and emails from actors about this never-existing movie. It was the only — and last — time I ever worked on a feature that never existed. If Dudley had just given me the money for the budget and let me handle everything, the movie would be completed and distributed at this point.

The Filmmakers were Asked:
What is the worst thing that ever happened to you while making a movie?

Glenn Andreiev: In 1993, we raised a large sum of money (let's say enough to buy a brand new car) towards making a larger budgeted film. The rest of the money was to come from a South Florida "finance company." That company stole that money using fraudulent documents for funds that didn't exist. I got the F.B.I. and the Florida State Comptroller's Office on them, and the scam artists went to jail. The money, of course, was never returned. One of the scammers fled and I believe has yet to be caught. Other than that, I badly scratched up my back doing a fight scene for *Silver Night*.

John Borowski: The worst experience I had while making a movie was when the first interviews for *Carl Panzram* were shot. We were shooting with a Panasonic camera and utilizing the new P2 card technology. During the shoot we had to continually transfer the footage to a master 1TB hard drive. After the shoot, I transferred all the footage to the hard drive. The hard drive crashed. What I did not know was that the hard drive was a raid containing two hard drives. So half of the information was written on one drive and half on the other. This made the retrieval of the data impossible. So, not only did I lose the footage from the weekend, but I also lost about ten years' worth of data that was on the drive. I was ready to quit the *Panzram* film and filmmaking. Because I am so dedicated to my films I eventually reshot the interviews. I now shoot on HDV, so I have a tape backup in case the data is ever damaged or lost.

Keith Crocker: When I was shooting the 16mm short, *One Grave Too Many*, in 1989, I made the mistake of shooting the grave-robbing scenes at what I thought was a deserted cemetery on a Sunday. Suddenly, the dilapidated doors to the church burst open and out poured the parishioners. They came right over to us and started reading us the riot act for not getting permission to shoot there in the first place. Lucky for me, Paul Richichi was in a chatty mood and decided to intervene, babbling on that this was a class project, that we had to shoot a horror-themed project and we had no clue the church was still being used, et cetera. Anyhow, the pastor was a female, and actually liked us and gave us *carte blanche* to

shoot as much as we needed. Thus, the benefit of being diplomatic. But the lesson here is simple: being a filmmaker does not give you the right to be disrespectful. Think about what's going on around you and act accordingly. We could have easily shot that footage on a Saturday and not risked offending the parishioners. I tell this story because it's so relevant to using your head as a filmmaker.

Richard Cunningham: A third-degree sprain to my right ankle. Out of all the dangerous stuff I did during *Lycian*, including fighting with a real sword for a sparring scene, the sprain happened pretty ingloriously. A reporter had shown up to do an interview. I was answering questions in the village we had constructed, and at the end of the interview the reporter wanted to take some publicity shots of us on the set. We had built a guard tower out of rough pine and it was an ideal photo op, so I climbed it, and when I hopped back down off the ladder I landed on a block of wood that twisted my ankle over. It instantly swelled up like a balloon. I had to cut the interview short with the woman to go to the emergency room.

I was also one of the lead actors in the film, and there are a few scenes where I'm noticeably walking with a limp, because I was on still on crutches.

Maurice Devereaux: During the shoot of *Blood Symbol*, my co-director and director of photography Tony Morello, for some strange reason, decided to stock all of our rushes into his big hockey duffel bag that he carried around with him at all times. He had over 150 reels (two weeks' worth of shooting) in his bag, and during an early 6 A.M. Sunday morning, we were shooting in a deserted cemetery. We had brought the main character's bedroom set into the cemetery for a dream sequence. We were busy shooting, when we looked around and Tony's bag was gone and all our rushes with it. We spent the rest of the day looking for it, to no avail. We were absolutely crushed. We got a call late that night around 11:30 P.M., and it was the police.

They wanted us to go to a police station far from where we were. Confused, we asked why. They would not tell us. We arrived at the police station and a cop pulls out Tony's duffel bag. I almost fainted. Then another cop approaches and, with a very stern voice, asks, "What were you doing in the cemetery?" "Shooting a film," "What kind of film? A porno? We can arrest you for that you know..." Me and Tony look at each other baffled... Suddenly the other cop starts laughing... They were just teasing. What happened was a man was taking a walk in the cemetery and saw all our stuff, and thought that we were robbers! So he took the duffel bag and brought it to the police! Unfortunately, Tony's wallet was also in the bag, with $100 bucks that mysteriously disappeared. But, luckily, we got our rushes back. Also, a few years later, after spending over $12,000 to transfer all my rushes to videotape (to edit the film), I had them in a suitcase and was taking the bus while reading Stephen King's *The Stand*, so I was distracted. Suddenly, I go to pick up the suitcase and it is gone... The world spun... I looked everywhere, and retraced where I had been... Nothing... I went home and was totally numb. Luckily, I had had the good sense beforehand to put my phone number on all the cassettes. Someone called me who had found the suitcase. Ever since, I always put my name and number on everything important.

On the shoot of *Lady of the Lake*, during a sword fight scene between our actors Eirik Rutherford and Chris Piggins (in full armor), Eirik fell to the ground and hit his jaw against Chris's armored knee and cut it deeply; he had to be brought to the hospital. I was terrified, but he was okay, [although he] needed stitches. So for the rest of the shoot I had to shoot Eirik from one side of his profile so as not to see his big bandage or, later, the stitches.

During *Slashers* we had non-union actors and, one day, reps from the unions sent big goons to push me around and try to make the film a union production. We did not have the money to do so, so after uttering many verbal threats to me, to no avail, they tried to bribe my actors to leave the set and quit the film, with the promise that if they did, they would receive full entry to be union members (something that usually takes years). Luckily, the actors didn't quit. I'm all for unions, but in this case, they wrongly though we were a BIG film trying to circumvent the union and not pay people, when were basically trying to get by with next-to-no money. Later, I learned that the producer (the one who at went bankrupt and left the project) had shafted the union before, and they though he was still involved with my film.

But, hands down, the worst thing that ever happened to me during a film was on *End of the Line*. You know, I always laugh when I hear about directors on big studio films that talk about "the pressure" they are under. Well, let me tell you, you do not know what real pressure is until you have sunk every dime you own and borrowed even more to make a film. That, my friend, is *real* pressure! When shooting *End of the Line*, it was my first union shoot (no visits from goons this time) and I was getting a discount from the Actor's Union on the rates for the actors' salaries, but in exchange I had to pay the complete payroll of all the actors for the entire film before the start of the shoot, and it was "non-refundable" (the amount was close to $100,000). So any canceled days due to unforeseen circumstances, would be all extra cost to me, as I could not afford the expensive, "all-inclusive" insurance packages that would cover various mishaps. Unfortunately, my father passed away during the shoot, and I could not take any time off, as it would've cost me thousands of extra dollars that I did not have, to cancel or even delay shooting days. So I had to plan and organize the funeral on my lunch breaks for the next available off day. I think anyone who has ever directed a movie can empathize how hard it must have been for me to keep going and keep my focus. Unfortunately, a week earlier, my girlfriend of four years left me, and my mom had died four years before, so I was all alone to deal with this very difficult situation. I don't think anything worse could ever happen to me during a shoot. But it's now October 2011 and I haven't been on a shoot since, so who knows... If ever I do another movie, I'll probably be in a horrible accident that will leave me crippled, disfigured, broke and homeless.

Donald Farmer: The dead body our actress found during *Cannibal Hookers* was pretty bad. Most of the other terrible movie incidents have happened after the fact. Like reading about the death of Margaux Hemingway just ten months after she'd starred for me in *Vicious Kiss*. The same with Dana Plato, although that was a few years after we made *Compelling Evidence*.

But one of the worst things to involve a movie I made happened 15 years after we wrapped production on *Deadly Run*. Our co-producer, Samuel Rael, had apparently consulted with a man named Gary Hilton to concoct the plot about a serial killer who stalks victims in the woods. Hilton also helped Rael find some of the out-of-the-way locations we used in the Georgia mountains. Eighteen years after that movie was released on video tape, Gary Michael Hilton would admit to a real-life murder in the Georgia mountains. He is now in prison, serving time for the kidnapping and murder of hiker Meredith Emerson, and [is also] a suspect in three other murders. Rael said that Hilton was never officially part of the production of *Deadly Run*, but he claims that Hilton would stop by, and would even offer advice to the main character.

In a final twist to this very strange story, when a search party gathered to hunt for the missing woman Hilton killed in the Georgia mountains, a member of that search team was a movie producer named Don Babb. Just a few months earlier, Babb had produced my film *Chainsaw Cheerleaders*. So, basically, the story of a real-life serial killer has intersected *two* of my movies. And, if that wasn't enough, one year later, in 2009, I'd co-star with future wife killer Ryan Jenkins when I appeared on the

VH1 reality show *Megan Wants a Millionaire*. Jenkins murdered his wife just three weeks after our show debuted, causing VH1 to immediately cancel all remaining episodes.

Jeff Forsyth: I really don't know. Maybe it's like a mother's experience after giving birth. It was difficult and painful but I don't really remember the bad in any of the experiences. And I know there was. But, generally, when I do remember those experiences, the memory is anchored with the memory of how I overcame the issue and persevered.

Richard W. Haines: The worst thing that ever happened to me was losing creative control during the production of *The Class of Nuke 'Em High*. Whoever controls the financing controls the content, which is why I produce my own movies now. I still subscribe to the auteur theory of filmmaking, even though it's fallen out of favor in the industry.

William Hopkins: As hard as both shoots were, I don't think anything was more depressing than having the money run out midway through production of *Sleepless Nights*. That was a low point. To have put that much work into something and then have it be shut down, with no way of knowing if we'd ever be able to complete it, was as bad a feeling as anything I've experienced on either film. But, in the end, we were able to get the production back on track and complete the film. And we learned a lot from the experience, and were able to put what we learned to work when we started on our second film.

Steve Hudgins: I got poison ivy while filming *Hell is Full* and we accidentally broke the window on the front door of a house that someone was gracious enough to let us use in our latest movie, *Spirit Stalkers*.

Rolfe Kanefsky: Well, if I had been the one who died during *Blonde and Blonder*, I guess that would have been the worst thing. But since it didn't happen to me I have to go with my experience making *Corpses*.

Corpses was actually a never-ending series of worst things. I could write an entire book about this called "How NOT to produce a movie: The Unmaking of *Corpses*," but right now I'll try to give you just the highlights.

Hire the ex-boyfriend of the head of the company to be the development person who has a personal grudge going on that has nothing to do to your project. Oh, and make sure he is also a frustrated screenwriter.

1. Get the greenlight to write the script a day before Christmas and make sure the deadline for delivery is a day before New Year's Eve. That's right. Give us a brilliant script in five days in the middle of the holidays. Fun times ahead.

2. Have the development guy call up the writer (me) on New Year's Eve, drunk, liking 90 percent of the script but upset about one point and then scream at the top of his lungs that "I will never work in this town again" so loudly that he pops a blood vessel in his eye!

3. Make sure half the company quits or is fired a week before production of your film begins, including the development guy.

4. As the head of the company, leave town for the entire production and bring in a new producer who has a personal agenda that has nothing to do with the success of the movie he's producing.

5. Hire a director of photography whose wife is pregnant and expects to have the baby right in the middle of the production.

6. Make a zombie film with a wardrobe budget of $300 so there won't be any duplicate clothes when the blood and gore happen, so you can't do another take even if you wanted to.

7. Force the director to shoot on 35mm when the budget is barely $50,000 so you can only shoot short ends (that's the leftover film that lasts five minutes — if your lucky — but usually runs out in 15 to 30 seconds into a take). Oh, and make sure it comes from different film stocks because it's cheaper. (38,000 feet of film for a full feature! Yay!)

8. Try to cast the movie with non-actors who are in the news, because, that way, you can have a name but not have to pay SAG wages. And I'm talking a list of names like "Monica Lewinsky," "Siegfried and Roy," "Pete Rose," "Heidi Fleiss." (NOTE: I went with the only actor on the list, Jeff Fahey. Thank God he agreed.)

9. To save money on locations, shoot in a real funeral home with real dead bodies everywhere — and I mean *everywhere*! I will not talk about the smell. You don't want to know.

10. Flip your two-week schedule around the weekend before shooting begins so none of the special effects, props, or anything else will be ready in time.

11. Make sure you don't have all your locations lined up so the night before filming you can still be wondering where you're going to be shooting the following day.

12. Make sure none of the cast is giving good directions to get to the location the night before so everyone gets lost.

13. Make sure there's no film for the camera for the first two hours of the shoot.

14. Hire a sound man who is narcoleptic. (I'm serious. It happened.)

15. Hire a make-up woman who is so mean she insults one of the leading actresses and sends her off, crying.

16. Find out a week into production that the lead actress is pregnant and it's unsafe for an unborn baby to be around the chemicals they use in embalming rooms, especially when you're shooting in a real, working funeral home.

17. Schedule the film around the funeral home's working hours so the whole cast and crew will be shooting nights, coming to set during rush hour at five to six P.M. and leaving at rush hour at 8:00 in the morning.

18. Make sure you have one make-up artist who has to get almost a dozen actors into zombie make-up so that he isn't done until two hours before wrap time.

19. Hire a new cameraman to take the place of the one whose wife had the baby to shoot the other half of a scene that he wasn't around for in the first place.

20. Have an editor cutting the scenes without director input so rough cuts can be shown on set that make it look like nothing cuts together properly.

21. Don't get permits for your location so you get kicked out at midnight when you were supposed to wrap at 5:00 A.M. and because of this...

22. ...put together a secret second unit to shoot a scene that was missed because of the lack of permits and DON'T TELL THE DIRECTOR about it!!!!! Also, don't tell the cameraman, script supervisor or sound mixer. Schedule it the next morning in a secret location right after production shot all night so the director won't be aware of it. (NOTE: The director *did* find out, threw a fit, discovered where the shoot was taking place, and ended up directing it anyway, after having worked all night, all day and then another all-nighter!) Also, shoot the scene without sound, even though there's tons of dialogue.

23. Don't add any days to the production and just cut out the 30 pages of the script that weren't shot. It'll make sense, right?

24. And, in post-production, allow one hour to color-correct an 85-minute movie.

There's actually a lot more I could add but I think that gives you an idea of the worst experience of my career ... so far. I didn't think it could be beaten, but this past year it came pretty close. However, that will be another book, this one entitled, "Making Seven Feature Films Simultaneously: Do NOT try at home ... or anywhere else!"

Brett Kelly: I got laryngitis during the making of *Pirates: Quest for Snake Island*. I was directing and was also the lead actor in that film, so to lose my voice was devastating. I ended up thinking on my feet and giving many of my lines to other characters. I also wrote new scenes on the set to make sure I shot my page count for the day. I would direct with hand signals, with my line producer calling out what I meant. Too weird.

Chris LaMartina: It's Murphy's Law. Anything that can go wrong will go wrong. We've seen it all: locations falling through at the last minute, actors double-booking, one-of-a-kind wardrobe disappearing. props breaking, car problems, hard drives failing and (my personal favorite) blood-stained carpets.

A week into shooting *Book of Lore*, one of our leads got mono, and our tight schedule was basically thrown out of the window. Our shoot was supposed to be a month long ... it ended-up stretching into four months (mostly nights and weekends).

Three weeks before we shot *President's Day*, [the reps for] our high school location decided a gory movie was not good for their reputation and pulled their involvement. We'd written the script specifically for that school, and we were screwed. The budget was already half spent on props, wardrobe, and effects. We scrambled, but, luckily, found a replacement at the last minute.

How *Witch's Brew* was even finished is an enigma to me. We faced every obstacle known to man. Our budget (from Kickstarter), didn't get deposited until two weeks before shooting ... which meant our effects crew and costume department were self-funding and waiting to be repaid. We had to fire an actor (a first for me); we had locations that weren't found until days before we shot; and — the worst, for me — was getting laid off from my job and realizing my healthcare costs were going to jump to terrifying heights (damn my dysfunctional pancreas). After our first day of shooting, I was an emotional mess and almost called the entire production off. Luckily, my partner, Jimmy George, is a good friend, my number-one cheerleader, and a hell of a producer. He saved that movie ... not just that day, but consistently. He never let me give up.

Jim Mickle: During the shoot for *Mulberry Street*, my girlfriend's brother died. She was producing my film and another film at the same time. It was devastating for both of us, but also a complete shock to happen during a shoot because you live in a bubble when you're making a film and something like that can snap you back into the real world pretty quick. Hurricane Katrina happened that week, too, and I knew nothing about it until weeks later. It was a very emotionally complex situation to go through an intense, personal, emotional experience like that while also making a first feature.

Damon Packard: Can't think of anything truly horrible, but there was a disastrous day of *Foxfur* shooting that never happened because of bad planning.

Brad Paulson: There have been so many bad things. Where should I begin?

Our lead actress had a father who had a heart attack a week into the shoot. Murphy's Law really had it out for us on that movie. Either that, or it was the Fates testing me to see if I was really prepared to make movies for a living. Making it through that movie cured my nerves for upcoming projects.

Jose Prendes: On the first day of shooting *Monster Man*, I had assembled the cast and we headed out toward our location, which was an hour away from anywhere in Homestead, which is Florida farm country. When we get there, we set out the snacks and the lunches and tripod. I grab the camera and set it up as I instruct my friend Javier Castineira, who was my assistant director, to open up the new pack of tapes. He responds with, "What tapes?" It turned out that I had had so much on my mind that I packed everything ... except the damn tapes. We had to scrap the whole day and the location, which was a major disappoint and got me so mad that I ripped the rearview mirror off of my car's windshield.

Paul Scrabo: The worst thing is the sudden, overwhelming chill that overtakes you that you are making a complete disaster, and why the hell am I involving other people in this? At some point this feeling occurs with any project I create for public consumption.

Eric Shapiro: After we finished shooting *Rule of Three*, the hard drive with all the footage on it crashed, and we had to go through a very painstaking, methodical, nervous-breakdown-inducing process to save it. Not a happy time, and I'm still somewhat shocked that we came out okay.

Anthony Straeger: The worst thing that ever happened to me was realizing that after two days into shooting *Call of the Hunter*, I hadn't really given myself enough time for the whole project. And the reason was simple enough: I didn't have enough money to pay for an extra two to five days.

It was late on the Monday night and after dinner we returned to the main location/house we were staying, and, after a nightcap, everyone went to bed. Stephen knew I was worried and asked if he could stay up with me, but I needed some time on my own and time to think. I sat at the table with a schedule that had already fallen behind, and I felt sick because I didn't know what to do to makeup the time. I already had a full schedule, and pulling back the scenes wasn't so easy. I worked and re-jigged the schedule, and the following morning I announced a new battle plan.

From that night on I had less than two hours of sleep per night and pushed myself to find the time and compress the schedule so that we could complete. We did shooting an average of seven minutes per day. The good news was, I succeeded. The bad news was that I had a migraine for about three days afterwards.

I do believe that [Murphy's Law], "If it can go wrong, it will!" really exist in the world of filmmaking. It doesn't matter how much you plan, something bad will happen, and at that point, as the director or producer, you have to make a stand and resolve it.

Marc Trottier: As I mentioned about almost being scammed... I hired someone to re-edit *Darkness Waits*, and they ended up trying to renegotiate the fee in the middle of editing. I had paid half up front, with the other half to be paid upon completion of the project, and they requested the second half to be paid beforehand, which I declined to do. It began to be apparent how much of a problem their social ineptitude was going to be to deal with. Then there were complaints about it being more work than they expected, saying that they wanted to be paid more, which I declined. Then they said that other jobs would take precedence during the day, leaving a couple of hours at night to work on my project. This finally escalated to the point where they manufactured an argument as an excuse to not finish the job, in which they said they'd keep the money since half the job was completed. At this point, with the conversations we were having, I realized that I was dealing with someone who appeared to have mental problems as well. After a stressful period, I was able to get the work that was done, but I have no doubts that I would've lost the second half of the fee as well if I had agreed to pay it early.

The hardest part was trying to remain calm while dealing with this individual, because after everything that had already happened, the situation could've ended very badly for them. The lesson learned was: You get what you pay for ... and sometimes when you deal with unstable individuals, you don't get anything at all.

Mike Watt: On *The Resurrection Game* we were in over our heads from day one, but we rolled with whatever came our way. If a location fell through, we rewrote and made do with whatever we could get. The rock bottom of that particular movie's production was when our lead actress's marriage fell apart during shooting and she abruptly decided to move to Greece. This required a recast and a quick rewrite of the character, and it set us back nearly four months. Which, of course, also meant a huge loss in film, processing and time.

Because of our limitations of equipment and experience on *The Resurrection Game*, most of our biggest problems came during the lengthy post-production period. The magnetic

film on which the dialogue had been transferred degraded after years of shuttling back and forth, so we were forced to retransfer all the original one-eighth-inch Nagra masters after the negative had, finally, been transferred to digital. Every line of dialogue had to be first re-synced — and our camera logs were so woefully kept that I basically had to do this by both eye and ear to make sure I was laying in the correct takes. After that, audio whiz Rich Conant (whom I met through *Absence of Light* director Patrick Desmond) was able to engineer all the dialogue tracks for consistency. Still, there were a number of lines we simply had to loop, which required tracking down the original cast.

If I had to choose the absolute "disaster" of *The Resurrection Game*— as well as our entire career —[that] came about due to a processing error. Much of the negative of the film's second reel suffered a chemical splash, resulting in little amoeba-like burns floating around during key sequences and permanently ruining the original camera negative. I had to learn After Effects and Photoshop over the course of a week in order to paint out the worst of these burns, and, to this day, I'm not 100 percent satisfied with the results. (I also discovered that the lab had transferred the negative to DV tape on EP speed, resulting in a slightly degraded and pixilated picture, but not until long after the lab had gone out of business. Go figure.)

All of those things were learning experiences, and, to date, we haven't duplicated the mistakes or suffered the same indignities. We've been amazingly lucky during our 15 years in the "business" in that we haven't encountered much disaster. Admittedly, only part of this is luck; the rest of it is anticipating disaster. The worst things that happened were usually on account of miscommunication.

One source of frustration on *Splatter Movie* was due to shooting during the haunt's off-season in mid-summer. Also, it was one of the hottest summers in Pittsburgh's history. Since the primary haunt season is autumn, none of the interior sets were air conditioned, naturally. Which meant we had to up the water and Gatorade supply for all involved. Being summer, volunteers and employees were also building and rebuilding parts of the haunt while we shot. We were able to work this into the script and story, though, so we could always explain the sudden whir of a circular saw or frantic hammering on the tracks. But the best (or worst) was that entire rooms would disappear overnight, which made shooting pick-ups quite challenging. Sometimes the rooms could be located (we've never needed an "on set location scout" before or since), but most of the time, they'd been repainted and redressed in the space of 12 hours. This also prevented us from orienting ourselves to any great degree. We'd go down a familiar hallway and the door that was there yesterday was suddenly a solid wall the next!

On *Demon Divas* there was a complete misunderstanding on our parts as to what bowling alleys had to go through for "league play." The owners told us that they'd be closed through the month of August, so when we began scheduling, we were under the impression that we had six good weekends to ourselves at the alley. As it turned out, four of those six weekends would be dedicated to reconditioning lanes, retraining staff and machine maintenance. Which meant that our six weekends became a mere six days of production time. Flights were rearranged, hotels had to be rebooked and a transportation chain had to be summoned from scratch. The resulting production felt so rushed and hectic that we were literally tearing pages from the script as we went along, purposefully staging scenes in front of some easily borrowed backdrop that could be relocated to another person's wall in the future, and many, many cast and crew doubled (shemped) for others. On one day, two or three different actresses wore Brinke Stevens's costume and were shot from the neck down to transition from one shot (from last week) to the next (shot the following week). This slight disaster resulted in our budget entirely

devoured over the course of two weeks, with more money having to be scrounged for post.

On other occasions, though, limitations magically became advantages, as I've illustrated above. Throwing money at the problems on *Demon Divas* didn't give us more time. Using only dedication, boldness and the sheer kick-assedness of the cast and crew on *Razor Days* saved us time down the line and resulted in magic. This is where being independent is truly the best direction. Hollywood demands perfection and will pay any price to achieve it. The indie world rewards risk and perseverance. Fortune favors the bold and resourcefulness begets art.

Ritch Yarber: The worst thing that ever happened to me while making a movie was the miserable experience of going through the computer crashes that plagued the production of *Murder Machine!* The frustration of getting to a certain point and then losing everything is indescribable. This happened more than once on this production and really caused the whole thing to grind to a halt. We did not have the means to quickly obtain new equipment, and had to wait for an interminable time to finally be able to move forward with post-production. The pressure from everybody who donated their time and efforts to the film were overwhelming, as they pressed to find out what the holdup was. I am adamant about my obligations and not being able to quickly fulfill my promises weighed greatly on my mind every day, causing great mental anguish, like a dread that lies thinly disguised, but never goes away, leaving an endless sick feeling in the pit of my stomach. I hope to never have to experience that again.

Ivan Zuccon: I don't know if it's the worst, but certainly the strangest and most disturbing thing was the first week of shooting of *Colour from the Dark*. We shot in an old and beautiful farmhouse and had an incredible series of misadventures. The first week was the most difficult, not because of the shooting schedule or the actors or anything like that, but because of some (actually, many...) strange episodes that dramatically slowed down production. Within a few days we had to replace two HD cameras that mysteriously stopped working properly; the second camera was actually recording and stopping by itself. Fortunately, the third camera did not give us problems. Both of my cars broke down: the first had brake failure, the other had a broken engine! And I could go on and on, telling about other accidents that happened almost everyday to people and things on set. We were shocked! After the first week we were so behind schedule that we had to work on days off. The executive producer of the movie, Roberta Marrelli, took some pictures during the shoot, and we found out there was a mysterious guest on set; in fact, through the smoke coming out from the smoke machine we glimpsed a sulky face, the same in each picture. From then on we began thinking about the presence of a ghost or a naughty poltergeist. Our visual effects supervisor took a couple of mysterious photos, too. There's an unbelievable photo sequence where you can spot a black, foggy substance taking human shape while rising from the ground of the yard in front of the farm: a really inexplicable and disturbing picture! However, after the first week, strange episodes became less and less frequent, so that we managed to finish shooting the movie.

Your Career as an Indie Filmmaker

When people ask me what I do for a living, I don't tell them I'm a "filmmaker." Nowadays that's a meaningless term and usually refers to someone who does this as a hobby or is still in school. I tell inquisitive minds that I'm an "independent movie producer," and more recently, a "television documentary producer," to set me apart from someone who just posts videos on YouTube. While there's nothing wrong with doing that, that's a beginning step and I've been doing this for over 20 years. And while I've never made a Hollywood movie, I am a professional.

Making the movies was always far more important than the idea of being able to make a living at it. When I first started making movies I was on the staff of a production house in New York City. A perk of that job was that I had access to their broadcast-quality cameras and could shoot on weekends. I spent my two-week summer vacation in 1990 shooting *Vampires & Other Stereotypes*. The next movie was shot on weekends, and the next was shot after work and on weekends. I made my income from my "real job," which I didn't particularly like. It was a means to an end — to make movies. It wasn't until my third movie, *Addicted to Murder*, that I began to make an income from them. This was the first Brimstone title that was distributed through Blockbuster video, which was a big deal in 1995. There were Blockbuster rental stores on every few blocks in New York City. Thousands of copies were sold. Then, I started making sales to distribution companies in other countries — England and Germany, to name but two. This influx of cash inspired me to continue to make more

movies and my library of titles grew. I even quit that staff job in '97, to do the independent filmmaking thing more than full-time. Because it's not just a job, it's a lifestyle.

When the horror/sci-fi market became over saturated at the beginning of the 21st century, and distributors were expecting movies for free (they promised residuals, and we all know what that means) I switched gears and began making independent feature documentaries. Money was obtained in a completely different way. I wasn't selling to individuals or stores. I was getting underwriters (advertisers) for the Public Television broadcasts. It took a bit more time and work on my part, but I was in control of all of this. And, as with the feature films, it was sheer determination that got them out there. I could never really dwell on how daunting a task it all was, from creating to selling a project on which I was earning my living. But, after ten years, the funding for documentaries began to dry up. Even documentary cable channels want your film for free, saying they'll give you lots of "exposure." With PBS no longer a factor, I decided to make a documentary that was a bit more risqué, and hearkened back to my horror roots — *The Life of Death*. I'm still shopping that around. Many distributors are interested, but not interested enough to pay money for licensing or broadcasts.

So it was back to doing other sorts of video jobs, like shooting/editing local commercials to supplement income and pay the bills. Does this make me less of an independent filmmaker? I don't think so. It's all a part of the deal. I'm still making films a though each day of not knowing where my income is coming from is, honestly, a bit stressful.

In fact, because there's no longer a paying market for documentaries I've come full circle and am planning on working on a new horror feature, *Cannibal Baby*, in the next few years.

There may not be much money in it, but that's not the reason I'm making it. I need to satisfy the creative itch and get that "movie in my mind" on screen. After all, I can't help it. I am an independent filmmaker.

The Filmmakers were asked:
Is it realistic for someone to make a living making low-budget independent movies?

Glenn Andreiev: Maybe up until the mid 1990s; not so much anymore. I feel making low-budget independent films can lead to second-hand sources of money—being able to teach filmmaking, screening your film to special-interest groups, getting work on other people's films—things like that.

John Borowski: It may be possible, but the key is to make films in volume. I would say an indie filmmaker may be able to make a living after having five or more films completed. But less than that it is pretty impossible to survive making indie films. If you have the luxury of being able to devote all your time to your filmmaking career and do not have to work a nine to five job, then you may be able to make some progress. It is extremely difficult to plan and make a film, publicize and promote it yourself, and seek other film work at the same time. Each of these aspects is a full-time job.

Keith Crocker: No, it's not realistic to assume you're going to make a living as an independent filmmaker. You're going to need to be more than that. I teach adult education courses on filmmaking and film genre. That's one way to supplement income. I still own and operate Cinefear Video, which also brings in money. I'm often hired to shoot and direct industrial training films. That's extra cash in the pocket. Films are a labor of love; you really have to want to do them. And, as I said earlier, you have to expect to be ripped off in distri-

bution—it happens, and it happens to the fullest extent of the law. In other words, books can be fudged, figures fucked with, and you are going to lose. But filmmakers should bask in the idea that their work is available for all to see and will outlive the filmmakers themselves. Making films makes you immortal, in a sense. But it might not pay your bills, so be prepared to put your oars in many different waters.

Richard Cunningham: I think at first it's good to assume that you're going to be spending some of your own hard-earned money (and time) making low-budget indie films, while you're progressing from one film to the next.

That being said, opportunities are opening up in the form of crowd funding online, i.e., Kickstarter, where a good idea and some aggressive outreaching can raise an entire budget for a small film, or cover the costs of distribution. Lately, I've also been seeing some of those aforementioned zombie fan sites forming production companies that release indie zombie films, and they're soliciting to a built-in fan base; so there are definitely new and creative ways that you can go about making low-budget films.

Maurice Devereaux: Not anymore. Years ago even hack filmmakers could make a living churning out bad B-movies, but the new realities of an abundance of films (now, *anyone* can make a film) and the easily available pirated downloads have changed the dynamics so much for the little guy. Yes, you can MAKE a film now, it's never been easier (or cheaper), but you will NOT make a LIVING doing so. Prices to buy indie films have plummeted. I'll give you a few examples. My film *End of the Line*, after months of negotiating, finally sold to the Sci-Fi channel/Chiller in the U.S., but, unfortunately, the price was a measly $5,000, minus U.S. taxes of 30 percent and a 10 percent commission to a lawyer who arranged the deal. I'm not going to retire on that amount. When I sold *End of the Line* at the AFM in 2007 to Japan for $50,000, this was high-end dollars, but ten years before it would have been $200,000 minimum. Today you're lucky to get $10,000 for a quality low-budget indie. One of my friends made three low-budget sci-fi flicks, in 2004, 2007 and 2009. Each film was better than the last, but each sold for less money as dwindling DVD markets crashed and piracy and illegal downloads went up. So, today, unless a film is completely financed through brokers using "investments portfolios" of many people (who will never get a dime back) and that you are PAID a salary to make the film, this is the only way to not lose money as a filmmaker. To be hired with a guaranteed salary. Even Francis Coppola, who self-financed his last two films, found out the hard way that, unlike his wine business (where he made the money to finance his last two films), the film business was a shark-filled ocean for the indie producer, he lost huge amounts on both films. So all his previous experiences as a hired hand on Hollywood films did not prepare him for the shocking realities of being an indie producer and then trying to sell your film and make money.

Donald Farmer: For every filmmaker who supports himself strictly through low-budget movies, you can probably point to hundreds more who don't. And movie work can rarely be counted on for a regular income. When you finish a project it may be months or years before you can work again. There are always exceptions, like the people who made *Paranormal Activity* or *The Blair Witch Project*, but they're very much the exceptions. For any-one who wants to do filmmaking, it's a good idea to have a day job. Maybe that day job could be video production services... I know several guys who [make] wedding and industrial films between movies. But, in today's economy, it's harder than ever to make a living off just movie-making alone. It was different in the '80s, when companies paid good advances for even the cheapest shot-on-video projects, but those days are SO gone!

Jeff Forsyth: You know, I am not really sure. I see it being done, so I have to say yes. I want to say yes.

Richard W. Haines: It was in the '80s and '90s, but the industry has changed so dramatically, it's much more difficult now. For instance, in the '80s, when I started my career, there were hundreds of independent cinemas, grind houses and drive-ins to book your movie in. They're all gone and were replaced with megaplexes, which only show studio product. There used to be many video companies, like Vestron and AIP, that gave advances to producers, but they folded, too. Many of the foreign sales reps I used passed on, like Walter Manley who made lucrative deals on *Splatter University* and *Space Avenger*. Indies always worked on the fringes of the film industry, and the marketing opportunities are more limited today than they were years ago. It's advisable to have another career, like teaching or writing, between productions. I'm a film historian and also give lectures at colleges between productions.

William Hopkins: It's not realistic for everyone who has a desire to make movies to expect to be able to make a living doing it. There just isn't that big a market for low-budget product for everyone who wants to be in the business to make money at it. But the few who are willing to stick with it may find their work catching on over time. Sheer persistence is often rewarded in this business.

Steve Hudgins: It can be realistic with LOTS of hard work! I don't think most people realize the amount of work that has to go into being an independent filmmaker. If you're going to make money, I think it's more likely to happen off of a large body of work, spanning many years, as opposed to making money off of one movie.

Rolfe Kanefsky: Absolutely! Piece of cake. All it takes is luck, hard work, luck, dedication, luck, determination, luck, talent and luck. And you might want to add "knowing the right people" to that list. In fact, you can get rid of all of that list except for luck and knowing the right people. But, seriously, is it realistic to make a living? No. But luckily, the film business isn't realistic to begin with. It's all make-believe and fantasy. The reality of working consistently in the film business is like winning the lottery many times over. There are no rules. To quote William Goldman, "Nobody knows anything." I and many others have always said that if you can be happy doing anything other than making films, do that. You have to be 100 percent obsessed with movies and just can't do anything else. If it's a hobby then let it be a hobby and have another job where you can make a living. But trying to have a family, a house, and work exclusively in the low-budget arena, I believe, is impossible. You might be able to start in low-budget movies and move up the ladder to the studio level and then make a comfortable living. But to stay in the low-budget field and get by ... highly doubtful. However, if you were to ask Fred Olen Ray or Jim Wynorski, they might tell you otherwise. The only rule is that there are always exceptions to the rule.

I've been in this business for over 20 years and some years have made as little as $14,000 for the entire year. My rent is $1,000 a month, so you do the math. But, in my case, with a little help from my parents when times get very tough, I've just managed to survive. I have squeaked out a living, but the things I've sacrificed to do this makes me wonder if it's been really worth it. Again, watch *Tomorrow by Midnight* for more insight on the subject... Oh, right, you can't. It never came out.

Brett Kelly: It's not easy, but I do. The odds are against it by a long shot these days. I started ten years ago when DVD was fairly new. Is it possible? Yes. Is it realistic? I honestly don't think so. You need a second gig.

Chris LaMartina: How you define "make a living" determines the answer to this. I know plenty of folks that make cheap movies full-time. They're not ordering the lobster or living like kings, but with everyone who produces low-budget content, they do it because they love it. I'd be impressed with anyone who pays their mortgage by doing what they love. It is remarkable that someone can function off micro-budget film revenue, however. If that is the case, they're probably involved in their own distribution avenues. The basic problem is the time it takes between finishing a film and the arrival of residual checks from a distributor. Even if it's a quick turnaround, sometimes those residual checks never even show up. Hell, most of the time they don't show. It's a sad truth.

To anyone who is living (in any sense) off of the fruits of their cinematic labor, I say "Bravo!" So what if they only eat bologna sandwiches and sleep on a pull-out couch? I'd still say they're living the dream, and that is highly commendable.

Jim Mickle: I'd love to say yes, but every indie director I know, including myself, has a day job. Maybe as distribution evolves and becomes more democratized, more money will go to the actual filmmakers, but for now it seems hard for anyone to make good money on a consistent basis without supplemental work.

Damon Packard: It depends on what scale you're talking about. Low-budget indie movies that get distributed and released on some scale? Like, for example, a Todd Solendz or Guy Maddin? Yes, they seem to manage. But, for the most part, absolutely not.

Brad Paulson: Nothing is impossible, but you're looking at Han Solo odds from *Star Wars*. In other words, not even close. What's realistic is to expect that you'll be delusional in keeping that dream alive while you're still broke. It's realistic to expect you'll be broke as fuck for far longer than it's hip to be below the level of the common man while you keep hoping it will get better one day. The truth is, only about 1 percent of people in L.A. actually make a living at being screenwriters, actors or directors. Sure, you may make a few dollars here and there, but nothing you can quit that shitty day job for.

Jose Prendes: No, unfortunately not. There is no money in no-money movie making. It's sad, but passion isn't a prerequisite for a paycheck. If you want to make movies, then MAKE THEM! No one should tell you any different. But don't expect to get rich filming your uncle dressed as vampire or your little cousin running away from a guy with a machete. There is a place and an audience for this, but it won't make you money. Hell, even the big studios are going under with their multi-million-dollar flops.

However, the one thing to remember when it comes to making movies is: THERE ARE NO GUARANTEES. Nothing is written in stone, and your little backyard opus could become the next *Blair Witch Project*. So I say forget the naysayers and just fucking do it. Prepare to starve, but stay hopeful.

Paul Scrabo: You can make money right away, but you are not going to make a profit right away! That's two different things. My projects are self-funded. It's silly for me to offer deferred payment to a cast or crew member. They showed up for me, they adjusted their schedule for me. Their pay is part of my film's budget. Some friends offered to work on the film for free. I took advantage of their generous offer and their talent and I made sure we fed them, and not fast food, but real meals.

Keep your budget low, and, hopefully, you can at least get your money back.

Eric Shapiro: Sure. I know numerous people who do. The majority who try never will — it's not some big pie we can all take a slice of. Though if you create a viable piece of work that sells to a healthy amount of territories around the world and manages to play in perpetuity, you can make a great living.

Anthony Straeger: NO, unless you get your small independent movie picked up and have a successful company like Lionsgate behind, it you will spend more than you can get as a return in promoting your film. Then you are hoping that you, as the filmmaker, will be picked up and paid to do another project.

I have seen some films that have been made for nothing more than a two or three thousand dollars, but, still, I can't see them making any money either, because most of them are simply awful.

If you can make money out of low-budget independent filmmaking, I think you need to have a film that WILL win festivals and gain acclaim, that is genre specific and that you have looked at and set in place every kind of marketing ploy under the sun.

For me, *Call of the Hunter* was a testing ground, and is a fabulous calling card. It proves that I can produce a certain quality within a certain budget — that I have a certain style and can deliver exactly what it says on the tin.

Ultra low/no budget films are nothing more than that. If you get into the range of half-million budgets, then maybe if you can maintain the quality — and we know how hard that is to do — you *might* be able to get by. But you sure won't get rich doing it.

Marc Trottier: That's hard for me to answer. I'll say, "Maybe." I would love to hear what other people think; those who have consistently put out content and successfully sold their product. I, myself, am curious to know how much of a profit there is to be made.

If you have good ideas and you have the resources to be able to make your films in a cost-effective manner, in a period of time that makes sense, then why not?

Mike Watt: No.

That's the short answer. The long answer is: absolutely not. But, strangely enough, with that realization comes freedom. Knowing ahead of time you will not make money or, even in the best of circumstances, likely even make your investment back, is comforting in its own way. The best thing about being an independent filmmaker is that first word: independent. You're not beholden to an audience or to any sort of studio expectations. There is no film by committee to undermine your base concept, only what you and your handpicked partners bring to it. Independence has its own myriad problems, of course, but at the end of production, the movie you made is 100 percent yours, to pass or fail on the merit of you and the crew that put its faith in your guidance.

If you are lucky enough to find investors (which we refer to as "angels"), let them know ahead of time that this is a risky venture and tell them (and understand yourself) to never invest more than one is prepared to lose. The compromises you'll have to make will either be budgetary, time-limited or conflict of schedules (and sometimes personalities, but the big boys suffer those things, too).

Don't like a predictable three-act script structure? Pitch it, but know what rules you're breaking. There's no one to enforce any "rules" upon you, such as having to have the plot in motion by page five. You can take the time to establish characters, if you want. You can put in as much gore and nudity as you like, or have none at all. Let the story dictate the elements of the movie and make the movie serve the story. You don't have to pander to the demands of corporate sponsors and product placement, you don't have to worry about a release date (in most situations) and you can truly make a movie that's an extension of you. If in the end, the pacing seems slow to you, change it. Too short? Shoot additional scenes or leave it the length it is.

But, in order to do yourself and your art the best service, make sure you know what story you want to tell and give consideration to who you want to entertain. Those are and should be your only restrictions. Be thoughtful and make the movie you want to make. It'll attract a large audience or a small one, but it won't matter when no one is dictating to you what you *have* to do.

Ritch Yarber: At this time, I do not feel that one can make any kind of real living making these types of films. There are just too many people making movies these days to be able to get enough commercial exposure for your films to pay the bills. Independent films are still an entertainment afterthought when it comes to audiences watching movies. The big studios still have the upper hand with huge-budgeted movies backed up by slickly produced trailers and commercials that demand your viewing dollars. Occasionally, an "independent" film will break the barrier and make a small fortune for a lucky filmmaker, but it is rare. I think that the reason to continue to make these small-budget independent films is to experience the challenge of reaching an audience and making them yours for a short while. The hope of being discovered and actually getting any kind of steady income rests like a lost treasure in each independent production, waiting to be discovered and added to the mother lode. It's all about the dream.

Ivan Zuccon: Yes, it is, but it's also a very difficult dream to fulfill. You'll have to make many sacrifices, more than you can imagine. The movie business is a tough one. Every morning I say to myself, "Okay, that's it, enough is enough. From now on I'm going to dedicate myself to something else. I'm tired, it's too hard, it's a battle I can never win." ... I feel like Don Quixote. My windmills are distributors, and they are so huge and monstrous that they give you the creeps. You get scared about the fact that your movie might end up in a limbo, or in the wrong hands. The fruit of your sacrifices, of your biggest effort, the blood of your blood could be thwarted by poor film distribution. Then, I find myself flickering through my new scripts, so I start writing, reviewing dialogue, thinking about the camera movements, and I finally say to myself, "I'm going ahead, but this time's the last time. This is going to be my last movie."

The Filmmakers were Asked:
What advice do you have for anyone who wants to be a "filmmaker," whether as a producer or director or writer? What are the three top things to do (and why) that would set them in the right direction?

Glenn Andreiev: Be yourself in your writing, filmmaking and producing. We don't need another Dario Argento tribute film, or a Scorsese-like Mafia movie. Everybody has a good story to tell. Don't try and do something like Hollywood, like your own low-budget version of *Salt*. Your car chase will never compare to Hollywood's. Just focus on telling a good story, a unique story—your story. Third, on so many low-budget film sets I watch filmmakers [take great pains to be] Stanley Kubrick–like perfectionists, that everything has to be just 100 percent right. (For example, I saw one filmmaker repeatedly reshoot a nightclub sequence because the light wasn't just right on an actor's face, or they found better extras and want to do retakes, and so on) You'll delay production, eat up what little funds you have, and possibly wind up with an unfinished film. A good filmmaker makes the minor flaws fly by unnoticed.

John Borowski: My advice is: DON'T DO IT! But if you feel you are strong enough, then go ahead. Lighting and sound are the most important elements when filming. If you select a genre, then you will have a niche market to exploit. You must have the drive to work on your films for years (and possibly the rest of your life) as you promote and sell them. You must believe in your work. Keep the quality at the highest [level] and never sacrifice story for modern equipment or special effects; they won't make the film any better. My motto is: I would rather watch a well-told [story] shot on the lowest [budget] available than a film which costs millions of dollars, where there is no emotional connection between the audience and the film.

Keith Crocker: You have to love being an artist. A filmmaker should be coming from the same intensity that drives a painter, poet, or sculptor. You have to let your desire to create art guide you, and you must not limit your dreams. Let that freak flag of yours fly high. Always remember: (1) you can do it; never let anyone make you believe you can't live a dream. Of course you can, no one will stop you if you have the desire; (2) Don't get discouraged. Learn how to troubleshoot problems at the drop of a hat. You need to think and be on your feet at all times so don't doze—not even for a minute, you might lose an opportunity; and (3) Be proud of your work, warts and all. Do the very best you can. Don't sell yourself short. Your voice matters in this over crowded world, you're not insignificant, you matter more than the next man. If you have something to say, say it! And, last but not least, have fun. Filmmaking is fun—it shouldn't be a burden. You can tire out, but if the energy and the drive keeps returning, then you know filmmaking is for you.

Richard Cunningham: I think it's important to push yourself and the work you do as hard and far as you can, however you go about it, be it teaching yourself, working in the field, or attending film school; develop within yourself an insatiable hunger to understand, master, and appreciate all the art forms that serve to ultimately constitute a movie, because whether you're a writer, a producer or a director, the more perspective you gain on the process, the better you can go about being a part of it.

Along those same lines, I think it's good to always keep moving ahead to the next project. Of course you want to give your finished movie its due run of promotion. Enter it into festivals, maybe try online distribution, even take the time to engage social media, so you can build up a targeted fan base. Do as much as you possibly can to exploit the movie you've toiled so greatly to make, but be sure, too, that you have projects lined up, or your next script is ready to go. There are invaluable lessons to learn that only the experience and the struggle of making a film can provide; so every time you put yourself in that situation, you are hurtling yourself light-years ahead in useful filmmaking know-how.

Last but not least: networking. Whether it's virtually via social media outlets, or passing your card or spec script off to someone in the business, producing with teams of like-minded filmmakers, or just having a conversation with people on other sets, the larger your network of talent, the more tools you will have available to put together a film when the time comes to commit.

Maurice Devereaux: Kids, don't try this at home ... seriously, don't do what I did. Don't spend your own money. It's better to work your way up to become a hotshot director of photography, shoot flashy music videos and commercials and you'll have a better chance of getting hired as a director (to do a remake of a classic horror film) than I do. Because EVEN if you make a film, (like my award-winning horror feature *End of the Line* that premiered at the Toronto International film festival and then played 39 other film festivals worldwide, garnered rave reviews and sold to many countries), this route gave me no job offers and left me thousands of dollars in debt. So, it's not recommended. It's unfortunate but true that the people who fund big films would rather hire someone who never directed a feature but did a bunch of expensive-looking, flashy commercials. Just look at the bios of the guys who made the remakes of *The Nightmare on Elm Street* or *The Texas Chainsaw Massacre*. That's the way it is and part of the reason why most horror films suck today. Keep the following points in mind:

1. Write something tailor made for a low budget (few actors and locations).
2. Make sure your script is ready and really tight, as you don't want to shoot anything you will later cut out (that means time and money wasted).
3. Don't spend your own money — you'll never get it back. But if you absolutely have no other choice, make sure you budget an amount you can easily [spend without seeing a return]. And then think that you will probably have to spend about 40 percent more for unforeseen expenses. Then look at the amount, and be true to yourself. Can you say goodbye to that money? ... If the answer is "Yes," then go into pre-production.
4. Get professional actors; whatever extra money you spend will be worth it. They will make your job easier and make you look like a better director. Use a casting agent, if needed, to find them.
5. Get professionals for key crew (Lighting, camera, sound, costumes, sets, make-up)
6. Make sure your locations are easily accessible, with available parking and low noise.
7. Once you start shooting, make sure you get your film completely "in the can," as you don't want to have to run after people for reshoots or unfinished scenes.
8. If you're producing, do NOT hand over your film to a sales agent. Accept only upfront cash deals. Because you will NEVER see any royalties and/or back-end money. No matter if it's a prestigious name company or not. Look at it as you would a drug deal — both of you hold guns at each other, the buyer holds money, and you hold a master copy of the film. Then you do the switch, never keeping your eyes off the other guy until you're paid. It's better to walk away from any deal, no matter how good it seems, if they do not pay you up front. You will always hear the classic excuses, "Send us the master and we promise we'll wire you the money next week," et cetera. Don't fall for it.

9. Don't give up. You only have one short life. If this is something you need to do, do it!

10. Don't listen to what anyone says, especially me.

Donald Farmer: Here are a few basic tips for anyone who wants to get into filmmaking:

1. Know how to network. Filmmaking is definitely a team activity, and you want to assemble the best team possible.

2. Try to know a little about the job of every crew member ... especially the cinematographer. The more you know about the responsibilities of your crew, the better you can supervise them. And know enough about lighting so you can make specific suggestions and requests to your director of photography, camera operator, et cetera. That's the area in which I tend to become the most vocal... I've learned the hard way not to always accept what a cinematographer wants to give you.

3. Learn the basics of promotion — make sure your target audience knows about your movie.

4. Thanks to audio commentaries on DVDs, everyone has access to a movie-making education that used to be the sole domain of film schools. You can't listen to too many directors' commentaries.

5. Visit the sets of other low-budget movies. Study how other directors and producers cope with tight schedules and little money. Talk to any directors you can corner at conventions or fan gatherings and pick their brains. That's basically what I was doing when I did magazine interviews with my favorite directors. I was picking their brains for tips I might be able to use later. For anyone wanting to be an indie filmmaker, it's a good place to start.

Jeff Forsyth: Besides seek therapy, I think a lot can be learned just by watching movies and analyzing them.

The top three things I would say to do are: read, connect, and shoot. Read all you can about the process and the equipment. Connect with people who are shooting. Learn from them and gain skills. And when you can, grab a camera and shoot — that's how you'll really put your skills into action.

Richard W. Haines: My first suggestion will probably be ignored by the majority of aspiring filmmakers, but I hope a few consider what I'm about to say. I think the most important thing for anyone making independent movies is to preserve their work. That means either shooting in 35mm or outputting their digital movie to a 35mm negative. They should retain either the camera negative or a duplicate negative of their feature and store it in a private temperature-and-humidity-controlled film vault. If they can't afford that, donate it to an archive for long-term preservation. You should never assume the distributor is preserving your film. They aren't archivists, they're salesmen and have no proprietary interest in the survival of your movie. I know of several indie filmmakers that can no longer find their camera negatives, since the distributor and lab folded.

Archival considerations aside, you cannot sell something that doesn't exist. If you want to have your film available for future sales you need a "hard copy" of the picture on film since digital imagery is an unreliable long-term storage medium, subject to data loss and degradation. Never give your only master to a distributor without keeping a duplicate element yourself.

My second suggestion is to shoot [using Alfred Hitchcock's methodical approach] rather than trying to improvise the shoot. The more pre-production, the better the technical specs will be. I know some people get away with making crude movies, and sometimes the crudeness is part of the appeal, but it's a risky way of making a picture. Technical ineptitude can be a distraction for audiences who are less tolerant about this than they were in the '60s, when directors were shooting in the cinéma vérité style. I suggest creating storyboards for every shot to make sure you have the coverage you need. Trying to "wing it" on your first feature film might prevent you from completing the movie or resulting in an amateurish production that won't be able to compete with more polished low-budget films.

My third suggestion is to make sure you negotiate a distribution deal that includes an advance that will recoup your production cost, or a deal where marketing expenses are either capped or recouped from the distributor's share of proceeds. If you sign a deal with unlimited marketing expenses recouped off the top or out of your share, you'll never see a dime. Or, take the DIY option by researching how to sell your movie in the available markets.

William Hopkins: I feel you should learn to do as much of it yourself as you can. Learn to write a good, solid screenplay; learn how to shoot it yourself; learn how to edit it yourself. For the indie filmmaker working on a tiny budget, there's no one you'll be able to afford to hire who will care as much about your film as you do, so you immediately put yourself in a better position if you hone your skills in as many areas of the filmmaking process as you can. That way you'll never be dependent on anyone else to get your film done the way you want it done. And, nowadays, with the cameras and software that are available, there's really no good reason why anyone should shy away from learning these things.

It's also important, I think, to carefully pick your projects. If you're going to be taking a project from inception through production and — eventually — distribution, that may represent an investment of a couple of years of your life. So you'd better feel strongly about the film you're making. You'd better like the story and the characters and feel comfortable in the world you're creating, because you'll be living in it for a while. Finally, it's important for people looking to have a career as indie filmmakers to develop a thick skin and a stubborn attitude about things. It's a tough business, and you'll face a lot of discouragement from people. It's hard to raise money for films

and it's hard to get productions going — it's a fight all the way. But you shouldn't give up. Always be working towards your next film, always have something on the drawing board. The only way to become a good filmmaker is to keep making films. The more you make, the better you'll get at it. So, keep writing scripts, keep networking with people who share your interests and goals and try to keep alive in yourself the spirit of enthusiasm and optimism you had when you were just starting out.

Steve Hudgins:

1. Don't expect someone to see your movie and suddenly offer you a million bucks for it. If that's what you're hoping for, you're setting yourself up for a big disappointment. That's a fairy tale. It just doesn't happen.

2. Get a distribution and marketing plan in place before you even start making your movie.

3. Get out there and start doing it. Don't talk about doing it. Don't work toward doing it, just do it!

Rolfe Kanefsky: Okay, let's switch gears from all this bitching and moaning to something positive. My father said that, in order to survive in this business, you have to believe everything and at the same time believe nothing. That means you have to think positively but keep a reality check in the back of your mind that it could all fall apart at any time. There's a lot of bullshit in this business. It's amazing that any movies get made. Many people have said that if we knew how difficult it was to do something, we would never do anything. But, to make movies, you almost have to have a kind of blind optimism. A kind of leap-before-you-look attitude. However, if you have no sense of reality you can get hurt, usually emotionally.

So, my advice is, if you have the drive and obsession to make movies, go for it. You know it's impossible, but you do it anyway. It's a case of mind over matter. Now, once you have the right mentality to take a shot at the film business and refuse to let anyone talk you out of it, you have to work your ass off. Nothing is just going to fall into your lap, and if it does, be prepared for it to jump back out again. You must network and meet as many people as you can. This business is all about connections and the people you know. Build relationships, and don't expect to be an overnight success. There are thousands of overnight successes that took ten, 20 years to get there. Try to find a group of friends who can give you an honest reaction to your work. Everyone in Hollywood is afraid to tell you what they really think. They can be ultra kind or ultra cruel. The real response is usually something in between. So, find a good sounding board of opinions you can trust. It will help keep your head on your shoulder so you don't get too suicidal or too full of yourself. Both are bad conditions in this business.

Next, you need to know what you're doing. Watch movies and learn the names of the producers, directors, and writers. Many people in the business — especially at the studios — really don't know much about the movies. Most memories go back about ten years or less. So, it really helps if you know what you're taking about and have the knowledge of film and filmmakers. Know your history. That way, when you're in the room, you don't have to bullshit. You'll know what you're taking about and can give references to what worked or didn't work in similar motion pictures. Also, if you do run into a film buff, you'll already have something in common. If you want to be a writer, read screenplays, both good and bad. You'll learn a lot about what works, why it works, and what to avoid. Compare the script to the final movie. See how it changed — what they pulled off and what they blew. In many ways, this can be just as good as taking a film/writing course.

Then you need to do the work. If you're a writer, write. Every day. Set goals for yourself. Force yourself to be productive. Make it a habit. If you want to be a producer or director, make movies any way you can. Basically, the more you're on a film set — either your own or someone else's — you will learn invaluable information.

I worked as a production assistant in the summers on independent films from the ages of 16 to 21. Even after I made my first film, *There's Nothing Out There*, I went back and worked as a production assistant on another film. The more you do, the better you get. You learn from your mistakes. And there is nothing that can compare to being on a movie set. All the theories and classes can give you some info, but you must do it for yourself to really see what making movies is all about.

Finish what you start. This is a key fact. If you expect someone to give you money to write, direct, and produce, they need to trust you. They have to feel confident that their money is in good hands. You have to show them you are responsible. So, I have always made a point to finish everything. If I'm writing a screenplay I will not stop until I reach the end. Even if I'm not happy with some of it, I barrel through to the conclusion. Maybe people start a project because they think it will be fun. Then, when it gets difficult, they walk away from it. Finishing something is what makes the difference between a hobby and a career. Even if you start to hate it, finish it, because once you reach the end, you will probably realize it's not as bad as you thought, and you can always go back to fix the problems. Prove you are capable of making a short, script, feature, and you will win over all of the naysayers. People will always tell you it can't be done. Well, if you do it, you win the argument hands down.

And, finally, keep at it. If you're serious about making it in this industry, you have to keep plugging away. Slamming your head into that wall until it breaks down. Many have said that the one who wins is the one who lasts the longest. If you've got the stamina to put up with all the heartaches, rejections, insults, abuse, poverty, backstabbers, people with hidden agendas, negative reactions, and boredom that comes with this job, then you may just make it in this town. It also helps to have a little luck. Did I mention that yet?

Well, that's about it. Good luck!

Brett Kelly: My advice is to take a class and watch a lot of films, especially movies that you think you won't like. You'll be surprised where inspiration comes from. Lastly, make a lot of short films, finish them, watch them and learn from them — do all this before you try a feature. Good luck!

Chris LaMartina: My first question for an aspiring filmmaker is: "What do you want to do as a filmmaker?" If someone just wants to make goofy short films, then ... go for it. Nothing is stopping you. Technology is getting cheaper and cheaper, and anyone can make movies now. If you want to make a living telling stories (features, web series, et cetera) ... then I'd sincerely suggest figuring out a business model while you hone your skills as a storyteller. It's show *business*, and in order to keep making films on a larger scale, you'll have to increase revenue. Plenty of folks I know have full-time "boring video" jobs that fund their dream projects ... but it's definitely taxing.

If I could break down my advice to three things, it would be these.

1. Respect your story. If you don't have a strong, primal screenplay that is marketable you're asking for trouble in every part of the filmmaking process. A lazy, sloppy, or derivative screenplay will murder any chance of great direction, solid editing, and, most importantly, distribution. Never forget that. Distribution is everything. Otherwise, no one will see the hard work you've put into this story.

2. Know what's within your means. Don't make your barbarian epic in your parents' backyard for $237. You won't be able to pull it off. I mean ... you can ... if you want it to be a comedy ... or maybe I'm wrong, and you can pull it off. The point is, you need to become a good judge of your abilities. Figure out what your strengths are

and play to them. If you have access to an amazing location, write a marketable story around it. If you wail on guitar, maybe you should score the film, too. On the other side of the token, if your girlfriend or boyfriend can't act to save their life ... do not cast them. Filmmaking, especially with no money, is about intelligent compromising and problem solving. Be smart. Work *your* advantages. Don't ask me what yours are. Everyone has their own.

3. Filmmaking is collaborative process, and, as someone who has written, directed, edited, and scored his own stuff, I know how easy it is to take all the credit. My co-producer and co-writer, Jimmy George, has been a backbone that not many people have acknowledged in various articles about my films. Similarly, you will have partners, and mini-armies of folks who are going to help your vision come alive. Most of them (if not all of them) will be working for peanuts. Say "Thank you" ... a lot! In general, we work harder for people who treat us with respect and dignity. Make sure you let people know that you appreciate their hard work. If I subtracted the time it takes me express my gratitude each shooting day, I'd probably have an extra 40 minutes for coverage ... but it's worth it to tell my cast/crew that I [appreciate] their efforts. Don't take anyone's work on your film for granted.

It's tough making movies, but nothing worth doing in life is easy. Just get ready to sacrifice all of your free time, push relationships to their limit, and challenge yourself to be more creative. If you've got the fire in your belly, you'll figure it out.

Jim Mickle:

1. Start making films right away. Don't wait around for the perfect opportunity or for Hollywood to hand you a budget. Make your movie your own way and give yourself a chance to get a film distributed. You'll learn from your mistakes and your voice will evolve the more you do it. Use a Flip

cam, a DV cam, an HD cam or a RED. Get iMovie or Final Cut Pro or Adobe Premiere and edit it yourself. Then go make another one.

2. Shorts are a great way to practice and don't require years of work to accomplish, but it's also very hard to find continued success making shorts exclusively. The finances are hard to pull off and chances for distribution are very small. Also, the SHORTER the BETTER. I made a 22-minute senior thesis after most professors advised against it, and when it came time for festivals it was very hard to get accepted anywhere. No festivals want to show a 20-minute film before a feature, and in a short film program, it's easier to schedule a lot of shorter films than to take up valuable time with longer films. And this was before YouTube and Vimeo, so attention spans have only gotten shorter. When making a short, try to remember what kind of an audience you're hoping for.

3. Work on as many films as possible. If you're interested in cameras, try to intern in the camera department. If you like lighting, talk to grips and electricians. If you don't know what you might be good at, look for production-assistant jobs or general intern work. Spend as much time on sets as you can and learn the workflow, so by the time you're directing or producing, you have some idea how things work. Or get an office-assistant job and spend time in a production office, or be an assistant editor and see how things come together in post. Be patient. A lot of people are looking for jobs and it helps to be in New York City or L.A., but when an opportunity comes, be on time and show a willingness to be helpful without being annoying. There's a lot of "hurry up and wait" times in filmmaking, but if the people that brought you on enjoy your company, they'll look you up for the next one. Stay busy.

Damon Packard: Just be prepared for a LOT of work and very few rewards or results.

You must be completely satisfied with your work. The world outside of yourself will not necessarily gratify you. But then there are many [others] who have better results on that end.

Brad Paulson: First and foremost, if you want to be a filmmaker, do it because you love movies. Don't do it because you want to be a glorified frat kid and think you'll get a bunch of Hollywood glitz and glam from the whole deal. Don't do it because you're a narcissistic asshole who wants to see your name in lights or your face in front of a camera. Don't do it because you think it will give you the attention you never got in high school. Don't do it because you think you're God's gift to cinema. No one likes a pretentious ass, and, from what I've seen in and out of school, those who talk about how great they are and berate others usually make terrible movies.

Second, be ready to live, sleep, and breathe movies. With the infusion of Netflix instant, and all the ways to get our hands on movies nowadays, people have no excuse to miss the classics. As we all know, nerds make the best movies. The names Martin Scorcese, Quentin Tarantino, Steven Spielberg, Peter Jackson and Stanley Kubrick are all household names, and these guys have one thing in common: they are all complete movie dorks. I remember seeing an interview with Spielberg where he was toading up *The Shining* and he talked about how he had seen the movie 25 times. I loved Spielberg after he said that. You really have to know your shit. If you know your shit, it impresses people. It legitimizes you in the eyes of filmmakers. Don't be the guy who has to look up the answer to a question on his phone. Be the guy who already knows the answer and is ready for several more.

Third, learn to embrace failure. I think this is why some people either work on movies for ten years or just, plain and simple, fuck up. Realizing that we're all human and not perfect is a terrifying reality but it's a fact of life we're all going to have to accept sooner or later, so it's best to fail as early on as possible and try and learn from our mistakes. What I'm saying is, don't be afraid to rush into new challenges and take on overwhelming jobs out of the fear you'll fail. You will. You'll endure humiliation and question yourself with every decision you make. But, that's okay. It's the name of the game. You'll get better and hone your skills with time and practice.

Fourth, and most importantly, learn to live like a broke starving artist for a long time. Being broke may be romanticized in the movies. Hollywood loves a Cinderella story. It fuels their machine. Living broke in real life, on the other hand, sucks rotting donkey balls. It's nonstop war with the worst enemy you can image: yourself. It's a battle of quiet desperation that never seems to end. I recommend you live out of your car for a few weeks, just to get a feel of what the pursuit of filmmaking in Los Angeles will be like. Tony Scott filmed this city through an orange filter several times in his films, but, in reality, if you go a couple blocks south of the Hollywood Walk of Fame you'll see drug deals in broad daylight and soak in the unmistakable scent of human urine on the streets. If you can make your peace with that and realize that it will most likely take years of suffering and prayers for the sweet release of death ... if you can ignore all the more-than-wise warnings to stay away from anything having to do with making movies and have a normal life before you end up killing yourself out of sheer desperation and misery ... then maybe, just maybe, you have what it takes to be a filmmaker. Good luck, brothers and sisters. Keep the dream alive. If you do make it through the heartless, soul-sucking trenches in one piece, I look forward to seeing your movies one day.

Jose Prendes: If you want to make movies in any capacity then JUST GO FUCKING DO IT. I hear from a lot of people [say], "I'm thinking of" or "I'd like to" or "One day I'm gonna" ... but the truth is, talk is cheap. Like Yoda says: "Do, or do not. There is no try." I hold that as my motto, and I think you should, too. If you want it, then go for it. It won't be

easy, so be ready to fight, be ready to get pinned to the ropes, be ready to sweat and cry and bleed, but keep swinging and eventually they will have to let you win. But know how to swing, first and foremost. Most persistent people fail because they don't really know what they're doing, so have a plan, know how to play, and come out swinging.

If there are three things you should know, they would probably be:

1. WATCH MOVIES. Watch all kinds movies from all over the world. You can't make movies if you don't know movies. I recommend a healthy dose of the Criterion Collection for great foreign films. This is crucial, and you'll see that most well-known film people are film scholars, too.
2. UNDERSTAND FORMAT & LINGO. If you are a writer, have a solid grasp of screenwriting format. Once you have format down to a science, then you can have fun with your scripts. If you're a director, learn all the terms for things so you don't look like an idiot to the seasoned pros. If you're a producer, maybe take a business course to understand financing and how to raise money and what terms go along with it, so you're not left in the cold. No one will give you money if you don't understand what they're talking about.
3. STICK TO IT. Most people give up when they realize how hard it is, or how long it takes. If you want it, then you fight for it. Stick to what you love like white on rice. Nothing worth doing is easy. Good luck.

Paul Scrabo: Most important, SAFETY FIRST.

We had a scene where Queen Exotica (Debbie Rochon) is blasted by a ray gun and becomes stiff as a board. The villain shows up with a hand truck, scoops the rigid queen up and exits. It was a quick, inexpensive gag. Debbie's apprehension became apparent.

"Okay. Just ... wait a second... I'm just getting over a back problem ... and..."

"No. Forget it. Don't worry about it. Give

us a second and we'll figure out something else to do."

"No. It's a funny bit. I can do it, but let ME be in control of how to do it."

So, instead of being scooped up in the hand truck, Debbie carefully placed herself on it beforehand, and it's a funnier bit now, because you just see her being carted away in the background. It can be dangerous getting caught up in any "big picture" and not being aware of any potential danger to a cast or crew member. You are already taking a risk with your own money, making your film. Let that be the only risk.

Listen to your cast and crew for any ideas. We were finishing the final scene of the film where Debbie and Trent sail off into the sunset. I was never really satisfied with the ending because I knew it needed something extra. Debbie was joking around, and she says, "And this is when a hand should come out of the water, and everybody screams!" And we all laugh, and I say, "Okay, that's it, everyone. We're done!" And we all pack up and go home. And then I realize that she was absolutely right. The next opportunity to use the location was in the beginning of winter, and I'm there in a rented wetsuit doing the hand-coming-out-of-the-water gag.

Finally, try not to be a perfectionist. You'll drive yourself crazy, and you'll also drive everybody else crazy. Take your project very seriously, but don't take *yourself* too seriously.

Eric Shapiro: The first thing is to get serious about the script. Don't view it as a process that sets you up for a shoot. View it as the most important part of the film — period. If you look at IMDb's list of the most beloved films, all of them vary in terms of style and sensibility, but those are some great fucking scripts, across the board. That's the most human and holy element, so don't rush it or underestimate it.

The second one is to go where your strengths are. Don't pretend to be something you're not. Don't make comedies if you have a morose worldview. I know I'll never be a techie, and everyone I shoot with knows it, too. I love orchestrating the visual side, but my obsession is the text and characters, so that's where I place my chips.

Third, you need to get comfortable with the idea of failing over and over again. There will be tons of rejection and negativity, even if you create a critically acclaimed masterpiece. At least a third of the people who watch anything will despise it. So don't go chasing after some objective, unassailable form of acceptance, because it doesn't exist for anyone. If you're good, you'll get enough people on your side to continue, and you should be grateful for whoever picks up what you're putting down.

Anthony Straeger: My advice is simple. First, don't take it personally. In this business, whether as an actor a member of the crew as the filmmaker, you will always find someone that will want to piss on your parade. Being strong and having a belief in what you do and are doing is very important. The other thing that you have to remember is that once you have made it, people might not like it. You find that someone on Amazon has called your film all the sons-of-bitches under the sun. But I believe that, if you put your head above the parapet, then expect to get it shot off!

Second, if you can't stand the heat, get out of the kitchen. This is a very hard process and you shouldn't go into it lightly. It is much easier to make a feature these days, but I would really hate myself if I felt I had wasted the time of everyone who had contributed to my project. If you can't be bothered to do it right, and if you want others to carry the can, then stop before you start.

Finally, you have got to give it everything until you don't want to give any more. This business attracts lots of "wannabes," but keeping yourself motivated is difficult when your rent is six months behind.

To conclude, what you have to do is be as clear about your aims as is possible. You have to include words like realistic — yeah, it's boring... But, being realistic doesn't exclude you from being artistic.

My three top tips for anyone wanting to get into independent filmmaking are as follows:

1. Planning is everything at every stage, be it budgets or schedules. You have to take the time and care to look under every stone and make sure you have checked, double-checked, triple-checked. Why? Because the less you leave to chance, the more chance you have of succeeding.

2. The script: read it with an objective mind, not a false sense that you have written God's gift to filmmaking. It doesn't matter whether this is your script as the director or someone else's work, as with *Call of the Hunter*. Understand what it is about and what it is you are trying to achieve with it. Rewrite it as many times as it takes and read-throughs to clear up any problems in the flow and understanding for the performers. Why? Because once you are in production, you want everyone quite literally on the same page, and rewriting something on set can be a hell of a nightmare.

3. Take advice from anyone who has more experience than you. Always remember good advice is always helpful but doesn't have to be taken. Consult anyone you know in the business, from the shops you hire the camera from to going to studios and asking editors for advice. Why? Forearmed is forewarned. I know everything about everyone's job.

Making *Call of the Hunter* was one of the best experiences of my life. It was some of the hardest work I have ever done and the most time I have ever invested in anything in my life. I am proud of my work and hope that anyone who watches will enjoy it. Making a film is one of the best buzzes in the world. But you really have to roll your sleeves up and get your hands dirty.

Mike Watt:

1. Feed your cast and crew. People don't like to work when they're hungry.

2. *Love* what you're doing. People don't like to watch half-assed movies.

3. Don't be an asshole. People don't do favors for assholes, and the indie world is built on favors.

Ritch Yarber: If asked to give advice to someone interested in becoming a filmmaker, I guess I would simply tell them the same thing I was told 11 years ago by New Jersey filmmaker Karl Petry (*Ironbound Vampire, The Larksville Ghost*). He said, "Quit talking about it and shoot something!" Conditions will never seem perfect for the beginning filmmaker to actually start a project, especially on the micro-budget level, making for a great opportunity to hide behind excuse after excuse as to what one would do if they only had the money, the time, the crew, the equipment, and on and on. Get a camera and start shooting something! Anything! Just take a topic and try to tell a story with moving images. Once the door is cracked open, the rest will come. Believe me, I know. I talked about making films for over ten years ... the conditions were never just right. And they still aren't, although I've now been making movies for over a decade. Writing, producing or directing, it all starts with the very first step. Start stepping!

I think the top three things to do in getting started making movies are as follows:

(1) obtain some type of camera; (2) come up with a story that you are interested in telling; and (3) take great care to use a script that is well-planned and complete. Once the ball is rolling, the other elements will come forward, or you will find ways to present the vision that is in your head. Filmmaking is like painting. You start with a blank canvas that is slowly filled with images, colors, music and sounds. Everything leads to the unveiling. Only then, judged solely by the audience's reaction, is the payoff to your efforts rendered. It is a highly sought after, fleeting moment of truth that will quickly validate or repudiate one's passion for filmmaking. If one has even an inkling of becoming a filmmaker, they owe it to themselves to give it at least one shot, on some level. The true filmmaker will be quickly addicted.

Ivan Zuccon: "Wanna make movies? Then start digging!" "This is what I'd like to say to budding filmmakers. I think art should, first of all, make people think. I don't like cinema without content, movies that are merely showy, even when I can't deny that I sometimes watch that kind of film in order to spend a carefree and relaxed evening. But when I work I personally try to find a meaning in everything I'm doing. So, as long as I find it, I begin to dig. Here, the term "digging" is the right one. At first I start digging deep inside myself until I find the right idea. From that idea the entire movie will be born. If you dig deep enough this is going to have a very positive affect on your work, and the chances of making an interesting movie are many.

Secondly, "Never give up." Even when everything seems to be against you, even when it seems that there's no way out, never stop believing in yourself and your ideas. If you have dug deep enough to find them, you'll have ideas worth fighting for. As I often say, "The life of independent filmmakers is like a struggle against windmills. We are the Don Quixote of movies." But this isn't a good reason to stop struggling and fighting. Third, be picky. Never be satisfied. The more your work improves technically and artistically, the more it will have commercial value.

Epilogue

As you may have surmised by now, being an independent filmmaker is not easy. You may be an amazing writer, yet when you try to shoot a feature in your neighborhood, you come to the realization that your community theater actors are unable to do your script justice. Or you may have the complete opposite happen and see that your dialogue is crap coming out of these great actors' mouths. There are also things, like equipment failures, cast and crew showing up late, and losing all of your shot footage from the camera's memory cards. The scariest part of all is that there is little support for independent filmmakers. YOU are the support and the glue so that things will not fall apart.

Ask yourself, "Is making a film something I *really* want to do?" Well, if the answer is "Yes," do it. And perhaps doing it again if you're happy with the experience... There is nothing quite like it!

Appendix: The Filmmakers and Their Films

Glenn Andreiev

Vampire's Embrace (1993, Camp Releasing)
Night (1997, Joseph Green Pictures)
Mad Wolf (1998)
Sharp and Sudden (2001)
Every Move You Make (2002)
Silver Night (2005, Echelon Pictures)
The Deed to Hell (2008, Echelon Pictures)
The Make Believers (2009)

John Borowski

H.H. Holmes: America's First Serial Killer (2004, Facets Video)
Albert Fish: In Sin He Found Salvation (2007, Facets Video)
Carl Panzram: The Spirit of Hatred and Vengeance (2012)

Keith Crocker

The Cinefear Sampler (1992, VHS Cinefear Video)
The Bloody Ape (1997, VHS Vanguard Distributors DVD Wildeye Releasing)
Blitzkrieg—Escape from Stalag 69 (2008, DVD Wildeye Releasing)

Richard Cunningham

Lycian (2002)
The Seven Kings: Scene Selections from Arcadium (2005)
She (2006)
America the Mental (2008)
Year Zero (2010)

Maurice Devereaux

Blood Symbol (1991, Atlas Entertainment [U.S.], also released in Russia and played on Polish TV under the title *Krwawe znami*)

Lady of the Lake (1998, MTI/Bedford Entertainment/Fangoria [U.S.]; Antarctic Video [France]; Stax Entertainment [UK]; also released by unknown distributors, through a sales agent, to Germany, South Africa, Hungary, Benelux, Israel, Spain, Greece, Latin America, Indonesia, Malaysia, Panama, Singapore, India. Also played on Canadian Pay-TV, and had a one-week theatrical run at the NFB theatre, in Montreal, in March 2000)

Slashers (2001, MTI/Bedford Entertainment/Fangoria [U.S.]; Kaboom/49th Parallel Censored 4/3 edition [Canada]; Ion New media [Germany]; Salvation films [UK]; Antarctic Video [France]; also had a four-weekend theatrical run at the Cinema du Parc, in Montreal, in September 2002)

PMS Survival Tips (2003)

End of the Line (2006) Anchor Bay (Canada/Australia/New Zealand); E1 (U.S.); MIG (Germany); AMG (Japan); Opening (France); Noble (Scandinavia); Popron (Czech Republic); The Entertainment Imitative (Benelux); International Production Associates (Thailand, Vietnam)

Donald Farmer

(Director on these titles unless noted otherwise)

Day of the Dead (1985) Actor
Demon Queen (1986) Actor
Cannibal Hookers (1987, Magnum Video)
No Justice (1989, Richfields Productions) Production Manager, Casting, Actor
Scream Dream (1989)
Vampire Cop (1990, Atlas Entertainment)
They Bite (1991, MTI Video) Assistant Casting Director, Actor
Invasion of the Scream Queens (1991, Mondo Video)
Savage Vengeance (1993, Magnum Video)
Red Lips (1995, Video Vamp)

Deadly Run (1995, Stratosphere Entertainment)

Compelling Evidence (1995, Stratosphere Entertainment)

Vicious Kiss (1995, Stratosphere Entertainment)

Demented (1996, Richfield Productions) Co-producer

Demolition Highway (1996, Stratosphere Entertainment)

Space Kid (1999, Velli Entertainment)

Blood and Honor (2000, David Heavener Entertainment)

Battle for Glory (2000, David Heavener Entertainment)

The Strike (2001, MTI Video)

Blood Feast 2 (2001, Shriek Show) Actor

Deadly Memories (2002, Brain Dead Films)

An Erotic Vampire in Paris (2002, E.I. Cinema)

Bollywood and Vine (2004, Stratosphere Entertainment)

Red Lips: Bloodlust (2005, Sub Rosa)

Red Lips: Eat the Living (2005, Sub Rosa)

Whose War? (2006, Indieflix)

Dorm of the Dead (2006, Under the Bed Films)

Chainsaw Cheerleaders (2008, Stratosphere Entertainment)

Megan Wants a Millionaire (2009, VH1) Actor

Country Strong (2011, Screen Gems) Actor

Twi-Hards (2011, Suicidal Productions)

Shark Exorcist (2012, Suicidal Productions)

Jeff Forsyth

Children of the Sky (2000, Brimstone Productions)

C.A.I.N. (2013) in post

What You Know (2012, short)

Richard W. Haines

Splatter University (Troma, 1983–1986, New Wave Distribution, 1986–2011)

Space Avenger (New Wave Film Distribution, 1989)

Head Games (New Wave Film Distribution, 1993)

Run for Cover (New Wave Film Distribution, 1995)

Unsavory Characters (New Wave Film Distribution, 2001)

Soft Money (New Wave Film Distribution, 2005)

What Really Frightens You? (New Wave Film Distribution, 2010)

William Hopkins

Children of the Night (Columbia Tristar Home Video, 1993) Writer

Sleepless Nights (Open Communications, 2003) Director, Writer, Editor

Demon Resurrection (Feature Resources, 2008) Director, Writer, Editor, Music, Special effects.

Steve Hudgins

The 3rd Floor (2007, Corn-O-Copia Productions)

Maniac on the Loose (2008, Big Biting Pig Productions)

Goatsucker (2009, Big Biting Pig Productions)

Widow (2009, Big Biting Pig Productions)

Hell Is Full (2010, Big Biting Pig Productions)

The Creepy Doll (2011, Big Biting Pig Productions)

Spirit Stalkers (2012, Big Biting Pig Productions)

Rolfe Kanefsky

There's Nothing Out There (1992, Image Entertainment; Troma, 2011) Writer, Director

My Family Treasure (1993, Arrow Entertainment) Story, Director

Red Line (1995, Orion/Triboro) Writer

The Ultimate Attraction (1996, New Concorde Entertainment) Writer, Director

The Alien Files a.k.a. *Alien Erotica* (1998, MTI Home Video/Bedford Entertainment) Writer, Directorse

Restless Souls (1998, New Concorde/Click Productions) Writer

Tomorrow by Midnight a.k.a. *Midnight 5* (1999, Hope Street Entertainment) Writer, Director

Pretty Cool (2000, MTI Home Video) Writer, Director

Rod Steele 0014: You Only Live Until You Die (2001, New Concorde Entertainment) Writer, Director

The Misadventures of the Invisible Man (2002, New Concorde Entertainment) Writer, Director

Shattered Lies (2003, Lantern Lane/Hart Sharp Entertainment) Writer

The Hazing a.k.a. *Dead Scared* (2003, Lightning Entertainment/MTI Video) Writer, Director

Corpses (2004. York Entertainment) Writer, Director

Jacquelyne Hyde (2004, Warner Home Video) Writer, Director, Producer

Nightmare Man (2005, Lions Gate/After Dark Films) Writer, Director, Producer

Pretty Cool Too! (2006, MTI Home Video) Writer, Director

Blonde and Blonder (2008, First Look Entertainment) Writer

1 in the Gun (2009, MTI Home Video) Writer, Director

Today Is Yesterday Tomorrow (2012, ASP Productions) Writer, Director

Emmanuelle in Wonderland (2012, ASP Productions) Writer, Director

Brett Kelly

The Feral Man (2001, Tempe Video)
The Bonesetter (2002, Tempe Video)
Final Curtain (2003, Tempe Video)
The Bonesetter Returns (2004, Tempe Video)
Spacemen, Go-Go Girls and the True Meaning of Christmas (2004, Tempe Video)
Spacemen, Go-Go Girls and the Great Easter Hunt (2004, Tempe Video)
My Dead Girlfriend (2005, Tempe Video)
Kingdom of the Vampire (2006, Tempe Video)
Prey for the Beast (2007, Brain Damage Films)
Attack of the Giant Leeches (2008, Brain Damage Films)
Pirates: Quest for Snake Island (2008, Brain Damage Films/Black Flag Pictures)
Iron Soldier (2008, Maverick Entertainment)
Avenging Force: The Scarab (2008, Japanese release)
She-Rex (2009, Self-distributed)
Blood Red Moon (2009, Brain Damage Films)
Rockland (2009, undistributed)
Thunderstorm: The Return of Thor (2010, TomCat Films)
Hell at My Heels (2011, Barnholtz Entertainment)
Jurassic Shark (2012, Tomcat Films)
My Fair Zombie (2013, in production)

Chris LaMartina

Dead Teenagers (2006, Brain Damage Films)
Book of Lore (2007, Camp Motion Pictures)
Grave Mistakes (2008, Camp Motion Pictures)
Faces of Schlock Segment: "One Foot in the Grave" (2009, Independent Entertainment)
President's Day (2010, Spy Music Group)
Lost Trailer Park: Never Coming Attractions (2010–2011, Web Series)
Witch's Brew (2011, unreleased)

Kevin Lindenmuth

(Producer/writer/director, unless otherwise noted)

Vampires and Other Stereotypes (1992) ... a.k.a. Hell's Belles
Twisted Tales (1994) Co-Director (with Mick McCleery, Rita Klus)
Addicted to Murder (1995)
Alien Agenda: Out of the Darkness (1996) Co-Director (with Mick McCleery)
Alien Agenda: Endangered Species (1996) Co-Director (with Tim Ritter, Ron Ford, Gabriel Campisi)

There & Back: Interviews with Near-Death-Experiencers (1997)
Alien Agenda: Under the Skin (1997) directed segment "The Guys in Black"
Addicted to Murder: Tainted Blood (1998)
Creaturealm: From the Dead (1998) segment "Eyes of the Ripper"
Creaturealm: Demons Wake (1998) Producer only
Caring for the Caregivers: Living with Cancer (1998) documentary Co-Producer, Co-Director (2000–2006, Films for the Humanities)
Walking Between the Raindrops (1999)
Rage of the Werewolf (1999)
Addicted to Murder 3: Blood Lust (2000) Co-Producer, Co-Director (with Tom Vollmann)
Beyond the Lost World: The Alien Conspiracy III (2001) Co-Director (with John Bowker, Tim Ritter)
Time Enough: The Alien Conspiracy (2002) Co-Director (with Ron Ford, Alexandre Michaud)
Grey Skies: The Alien Conspiracy (2002) Co-Director (with Tom Nondorf & Les Sekely)
Blood of the Werewolf (2002) Co-Director (with Bruce G. Hallenbeck, Joe Bagnardi)
"But You Look So Well..." (2002, documentary) Broadcast nationally on PBS 2003–2008
Werewolf Tales (2003) Producer, Co-Writer
Turning American: A German Immigrant's Story (2004, PBS documentary)
"But You Still Look So Well...": Living with Multiple Sclerosis (2005) Broadcast nationally on PBS, 2006–2011 [completely different from the 2002]
The Healing Prophet: Solanus Casey (2006) Broadcast internationally, beginning in July 2007
"I'm Not Nuts": Living with Food Allergies (2008) Broadcast nationally on PBS, beginning May 2009
The Life of Death (2011)
Blood of the Werewolf II: Wolves & Zombies (2012)

Jim Mickle

The Underdogs (2003, senior thesis short film)
Mulberry Street (2007, Lionsgate/After Dark Films)
One Night in December (2008, short film)
Stake Land (2010, Dark Sky Films/IFC)

Damon Packard

Afterlife/Amazing Stories (1983–84)
Dawn of an Evil Millennium (1988)
Apple (1992)
The Early 70's Horror Trailer (1999)
Reflections of Evil (2002)
Untitled Star Wars *Mockumentary* (2003)

SpaceDisco One (2007)
Nausicaa (2009)
Foxfur (2011)

Brad Paulson

The Van (2003, Brimstone)
The Bloodstained Bride (2006, Brain Damage Films)
Evil Ever After (2006, Cryptkeeper Films)
Reservoir Drunks (2008, Aleheads Apart)
Dead Harvey TV: Episode One (2009, Cape Fear Imageworks)
Paranormal Inactivity (2011, FSD)
Suicide Poet (2011, Straight Stumble)
Satisfied (2011, UBFilm) Screenplay
Guns, Hookers and a Pound of Coke (pre-production, The Ford Austin Company) Screenplay
Zebra Room (pre-production, The Ford Austin Company) Screenplay

Jose Prendes

The Monster Man (2001, Brimstone) Writer, Director
Vampire Resurrection (2001, Full Moon) Writer
Corpses Are Forever (2003, Asylum Entertainment) Writer, Director
Countdown: Jerusalem (2009, Asylum) Writer
The Terminators (2009, Asylum) Writer
Haunting of Winchester House (2009, Asylum) Writer
Final Girl (2012, Aviator Ent) Writer, Director

Paul Scrabo

Dr. Horror's Erotic House of Idiots (2004, self-distributed)

Eric Shapiro

Rule of Three (2010, Big Screen Entertainment Group)
Mail Order (2011, Wildlight Entertainment)
Girl Zero (due 2012, Big Screen Entertainment Group)

Anthony Straeger

Call of the Hunter (2009, U.S.—RSquared Films, UK—Quid In Shrapnel Productions)

Marc Trottier

The Job (2003, undistributed)

Darkness Waits (2009, Screamkings.com)
Resolute (2011, undistributed)

Mike Watt

Tenants (1997) Writer, Director, Editor
The Resurrection Game (2001) Writer, Director, Co-Producer
American Nightmare (2002) Production Assistant
Weregrrl (2002) Writer, Editor
Cannibal Aneurysm (2003) Camera
Severe Injuries (2003) Writer, Editor
Dr. Horror's Erotic House of Idiots (2004) Actor
My Demon Nights (2004) Director of Photography
Spicy Sister Slumber Party (2004) Director of Photography
Dead Men Walking (2005) Screenwriter
A Feast of Flesh (2007) Writer, Director, Editor
Blood Bath: Blood Wrestling Volume I (2007) Photographer, Editor
The Screening ((2007) Screenwriter
Splatter Movie: The Director's Cut (2008) Co-Producer, Editor, Photographer
Demon Divas and the Lanes of Damnation (2009) Writer, Director, Editor
I Spit on Eli Roth (2009) Director of Photography)
The Night We Didn't Discuss Myra Breckinridge (2009) Writer, Director
Countess Bathoria's Graveyard Picture Show (2011) ("Retreat" segment) Writer, Director, Editor
Razor Days (2012) Writer, Director, Editor
Tales of Poe (2012) Actor, Associate Producer

Ritch Yarber

Transylvania Police: Monster Squad (1999, Alpha Home Entertainment)
The Gobbler (2001, unreleased)
The Deep Dark Woods (2003, self-distributed)
The Deep Dark Woods: No Witnesses (2005, recut version 2009, self-distributed)
The Tricky Treat (2007, Short Film)
The Marc Norton Show (2009)
Murder Machine! (2010, self-distributed)

Ivan Zuccon

The Darkness Beyond (2000, Epix Media)
Unknown Beyond (2001, Leo Films)
The Shunned House (2003, Brain Damage Films)
Bad Brains (2005, Epix Media)
NyMpha (2006, MTI Video)
Colour from the Dark (2008, Vanguard Cinema)
Wrath of the Crows (2011, in production)

Index